Literary Essays
of
Ezra Pound

BY EZRA POUND

ABC OF READING

THE CANTOS

THE CLASSIC NOH THEATRE OF JAPAN

COLLECTED EARLY POEMS OF EZRA POUND

CONFUCIUS (ENGLISH VERSIONS)

CONFUCIUS TO CUMMINGS (WORLD POETRY ANTHOLOGY)

A DRAFT OF XXX CANTOS

ELEKTRA

EZRA POUND AND DOROTHY SHAKESPEAR: THEIR LETTERS 1909-1914

EZRA POUND AND MUSIC

EZRA POUND AND THE VISUAL ARTS

GAUDIER-BRZESKA

GUIDE TO KULCHUR

LITERARY ESSAYS

PAVANNES AND DIVAGATIONS

PERSONAE

POUND/FORD: THE STORY OF A LITERARY FRIENDSHIP

POUND/JOYCE: LETTERS & ESSAYS

POUND/LEWIS: THE LETTERS OF EZRA POUND AND WYNDHAM LEWIS

POUND/ZUKOFSKY

SELECTED CANTOS

SELECTED LETTERS

SELECTED POEMS

SELECTED PROSE (1909-1965)

THE SPIRIT OF ROMANCE

TRANSLATIONS

WOMEN OF TRACHIS (SOPHOKLES)

LITERARY ESSAYS
OF
EZRA POUND

Edited with an Introduction

by

T. S. ELIOT

A NEW DIRECTIONS BOOK

CONTENTS

INTRODUCTION

The editor of this volume is alone responsible for the choice of essays and reviews included; and he is therefore called upon to give account of his principles of selection. I have not aimed at including everything, in the area of literary criticism, that seemed to me worth preserving: there is enough material for another volume. Limitation of size has imposed the exclusion of much; so I have tried only to give a representative choice from Ezra Pound's literary criticism over a period of some thirty years. Being a retrospective selection, this book differs from the four books of critical papers from which the bulk of the material has been taken, and to the publishers of which I make acknowledgement: *Pavannes and Divisions* (A. A. Knopf, New York, 1918), *Instigations* (Boni & Liveright, New York, 1920), *Make It New* (Faber & Faber, London, and the Yale University Press, 1934) and *Polite Essays* (Faber & Faber, London, 1937). These collections were assembled in a form which does not seem to me permanently satisfactory: they have served their purpose in prolonging the effect at which the various papers were aimed on their original publication in periodicals. The books themselves have become more difficult to obtain; and there is furthermore some overlapping of contents between the American and the English collections. I have included also shorter pieces rescued from the files of periodicals: amongst such, I have made selection from photostats from American magazines, supplied to me by Mr James Laughlin. There must be other uncollected writings which have escaped our notice: Pound has contributed indefatigably to little magazines. There remain two books from which I have taken nothing: *Guide to Kulchur* (Faber & Faber, 1938) and the early but very important *The Spirit of Romance* (Dent, London, 1910). Both these books have been out of print, but have recently been republished by New Directions: they should both be read entire.

The present book is designed differently from any previous collection of Pound's essays; so I believe there is justification for its having been entrusted to another hand than that of the author. The author—like any author—would make a somewhat different choice from that of his editor; he has, in fact, expressed regret at certain omissions, and deprecated the inclusion of several items which appear to the editor to be of more lasting value than they do to him. But Mr. Pound has never valued his literary criticism except in terms of its immediate impact; the editor, on the other hand, wished to regard the material in historical perspective, to put a new generation of readers, into whose hands the earlier collections and scattered essays did not come when they were new, into a position to appreciate the central importance of Pound's critical writing in the development of poetry during the first half of the twentieth century.

I hope, furthermore, that this volume will demonstrate that Pound's literary criticism is the most important contemporary criticism of its kind. Of a very important kind—perhaps the kind that we can least afford to do without: what the kind is I shall have to consider presently. If this selection succeeds in its purpose, it will show (1) that Pound has said much about the art of writing and of writing poetry in particular, that is permanently valid and useful. Very few critics have done that. It will show (2) that he said much that was peculiarly pertinent to the needs of the time at which it was written; (3) that he forced upon our attention not only individual authors, but whole areas of poetry, which no future criticism can afford to ignore. And finally (what will matter less to *him* than any of the foregoing achievements) that he has shown a more immediate and generous appreciation of authors whose work one would not expect him to find sympathetic, than is generally known. It is for this last reason that I have included early reviews of poems by Robert Frost and D. H. Lawrence. For this reason also I have included the early essay on Lionel Johnson, otherwise unobtainable: the edition of Lionel Johnson's poems of which this essay formed the Introduction was withdrawn immediately after publication. Mr. Pound tells me that his Introduction aroused hostility: it is difficult for me, and I think it will be difficult for other readers now, to understand why. This essay is of interest, not only for what Pound says about Johnson, but for Johnson's own opinions, there quoted, about his contemporaries—judgements to which, by the fact of quoting them, Pound seems to have given implicit assent.

To appreciate any retrospective collection of literary opinions and judgements, it is necessary to pay attention to the dates at which they were written. I have tried to establish as nearly as possible, the dates of all the pieces included; and here must make acknowledgement of invaluable help from Mr. Hugh Kenner[1] of the University of California, and from Mr. Norman Holmes Pearson of Yale University. Such dating is essential. Malevolent critics have two well-known resources: to quote and collate isolated sentences torn from their context, and to quote what a writer said twenty or thirty years ago as if it was something he had said yesterday. Every collection of statements written at different times and in different contexts must be protected as far as possible against such misrepresentation. The views of any writer, if his mind develops and matures, will change or will be modified by events; a statement may lose the validity which it had when it was written; but if it was valid for its place and time, it may still have permanent value. Much of the *permanence* of Mr. Pound's criticism is due simply to his having seen so clearly what needed to be said at a particular time; his occupation with his own moment and its needs has led him to say many things which are of permanent value, but the value of which may not be immediately appreciated by later readers who lack the sense of historical situation.

Inevitably, after the passage of time, such a critic as Mr. Pound (who has never been afraid of his own insights) will appear to have exaggerated the importance of some principles, or of some authors, and to have unjustly depreciated others. He has enlarged criticism by his interpretation of neglected authors and literatures, and by his rehabilitation of misesteemed authors. As for the reputations that he has attacked, we must recall the reaction against the Augustan Age initiated by the Lake Poets. Any pioneer of a revolution in poetry— and Mr. Pound is more responsible for the XXth Century revolution in poetry than is any other individual—is sure to attack some venerated names. For the real point of attack is the idolatry of a great artist by unintelligent critics, and his imitation by uninspired practitioners. A great writer can have, at a particular time, a pernicious or merely deadening influence; and this influence can be most effectively attacked by pointing out those faults which ought not to be copied, and those virtues any emulation of which is anachronistic. Pound's disparagement of Milton, for instance, was, I am convinced,

[1] Mr Kenner is the author of *The Poetry of Ezra Pound* (Faber & Faber, London; and New Directions, New York: both 1951).

most salutary twenty and thirty years ago; I still agree with him against the academic admirers of Milton; though to me it seems that the situation has changed.

It is necessary to consider Pound's literary pronouncements in the light of the circumstances in which they were written, both in order to grasp the extent of the revolution of taste and practice which he has brought about, and in order to understand the particular kind of critic of which he is so eminent an example. He has always been, first and foremost, a teacher and a campaigner. He has always been impelled, not merely to find out for himself how poetry should be written, but to pass on the benefit of his discoveries to others; not simply to make these benefits available, but to insist upon their being received. He would cajole, and almost coerce, other men into writing well: so that he often presents the appearance of a man trying to convey to a very deaf person the fact that the house is on fire. Every change he has advocated has always struck him as being of instant urgency. This is not only the temperament of the teacher: it represents also, with Pound, a passionate desire, not merely to write well himself, but to live in a period in which he could be surrounded by equally intelligent and creative minds. Hence his impatience. For him, to discover a new writer of genius is as satisfying an experience, as it is for a lesser man to believe that he has written a great work of genius himself. He has cared deeply that his contemporaries and juniors should write well; he has cared less for his personal achievement than for the life of letters and art. One of the lessons to be learnt from his critical prose and from his correspondence is the lesson to care unselfishly for the art one serves.

Pound's criticism is always addressed, implicitly, first of all to his fellow craftsmen; to all those who write the English language, though his especial concern and care has been for his fellow craftsmen in America. But it is precisely this address to *writers* that gives Pound's criticism a special and permanent value for *readers*. One learns from him appreciation of literature by learning to understand the preparation, study and training to which the writer should submit himself. Whether Pound is giving his attention to the enunciation of general principles, or to the reassessment of neglected authors and to expounding neglected literatures, or whether he is advertising the merits of new writers (corresponding to the three sections into which I have divided this book) the motive is fundamentally the same: the refreshment, revitalisation, and 'making new' of literature in our own time.

It is something, but not much, for the classification of Pound's criticism, to place it with the other notable contributions of poets to criticism: the essays and prefaces of Dryden, the two prefaces of Wordsworth, the *Biographia Literaria* of Coleridge: all of whom were concerned with 'making new' in their own time. (I should like to add, to please myself, Samuel Johnson; and, to please Pound, Walter Savage Landor.) But none of these was so consistently concerned with teaching others how to write. And of no other poet can it be more important to say, that his criticism and his poetry, his precept and his practice, compose a single *oeuvre*. It is necessary to read Pound's poetry to understand his criticism, and to read his criticism to understand his poetry. I am not interested—it is inessential to my purpose—to assert that one kind of criticism is of higher value than another. What does seem to me true, and necessary to say, is that Pound's critical writings, scattered and occasional as they have been, form the *least dispensable* body of critical writing in our time. They began at a moment when they were very much needed: the situation of poetry in 1909 or 1910 was stagnant to a degree difficult for any young poet of to-day to imagine. Pound himself had a long way to go: and he has gone it. Comparison of his earliest with his latest verse should give ample evidence of how much he himself has learnt from his own critical meditations and from study of the authors about whom he has written.

To say that any kind of criticism has its limitations is not to belittle it, but to contribute towards its definition and understanding. The limitation of Pound's kind is in its concentration upon the craft of letters, and of poetry especially. (The fact that he ignores consideration of dramatic verse, which he regards, quite rightly, as a distinct form or application of verse, and which is a form or application in which he is not interested, is a deliberate limitation worth noting, but not otherwise important.) On the one hand, this very limitation gives him a wider range: Pound's contribution, by calling our attention to the merits of poetry of remote or alien societies— Anglo-Saxon, Provençal, early Italian, Chinese and Japanese, to say nothing of his beneficial, though irritating and sometimes disputable knocking about of accepted valuations in Latin and Greek literature— is immense. But when we want to try to understand what a foreign literature means, or meant, to the people to whom it belongs, when we want to acquaint ourselves with the spirit of a whole civilisation through the whole of its literature, we must go elsewhere. With some literatures, as the Provençal, that literature may, for aught I know, be comprehensively exhibited by the specimens of it which Pound recommends for study by the contemporary writer of English. For those literatures whose summits have been mostly in the drama, the exclusion of drama is serious: but Pound has never yet written about a form of verse which he would not care to practise. And (to take the foreign literature which I know best) Pound performed a great service (especially in *The Spirit of Romance*) for the English-speaking reader in emphasising the greatness of Villon. He was quick to appreciate the originality of Laforgue and Corbière. He showed a discriminating taste among the minor poets of the 'Symbolist Movement'. But he ignores Mallarmé; he is uninterested in Baudelaire; and to his interests such poets as Malherbe and La Fontaine are irrelevant. In Elizabethan literature, apart from the drama, and apart from the songs about which he has spoken well, what about such poetry as that of Jonson or Chapman? I mention these omissions, not as cautious reservations in my admiration for Pound's criticism, but the better to praise it for what it is. You can't ask everything of anybody; and it is an illusion fostered by academic authorities on literature, that there is only one kind of criticism, the kind that is delivered on academic foundations, to be printed afterwards in the 'proceedings' or as a brochure in a series.

I must add a word about footnotes. I have tried to avoid notes (with the exception of one modest correction bearing my initials) except to supply dates. Any notes newly contributed by Mr. Pound are initialled E. P. Notes with no such indication are the author's notes to the text as originally published.

Mr. Pound regrets the omission (for which the editor is responsible) of an essay on René Crevel; he regrets that he has not yet written a study of the work of Jean Cocteau, and that he has not produced a more recent and comprehensive study of the work of Wyndham Lewis. And I gather that he has recently been giving thought to Sophocles—an excursion into new territory, the fruits of which should be interesting. Other papers which he would have liked me to include struck me as being outside the frame of a volume entitled 'Literary Essays'.

I should add that amongst the papers excluded from this volume of literary essays, are those on music, painting and sculpture, with two exceptions: the notes on Dolmetsch and Brancusi which I have appended as a reminder to the reader of all the other essays on the arts, which fall outside the scope of the present volume.

T. S. ELIOT

PART ONE
The Art of Poetry

A RETROSPECT[1]

There has been so much scribbling about a new fashion in poetry, that I may perhaps be pardoned this brief recapitulation and retrospect.

In the spring or early summer of 1912, 'H. D.', Richard Aldington and myself decided that we were agreed upon the three principles following:

1. Direct treatment of the 'thing' whether subjective or objective.

2. To use absolutely no word that does not contribute to the presentation.

3. As regarding rhythm: to compose in the sequence of the musical phrase, not in sequence of a metronome.

Upon many points of taste and of predilection we differed, but agreeing upon these three positions we thought we had as much right to a group name, at least as much right, as a number of French 'schools' proclaimed by Mr Flint in the August number of Harold Monro's magazine for 1911.

This school has since been 'joined' or 'followed' by numerous people who, whatever their merits, do not show any signs of agreeing with the second specification. Indeed *vers libre* has become as prolix and as verbose as any of the flaccid varieties that preceded it. It has brought faults of its own. The actual language and phrasing is often as bad as that of our elders without even the excuse that the words are shovelled in to fill a metric pattern or to complete the noise of a rhyme-sound. Whether or no the phrases followed by the followers are musical must be left to the reader's decision. At times I can find a marked metre in 'vers libres', as stale and hackneyed as any pseudo-Swinburnian, at times the writers seem to follow no musical structure whatever. But it is, on the whole, good that the field should be ploughed. Perhaps a few good poems have come from the new method, and if so it is justified.

[1] A group of early essays and notes which appeared under this title in *Pavannes and Divisions* (1918). 'A Few Dont's' was first printed in *Poetry*, I, 6 (March, 1913).

Criticism is not a circumscription or a set of prohibitions. It provides fixed points of departure. It may startle a dull reader into alertness. That little of it which is good is mostly in stray phrases; or if it be an older artist helping a younger it is in great measure but rules of thumb, cautions gained by experience.

I set together a few phrases on practical working about the time the first remarks on imagisme were published. The first use of the word 'Imagiste' was in my note to T. E. Hulme's five poems, printed at the end of my 'Ripostes' in the autumn of 1912. I reprint my cautions from *Poetry* for March, 1913.

A FEW DON'TS

An 'Image' is that which presents an intellectual and emotional complex in an instant of time. I use the term 'complex' rather in the technical sense employed by the newer psychologists, such as Hart, though we might not agree absolutely in our application.

It is the presentation of such a 'complex' instantaneously which gives that sense of sudden liberation; that sense of freedom from time limits and space limits; that sense of sudden growth, which we experience in the presence of the greatest works of art.

It is better to present one Image in a lifetime than to produce voluminous works.

All this, however, some may consider open to debate. The immediate necessity is to tabulate A LIST OF DON'TS for those beginning to write verses. I can not put all of them into Mosaic negative.

To begin with, consider the three propositions (demanding direct treatment, economy of words, and the sequence of the musical phrase), not as dogma—never consider anything as dogma—but as the result of long contemplation, which, even if it is some one else's contemplation, may be worth consideration.

Pay no attention to the criticism of men who have never themselves written a notable work. Consider the discrepancies between the actual writing of the Greek poets and dramatists, and the theories of the Graeco-Roman grammarians, concocted to explain their metres.

LANGUAGE

Use no superfluous word, no adjective which does not reveal something.

Don't use such an expression as 'dim lands *of peace*'. It dulls the image. It mixes an abstraction with the concrete. It comes from the writer's not realizing that the natural object is always the *adequate* symbol.

Go in fear of abstractions. Do not retell in mediocre verse what has already been done in good prose. Don't think any intelligent person is going to be deceived when you try to shirk all the difficulties of the unspeakably difficult art of good prose by chopping your composition into line lengths.

What the expert is tired of today the public will be tired of tomorrow.

Don't imagine that the art of poetry is any simpler than the art of music, or that you can please the expert before you have spent at least as much effort on the art of verse as the average piano teacher spends on the art of music.

Be influenced by as many great artists as you can, but have the decency either to acknowledge the debt outright, or to try to conceal it.

Don't allow 'influence' to mean merely that you mop up the particular decorative vocabulary of some one or two poets whom you happen to admire. A Turkish war correspondent was recently caught red-handed babbling in his despatches of 'dove-grey' hills, or else it was 'pearl-pale', I can not remember.

Use either no ornament or good ornament.

RHYTHM AND RHYME

Let the candidate fill his mind with the finest cadences he can discover, preferably in a foreign language,[1] so that the meaning of the words may be less likely to divert his attention from the movement; e.g. Saxon charms, Hebridean Folk Songs, the verse of Dante, and the lyrics of Shakespeare—if he can dissociate the vocabulary from the cadence. Let him dissect the lyrics of Goethe coldly into their component sound values, syllables long and short, stressed and unstressed, into vowels and consonants.

It is not necessary that a poem should rely on its music, but if it does rely on its music that music must be such as will delight the expert.

[1] This is for rhythm, his vocabulary must of course be found in his native tongue.

Let the neophyte know assonance and alliteration, rhyme immediate and delayed, simple and polyphonic, as a musician would expect to know harmony and counterpoint and all the minutiae of his craft. No time is too great to give to these matters or to any one of them, even if the artist seldom have need of them.

Don't imagine that a thing will 'go' in verse just because it's too dull to go in prose.

Don't be 'viewy'—leave that to the writers of pretty little philosophic essays. Don't be descriptive; remember that the painter can describe a landscape much better than you can, and that he has to know a deal more about it.

When Shakespeare talks of the 'Dawn in russet mantle clad' he presents something which the painter does not present. There is in this line of his nothing that one can call description; he presents.

Consider the way of the scientists rather than the way of an advertising agent for a new soap.

The scientist does not expect to be acclaimed as a great scientist until he has *discovered* something. He begins by learning what has been discovered already. He goes from that point onward. He does not bank on being a charming fellow personally. He does not expect his friends to applaud the results of his freshman class work. Freshmen in poetry are unfortunately not confined to a definite and recognizable class room. They are 'all over the shop'. Is it any wonder 'the public is indifferent to poetry?'

Don't chop your stuff into separate *iambs*. Don't make each line stop dead at the end, and then begin every next line with a heave. Let the beginning of the next line catch the rise of the rhythm wave, unless you want a definite longish pause.

In short, behave as a musician, a good musician, when dealing with that phase of your art which has exact parallels in music. The same laws govern, and you are bound by no others.

Naturally, your rhythmic structure should not destroy the shape of your words, or their natural sound, or their meaning. It is improbable that, at the start, you will be able to get a rhythm-structure strong enough to affect them very much, though you may fall a victim to all sorts of false stopping due to line ends and cæsurae.

The Musician can rely on pitch and the volume of the orchestra. You can not. The term harmony is misapplied in poetry; it refers to simultaneous sounds of different pitch. There is, however, in the best verse a sort of residue of sound which remains in the ear of the hearer and acts more or less as an organ-base.

A rhyme must have in it some slight element of surprise if it is to give pleasure; it need not be bizarre or curious, but it must be well used if used at all.

Vide further Vildrac and Duhamel's notes on rhyme in '*Technique Poétique*'.

That part of your poetry which strikes upon the imaginative *eye* of the reader will lose nothing by translation into a foreign tongue; that which appeals to the ear can reach only those who take it in the original.

Consider the definiteness of Dante's presentation, as compared with Milton's rhetoric. Read as much of Wordsworth as does not seem too unutterably dull.[1]

If you want the gist of the matter go to Sappho, Catullus, Villon, Heine when he is in the vein, Gautier when he is not too frigid; or, if you have not the tongues, seek out the leisurely Chaucer. Good prose will do you no harm, and there is good discipline to be had by trying to write it.

Translation is likewise good training, if you find that your original matter 'wobbles' when you try to rewrite it. The meaning of the poem to be translated can not 'wobble'.

If you are using a symmetrical form, don't put in what you want to say and then fill up the remaining vacuums with slush.

Don't mess up the perception of one sense by trying to define it in terms of another. This is usually only the result of being too lazy to find the exact word. To this clause there are possibly exceptions.

The first three simple prescriptions will throw out nine-tenths of all the bad poetry now accepted as standard and classic; and will prevent you from many a crime of production.

' . . . *Mais d'abord il faut être un poète*', as MM. Duhamel and Vildrac have said at the end of their little book, '*Notes sur la Technique Poétique.*'

Since March 1913, Ford Madox Hueffer has pointed out that Wordsworth was so intent on the ordinary or plain word that he never thought of hunting for *le mot juste*.

John Butler Yeats has handled or man-handled Wordsworth and

[1] Vide infra.

the Victorians, and his criticism, contained in letters to his son, is now printed and available.

I do not like writing *about* art, my first, at least I think it was my first essay on the subject, was a protest against it.

PROLEGOMENA[1]

Time was when the poet lay in a green field with his head against a tree and played his diversion on a ha'penny whistle, and Caesar's predecessors conquered the earth, and the predecessors of golden Crassus embezzled, and fashions had their say, and let him alone. And presumably he was fairly content in this circumstance, for I have small doubt that the occasional passerby, being attracted by curiosity to know why any one should lie under a tree and blow diversion on a ha'penny whistle, came and conversed with him, and that among these passers-by there was on occasion a person of charm or a young lady who had not read *Man and Superman;* and looking back upon this naïve state of affairs we call it the age of gold.

Metastasio, and he should know if any one, assures us that this age endures—even though the modern poet is expected to holloa his verses down a speaking tube to the editors of cheap magazines— S. S. McClure, or some one of that sort—even though hordes of authors meet in dreariness and drink healths to the 'Copyright Bill'; even though these things be, the age of gold pertains. Imperceivably, if you like, but pertains. You meet unkempt Amyclas in a Soho restaurant and chant together of dead and forgotten things—it is a manner of speech among poets to chant of dead, half-forgotten things, there seems no special harm in it; it has always been done—and it's rather better to be a clerk in the Post Office than to look after a lot of stinking, verminous sheep—and at another hour of the day one substitutes the drawing-room for the restaurant and tea is probably more palatable than mead and mare's milk, and little cakes than honey. And in this fashion one survives the resignation of Mr Balfour, and the iniquities of the American customs-house, *e quel bufera infernal,* the periodical press. And then in the middle of it, there being apparently no other person at once capable and available one is stopped and asked to explain oneself.

[1] *Poetry and Drama* (then the *Poetry Review,* edited by Harold Monro), Feb. 1912.

I begin on the chord thus querulous, for I would much rather lie on what is left of Catullus' parlour floor and speculate the azure beneath it and the hills off to Salo and Riva with their forgotten gods moving unhindered amongst them, than discuss any processes and theories of art whatsoever. I would rather play tennis. I shall not argue.

CREDO

Rhythm.—I believe in an 'absolute rhythm', a rhythm, that is, in poetry which corresponds exactly to the emotion or shade of emotion to be expressed. A man's rhythm must be interpretative, it will be, therefore, in the end, his own, uncounterfeiting, uncounterfeitable.

Symbols.—I believe that the proper and perfect symbol is the natural object, that if a man use 'symbols' he must so use them that their symbolic function does not obtrude; so that *a* sense, and the poetic quality of the passage, is not lost to those who do not understand the symbol as such, to whom, for instance, a hawk is a hawk.

Technique.—I believe in technique as the test of a man's sincerity; in law when it is ascertainable; in the trampling down of every convention that impedes or obscures the determination of the law, or the precise rendering of the impulse.

Form.—I think there is a 'fluid' as well as a 'solid' content, that some poems may have form as a tree has form, some as water poured into a vase. That most symmetrical forms have certain uses. That a vast number of subjects cannot be precisely, and therefore not properly rendered in symmetrical forms.

'Thinking that alone worthy wherein the whole art is employed'.[1] I think the artist should master all known forms and systems of metric, and I have with some persistence set about doing this, searching particularly into those periods wherein the systems came to birth or attained their maturity. It has been complained, with some justice, that I dump my note-books on the public. I think that only after a long struggle will poetry attain such a degree of development, or, if you will, modernity, that it will vitally concern people who are accustomed, in prose, to Henry James and Anatole France, in music to Debussy. I am constantly contending that it took two centuries of Provence and one of Tuscany to develop the media of Dante's masterwork, that it took the latinists of the Renaissance, and the

[1] Dante, *De Volgari Eloquio.*

Pleiade, and his own age of painted speech to prepare Shakespeare his tools. It is tremendously important that great poetry be written, it makes no jot of difference who writes it. The experimental demonstrations of one man may save the time of many—hence my furore over Arnaut Daniel—if a man's experiments try out one new rime, or dispense conclusively with one iota of currently accepted nonsense, he is merely playing fair with his colleagues when he chalks up his result.

No man ever writes very much poetry that 'matters'. In bulk, that is, no one produces much that is final, and when a man is not doing this highest thing, this saying the thing once for all and perfectly; when he is not matching Ποικιλόθρον’, ἀθάνατ’ ’Αφρόδιτα, or 'Hist—said Kate the Queen', he had much better be making the sorts of experiment which may be of use to him in his later work, or to his successors.

'The lyf so short, the craft so long to lerne.' It is a foolish thing for a man to begin his work on a too narrow foundation, it is a disgraceful thing for a man's work not to show steady growth and increasing fineness from first to last.

As for 'adaptations'; one finds that all the old masters of painting recommend to their pupils that they begin by copying masterwork, and proceed to their own composition.

As for 'Every man his own poet', the more every man knows about poetry the better. I believe in every one writing poetry who wants to; most do. I believe in every man knowing enough of music to play 'God bless our home' on the harmonium, but I do not believe in every man giving concerts and printing his sin.

The mastery of any art is the work of a lifetime. I should not discriminate between the 'amateur' and the 'professional'. Or rather I should discriminate quite often in favour of the amateur, but I should discriminate between the amateur and the expert. It is certain that the present chaos will endure until the Art of poetry has been preached down the amateur gullet, until there is such a general understanding of the fact that poetry is an art and not a pastime; such a knowledge of technique; of technique of surface and technique of content, that the amateurs will cease to try to drown out the masters.

If a certain thing was said once for all in Atlantis or Arcadia, in 450 Before Christ or in 1290 after, it is not for us moderns to go saying it over, or to go obscuring the memory of the dead by saying the same thing with less skill and less conviction.

My pawing over the ancients and semi-ancients has been one struggle to find out what has been done, once for all, better than it can ever be done again, and to find out what remains for us to do, and plenty does remain, for if we still feel the same emotions as those which launched the thousand ships, it is quite certain that we come on these feelings differently, through different nuances, by different intellectual gradations. Each age has its own abounding gifts yet only some ages transmute them into matter of duration. No good poetry is ever written in a manner twenty years old, for to write in such a manner shows conclusively that the writer thinks from books, convention and *cliché*, and not from life, yet a man feeling the divorce of life and his art may naturally try to resurrect a forgotten mode if he finds in that mode some leaven, or if he think he sees in it some element lacking in contemporary art which might unite that art again to its sustenance, life.

In the art of Daniel and Cavalcanti, I have seen that precision which I miss in the Victorians, that explicit rendering, be it of external nature, or of emotion. Their testimony is of the eyewitness, their symptoms are first hand.

As for the nineteenth century, with all respect to its achievements, I think we shall look back upon it as a rather blurry, messy sort of a period, a rather sentimentalistic, mannerish sort of a period. I say this without any self-righteousness, with no self-satisfaction.

As for there being a 'movement' or my being of it, the conception of poetry as a 'pure art' in the sense in which I use the term, revived with Swinburne. From the puritanical revolt to Swinburne, poetry had been merely the vehicle—yes, definitely, Arthur Symon's scruples and feelings about the word not withholding—the ox-cart and post-chaise for transmitting thoughts poetic or otherwise. And perhaps the 'great Victorians', though it is doubtful, and assuredly the 'nineties' continued the development of the art, confining their improvements, however, chiefly to sound and to refinements of manner.

Mr Yeats has once and for all stripped English poetry of its perdamnable rhetoric. He has boiled away all that is not poetic—and a good deal that is. He has become a classic in his own lifetime and *nel mezzo del cammin.* He has made our poetic idiom a thing pliable, a speech without inversions.

Robert Bridges, Maurice Hewlett and Frederic Manning are[1] in their different ways seriously concerned with overhauling the metric, in testing the language and its adaptability to certain modes. Ford Hueffer is making some sort of experiments in modernity. The Provost of Oriel continues his translation of the *Divina Commedia.*

As to Twentieth century poetry, and the poetry which I expect to see written during the next decade or so, it will, I think, move against poppy-cock, it will be harder and saner, it will be what Mr Hewlett calls 'nearer the bone'. It will be as much like granite as it can be, its force will lie in its truth, its interpretative power (of course, poetic force does always rest there); I mean it will not try to seem forcible by rhetorical din, and luxurious riot. We will have fewer painted adjectives impeding the shock and stroke of it. At least for myself, I want it so, austere, direct, free from emotional slither.

What is there now, in 1917, to be added?

RE VERS LIBRE

I think the desire for vers libre is due to the sense of quantity reasserting itself after years of starvation. But I doubt if we can take over, for English, the rules of quantity laid down for Greek and Latin, mostly by Latin grammarians.

I think one should write vers libre only when one 'must', that is to say, only when the 'thing' builds up a rhythm more beautiful than that of set metres, or more real, more a part of the emotion of the 'thing', more germane, intimate, interpretative than the measure of regular accentual verse; a rhythm which discontents one with set iambic or set anapaestic.

Eliot has said the thing very well when he said, 'No *vers* is *libre* for the man who wants to do a good job.'

As a matter of detail, there is vers libre with accent heavily marked as a drum-beat (as par example my 'Dance Figure'), and on the other hand I think I have gone as far as can profitably be gone in the other direction (and perhaps too far). I mean I do not think one can use to any advantage rhythms much more tenuous and imper-

[1] (Dec. 1911)

ceptible than some I have used. I think progress lies rather in an attempt to approximate classical quantitative metres (NOT to copy them) than in a carelessness regarding such things.[1]

I agree with John Yeats on the relation of beauty to certitude. I prefer satire, which is due to emotion, to any sham of emotion.

I have had to write, or at least I have written a good deal about art, sculpture, painting and poetry. I have seen what seemed to me the best of contemporary work reviled and obstructed. Can any one write prose of permanent or durable interest when he is merely saying for one year what nearly every one will say at the end of three or four years? I have been battistrada for a sculptor, a painter, a novelist, several poets. I wrote also of certain French writers in *The New Age* in nineteen twelve or eleven.

I would much rather that people would look at Brzeska's sculpture and Lewis's drawings, and that they would read Joyce, Jules Romains, Eliot, than that they should read what I have said of these men, or that I should be asked to republish argumentative essays and reviews.

All that the critic can do for the reader or audience or spectator is to focus his gaze or audition. Rightly or wrongly I think my blasts and essays have done their work, and that more people are now likely to go to the sources than are likely to read this book.

Jammes's 'Existences' in '*La Triomphe de la Vie*' is available. So are his early poems. I think we need a convenient anthology rather than descriptive criticism. Carl Sanburg wrote me from Chicago, 'It's hell when poets can't afford to buy each other's books.' Half the people who care, only borrow. In America so few people know each other that the difficulty lies more than half in distribution. Perhaps one should make an anthology: Romains's 'Un Etre en Marche' and 'Prières', Vildrac's 'Visite'. Retrospectively the fine wrought work of Laforgue, the flashes of Rimbaud, the hard-bit lines of Tristan Corbière, Tailhade's sketches in 'Poèmes Aristophanesques', the 'Litanies' of De Gourmont.

It is difficult at all times to write of the fine arts, it is almost impossible unless one can accompany one's prose with many reproductions. Still I would seize this chance or any chance to reaffirm my belief in Wyndham Lewis's genius, both in his drawings

[1] Let me date this statement 20 Aug. 1917

and his writings. And I would name an out of the way prose book, the '*Scenes and Portraits*' of Frederic Manning, as well as James Joyce's short stories and novel, 'Dubliners' and the now well known 'Portrait of the Artist' as well as Lewis' 'Tarr', if, that is, I may treat my strange reader as if he were a new friend come into the room, intent on ransacking my bookshelf.

ONLY EMOTION ENDURES

'ONLY emotion endures.' Surely it is better for me to name over the few beautiful poems that still ring in my head than for me to search my flat for back numbers of periodicals and rearrange all that I have said about friendly and hostile writers.

The first twelve lines of Padraic Colum's 'Drover'; his 'O Woman shapely as a swan, on your account I shall not die'; Joyce's 'I hear an army'; the lines of Yeats that ring in my head and in the heads of all young men of my time who care for poetry: Braseal and the Fisherman, 'The fire that stirs about her when she stirs'; the later lines of 'The Scholars', the faces of the Magi; William Carlos Williams's 'Postlude', Aldington's version of 'Atthis', and 'H. D.'s' waves like pine tops, and her verse in 'Des Imagistes' the first anthology; Hueffer's 'How red your lips are' in his translation from Von der Vogelweide, his 'Three Ten', the general effect of his 'On Heaven'; his sense of the prose values or prose qualities in poetry; his ability to write poems that half-chant and are spoiled by a musician's additions; beyond these a poem by Alice Corbin, 'One City Only', and another ending 'But sliding water over a stone'. These things have worn smooth in my head and I am not through with them, nor with Aldington's 'In Via Sestina' nor his other poems in 'Des Imagistes', though people have told me their flaws. It may be that their content is too much embedded in me for me to look back at the words.

I am almost a different person when I come to take up the argument for Eliot's poems.

HOW TO READ[1]

PART ONE: INTRODUCTION

Largely Autobiographical, Touching the Present, and More or Less Immediately Past, 'State of Affairs'.

Literary instruction in our 'institutions of learning'[2] was, at the beginning of this century, cumbrous and inefficient. I dare say it still is. Certain more or less mildly exceptional professors were affected by the 'beauties' of various authors (usually deceased), but the system, as a whole, lacked sense and co-ordination. I dare say it still does. When studying physics we are not asked to investigate the biographies of all the disciples of Newton who showed interest in science, but who failed to make any discovery. Neither are their unrewarded gropings, hopes, passions, laundry bills, or erotic experiences thrust on the hurried student or considered germane to the subject.

The general contempt of 'scholarship', especially any part of it connected with subjects included in university 'Arts' courses; the shrinking of people in general from any book supposed to be 'good'; and, in another mode, the flamboyant advertisements telling 'how to seem to know it when you don't', might long since have indicated to the sensitive that there is something defective in the contemporary methods of purveying letters.

As the general reader has but a vague idea of what these methods are at the 'centre', i.e. for the specialist who is expected to serve the general reader, I shall lapse or plunge into autobiography.

In my university I found various men interested (or uninterested) in their subjects, but, I think, no man with a view of literature as a whole, or with any idea whatsoever of the relation of the part he himself taught to any other part.

Those professors who regarded their 'subject' as a drill manual rose most rapidly to positions of executive responsibility (one case

---

[1] *New York Herald Tribune,* 'Books', 1929.

[2] Foot-note a few decades later: The proper definition would be 'Institutions for the obstruction of learning.'

is now a provost). Those professors who had some natural aptitude for comprehending their authors and for communicating a general sense of comfort in the presence of literary masterwork remained obscurely in their less exalted positions.

A professor of Romanics admitted that the *Chanson de Roland* was inferior to the *Odyssey*, but then the Middle Ages were expected to present themselves with apologies, and this was, if I remember rightly, an isolated exception. English novelists were not compared with the French. 'Sources' were discussed; forty versions of a Chaucerian anecdote were 'compared', but not on points of respective literary merit. The whole field was full of redundance. I mean that what one had learned in one class, in the study of one literature, one was told again in some other.

One was asked to remember what some critic (deceased) had said, scarcely to consider whether his views were still valid, or ever had been very intelligent.

In defence of this dead and uncorrelated system, it may be urged that authors like Spengler, who attempt a synthesis, often do so before they have attained sufficient knowledge of detail: that they stuff expandable and compressible objects into rubber-bag categories, and that they limit their reference and interest by supposing that the pedagogic follies which they have themselves encountered, constitute an error universally distributed, and encountered by every one else. In extenuation of their miscalculations we may admit that any error or clumsiness of method that has sunk into, or been hammered into one man, over a period of years, probably continues as an error— not merely passively, but as an error still being propagated, consciously or unconsciously, by a number of educators, from laziness, from habits, or from natural cussedness.

'Comparative literature' sometimes figures in university curricula, but very few people know what they mean by the term, or approach it with a considered conscious method.

To tranquillize the low-brow reader, let me say at once that I do not wish to muddle him by making him read more books, but to allow him to read fewer with greater result. (I am willing to discuss this privately with the book trade.) I have been accused of wanting to make people read all the classics; which is not so. I have been accused of wishing to provide a 'portable substitute for the British Museum', which I would do, like a shot, were it possible. It isn't.

American 'taste' is less official than English taste, but more derivative. When I arrived in England (A.D. 1908), I found a greater darkness in the British 'serious press' than had obtained on the banks of the Schuylkill. Already in my young and ignorant years they considered me 'learned'. It was impossible, at first, to see why and whence the current opinion of British weeklies. It was incredible that literate men—men literate enough, that is, to write the orderly paragraphs that they did write constantly in their papers—believed the stupidities that appeared there with such regularity. (Later, for two years, we ran fortnightly in the *Egoist,* the sort of fool-column that the French call a *sottisier,* needing nothing for it but quotations from the *Times Literary Supplement.* Two issues of the *Supplement* yielding, easily, one page of the *Egoist.*) For years I awaited enlightenment. One winter I had lodgings in Sussex. On the mantel-piece of the humble country cottage I found books of an earlier era, among them an anthology printed in 1830, and yet another dated 1795, and there, there by the sox of Jehosaphat was the British taste of this century, 1910, 1915, and even the present, A.D. 1931.

I had read Stendhal's remark that it takes eighty years for any-thing to reach the general public, and looking out on the waste heath, under the December drizzle, I believed him. But that is not all of the story. Embedded in that naïve innocence that does, to their credit, pervade our universities, I ascribed the delay to mere time. I still thought: With the attrition of decades, ah, yes, in another seventy, in another, perhaps, ninety years, they will admit that . . . etc.

I mean that I thought they wanted to, but were hindered.

Later it struck me that the best history of painting in London was the National Gallery, and that the best history of literature, more particularly of poetry, would be a twelve-volume anthology in which each poem was chosen not merely because it was a nice poem or a poem Aunt Hepsy liked, but because it contained an invention, a definite contribution to the art of verbal expression. With this in mind, I approached a respected agent. He was courteous, he was even openly amazed at the list of three hundred items which I offered as an indication of outline. No autochthonous Briton had ever, to his professed belief, displayed such familiarity with so vast a range, but he was too indolent to recast my introductory letter into a form suited to commerce. He, as they say, 'repaired' to an equally august and long-established publishing house (which had already served his and my interest). In two days came a hasty summons: would I see him in person. I found him awed, as if one had killed a cat in the sacristy. Did I know what I had said in my letter? I did. Yes, but about Palgrave? I did. I had said: 'It is time we had something to replace that doddard Palgrave.' 'But don't you know', came the awstruck tones, 'that the whole fortune of X & Co. is founded on Palgrave's *Golden Treasury*?'

From that day onward no book of mine received a British imprimatur until the appearance of Eliot's castrated edition of my poems.

I perceived that there were thousands of pounds sterling invested in electro-plate, and the least change in the public taste, let alone swift, catastrophic changes, would depreciate the value of those electros (of Hemans, let us say, or of Collins, Cowper, and of Churchill, who wrote the satiric verses, and of later less blatant cases, touched with a slighter flavour of mustiness).

I sought the banks of the Seine. Against ignorance one might struggle, and even against organic stupidity, but against a so vast vested interest the lone odds were too heavy.

Two years later a still more august academic press reopened the question. *They* had ventured to challenge Palgrave: they had been 'interested'—would I send back my prospectus? I did. They found the plan 'too ambitious'. They said they might do 'something', but that if they did it would be 'more in the nature of gems'.

FOR A METHOD

Nevertheless, the method I had proposed was simple, it is perhaps the only one that can give a man an orderly arrangement of his perception in the matter of letters. In opposition to it, there are the forces of superstition, of hang-over. People regard literature as something vastly more flabby and floating and complicated and indefinite than, let us say, mathematics. Its subject-matter, the human consciousness, is more complicated than are number and space. It is not, however, more complicated than biology, and no one ever supposed that it was. We apply a loose-leaf system to book-keeping so as to have the live items separated from the dead ones. In the study of physics we begin with simple mechanisms, wedge, lever and fulcrum, pulley and inclined plane, all of them still as useful as when they were first invented. We proceed by a study of discoveries.

We are not asked to memorize a list of the parts of a side-wheeler engine.

And we could, presumably, apply to the study of literature a little of the common sense that we currently apply to physics or to biology. In poetry there are simple procedures, and there are known discoveries, clearly marked. As I have said in various places in my unorganized and fragmentary volumes: in each age one or two men of genius find something, and express it. It may be in only a line or in two lines, or in some quality of a cadence; and thereafter two dozen, or two hundred, or two or more thousand followers repeat and dilute and modify.

And if the instructor would select his specimens from works that contain these discoveries and solely on the basis of discovery— which may lie in the dimension of depth, not merely of some novelty on the surface—he would aid his student far more than by presenting his authors at random, and talking about them *in toto*.

Needless to say, this presentation would be entirely independent of consideration as to whether the given passages tended to make the student a better republican, monarchist, monist, dualist, rotarian, or other sectarian. To avoid confusion, one should state at once that such method has nothing to do with those allegedly scientific methods which approach literature as if it were something *not literature*, or with scientists' attempts to sub-divide the elements in literature according to some non-literary categoric division.

You do not divide physics or chemistry according to racial or religious categories. You do not put discoveries by Methodists and Germans into one category, and discoveries by Episcopalians or Americans or Italians into another.

DEFECTIVE RELATIVITIES

It is said that in America nothing is ever consciously related to anything else. I have cited as an exception the forty versions of the Chaucerian anecdote; they and the great edition of Horace with the careful list and parallel display of Greek sources for such line or such paragraph, show how the associative faculty can be side-tracked. Or at any rate they indicate the first gropings of association. Let us grant that some bits of literature have been, in special cases, displayed in relation to some other bits; usually some verbose gentleman writes a trilogy of essays, on three grandiose figures, comparing their 'philosophy' or personal habits.

Let us by all means glance at 'philology' and the 'germanic system'. Speaking as an historian, 'we' may say that this system was designed to inhibit thought. After 1848 it was, in Germany, observed that some people thought. It was necessary to curtail this pernicious activity, the thinkists were given a china egg labelled scholarship, and were gradually unfitted for active life, or for any contact with life in general. Literature was permitted as a subject of study. And its study was so designed as to draw the mind of the student away from literature into inanity.

WHY BOOKS?

I

This simple first question was never asked.

The study of literature, or more probably of morphology, verbroots, etc., was permitted the German professor in, let us say, 1880–1905, to keep his mind off life in general, and off public life in particular.

In America it was permitted from precedent; it was known to be permitted in Germany; Germany had a 'great university tradition', which it behoved America to equal and perhaps to surpass.

This study, or some weaker variety of it, was also known to be permitted at Oxford, and supposed to have a refining influence on the student.

II

The practice of literary composition in private has been permitted since 'age immemorial', like knitting, crocheting, etc. It occupies the practitioner, and, so long as he keeps it to himself, *ne nuit pas aux autres*, it does not transgress the definition of liberty which we find in the declaration of the *Droits de l'Homme*: Liberty is the right to do anything which harms not others. All of which is rather negative and unsatisfactory.

III

It appears to me quite tenable that the function of literature as a generated prize-worthy force is precisely that it does incite humanity to continue living; that it eases the mind of strain, and feeds it, I mean definitely as *nutrition of impulse*.

This idea may worry lovers of order. Just as good literature does often worry them. They regard it as dangerous, chaotic, subversive. They try every idiotic and degrading wheeze to tame it down. They try to make a bog, a marasmus, a great putridity in place of a sane and active ebullience. And they do this from sheer simian and pig-like stupidity, and from their failure to understand the function of letters.

IV

Has literature a function in the state, in the aggregation of humans, in the republic, in the *res publica*, which ought to mean the public convenience (despite the slime of bureaucracy, and the execrable taste of the populace in selecting its rulers)? It has.

And this function is *not* the coercing or emotionally persuading, or bullying or suppressing people into the acceptance of any one set or any six sets of opinions as opposed to any other one set or half-dozen sets of opinions.

It has to do with the clarity and vigour of 'any and every' thought and opinion. It has to do with maintaining the very cleanliness of the tools, the health of the very matter of thought itself. Save in the rare and limited instances of invention in the plastic arts, or in mathematics, the individual cannot think and communicate his thought, the governor and legislator cannot act effectively or frame his laws, without words, and the solidity and validity of these words is in the care of the damned and despised *litterati*. When their work goes rotten—by that I do not mean when they express indecorous thoughts—but when their very medium, the very essence of their work, the application of word to thing goes rotten, i.e. becomes slushy and inexact, or excessive or bloated, the whole machinery of social and of individual thought and order goes to pot. This is a lesson of history, and a lesson not yet half learned.

The great writers need no debunking.

The pap is not in them, and doesn't need to be squeezed out. They do not lend themselves to imperial and sentimental exploitations. A civilization was founded on Homer, civilization not a mere bloated empire. The Macedonian domination rose and grew after the sophists. It also subsided.

It is not only a question of rhetoric, of loose expression, but also of the loose use of individual words. What the renaissance gained in direct examination of natural phenomena, it in part lost in losing the feel and desire for exact descriptive terms. I mean that the medieval mind had little but words to deal with, and it was more careful in its definitions and verbiage. It did not define a gun in terms that would just as well define an explosion, nor explosions in terms that would define triggers.

Misquoting Confucius, one might say: It does not matter whether the author desire the good of the race or acts merely from personal vanity. The thing is mechanical in action. In proportion as his work is exact, i.e., true to human consciousness and to the nature of man, as it is exact in formulation of desire, so is it durable and so is it 'useful'; I mean it maintains the precision and clarity of thought, not merely for the benefit of a few dilettantes and 'lovers of literature', but maintains the health of thought outside literary circles and in non-literary existence, in general individual and communal life.

Or *'dans ce genre on n'émeut que par la clarté'*. One 'moves' the reader only by clarity. In depicting the motions of the 'human heart' the durability of the writing depends on the exactitude. It is the thing that is true and stays true that keeps fresh for the new reader.

With this general view in mind, and subsequent to the events already set forth in this narrative, I proposed (from the left bank of the Seine, and to an American publishing house), not the twelve-volume anthology, but a short guide to the subject. That was after a few years of 'pause and reflection'. The subject was pleasantly received and considered with amity, but the house finally decided that it would pay neither them to print nor me to write the book, because we 'weren't in the text-book ring'. For the thing would have been a text-book, its circulation would have depended on educators, and educators have been defined as 'men with no intellectual interests'.

Hence, after a lapse of four years, this essay, dedicated to Mr Glenn Frank, and other starters of ideal universities, though not with any great hope that it will rouse them.

PART II: OR WHAT MAY BE AN INTRODUCTION TO METHOD

It is as important for the purpose of thought to keep language efficient as it is in surgery to keep tetanus bacilli out of one's bandages.

In introducing a person to literature one would do well to have

him examine works where language is efficiently used; to devise a
system for getting directly and expeditiously at such works, despite
the smokescreens erected by half-knowing and half-thinking critics.
To get at them, despite the mass of dead matter that these people
have heaped up and conserved round about them in the proportion:
one barrel of sawdust to each half-bunch of grapes.

Great literature is simply language charged with meaning to the
utmost possible degree.

When we set about examining it we find that this charging has
been done by several clearly definable sorts of people, and by a
periphery of less determinate sorts.

(*a*) *The inventors*, discoverers of a particular process or of more
than one mode and process. Sometimes these people are known, or
discoverable; for example, we know, with reasonable certitude, that
Arnaut Daniel introduced certain methods of rhyming, and we know
that certain finenesses of perception appeared first in such a troubadour or in G. Cavalcanti. We do not know, and are not likely to
know, anything definite about the precursors of Homer.

(*b*) *The masters*. This is a very small class, and there are very
few real ones. The term is properly applied to inventors who, apart
from their own inventions, are able to assimilate and co-ordinate a
large number of preceding inventions. I mean to say they either
start with a core of their own and accumulate adjuncts, or they digest
a vast mass of subject-matter, apply a number of known modes of
expression, and succeed in pervading the whole with some special
quality or some special character of their own, and bring the whole
to a state of homogeneous fullness.

(*c*) *The diluters*, these who follow either the inventors or the
'great writers', and who produce something of lower intensity, some
flabbier variant, some diffuseness or tumidity in the wake of the
valid.

(*d*) (And this class produces the great bulk of all writing.) The
men who do more or less good work in the more or less good style of
a period. Of these the delightful anthologies, the song books, are
full, and choice among them is the matter of taste, for you prefer
Wyatt to Donne, Donne to Herrick, Drummond of Hawthornden
to Browne, in response to some purely personal sympathy, these
people add but some slight personal flavour, some minor variant of a
mode, without affecting the main course of the story.

At their faintest '*Ils n'existent pas, leur ambiance leur confert une existence.*' They do not exist: their ambience confers existence upon them. When they are most prolific they produce dubious cases like Virgil and Petrarch, who probably pass, among the less exigeant, for colossi.

(*e*) *Belles Lettres.* Longus, Prévost, Benjamin Constant, who are not exactly 'great masters', who can hardly be said to have originated a form, but who have nevertheless brought some mode to a very high development.

(*f*) And there is a supplementary or sixth class of writers, the starters of crazes, the Ossianic McPhersons, the Gongoras[1] whose wave of fashion flows over writing for a few centuries or a few decades, and then subsides, leaving things as they were.

It will be seen that the first two classes are the more sharply defined: that the difficulty of classification for particular lesser authors increases as one descends the list, save for the last class, which is again fairly clear.

The point is, that if a man knows the facts about the first two categories, he can evaluate almost any unfamiliar book at first sight. I mean he can form a just estimate of its worth, and see how and where it belongs in this schema.

As to crazes, the number of possible diseases in literature is perhaps not very great, the same afflictions crop up in widely separated countries without any previous communication. The good physician will recognize a known malady, even if the manifestation be superficially different.

The fact that six different critics will each have a different view concerning what author belongs in which of the categories here given, does not in the least invalidate the categories. When a man knows the facts about the first two categories, the reading of work in the other categories will not greatly change his opinion about those in the first two.

LANGUAGE

Obviously this knowledge cannot be acquired without knowledge of various tongues. The same discoveries have served a number of races. If a man has not time to learn different languages he can at

[1] One should perhaps apologize, or express a doubt as to the origin of Gongorism, or redefine it or start blaming it on some other spaniard.

least, and with very little delay, be told what the discoveries were. If he wish to be a good critic he will have to look for himself.

Bad critics have prolonged the use of demoded terminology, usually a terminology originally invented to describe what had been done before 300 B.C., and to describe it in a rather exterior fashion. Writers of second order have often tried to produce works to fit some category or term not yet occupied in their own local literature. If we chuck out the classifications which apply to the outer shape of the work, or to its occasion, and if we look at what actually happens, in, let us say, poetry, we will find that the language is charged or energized in various manners.

That is to say, there are three 'kinds of poetry':

MELOPŒIA, wherein the words are charged, over and above their plain meaning, with some musical property, which directs the bearing or trend of that meaning.

PHANOPŒIA, which is a casting of images upon the visual imagination.

LOGOPŒIA, 'the dance of the intellect among words', that is to say, it employs words not only for their direct meaning, but it takes count in a special way of habits of usage, of the context we *expect* to find with the word, its usual concomitants, of its known acceptances, and of ironical play. It holds the aesthetic content which is peculiarly the domain of verbal manifestation, and cannot possibly be contained in plastic or in music. It is the latest come, and perhaps most tricky and undependable mode.

The *melopœia* can be appreciated by a foreigner with a sensitive ear, even though he be ignorant of the language in which the poem is written. It is practically impossible to transfer or translate it from one language to another, save perhaps by divine accident, and for half a line at a time.

Phanopœia can, on the other hand, be translated almost, or wholly, intact. When it is good enough, it is practically impossible for the translator to destroy it save by very crass bungling, and the neglect of perfectly well-known and formulative rules.

Logopœia does not translate; though the attitude of mind it expresses may pass through a paraphrase. Or one might say, you can *not* translate it 'locally', but having determined the original author's state of mind, you may or may not be able to find a derivative or an equivalent.

PROSE

The language of prose is much less highly charged, that is perhaps the only availing distinction between prose and poesy. Prose permits greater factual presentation, explicitness, but a much greater amount of language is needed. During the last century or century and a half, prose has, perhaps for the first time, perhaps for the second or third time, arisen to challenge the poetic pre-eminence. That is to say, *Cœur Simple*, by Flaubert, is probably more important than Théophile Gautier's *Carmen*, etc.

The total charge in certain nineteenth-century prose works possibly surpasses the total charge found in individual poems of that period; but that merely indicates that the author has been able to get his effect cumulatively, by a greater heaping up of factual data; imagined fact, if you will, but nevertheless expressed in factual manner.

By using several hundred pages of prose, Flaubert, by force of architectonics, manages to attain an intensity comparable to that in Villon's *Heaulmière*, or his prayer for his mother. This does not invalidate my dissociation of the two terms: poetry, prose.

In *Phanopœia* we find the greatest drive toward utter precision of word; this art exists almost exclusively by it.

In *melopœia* we find a contrary current, a force tending often to lull, or to distract the reader from the exact sense of the language. It is poetry on the borders of music and music is perhaps the bridge between consciousness and the unthinking sentient or even in-sentient universe.

All writing is built up of these three elements, plus 'architectonics' or 'the form of the whole', and to know anything about the relative efficiency of various works one must have some knowledge of the maximum already attained by various authors, irrespective of where and when.[1]

It is not enough to know that the Greeks attained to the greatest skill in melopœia, or even that the Provençaux added certain diverse developments and that some quite minor, nineteenth-century Frenchmen achieved certain elaborations.

It is not quite enough to have the general idea that the Chinese

---

[1] Lacuna at this point to be corrected in criticism of Hindemith's 'Schwanen-dreher'. E.P. Sept. 1938.

(more particularly Rihaku and Omakitsu) attained the known maximum of *phanopœia*, due perhaps to the nature of their written ideograph, or to wonder whether Rimbaud is, at rare moments, their equal. One wants one's knowledge in more definite terms.

It is an error to think that vast reading will automatically produce any such knowledge or understanding. Neither Chaucer with his forty books, nor Shakespeare with perhaps half a dozen, in folio, can be considered illiterate. A man can learn more music by working on a Bach fugue until he can take it apart and put it together, than by playing through ten dozen heterogeneous albums.

You may say that for twenty-seven years I have thought consciously about this particular matter, and read or read at a great many books, and that with the subject never really out of my mind, I don't yet know half there is to know about *melopœia*.

There are, on the other hand, a few books that I still keep on my desk, and a great number that I shall never open again. But the books that a man needs to know in order to 'get his bearings', in order to have a sound judgement of any bit of writing that may come before him, are very few. The list is so short, indeed, that one wonders that people, professional writers in particular, are willing to leave them ignored and to continue dangling in mid-chaos emitting the most imbecile estimates, and often vitiating their whole lifetime's production.

Limiting ourselves to the authors who actually invented something, or who are the 'first known examples' of the process in working order, we find:

OF THE GREEKS: Homer, Sappho. (The 'great dramatists' decline from Homer, and depend immensely on him for their effects; their 'charge', at its highest potential, depends so often, and so greatly on their being able to count on their audience's knowledge of the *Iliad*. Even Æschylus is rhetorical.)[1]

OF THE ROMANS: As we have lost Philetas, and most of Callimachus, we may suppose that the Romans added a certain sophistication; at any rate, Catullus, Ovid, Propertius, all give us something we cannot find now in Greek authors.

A specialist may read Horace if he is interested in learning the precise demarcation between what can be learned about writing, and

---

[1] E.P.'s later and unpublished notes, revise all this in so far as they demand much greater recognition of Sophokles.

what cannot. I mean that Horace is the perfect example of a man who acquired all that is acquirable, without having the root. I beg the reader to observe that I am being exceedingly iconoclastic, that I am omitting thirty established names for every two I include. I am chucking out Pindar, and Virgil, without the slightest compunction. I do not suggest a 'course' in Greek or Latin literature, I name a few isolated writers; five or six pages of Sappho. One can throw out at least one-third of Ovid. That is to say, I am omitting the authors who can teach us no new or no more effective method of 'charging words.

OF THE MIDDLE AGES: The Anglo-Saxon *Seafarer,* and some more cursory notice of some medieval narrative, it does not so greatly matter what narrative, possibly the *Beowulf,* the *Poema del Cid,* and the sagas of *Grettir* and *Burnt Nial.* And then, in contrast, troubadours, perhaps thirty poems in Provençal, and for comparison with them a few songs by Von Morungen, or Wolfram von Essenbach, and von der Vogelweide; and then Bion's *Death of Adonis.*

From which mixture, taken in this order, the reader will get his bearings on the art of poetry made to be sung; for there are three kinds of *melopœia*: (1) that made to be sung to a tune; (2) that made to be intoned or sung to a sort of chant; and (3) that made to be spoken; and the art of joining words in each of these kinds is different, and cannot be clearly understood until the reader knows that there are three different objectives.

OF THE ITALIANS: Guido Cavalcanti and Dante; perhaps a dozen and a half poems of Guido's, and a dozen poems by his contemporaries, and the *Divina Commedia.*

In Italy, around the year 1300, there were new values established, things said that had not been said in Greece, or in Rome or elsewhere.

VILLON: After Villon and for several centuries, poetry can be considered as *fioritura,* as an efflorescence, almost an effervescence, and without any new roots. Chaucer is an enrichment, one might say a more creamy version of the 'matter of France', and he in some measure preceded the verbal richness of the classic revival, but beginning with the Italians after Dante, coming through the Latin writers of the Renaissance, French, Spanish, English, Tasso, Ariosto, etc., the Italians always a little in the lead, the whole is elaboration, medieval basis, and wash after wash of Roman or Hellenic influence. I mean one need not read any particular part of it for purpose of learning one's comparative values.

If one were studying history and not poetry, one might discover the medieval mind more directly in the opening of Mussato's *Ecerinus* than even in Dante. The culture of Chaucer is the same as that which went contemporaneously into Ferrara, with the tongue called ' *francoveneto* '.

One must emphasize one's contrasts in the quattrocento. One can take Villon as pivot for understanding them. After Villon, and having begun before his time, we find this *fioritura*, and for centuries we find little else, Even in Marlowe and Shakespeare there is this embroidery of language, this talk about the matter, rather than presentation. I doubt if anyone ever acquired discrimination in studying 'The Elizabethans'. You have grace, richness of language, abundance, but you have probably nothing that isn't replaceable by something else, no ornament that wouldn't have done just as well in some other connection, or for which some other figure of rhetoric couldn't have served, or which couldn't have been distilled from literary antecedents.

The 'language' had not been heard on the London stage, but it had been heard in the Italian law courts, etc.; there were local attempts, all over Europe, to teach the public (in Spain, Italy, England) Latin diction. 'Poetry' was considered to be (as it still is considered by a great number of drivelling imbeciles) synonymous with 'lofty and flowery language'.

One Elizabethan specialist has suggested that Shakespeare, disgusted with his efforts, or at least despairing of success, as a poet, took to the stage. The drama is a mixed art; it does not rely on the charge that can be put into the word, but calls on gesture and mimicry and 'impersonation' for assistance. The actor must do a good half of the work. One does no favour to drama by muddling the two sets of problems.

Apologists for the drama are continually telling us in one way or another that drama either cannot use at all, or can make but a very limited use of words charged to their highest potential. This is perfectly true. Let us try to keep our minds on the problem we started with, i.e., the art of writing, the art of 'charging' language with meaning.

After 1450 we have the age of *fioritura;* after Marlowe and

Shakespeare came what was called a 'classic' movement, a movement that restrained without inventing. Anything that happens
to mind in England has usually happened somewhere else first.
Someone invents something, then someone develops, or some dozens
develop a frothy or at any rate creamy enthusiasm or over-abundance, then someone tries to tidy things up. For example, the
estimable Pleiad emasculating the French tongue, and the French
classicists, and the English classicists, etc., all of which things should
be relegated to the subsidiary zone: period interest, historical interest,
bric-à-brac for museums.

At this point someone says: 'O, but the ballads'. All right, I will
allow the voracious peruser a half-hour for ballads (English and
Spanish, or Scottish, Border, and Spanish). There is nothing easier
than to be distracted from one's point, or from the main drive of
one's subject by a desire for utterly flawless equity and omniscience.

Let us say, but directly in parenthesis, that there was a very
limited sort of *logopœia* in seventeenth- and eighteenth-century satire.
And that Rochester and Dorset may have introduced a new note, or
more probably re-introduced an old one, that reappears later in
Heine.

Let us also cut loose from minor details and minor exceptions: the
main fact is that we 'have come' or that 'humanity came' to a point
where verse-writing can or could no longer be clearly understood
without the study of prose-writing.

Say, for the sake of argument, that after the slump of the Middle
Ages, prose 'came to' again in Machiavelli; admit that various sorts
of prose had existed, in fact nearly all sorts had existed. Herodotus
wrote history that is literature. Thucydides was a journalist. (It is
a modern folly to suppose that vulgarity and cheapness have the
merit of novelty; they have always existed, and are of no interest in
themselves.)

There have been bombast, oratory, legal speech, balanced sentences, Ciceronian impressiveness; Petronius had written a satiric
novel, Longus had written a delicate nouvelle. The prose of the
Renaissance leaves us Rabelais, Brantôme, Montaigne. A determined
specialist can dig interesting passages, or sumptuous passages, or
even subtle passages out of Pico, the medieval mystics, scholastics,
platonists, none of which will be the least use to a man trying to
learn the art of 'changing language'.

I mean to say that from the beginning of literature up to A.D. 1750 poetry was the superior art, and was so considered to be, and if we read books written before that date we find the number of interesting books in verse at least equal to the number of prose books still readable; and the poetry contains the quintessence. When we want to know what people were like before 1750, when we want to know that they had blood and bones like ourselves, we go to the poetry of the period.

But, as I have said, the '*fioritura* business' set in. And one morning Monsieur Stendhal, not thinking of Homer, or Villon, or Catullus, but having a very keen sense of actuality, noticed that 'poetry', *la poésie*, as the term was then understood, the stuff written by his French contemporaries, or sonorously rolled at him from the French stage, was a damn nuisance. And he remarked that poetry, with its bagwigs and its bobwigs, and its padded calves and its periwigs, its 'fustian à la Louis XIV', was greatly inferior to prose for conveying a clear idea of the diverse states of our consciousness ('les mouvements du cœur').

And at that moment the serious art of writing 'went over to prose', and for some time the important developments of language as means of expression were the developments of prose. And a man cannot clearly understand or justly judge the value of verse, modern verse, any verse, unless he has grasped this.

PART III: CONCLUSIONS, EXCEPTIONS, CURRICULA

Before Stendhal there is probably nothing in prose that does not also exist in verse or that can't be done by verse just as well as by prose. Even the method of annihilating imbecility employed by Voltaire, Bayle, and Lorenzo Valla can be managed quite as well in rhymed couplets.

Beginning with the Renaissance, or perhaps with Boccaccio, we have prose that is quite necessary to the clear comprehension of things in general: with Rabelais, Brantôme, Montaigne, Fielding, Sterne, we begin to find prose recording states of consciouness that their verse-writing contemporaries scamp. And this fuller consciousness, in more delicate modes, appears in l'Abbé Prévost, Benjamin Constant, Jane Austen. So that Stendhal had already 'something back of him' when he made his remarks about the inferiority of 'La Poésie'.

During the nineteenth century the superiority, if temporary, is at any rate obvious, and to such degree that I believe no man can now write really good verse unless he knows Stendhal and Flaubert. Or, let us say, Le Rouge et le Noir, the first half of La Chartreuse, Madame Bovary, L'Education, Les Trois Contes, Bouvard et Pécuchet. To put it perhaps more strongly, he will learn more about the art of charging words from Flaubert than he will from the floribund sixteenth-century dramatists.

The main expression of nineteenth-century consciousness is in prose. The art continues in Maupassant, who slicked up the Flaubertian mode. The art of popular success lies simply in never putting more on any one page than the most ordinary reader can lick off it in his normally rapid, half-attentive skim-over. The Goncourts struggled with praiseworthy sobriety, noble, but sometimes dull. Henry James was the first person to add anything to the art of the nineteenth-century novel not already known to the French.

Thought was churned up by Darwin, by science, by industrial machines, Nietzsche made a temporary commotion, but these things are extraneous to our subject, which is the *art of getting meaning into words*. There is an 'influence of Ibsen', all for the good, but now exploited by cheap-jacks. Fabre and Frazer are both essential to contemporary clear thinking. I am not talking about the books that have poured something into the general consciousness, but of books that show *how* the pouring is done or display the implements, newly discovered, by which one can pour.

The nineteenth-century novel is such an implement. The Ibsen play is, or perhaps we must say was, such an implement.

It is for us to think whether these implements are more effective than poetry: (*a*) as known before 1800; (*b*) as known during the nineteenth century and up to the present.

FRANCE

The decline of England began on the day when Landor packed his trunks and departed to Tuscany. Up till then England had been able to contain her best authors; after that we see Shelley, Keats, Byron, Beddoes on the Continent, and still later observe the edifying spectacle of Browning in Italy and Tennyson in Buckingham Palace.

In France, as the novel developed, spurred on, shall we say, by the activity in the prose-media, the versifiers were not idle.

Departing from *Albertus*, Gautier developed the medium we find in the *Emaux et Camées*. England in the 'nineties had got no further than the method of the *Albertus*. If Corbière invented no process he at any rate restored French verse to the vigour of Villon and to an intensity that no Frenchman had touched during the intervening four centuries.

Unless I am right in discovering *logopœia* in Propertius (which means unless the academic teaching of Latin displays crass insensitivity as it probably does), we must almost say that Laforgue invented *logopœia* observing that there had been a very limited range of *logopœia* in all satire, and that Heine occasionally employs something like it, together with a dash of bitters, such as can (though he may not have known it) be found in a few verses of Dorset and Rochester. At any rate Laforgue found or refound *logopœia*. And Rimbaud brought back to *phanopœia* its clarity and directness.

All four of these poets, Gautier, Corbière, Laforgue, Rimbaud, redeem poetry from Stendhal's condemnation. There is in Corbière something one finds nowhere before him, unless in Villon.

Laforgue is not like any preceding poet. He is not ubiquitously like Propertius.

In Rimbaud the image stands clean, unencumbered by non-functioning words; to get anything like this directness of presentation one must go back to Catullus, perhaps to the poem which contains *dentes habet*.

If a man is too lazy to read the brief works of these poets, he cannot hope to understand writing, verse writing, prose writing, any writing.

ENGLAND

Against this serious action England can offer only Robert Browning. He has no French or European parallel. He has, indubitably, grave limitations, but *The Ring and the Book* is serious experimentation. He is a better poet than Landor, who was perhaps the only complete and serious man of letters ever born in these islands.

We are so encumbered by having British literature in our foreground that even in this brief survey one must speak of it in disproportion. It was kept alive during the last century by a series of

exotic injections. Swinburne read Greek and took English metric in
hand; Rossetti brought in the Italian primitives; FitzGerald made the
only good poem of the time that has gone to the people; it is called,
and is to a great extent, a trans- or mistrans-lation.

There was a faint waft of early French influence. Morris translated sagas, the Irish took over the business for a few years; Henry
James led, or rather preceded, the novelists, and then the Britons
resigned *en bloc;* the language is now in the keeping of the Irish
(Yeats and Joyce); apart from Yeats, since the death of Hardy, poetry
is being written by Americans. All the developments in English
verse since 1910 are due almost wholly to Americans. In fact, there
is no longer any reason to call it English verse, and there is no present
reason to think of England at all.

We speak a language that was English. When Richard Cœur de
Lion first heard Turkish he said: 'He spik lak a fole Britain.' From
which orthography one judges that Richard himself probably spoke
like a French-Canadian.

It is a magnificent language, and there is no need of, or advantage
in, minimizing the debt we owe to Englishmen who died before 1620.
Neither is there any point in studying the 'History of English Literature' as taught. Curiously enough, the histories of Spanish and
Italian literature always take count of translators. Histories of English
literature always slide over translation—I suppose it is inferiority
complex—yet some of the best books in English are translations.
This is important for two reasons. First, the reader who has been
appalled by the preceding parts and said, 'Oh, but I can't learn all
these languages', may in some measure be comforted. He can learn
the art of writing precisely where so many great local lights learned
it; if not from the definite poems I have listed, at least from the men
who learned it from those poems in the first place.

We may count the *Seafarer*, the *Beowulf*, and the remaining Anglo-
Saxon fragments as indigenous art; at least, they dealt with a native
subject, and by an art not newly borrowed. Whether alliterative
metre owes anything to Latin hexameter is a question open to
debate; we have no present means of tracing the debt. Landor
suggests the problem in his dialogue of Ovid and the Prince of the
Gaetae.

After this period English literature lives on translation, it is
fed by translation; every new exuberance, every new heave is stimu-

lated by translation, every allegedly great age is an age of translations, beginning with Geoffrey Chaucer, Le Grand Translateur, translator of the *Romaunt of the Rose*, paraphraser of Virgil and Ovid, condenser of old stories he had found in Latin, French, and Italian.

After him even the ballads that tell a local tale tell it in art indebted to Europe. It is the natural spreading ripple that moves from the civilized Mediterranean centre out through the half-civilized and into the barbarous peoples.

The Britons never have shed barbarism; they are proud to tell you that Tacitus said the last word about Germans. When Mary Queen of Scots went to Edinburgh she bewailed going out among savages, and she herself went from a sixteenth-century court that held but a barbarous, or rather a drivelling and idiotic and superficial travesty of the Italian culture as it had been before the débâcle of 1527. The men who tried to civilize these shaggy and uncouth marginalians by bringing them news of civilization have left a certain number of translations that are better reading today than are the works of the ignorant islanders who were too proud to translate. After Chaucer we have Gavin Douglas's *Eneados*, better than the original, as Douglas had heard the sea. Golding's *Metamorphoses*, from which Shakespeare learned so much of his trade. Marlowe's translation of Ovid's *Amores*. We have no satisfactory translation of any Greek author. Chapman and Pope have left Iliads that are of interest to specialists; so far as I know, the only translation of Homer that one can read with continued pleasure is in early French by Hugues Salel; he, at least, was intent on telling the story, and not wholly muddled with accessories. I have discussed the merits of these translators elsewhere. I am now trying to tell the reader what he can learn of comparative literature through translations that are in themselves better reading than the 'original verse' of their periods. He can study the whole local development, or, we had better say, the sequence of local fashion in British verse by studying the translations of Horace that have poured in uninterrupted sequence from the British Press since 1650. That is work for a specialist, an historian, not for a man who wants simply to establish his axes of reference by knowing *the best of each kind* of written thing; as he would establish his axes of reference for painting by knowing a few pictures by Cimabue, Giotto, Piero della Francesca, Ambrogio de Predis, etc.; Velasquez, Goya, etc.

It is one thing to be able to spot the best painting and quite another and far less vital thing to know just where some secondary or tertiary painter learned certain defects.

Apart from these early translations, a man may enlarge his view of international poetry by looking at Swinburne's Greek adaptations. The Greeks stimulated Swinburne; if he had defects, let us remember that, apart from Homer, the Greeks often were rather Swinburnian. Catullus wasn't, or was but seldom. From which one may learn the nature of the Latin, non-Greek contribution to the art of expression.[1]

Swinburne's Villon is not Villon very exactly, but it is perhaps the best Swinburne we have. Rossetti's translations were perhaps better than Rossetti, and his *Vita Nuova* and early Italian poets guide one to originals, which he has now and again improved. Our contact with Oriental poetry begins with FitzGerald's Rubáiyát. Fenollosa's essay on the Chinese written character opens a door that the earlier students had, if not 'howled without', at least been unable to open.

In mentioning these translations, I don't in the least admit or imply that any man in our time can think with only one language. He may be able to invent a new carburettor, or even work effectively in a biological laboratory, but he probably won't even try to do the latter without study of at least one foreign tongue. Modern science has always been multilingual. A good scientist simply would not be bothered to limit himself to one language and be held up for news of discoveries. The writer or reader who is content with such ignorance simply admits that his particular mind is of less importance than his kidneys or his automobile. The French who know no English are as fragmentary as the Americans who know no French. One simply leaves half of one's thought untouched in their company.

Different languages—I mean the actual vocabularies, the idioms— have worked out certain mechanisms of communication and registration. No one language is complete. A master may be continually expanding his own tongue, rendering it fit to bear some charge hitherto borne only by some other alien tongue, but the process does not stop with any one man. While Proust is learning Henry James, preparatory to breaking through certain French paste-board partitions, the whole American speech is churning and chugging, and every other tongue doing likewise.

To be 'possible' in mentally active company the American has to

[1] To be measured against the Sophoklean economy.

learn French, the Frenchman has to learn English or American. The Italian has for some time learned French. The man who does not know the Italian of the duocento and trecento has in him a painful lacuna, not necessarily painful to himself, but there are simply certain things he don't know, and can't; it is as if he were blind to some part of the spectrum. Because of the determined attempt of the patriotic Latinists of Italy in the renaissance to 'conquer' Greek by putting every Greek author effectively into Latin it is now possible to get a good deal of Greek through Latin cribs. The disuse of Latin cribs in Greek study, beginning, I suppose, about 1820, has caused no end of damage to the general distribution of 'classic culture'.

Another point miscomprehended by people who are clumsy at languages is that one does not need to learn a whole language in order to understand some one or some dozen poems. It is often enough to understand thoroughly the poem, and every one of the few dozen or few hundred words that compose it.

This is what we start to do as small children when we memorize some lyric of Goethe or Heine. Incidentally, this process leaves us for life with a measuring rod (*a*) for a certain type of lyric, (*b*) for the German language, so that, however bored we may be by the *Grundriss von Groeber*, we never wholly forget the feel of the language.

VACCINE

Do I suggest a remedy? I do. I suggest several remedies. I suggest that we throw out all critics who use vague general terms. Not merely those who use vague terms because they are too ignorant to have a meaning; but the critics who use vague terms to *conceal* their meaning, and all critics who use terms so vaguely that the reader can think he agrees with them or assents to their statements when he doesn't.

The first credential we should demand of a critic is *his* ideograph of the good; of what he considers valid writing, and indeed of all his general terms. Then we know where he is. He cannot simply stay in London writing of French pictures that his readers have not seen. He must begin by stating that such and such *particular* works seem to him 'good', 'best', 'indifferent', 'valid', 'non-valid'. I suggest a definite curriculum in place of the present *émiettements*, of breaking the subject up into crumbs quickly dryable. A curriculum for instructors, for obstreperous students who wish to annoy dull instructors, for men who haven't had time for systematized college courses. Call it the minimum basis for a sound and liberal education in letters (with French and English 'aids' in parenthesis).

CONFUCIUS—In full (there being no complete and intelligent English version, one would have either to learn Chinese or make use of the French version by Pauthier).

HOMER—in full (Latin cribs, Hugues Salel in French, no satisfactory English, though Chapman can be used as reference).

OVID—And the Latin 'personal' poets, Catullus and Propertius. (Golding's *Metamorphoses*, Marlowe's *Amores*. There is no useful English version of Catullus.)

A PROVENÇAL SONG BOOK—With cross reference to Minnesingers, and to Bion, perhaps thirty poems in all.

DANTE—'And his circle'; that is to say Dante, and thirty poems by his contemporaries, mostly by Guido Cavalcanti.

VILLON—

PARENTHETICALLY—Some other medieval matter might be added, and some general outline of history of thought through the Renaissance.

VOLTAIRE—That is to say, some incursion into his critical writings, not into his attempts at fiction and drama, and some dip into his contemporaries (prose).

STENDHAL—(At least a book and half).

FLAUBERT (omitting *Salambô* and the *Tentation*)—And the Goncourts.

GAUTIER, CORBIÈRE, RIMBAUD.

This would not overburden the three- or four-year student. After this inoculation he could be 'with safety exposed' to modernity or anything else in literature. I mean he wouldn't lose his head or ascribe ridiculous values to works of secondary intensity. He would have axes of reference and, would I think, find them dependable.

For the purposes of general education we could omit all study of monistic totemism and voodoo for at least fifty years and study of Shakespeare for thirty on the ground that acquaintance with these subjects is already very widely diffused, and that one absorbs quite enough knowledge of them from boring circumjacent conversation.

This list does not, obviously, contain the names of every author who has ever written a good poem or a good octave or sestet. It is the result of twenty-seven years' thought on the subject and a résumé of conclusions. That may be a reason for giving it some consideration. It is not a reason for accepting it as a finality. Swallowed whole it is useless. For practical class work the instructor should try, and incite his students to try, to pry out some element that I have included and to substitute for it something more valid. The intelligent lay reader will instinctively try to do this for himself.

I merely insist that *without* this minimum the critic has almost no chance of sound judgment. Judgment will gain one more chance of soundness if he can be persuaded to consider Fenollosa's essay or some other, and to me unknown but equally effective, elucidation of the Chinese written character.

Before I die I hope to see at least a few of the best Chinese works printed bilingually, in the form that Mori and Ariga prepared certain texts for Fenollosa, a 'crib', the picture of each letter accompanied by a full explanation.

For practical contact with all past poetry that was actually *sung* in its own day I suggest that each dozen universities combine in employing a couple of singers who understand the meaning of words. Men like Yves Tinayre and Robert Maitland are available. A half-dozen hours spent in listening to the lyrics actually performed would give the student more knowledge of that sort of *melopœia* than a year's work in philology. The Kennedy-Frasers have dug up music that fits the *Beowulf*. It was being used for heroic song in the Hebrides. There is other available music, plenty of it, from at least the time of Faidit (A.D. 1190).

I cannot repeat too often or too forcibly my caution against so-called critics who talk 'all around the matter', and who do not define their terms, and who won't say frankly that certain authors are demnition bores. Make a man tell you *first* and specially what writers he thinks are good writers, after that you can listen to his explanation.

Naturally, certain professors who have invested all their intellectual capital, i.e., spent a lot of time on some perfectly dead period, don't like to admit they've been sold, and they haven't often the courage to cut a loss. There is no use in following them into the shadows.

In the above list I take full responsibility for my omissions. I have omitted 'the Rhooshuns'. All right. Let a man judge them after he has encountered Charles Bovary; he will read them with better balance. I have omitted practically all the fustian included in curricula of French literature in American universities (Bossuet, Corneille, etc.) and in so doing I have not committed an oversight. I have touched German in what most of you will consider an insufficient degree. All right. I have done it. I rest my case.

If one finds it convenient to think in chronological cycles, and wants to 'relate literature to history', I suggest the three convenient 'breaks' or collapses. The fall of Alexander's Macedonian empire; the fall of the Roman empire; the collapse of Italy after 1500, the fall of Lodovico Moro, and the sack of Rome. That is to say, human lucidity appears to have approached several times a sort of maximum, and then suffered a set-back.

The great break in the use of language occurs, however, with the change from inflected to uninflected speech. It can't be too clearly understood that certain procedures are good for a language in which every word has a little final tag telling what part of speech it is, and what case it is in, and whether it is a subject, or an object or an accessory; and that these procedures are not good in English or French. Milton got into a mess trying to write English as if it were Latin. Lack of this dissociation is largely responsible for late renaissance floridity. One cannot at this point study all the maladies and all their variations. The study of misguided Latinization needs a treatise to itself.[1]

---

[1] Argument of this essay is elaborated in the author's *ABC of Reading*.

THE SERIOUS ARTIST

I

It is curious that one should be asked to rewrite Sidney's *Defence of Poesy* in the year of grace 1913. During the intervening centuries, and before them, other centres of civilization had decided that good art was a blessing and that bad art was criminal, and they had spent some time and thought in trying to find means whereby to distinguish the true art from the sham. But in England now, in the age of Gosse as in the age of Gosson we are asked if the arts are moral. We are asked to define the relation of the arts to economics, we are asked what position the arts are to hold in the ideal republic. And it is obviously the opinion of many people less objectionable than the Sydney Webbs that the arts had better not exist at all.

I take no great pleasure in writing prose about æsthetic. I think one work of art is worth forty prefaces and as many apologiæ. Nevertheless I have been questioned earnestly and by a person certainly of good will. It is as if one said to me: what is the use of open spaces in this city, what is the use of rose-trees and why do you wish to plant trees and lay out parks and gardens? There are some who do not take delight in these things. The rose springs fairest from some buried Cæsar's throat and the dogwood with its flower of four petals (our dogwood, not the tree you call by that name) is grown from the heart of Aucassin, or perhaps this is only fancy. Let us pursue the matter in ethic.

It is obvious that ethics are based on the nature of man, just as it is obvious that civics are based upon the nature of men when living together in groups.

It is obvious that the good of the greatest number cannot be attained until we know in some sort of what that good must consist. In other words we must know what sort of an animal man is, before we can contrive his maximum happiness, or before we can decide what percentage of that happiness he can have without causing too great a percentage of unhappiness to those about him.

[1] From *The Egoist* A.D. 1913

41

The arts, literature, poesy, are a science, just as chemistry is a science. Their subject is man, mankind and the individual. The subject of chemistry is matter considered as to its composition.

The arts give us a great percentage of the lasting and unassailable data regarding the nature of man, of immaterial man, of man considered as a thinking and sentient creature. They begin where the science of medicine leaves off or rather they overlap that science. The borders of the two arts overcross.

From medicine we learn that man thrives best when duly washed, aired and sunned. From the arts we learn that man is whimsical, that one man differs from another. That men differ among themselves as leaves upon trees differ. That they do not resemble each other as do buttons cut by machine.

From the arts also we learn in what ways man resembles and in what way he differs from certain other animals. We learn that certain men are often more akin to certain animals than they are to other men of different composition. We learn that all men do not desire the same things and that it would therefore be inequitable to give to all men two acres and a cow.

It would be manifestly inequitable to treat the ostrich and the polar bear in the same fashion, granted that it is not unjust to have them pent up where you can treat them at all.

An ethic based on a belief that men are different from what they are is manifestly stupid. It is stupid to apply such an ethic as it is to apply laws and morals designed for a nomadic tribe, or for a tribe in the state of barbarism, to a people crowded into the slums of a modern metropolis. Thus in the tribe it is well to beget children, for the more strong male children you have in the tribe the less likely you are to be bashed on the head by males of the neighbouring tribes, and the more female children the more rapidly the tribe will increase. Conversely it is a crime rather worse than murder to beget children in a slum, to beget children for whom no fitting provision is made, either as touching their physical or economic wellbeing. The increase not only afflicts the child born but the increasing number of the poor keeps down the wage. On this count the bishop of London, as an encourager of this sort of increase, is a criminal of a type rather lower and rather more detestable than the souteneur.

I cite this as one example of inequity persisting because of a continued refusal to consider a code devised for one state of society,

in its (the code's) relation to a different state of society. It is as if, in physics or engineering, we refused to consider a force designed to affect one mass, in its relation (i.e. the force's) to another mass wholly differing, or in some notable way differing, from the first mass.

As inequities can exist because of refusals to consider the actualities of a law in relation to a social condition, so can inequities exist through refusal to consider the actualities of the composition of the masses, or of the individuals to which they are applied.

If all men desired above everything else two acres and a cow, obviously the perfect state would be that state which gave to each man two acres and a cow.

If any science save the arts were able more precisely to determine what the individual does not actually desire, then that science would be of more use in providing the data for ethics.

In the like manner, if any sciences save medicine and chemistry were more able to determine what things were compatible with physical wellbeing, then those sciences would be of more value for providing the data of hygiene.

This brings us to the immorality of bad art. Bad art is inaccurate art. It is art that makes false reports. If a scientist falsifies a report either deliberately or through negligence we consider him as either a criminal or a bad scientist according to the enormity of his offence, and he is punished or despised accordingly.

If he falsifies the reports of a maternity hospital in order to retain his position and get profit and advancement from the city board, he may escape detection. If he declines to make such falsification he may lose financial rewards, and in either case his baseness or his pluck may pass unknown and unnoticed save by a very few people. Nevertheless one does not have to argue his case. The layman knows soon enough on hearing it whether the physician is to be blamed or praised.

If an artist falsifies his report as to the nature of man, as to his own nature, as to the nature of his ideal of the perfect, as to the nature of his ideal of this, that or the other, of god, if god exist, of the life force, of the nature of good and evil, if good and evil exist, of the force with which he believes or disbelieves this, that or the other, of the degree in which he suffers or is made glad; if the artist falsifies his reports on these matters or on any other matter in order that he

may conform to the taste of his time, to the proprieties of a sovereign, to the conveniences of a preconceived code of ethics, then that artist lies. If he lies out of deliberate will to lie, if he lies out of carelessness, out of laziness, out of cowardice, out of any sort of negligence whatsoever, he nevertheless lies and he should be punished or despised in proportion to the seriousness of his offence. His offence is of the same nature as the physician's and according to his position and the nature of his lie he is responsible for future oppressions and for future misconceptions. Albeit his lies are known to only a few, or his truth-telling to only a few. Albeit he may pass without censure for one and without praise for the other. Albeit he can only be punished on the plane of his crime and by nothing save the contempt of those who know of his crime. Perhaps it is caddishness rather than crime. However there is perhaps nothing worse for a man than to know that he is a cur and to know that someone else, if only one person, knows it.

We distinguish very clearly between the physician who is doing his best for a patient, who is using drugs in which he believes, or who is in a wilderness, let us say, where the patient can get no other medical aid. We distinguish, I say, very clearly between the failure of such a physician, and the act of that physician, who ignorant of the patient's disease, being in reach of more skilful physicians, deliberately denies an ignorance of which he is quite conscious, refuses to consult other physicians, tries to prevent the patient's having access to more skilful physicians, or deliberately tortures the patient for his own ends.

One does not need to read black print to learn this ethical fact about physicians. Yet it takes a deal of talking to convince a layman that bad art is 'immoral'. And that good art however 'immoral' it is, is wholly a thing of virtue. Purely and simply that good art can NOT be immoral. By good art I mean art that bears true witness, I mean the art that is most precise. You can be wholly precise in representing a vagueness. You can be wholly a liar in pretending that the particular vagueness was precise in its outline. If you cannot understand this with regard to poetry, consider the matter in terms of painting.

If you have forgotten my statement that the arts bear witness and define for us the inner nature and conditions of man, consider the Victory of Samothrace and the Taj of Agra. The man who carved the one and the man who designed the other may either or both of them

have looked like an ape, or like two apes respectively. They may have looked like other apelike or swinelike men. We have the Victory and the Taj to witness that there was something within them differing from the contents of apes and of the other swinelike men. Thus we learn that humanity is a species or genus of animals capable of a variation that will produce the desire for a Taj or a Victory, and moreover capable of effecting that Taj or Victory in stone. We know from other testimony of the arts and from ourselves that the desire often overshoots the power of efficient presentation; we therefore conclude that other members of the race may have desired to effect a Taj or a Victory. We even suppose that men have desired to effect more beautiful things although few of us are capable of forming any precise mental image of things, in their particular way, more beautiful than this statue or this building. So difficult is this that no one has yet been able to effect a restoration for the missing head of the Victory. At least no one has done so in stone, so far as I know. Doubtless many people have stood opposite the statue and made such heads in their imagination.

As there are in medicine the art of diagnosis and the art of cure, so in the arts, so in the particular arts of poetry and of literature, there is the art of diagnosis and there is the art of cure. They call one the cult of ugliness and the other the cult of beauty.

The cult of beauty is the hygiene, it is sun, air and the sea and the rain and the lake bathing. The cult of ugliness, Villon, Baudelaire, Corbière, Beardsley are diagnosis. Flaubert is diagnosis. Satire, if we are to ride this metaphor to staggers, satire is surgery, insertions and amputations.

Beauty in art reminds one what is worth while. I am not now speaking of shams. I mean beauty, not slither, not sentimentalizing about beauty, not telling people that beauty is the proper and respectable thing. I mean beauty. You don't argue about an April wind, you feel bucked up when you meet it. You feel bucked up when you come on a swift moving thought in Plato or on a fine line in a statue.

Even this pother about gods reminds one that something is worth while. Satire reminds one that certain things are not worth while. It draws one to consider time wasted.

The cult of beauty and the delineation of ugliness are not in mutual opposition.

II

I have said that the arts give us our best data for determining what sort of creature man is. As our treatment of man must be determined by our knowledge or conception of what man is, the arts provide data for ethics.

These data are sound and the data of generalizing psychologists and social theoricians are usually unsound, for the serious artist is scientific and the theorist is usually empiric in the medieval fashion. That is to say a good biologist will make a reasonable number of observations of any given phenomenon before he draws a conclusion, thus we read such phrases as 'over 100 cultures from the secretions of the respiratory tracts of over 500 patients and 30 nurses and attendants'. The results of each observation must be precise and no single observation must in itself be taken as determining a general law, although, after experiment, certain observations may be held as typical or normal. The serious artist is scientific in that he presents the image of his desire, of his hate, of his indifference as precisely that, as precisely the image of his own desire, hate or indifference. The more precise his record the more lasting and unassailable his work of art.

The theorist, and we see this constantly illustrated by the English writers on sex, the theorist constantly proceeds as if his own case, his own limits and predilections were the typical case, or even as if it were the universal. He is constantly urging someone else to behave as he, the theorist, would like to behave. Now art never asks anybody to do anything, or to think anything, or to be anything. It exists as the trees exist, you can admire, you can sit in the shade, you can pick bananas, you can cut firewood, you can do as you jolly well please.

Also you are a fool to seek the kind of art you don't like. You are a fool to read classics because you are told to and not because you like them. You are a fool to aspire to good taste if you haven't naturally got it. If there is one place where it is idiotic to sham that place is before a work of art. Also you are a fool not to have an open mind, not to be eager to enjoy something you might enjoy but don't know how to. But it is not the artist's place to ask you to learn, or to defend his particular works of art, or to insist on your reading his books. Any artist who wants your particular admiration is, by just so much, the less artist.

The desire to stand on the stage, the desire of plaudits has nothing to do with serious art. The serious artist may like to stand on the stage, he may, apart from his art, be any kind of imbecile you like, but the two things are not connected, at least they are not concentric. Lots of people who don't even pretend to be artists have the same desire to be slobbered over, by people with less brains than they have.

The serious artist is usually, or is often as far from the ægrum vulgus as is the serious scientist. Nobody has heard of the abstract mathematicians who worked out the determinants that Marconi made use of in his computations for the wireless telegraph. The public, the public so dear to the journalistic heart, is far more concerned with the shareholders in the Marconi company.

The permanent property, the property given to the race at large is precisely these data of the serious scientist and of the serious artist; of the scientist as touching the relations of abstract numbers, of molecular energy, of the composition of matter, etc.; of the serious artist, as touching the nature of man, of individuals.

Men have ceased trying to conquer the world[1] and to acquire universal knowledge. Men still try to promote the ideal state. No perfect state will be founded on the theory, or on the working hypothesis that all men are alike. No science save the arts will give us the requisite data for learning in what ways men differ.

The very fact that many men hate the arts is of value, for we are enabled by finding out what part of the arts they hate, to learn something of their nature. Usually when men say they hate the arts we find that they merely detest quackery and bad artists.

In the case of a man's hating one art and not the others we may learn that he is of defective hearing or of defective intelligence. Thus an intelligent man may hate music or a good musician may detest very excellent authors.

And all these things are very obvious.

Among thinking and sentient people the bad artist is contemned as we would contemn a negligent physician or a sloppy, inaccurate scientist, and the serious artist is left in peace, or even supported and encouraged. In the fog and the outer darkness no measures are taken to distinguish between the serious and the unserious artist. The unserious artist being the commoner brand and greatly

[1] *Blind Optimism* A.D. 1913.

outnumbering the serious variety, and it being to the temporary and apparent advantage of the false artist to gain the rewards proper to the serious artist, it is natural that the unserious artist should do all in his power to obfuscate the lines of demarcation.

Whenever one attempts to demonstrate the difference between serious and unserious work, one is told that 'it is merely a technical discussion'. It has rested at that—in England it has rested at that for more than three hundred years. The people would rather have patent medicines than scientific treatment. They will occasionally be told that art as art is not a violation of God's most holy laws. They will not have a specialist's opinion as to what art is good. They will not consider the 'problem of style'. They want 'The value of art to life' and 'Fundamental issues'.

As touching fundamental issues: The arts give us our data of psychology, of man as to his interiors, as to the ratio of his thought to his emotions, etc., etc., etc.

The touchstone of an art is its precision. This precision is of various and complicated sorts and only the specialist can determine whether certain works of art possess certain sorts of precision. I don't mean to say that any intelligent person cannot have more or less sound judgement as to whether a certain work of art is good or not. An intelligent person can usually tell whether or not a person is in good health. It is none the less true that it takes a skilful physician to make certain diagnoses or to discern the lurking disease beneath the appearance of vigour.

It is no more possible to give in a few pages full instructions for knowing a masterpiece than it would be to give full instructions for all medical diagnosis.

III

EMOTION AND POESY

Obviously, it is not easy to be a great poet. If it were, many more people would have done so. At no period in history has the world been free of people who have mildly desired to be great poets and not a few have endeavoured conscientiously to be such.

I am aware that adjectives of magnitude are held to savour of barbarism. Still there is no shame in desiring to give great gifts and an enlightened criticism does not draw ignominious comparisons between Villon and Dante. The so-called major poets have most of them given their *own* gift but the peculiar term 'major' is rather a gift to them from Chronos. I mean that they have been born upon the stroke of their hour and that it has been given them to heap together and arrange and harmonize the results of many men's labour. This very faculty for amalgamation is a part of their genius and it is, in a way, a sort of modesty, a sort of unselfishness. They have not wished for property.

The men from whom Dante borrowed are remembered as much for the fact that he did borrow as for their own compositions. At the same time he gave of his own, and no mere compiler and classifier of other men's discoveries is given the name of 'major poet' for more than a season.

If Dante had not done a deal more than borrow rhymes from Arnaut Daniel and theology from Aquinas he would not be published by Dent in the year of grace 1913.

We might come to believe that the thing that matters in art is a sort of energy, something more or less like electricity or radio-activity, a force transfusing, welding, and unifying. A force rather like water when it spurts up through very bright sand and sets it in swift motion. You may make what image you like.

I do not know that there is much use in composing an answer to the often asked question: What is the difference between poetry and prose?

I believe that poetry is the more highly energized. But these things are relative. Just as we say that a certain temperature is hot and another cold. In the same way we say that a certain prose passage 'is poetry' meaning to praise it, and that a certain passage of verse is 'only prose' meaning dispraise. And at the same time 'Poetry!!!' is used as a synonym for 'Bosh! Rott!! Rubbish!!!' The thing that counts is 'Good writing'.

And 'Good writing' is perfect control. And it is quite easy to control a thing that has in it no energy—provided that it be not too heavy and that you do not wish to make it move.

And, as all the words that one would use in writing about these things are the vague words of daily speech, it is nearly impossible to write with scientific preciseness about 'prose and verse' unless one writes a complete treatise on the 'art of writing', defining each word as one would define the terms in a treatise on chemistry. And on this account all essays about 'poetry' are usually not only dull but inaccurate and wholly useless. And on like account if you ask a good painter to tell you what he is trying to do to a canvas he will very probably wave his hands helplessly and murmur that 'He — eh — eh — he can't talk about it'. And that if you 'see anything at all, he is quite — eh — more or less — eh — satisfied'.

Nevertheless it has been held for a shameful thing that a man should not be able to give a reason for his acts and words. And if one does not care about being taken for a mystificateur one may as well try to give approximate answers to questions asked in good faith. It might be better to do the thing thoroughly, in a properly accurate treatise, but one has not always two or three spare years at one's disposal, and one is dealing with very subtle and complicated matter, and even so, the very algebra of logic is itself open to debate.

Roughly then, Good writing is writing that is perfectly controlled, the writer says just what he means. He says it with complete clarity and simplicity. He uses the smallest possible number of words. I do not mean that he skimps paper, or that he screws about like Tacitus to get his thought crowded into the least possible space. But, granting that two sentences are at times easier to understand than one sentence containing the double meaning, the author tries to communicate with the reader with the greatest possible despatch, save where for any one of forty reasons he does not wish to do so.

Also there are various kinds of clarity. There is the clarity of the request: Send me four pounds of ten-penny nails. And there is the syntactical simplicity of the request: Buy me the kind of Rembrandt I like. This last is an utter cryptogram. It presupposes a more complex and intimate understanding of the speaker than most of us ever acquire of anyone. It has as many meanings, almost, as there are persons who might speak it. To a stranger it conveys nothing at all.

It is the almost constant labour of the prose artist to translate this latter kind of clarity into the former; to say 'Send me the kind of Rembrandt I like' in the terms of 'Send me four pounds of ten-penny nails'.

The whole thing is an evolution. In the beginning simple words were enough: Food; water; fire. Both prose and poetry are but an extension of language. Man desires to communicate with his fellows. He desires an ever increasingly complicated communication. Gesture serves up to a point. Symbols may serve. When you desire something not present to the eye or when you desire to communicate ideas, you must have recourse to speech. Gradually you wish to communicate something less bare and ambiguous than ideas. You wish to communicate an idea and its modifications, an idea and a crowd of its effects, atmospheres, contradictions. You wish to question whether a certain formula works in every case, or in what per cent of cases, etc., etc., etc., you get the Henry James novel.

You wish to communicate an idea and its concomitant emotions, or an emotion and its concomitant ideas, or a sensation and its derivative emotions, or an impression that is emotive, etc., etc., etc. You begin with the yeowl and the bark, and you develop into the dance and into music, and into music with words, and finally into words with music, and finally into words with a vague adumbration of music, words suggestive of music, words measured, or words in a rhythm that preserves some accurate trait of the emotive impression, or of the sheer character of the fostering or parental emotion.

When this rhythm, or when the vowel and consonantal melody or sequence seems truly to bear the trace of emotion which the poem (for we have come at last to the poem) is intended to communicate, we say that this part of the work is good. And 'this part of the work' is by now 'technique'. That 'dry, dull, pedantic' technique, that all bad artists rail against. It is only a part of technique, it is rhythm, cadence, and the arrangement of sounds.

Also the 'prose', the words and their sense must be such as fit the emotion. Or, from the other side, ideas, or fragments of ideas, the emotion and concomitant emotions of this 'Intellectual and Emotional Complex' (for we have come to the intellectual and emotional complex) must be in harmony, they must form an organism, they must be an oak sprung from an acorn.

When you have words of a lament set to the rhythm and tempo of *There'll be a Hot Time in the Old Town to-night* you have either an intentional burlesque or you have rotten art. Shelley's *Sensitive Plant* is one of the rottenest poems ever written, at least one of the worst ascribable to a recognized author. It jiggles to the same tune as *A little peach in the orchard grew*. Yet Shelley recovered and wrote the fifth act of the Cenci.

IV

It is occasionally suggested by the wise that poets should acquire the graces of prose. That is an extension of what has been said above anent control. Prose does not need emotion. It may, but it need not, attempt to portray emotion.

Poetry is a centaur. The thinking word-arranging, clarifying faculty must move and leap with the energizing, sentient, musical faculties. It is precisely the difficulty of this amphibious existence that keeps down the census record of good poets. The accomplished prose author will tell you that he 'can only write poetry when he has a bellyache' and thence he will argue that poetry just isn't an art.

I dare say there are very good marksmen who just can't shoot from a horse.

Likewise if a good marksman only mounted a few times he might never acquire any proficiency in shooting from the saddle. Or leaving metaphor, I suppose that what, in the long run, makes the poet is a sort of persistence of the emotional nature, and, joined with this, a peculiar sort of control.

The saying that 'a lyric poet might as well die at thirty' is simply saying that the emotional nature seldom survives this age, or that it becomes, at any rate, subjected and incapable of moving the whole man. Of course this is a generality, and, as such, inaccurate.

It is true that most people poetize more or less, between the ages of seventeen and twenty-three. The emotions are new, and, to their possessor, interesting, and there is not much mind or personality to be moved. As the man, as his mind, becomes a heavier and heavier machine, a constantly more complicated structure, it requires a constantly greater voltage of emotional energy to set it in harmonious motion. It is certain that the emotions increase in vigour as a vigorous man matures. In the case of Guido we have his strongest work at fifty. Most important poetry has been written by men over thirty.

'En l'an trentiesme de mon eage', begins Villon and considering the nature of his life thirty would have seen him more spent than forty years of more orderly living.

Aristotle will tell you that 'The apt use of metaphor, being as it is, the swift perception of relations, is the true hall-mark of genius'. That abundance, that readiness of the figure is indeed one of the surest proofs that the mind is upborne upon the emotional surge.

By 'apt use', I should say it were well to understand, a swiftness, almost a violence, and certainly a vividness. This does not mean elaboration and complication.

There is another poignancy which I do not care to analyse into component parts, if, indeed, such vivisection is possible. It is not the formal phrasing of Flaubert much as such formality is desirable and noble. It is such phrasing as we find in

> Era gìa l'ora che volge il disio
> Ai naviganti....

Or the opening of the ballata which begins:

> Perch 'io non spero di tornar già mai
> Ballatetta, in Toscana.

Or:

> S'ils n 'ayment fors que pour l'argent,
> On ne les ayme que pour l'heure.

Or, in its context:

> The fire that stirs about her, when she stirs,

or, in its so different setting,

> Ne maeg werigmod wryde withstondan
> ne se hreo hyge helpe gefremman:
> forthon domgeorne dreorigne oft
> in hyra breostcofan bindath faeste.

These things have in them that passionate simplicity which is beyond the precisions of the intellect. Truly they are perfect as fine prose is perfect, but they are in some way different from the clear statements of the observer. They are in some way different from that so masterly ending of the Herodias: 'Comme elle était très lourde ils la portaient alternativement' or from the constatation in St. Julian Hospitalier: 'Et l'idée lui vient d'employer son existence au service des autres.'

The prose author has shown the triumph of his intellect and one knows that such triumph is not without its sufferings by the way, but by the verses one is brought upon the passionate moment. This moment has brought with it nothing that violates the prose simplicities. The intellect has not found it but the intellect has been moved.

There is little but folly in seeking the lines of division, yet if the two arts must be divided we may as well use that line as any other. In the verse something has come upon the intelligence. In the prose the intelligence has found a subject for its observations. The poetic fact pre-exists.

In a different way, of course, the subject of the prose pre-exists. Perhaps the difference is undemonstrable, perhaps it is not even communicable to any save those of good will. Yet I think this orderliness in the greatest poetic passages, this quiet statement that partakes of the nature of prose and is yet floated and tossed in the emotional surges, is perhaps as true a test as that mentioned by the Greek theorician.

v

La poésie, avec ses comparaisons obligées, sa mythologie que ne croit pas le poète, sa dignité de style à la Louis XIV, et tout l'attirail de ses ornements appelés poétiques, est bien au-dessous de la prose dès qu'il s'agit de donner une idée claire et précise des mouvements du coeur; or, dans ce genre, on n'émeut que par la clarté.—*Stendhal*

And that is precisely why one employs oneself in seeking precisely the poetry that shall be without this flummery, this fustian *à la Louis XIV*, *'farcie de comme'*. The above critique of Stendhal's does not apply to the Poema del Cid, nor to the parting of Odysseus and Calypso. In the writers of the duo-cento and early tre-cento we find a precise psychology, embedded in a now almost unintelligible jargon, but there nevertheless. If we cannot get back to these things; if the serious artist cannot attain this precision in verse, then he must either take to prose or give up his claim to being a serious artist.

It is precisely because of this fustian that the Parnassiads and epics of the eighteenth century and most of the present-day works of most of our contemporary versifiers are pests and abominations.

As the most efficient way to say nothing is to keep quiet, and as technique consists precisely in doing the thing that one sets out to do, in the most efficient manner, no man who takes three pages to say nothing can expect to be seriously considered as a technician. To take three pages to say nothing is not style, in the serious sense of that word.

There are several kinds of honest work. There is the thing that will out. There is the conscientious formulation, a thing of infinitely greater labour, for the first is not labour at all, though the efficient doing of it may depend on a deal of labour foregoing.

There is the 'labour foregoing', the patient testing of media, the patient experiment which shall avail perhaps the artist himself, but is as likely to avail some successor.

The first sort of work may be poetry.

The second sort, the conscientious formulation, is more than likely to be prose.

The third sort of work savours of the laboratory, it concerns the specialist, and the dilettante, if that word retains any trace of its finer and original sense. A dilettante proper is a person who takes delight in the art, not a person who tries to interpose his inferior productions between masterwork and the public.

I reject the term connoisseurship, for 'connoisseurship' is so associated in our minds with a desire for acquisition. The person possessed of connoisseurship is so apt to want to buy the rare at one price and sell it at another. I do not believe that a person with this spirit has ever *seen* a work of art. Let me restore the foppish term dilettante, the synonym for folly, to its place near the word *diletto*.

The dilettante has no axe to grind for himself. If he be artist as well, he will be none the less eager to preserve the best precedent work. He will drag out 'sources' that prove him less original than his public would have him.

As for Stendhal's stricture, if we can have a poetry that comes as close as prose, *pour donner une idée claire et précise,* let us have it, '*E di venire a ciò io studio quanto posso . . . che la mia vita per alquanti anni duri.*' . . . And if we cannot attain to such a poetry, noi altri poeti, for God's sake let us shut up. Let us 'Give up, go down', etcetera; let us acknowledge that our art, like the art of dancing in armour, is out of date and out of fashion. Or let us go to our ignominious ends knowing that we have strained at the cords, that we have spent our strength in trying to pave the way for a new sort of poetic art—it is not a new sort but an old sort—but let us know that we have tried to make it more nearly possible for our successors to recapture this art. To write a poetry that can be carried as a communication between intelligent men.

To this end *io studio quanto posso*. I have tried to establish a clear demarcation. I have been challenged on my use of the phrase 'great art' in an earlier article. It is about as useless to search for a definition of 'great art' as it is to search for a scientific definition of life. One knows fairly well what one means. One means something more or less proportionate to one's experience. One means something quite different at different periods of one's life.

It is for some such reason that all criticism should be professedly personal criticism. In the end the critic can only say 'I like it', or 'I am moved', or something of that sort. When he has shown us himself we are able to understand him.

Thus, in painting, I mean something or other vaguely associated in my mind with work labelled Dürer, and Rembrandt, and Velasquez, etc., and with the painters whom I scarcely know, possibly of T'ang and Sung—though I dare say I've got the wrong labels—and with some Egyptian designs that should probably be thought of as sculpture.

And in poetry I mean something or other associated in my mind with the names of a dozen or more writers.

On closer analysis I find that I mean something like 'maximum efficiency of expression'; I mean that the writer has expressed something interesting in such a way that one cannot re-say it more effectively. I also mean something associated with discovery. The artist must have discovered something—either of life itself or of the means of expression.

Great art must of necessity be a part of good art. I attempted to define good art in an earlier chapter. It must bear true witness. Obviously great art must be an exceptional thing. It cannot be the sort of thing anyone can do after a few hours' practice. It must be the result of some exceptional faculty, strength, or perception. It must almost be that strength of perception working with the connivance of fate, or chance, or whatever you choose to call it.

And who is to judge? The critic, the receiver, however stupid or ignorant, must judge for himself. The only really vicious criticism is the academic criticism of those who make the grand abnegation, who refuse to say what they think, if they do think, and who quote accepted opinion; these men are the vermin, their treachery to the great work of the past is as great as that of the false artist to the present. If they do not care enough for the heritage to have a personal conviction then they have no licence to write.

Every critic should give indication of the sources and limits of his knowledge. The criticism of English poetry by men who knew no language but English, or who knew little but English and school-classics, has been a marasmus.

When we know to what extent each sort of expression has been driven, in, say, half a dozen great literatures, we begin to be able to tell whether a given work has the excess of great art. We would not think of letting a man judge pictures if he knew only English pictures, or music if he knew only English music—or only French or German music for that matter.

The stupid or provincial judgment of art bases itself on the belief that great art must be like the art that it has been reared to respect.

THE TEACHER'S MISSION [1]

I

'Artists are the antennae of the race.' If this statement is incomprehensible and if its corollaries need any explanation, let me put it that a nation's writers are the voltometers and steam-gauges of that nation's intellectual life. They are the registering instruments, and if they falsify their reports there is no measure to the harm that they do. If you saw a man selling defective thermometers to a hospital, you would consider him a particularly vile kind of cheat. But for 50 years an analogous treatment of thought has gone on in America without throwing any discredit whatever on its practitioners.

For this reason I personally would not feel myself guilty of manslaughter if by any miracle I ever had the pleasure of killing Canby or the editor of the *Atlantic Monthly* and their replicas, or of ordering a wholesale death and/or deportation of a great number of affable, suave, moderate men, all of them perfectly and snugly convinced of their respectability, and all incapable of any twinge of conscience on account of any form of mental cowardice or any falsification of reports whatsoever.

Criminals have no intellectual interests. Is it clear to the teacher of literature that writers who falsify their registration, sin against the well-being of the nation's mind? Is there any possible 'voice from the audience' that can be raised to sustain the contrary? Is there any reader so humble of mind as to profess incomprehension of this statement?

In so far as education and the press have NOT blazoned this view during our time, the first step of educational reform is to proclaim the necessity of HONEST REGISTRATION, and to exercise an antiseptic intolerance of all inaccurate reports about letters—intolerance of the same sort that one would exercise about a false hospital chart or a false analysis in a hospital laboratory.

This means abolition of personal vanity in the reporting; it means abolition of this vanity, whether the writer is reporting on society at

[1] *English Journal,* 1934

large; on the social and economic order, or on literature itself. It means the abolition of local vanity. You would not tolerate a doctor who tried to tell you the fever temperature of patients in Chicago was always lower than that of sufferers from the same kind of fever in Singapore (unless accurate instruments registered such a difference).

As the press, daily, weekly, and monthly, is utterly corrupted, either from economic or personal causes, it is manifestly UP TO the teaching profession to act for themselves without waiting for the journalists and magazine blokes to assist them.

The mental life of a nation is no man's private property. The function of the teaching profession is to maintain the HEALTH OF THE NATIONAL MIND. As there are great specialists and medical discoverers, so there are 'leading writers'; but once a discovery is made, the local practitioner is just as inexcusable as the discoverer himself if he fails to make use of known remedies and known prophylactics.

A vicious economic system has corrupted every ramification of thought. There is no possibility of ultimately avoiding the perception of this. The first act is to recognize the disease, the second to cure it.

II

The shortcomings of education and of the professor are best tackled by each man for himself; his first act must be an examination of his consciousness, and his second, the direction of his will toward the light.

The first symptom he finds will, in all probability, be mental LAZINESS, lack of curiosity, desire to be undisturbed. This is not in the least incompatible with the habit of being very BUSY along habitual lines.

Until the teacher wants to know all the facts, and to sort out the roots from the branches, the branches from the twigs, and to grasp the MAIN STRUCTURE of his subject, and the relative weights and importances of its parts, he is just a lump of the dead clay in the system.

The disease of the last century and a half has been 'abstraction'. This has spread like tuberculosis.

Take the glaring example of 'Liberty'. Liberty became a goddess in the eighteenth century, and had a FORM. That is to say, Liberty was 'defined' in the *Rights of Man* as 'the right to do anything that doesn't hurt someone else'. The restricting and highly ethical limiting clause was, within a few decades, REMOVED. The idea of liberty degenerated into meaning mere irresponsibility and the right to be just as pifflingly idiotic as the laziest sub-human pleased, and to exercise almost 'any and every' activity utterly regardless of its effect on the commonweal.

I take a non-literary example, on purpose. Observing the same mental defection in literary criticism or in proclaimed programmes, we stigmatize writing which consists of 'general terms'. These general terms finally have NO meaning, in the sense that each teacher uses them with a meaning so vague as to *convey* nothing to his students.

All of which is inexcusable AFTER the era of 'Agassiz and the fish'— by which I mean now that general education is in position to profit by the parallels of biological study based on EXAMINATION and COMPARISON of particular specimens.

All teaching of literature should be performed by the presentation and juxtaposition of specimens of writing and NOT by discussion of some other discusser's opinion *about* the general standing of a poet or author. Any teacher of biology would tell you that knowledge can NOT be transmitted by general statement without knowledge of particulars. By this method of presentation and juxtaposition even a moderately ignorant teacher can transmit most of what he knows WITHOUT filling the student's mind with a great mass of prejudice and error. The teaching may be incomplete but it will not be idiotic or vicious. Ridiculous prejudice in favour of known authors, or in favour of modern as against ancient, or ancient against modern work, would of necessity disappear.

The whole system of intercommunication via the printed page in America is now, and has been, a mere matter of successive *dilutions* of knowledge. When some European got tired of an idea he wrote it down, it was printed after an interval, and it was reviewed in, say, London, by a hurried and harassed reviewer, usually lazy, almost always indifferent. The London periodicals were rediluted by still more hurried and usually incompetent New York reviewers, and their 'opinion' was dispersed and watered down via American trade distribution. Hence the 15 to 20 years' delay with which all and every idea, and every new kind of literature, reaches the 'American reader' or 'teacher'.

The average reader under such a system has no means whatsoever of controlling the facts. He has been brought up on vague general statements, which have naturally blunted his curiosity. The simple ignorance displayed, even in the *English Journal*, is appalling, and the individuals cannot always be blamed.

A calm examination of the files of the *Little Review* for 1917-19 will show the time-lag between publication and reception of perfectly simple facts. The Douglas economics now being broadcast by Senator Cutting, and receiving 'thoughtful attention from the Administration', were available in 1919, and mentionable in little magazines in America in 1920. Many people think they would have saved us from the crisis, and would have already abolished poverty, had they received adequate attention and open discussion, and started toward being put into effect at that time. I mention this to show that the time-lag in American publishing and teaching is NOT CONFINED to what are called 'merely cultural subjects' but that it affects even matters of life and death, eating or starvation, the comfort and suffering of great masses of the people.

III

Our editor asks: What ought to be done?

1. Examination of conscience and consciousness, by each teacher for himself or herself.

2. Direction of the will toward the light, with concurrent sloughing off of laziness and prejudice.

3. An inexorable demand for the facts.

4. Dispassionate examination of the ideogrammic method (the examination and juxtaposition of particular specimens—e.g. particular works, passages of literature) as an implement for acquisition and transmission of knowledge.

5. A definite campaign against human deadwood still clogging the system. A demand either that the sabotage cease, or that the saboteurs be removed.

As concomitant and result, there would naturally be a guarantee that the dismissal of professors and teachers *for having* EXAMINED facts and having discussed ideas, should cease. Such suppression of the searchers for Truth is NOT suited to the era of the New Deal, and should be posted on the pillar of infamy as a symptom of the Wilson-Harding-Coolidge-Hoover epoch. To remove any teacher or professor for his IDEAS, it should be necessary to prove that these ideas had been preached from malice and against the mental health of the nation. As in our LAW a man is assumed innocent until the contrary is proved, so a man must be assumed to be of good-will until the contrary is proved.

A man of good-will abandons a false idea as soon as he is made aware of its falsity, he abandons a mis-statement of fact as soon as corrected. In the case of a teacher misinforming his students, it is the business of his higher officers to INSTRUCT him, not merely to suppress him. In the case of professors, etc., the matter should be carried in open debate.

When the University of Paris was alive (let us say in the time of Abelard) even highly technical special debates were a public exhilaration. Education that does not bear on LIFE and on the most vital and immediate problems of the day is not education but merely suffocation and sabotage.

Retrospect is inexcusable, especially in education, save when used distinctly AS a leverage toward the future. An education that is not focused on the life of to-day and to-morrow is treason to the pupil. There are no words permitted in a polite educational bulletin that can describe the dastardliness of the American university system as we have known it. By which I don't mean that the surface hasn't been, often, charming. I mean that the *fundamental* perversion has been damnable. It has tended to unfit the student for his part in his era. Some college presidents have been chosen rather for their sycophantic talents than for their intellectual acumen or their desire to enliven and build intellectual life. Others with good intentions have seen their aims thwarted and their best intended plans side-tracked, and have been compelled to teeter between high aim and constriction. The evil, like all evil, is in the direction of the will. For that phrase to have life, there must be both will *and* direction.

There may have been an excuse, or may have been extenuating circumstances for my generation, but there can be no *further* excuse. When I was in prep school Ibsen was a joke in the comics, and the great authors of the weekly 'literary' press and the 'better magazines' were . . . a set of names that are now known only to 'students of that period', and to researchers. Then came the Huneker-Brentano sabotage. New York's advanced set abandoned the Civil War, and stopped at the London nineties or the mid-European sixties and eighties.

That is, the London nineties were maintained in New York up to 1915. Anything else was considered as bumptious silliness. The *Atlantic Monthly's* view of French literature in 1914 was as comic as Huey Long's opinion of Aquinas. And the pretenders, the men who then set themselves up as critics and editors, still prosper, and still prevent contemporary ideas from penetrating the Carnegie library system or from reaching the teaching profession, until they have gathered a decade's mildew—or two decades' mildew.

The humblest teacher in grammar school CAN CONTRIBUTE to the national education if he or she refuse to let printed inaccuracy pass unreproved:

(A) By acquiring even a little accurate knowledge based on examination and comparison of PARTICULAR books.

(B) By correcting his or her own errors gladly and as a matter of course, at the earliest possible moment.

For example, a well-known anthology by a widely accepted anthologist contains a mass of simple inaccuracies, statements contrary to simple, ascertainable chronology. I have not seen any complaints. In the *English Journal* inaccuracies of fact occur that ought to be corrected NOT by established authors, but by junior members of the teaching profession. This would lead inevitably to a higher intellectual morale. Some teachers would LIKE it, others would have to accept it because they would not be able to continue without it. False witness in the teaching of letters OUGHT to be just as dishonourable as falsification in medicine.

THE CONSTANT PREACHING
TO THE MOB[1]

Time and again the old lie. There is no use talking to the ignorant about lies, for they have no criteria. Deceiving the ignorant is by some regarded as evil, but it is the demagogue's business to bolster up his position and to show that God's noblest work is the demagogue. Therefore we read again for the one-thousand-one-hundred-and-eleventh time that poetry is made to entertain. As follows: 'The beginnings of English poetry . . . made by a rude war-faring people for the entertainment of men-at-arms, or for men at monks' tables.'

Either such statements are made to curry favor with other people sitting at fat sterile tables, or they are made in an ignorance which is charlatanry when it goes out to vend itself as sacred and impeccable knowledge.

'The beginnings—for entertainment'—has the writer of this sentence read *The Seafarer* in Anglo-Saxon? Will the author tell us for whose benefit these lines, which alone in the works of our fore-bears are fit to compare with Homer—for whose entertainment were they made? They were made for no man's entertainment, but because a man believing in silence found himself unable to withhold himself from speaking. And that more uneven poem, *The Wanderer*, is like to this, a broken man speaking:

> Ne maeg werigmod wryde withstondan
> ne se hreo hyge helpe gefremman:
> forthon domgeorne dreorigne oft
> in hyra breostcofan bindath faeste.

'For the doom-eager bindeth fast his blood-bedraggled heart in his breast'—an apology for speaking at all, and speech only pardoned because his captain and all the sea-faring men and companions are dead; some slain of wolves, some torn from the cliffs by sea-birds whom they had plundered.

[1] *Poetry*, VIII, 3 (June, 1916).

Such poems are not made for after-dinner speakers, nor was the eleventh book of the Odyssey. Still it flatters the mob to tell them that their importance is so great that the solace of lonely men, and the lordliest of the arts, was created for their amusement.

MR HOUSMAN AT LITTLE BETHEL[1]

This volume[2] reaches me with a friend's note stating that it has 'upset a lot of the Cambridge critics'. My first hope was, naturally, that the upset had occurred in the highest possible seas and at furthest possible from any danger of rescue.

A. E. H., with consummate caution, takes the ground that he is incompetent to discuss the subject and defies Zeus and Thersites to dislodge him therefrom. So far so good, I might be the last to raise an objection; it is only on page 8 that the eyebrow of the reader tends almost irresistibly to rise: 'The artifice of versification ... little explored by critics' (that's true enough), 'a few pages of C. Patmore and F. Myers contain all, so far as I know, or all of value, which has been written on such matters; and to these I could add a few more.'

As autobiography one cannot question the first statement, and as Mr Housman refrains from the adumbrated 'adding' one has no means of knowing whether he be launched into vain jactancy or merely stating a fact.

The marvel is, or would be to any foreigner unacquainted with England, that any professor of Latin in a recognized institution of learning, or any man alleging that his 'favourite recreation has been the best literature of several languages', could rest for the twenty-two years of his professorate in that phase of 'so far as I know'. Perhaps they have overworked him; left him scant for his predilected recreation.

He is an ally of righteousness when he alleges that 'good literature read for pleasure must ... do some good to the reader, quicken his perception ... sharpen discrimination ... mellow rawness of personal opinion'.

This bit of dog sense has I suppose upset the clique of critics of critics, who take the ground that Jojo's opinion of Jimjim's explanation of Shakespeare will shed greater light on the reader and initiate him to a higher degree of perception than would perusal of the Bard's original text.

My initial and thirty-year-old divergence from both their houses being that as long as the British critic is damn ignorant of so much of

<hr>

[1] The *Criterion*, January 1934.   [2] *The Name and Nature of Poetry.*

the best literature and even of half a dozen *kinds* of the best literature, English critical writing will be limited in its scope and unsatisfactory not only to the serious writer, but to the reader whose pleasure has been taken in further uplands, or in more wide-lying pastures.

During the twenty-five years wherein my acquaintance with letters has been anything but casual and my observance of English production far from disinterested, I have barged into no single indication that Mr Housman was aware of the world of my contemporaries. That is natural enough, and few men in any country cast a very thoughtful eye on their successors. But even among the writers of Housman's day there must have been a stray hint, a line here and there in, say, the gentle murmurs of Bridges or Hopkins that could have been added to the wisdom of Patmore, or to the astuteness of Fred Myers (whose verse, if any, is unknown to me). None of it, so far as I know, appears in the worst accepted anthologies, nor has it been edited by Mr Housman.

I could, if Mr Housman is interested, supply him with a list of works, which if not specifically catalogued as 'treatises on metric', 'prosody taught in ten lessons', 'tiny tots' guide to the muses', would at least supply him with an idea here or there, not that I want to impinge on any man's recreation.

All of which doesn't diminish the fact that Housman's note in fine print on page 8 is one of the most masterly summaries of a small section of the problems of metric that I have ever had the pleasure to come on. I doubt if anyone has done anything better in English, that is to say, listed a larger number of more important—some of them possibly fundamental—issues, in so small a compass.

The marvel is that he should have been willing to rest on Myers and Patmore. Specific doubt rises with Housman's specific examples of presumably particular triumph. Why, for example, are we 'ceasing to gallop with Callender's horse and beginning to fly with Pegasus' (like astripitent eagles, etc.) when we come on a verse writ to the following measure, easier almost to parody than to transcribe?

> Come, tumtum Greek, Ulysses, come[1]
> Caress these shores with me:
> The windblown seas have wet my bum
> And here the beer is free.

[1] Or 'tum' as the case may be.

No! While Dr Bridges' actual verse does not always leap with the springbok, buck with the mustang, course lightly with the gay gazelle, or in any way fill the chest with 'surge and thunder'; and while Gerard Hopkins does not by habit vary his movement with the change of what one would expect to be the underlying emotion, I cannot believe that either Bridges or Hopkins would have been wholly content with Housman's selected illustration.

Mr Housman's prose proceeds with a suavity which the present writer is perfectly willing to envy. Only a biased judgment would deny this, and only a man writing in irritation would, it seems to me, be unaware. One goes from contrast to contrast, Mr Housman's well-known competence up to a point, and the surprising and sudden limits of his cognizance; were he a yokel or yellow press hack, there would be no surprise that he quotes Johnson as the source of J.'s repetition of Aristotle; but from a professor of Latin, a reader, for recreation, of 'several languages'? Ah well, Aristotle was a Greek?

And as for 'the dawn in russet mantle', which is a perfectly good example of the Aristotle via Johnson's 'hall mark of genius', I fail utterly to see *why* it should give only a pleasure purely intellectual and intellectually frivolous, and be of no more virtue than an anagram.

Perhaps the suavity of Housman's writing is not co-partner with precision of thought.

On page 19 I would offer an emendation. As the text stands we are invited to suppose that 'the intelligence' (they are discussing the eighteenth century) involved 'some repressing and silencing of poetry'.

The intelligence never did anything of the sort. (Ref. 'Donne's 'Ecstacy', Voi ch'avete intelletto d'amore', 'Voi ch' intendendo il terzo ciel movete', or the pawky comments of Homer!)

The particular form of abstract statement, Voltairian (out of Bayle, out of Quevedo, out of antiquity) kind of reduction *ad absurdum*, etc., dear to the eighteenth century, had an effect on verse. They had no ideogrammic method or hadn't erected it into a system and hadn't heard about Professor Agassiz's fish, but to confuse a tendency to abstract general statement with *tout bonnement* 'intelligence' is to sin against all those most admirable canons of nomenclature which Mr Housman has just so (on his preceding two pages) eulogized.

'The poetry of the eighteenth century', says Mr Housman, 'was most satisfactory when it did not try to be poetical.' And in other centuries? Again we find a curious trilogy 'satire, controversy and burlesque'. What has satire done, that it should be found so confounded? And what did Hermes say to Calypso?

Mr Housman must be being hortatory, we must indeed be headed for the loftiest possible heights where Homer, Ovid, Dante and Chaucer are not to be quite given the entrée. His bethel must be contracting.

'Le pointe de la pyramide,' says Brancusi, 'on est là, on ne peut pas bouger.'

Housman's remark on 'great parsimony and tact' perhaps covers him. If the samples of nineteenth and eighteenth century faded prettiness (on page 22) are to be graded, I candidly doubt whether the latter is inferior to the former. Content more or less kiff/kiff and the eighteenth-century metric rather cleaner?

The general trend of Housman's sermon on the undesirability of confusing poetry with 'lofty thoughts expressed in beeyeewteeful and flowery langwidg', can however confer nothing save benefit on his readers. I suppose by 'eighteenth century' he means that century *in* England.

Again the pedant in me (who am not like Mr Housman a professor with honours, benefice, ecclesiastical preferments) arises on a matter of nomenclature. Housman has dragged in an 'eighteenth century' which he defines as a condition and not a chronological measure, and for this extension of language he can find plenty of justification, though it be just a little off the stipulated colour of his doctrine.

But is it well found? Dryden, according to my dictionary of dates, breathed between 1631 and 1700, Crabbe between 1754 and 1832.

I have never told anyone to read Dryden, who seems to be the chief and anti-Eliotic demon in Professor Housman's cosmos, but was Crabbe up till the forty-sixth year of his age an eighteenth-century writer by chronology or by spiritual definition? and wasn't Landor even well into the woollier days of Queen Victoria, not only by the chronology of his adolescence, but by affinity with Mr Housman's own definition?

Again the ways of Housman's mind are recondite; having damned burlesque and disparaged Gilpin as lacking sublimity, he produces:

Uprose the sun and up rose Emily

as Chaucerian unbetterableness. Heaven knows I don't want to improve it, but is it the height of seriousness, here attained, or have we Chaucerian chuckle? Or at any rate can the reader familiar with Chaucer, but without looking up the context, suppose this line to be any more expressive, any closer to the heart of another's dark forest, etc., than some line of spitfire Alex?

Heaven be my witness that I, at any rate, and of all men, don't want Johnnie Dryden dug up again. Whether by maturity of wit, or whether it be that from early, very early childhood I have been protected by the association of ideas inherent in the first syllable of John's patronymic—Mr Eliot's endeavours having served only to strengthen my resolve never, never again, to open either John Dryden, his works or any comment upon them, but if anything could stir an interest in that outstanding aridity it would be the isolation of some quite sensible remark about Chaucer illustrated pro and con; con by three brays as blatant as Milton; and pro? well, perhaps not very successfully.

In short, Dryden found a rather good critical term, but being by nature a lunk-head, was unable to derive much light from that accident. The marvel, to me, is how any man bent on recreation 'among the best', and yet so limited a range (apparently) in his selected reading matter, should between beer and the hedgerows have pervaded, transgressed, wandered into, even to the extent of so many quoted lines, Mr Dryden's plasterings upon Chaucer.

On the other hand, Mr Housman has obviously been protected by Heaven. The curse of Isaiah which he shudders to think *had* fallen in the dim years of the treaty of Utrecht, has fairly deluged his country during the literary regencies of Marsh and Abercrombie (1910 to 1930), and Mr Housman has heard nothing about it.

And the North Pole said to the South Pole: 'Heteroclite is man and there is surely room for a great deal of difference.'

Anyone who can write such neat suave sentences as Mr Housman with such open sincerity is a blessing to . . . oh, to the present reader —if only to come bang up against another point of view so alien to any preconception, and of a so antipodal difference of disposition.

'No truth', says Housman, 'too precious, observation too profound, sentiment too exalted to be expressed in prose.'

I am unqualified to speak of exalted sentiment, but I should say no idea worth carrying in the mind from one year's end to another, and no story really good enough to make me at least want to tell it, but chafes at the flatness of prose, but suffers from inadequate statement, but leaves me feeling it is but half said, or said in abstraction, defined in terms so elastic that any god's ape can stretch its definition to meet his own squalor or to fit his own imbecility, until it be conjoined with music, or at least given rhythmic definition even though one do not arrive at defining its total articulation.

As for 'some ideas do, some do not', etc., Mr Housman is being too 'choosey'. Not the idea but the degree of its definition determines its aptitude for reaching to music.

We have obviously come to a parting of the ways: 'If poetry has a meaning it may be inadvisable to draw it out', *Housman;* 'The intellectual love of a thing consists in the understanding of its perfections', *Spinoza.* Also 'le style c'est l'homme', *vir quidem,* who may for all I care have been the whole of Latinity, the Mediterranean Everyman, made verb and articulate.

On page 38, Mr Housman descends to bathos, slop, ambiguity, word-twisting, and is like to finish off the respect one had been feeling for him. If the Greek word there translated means 'madness' in the sense of Smart's and Collins' and Willie Blake's being occasionally sent off to do a week-end in an asylum; if it means anything more than a certain tenseness of emotion, a mental excess, no more insane than the kind of physical excess that enabled black Siki to dance back to back with his opponent in a boxing ring, delivering blows over his head or that enables the sabre ant to cup up a spider, then Plato was an hog, an ape, the louse of a louse, an unprincipled impertinent liar, cutting loose from all the known facts of Greek poetry, none of whose great makers were either lunatics, moon-chewers, village idiots, or general imbeciles, nor were the best Latins, nor was Dante, nor Guido, nor Villon, nor Gautier, Corbière, Browning; and Mr Housman can pack that sentimental drool in his squiffer, and turn his skill to throwing the dart in the pub next adjacent.

Saxpence reward for any authenticated case of intellect having stopped a chap's writing poesy! You might as well claim that railway tracks stop the engine. No one ever claimed they would make it go.

The worship of the village idiot is perhaps peculiar to England? Even the Irish prefer to think the man's mind exists somewhere though it be gone to the fairies.

When it comes to Shakespeare writing 'nonsense', or to the given example: A. The sample is by no means nonsense. B. The intellect has been in plenary function, Shakespeare being the greatest English technician bar none, and having had the wit to concentrate his technique where the most enlightened intellect would naturally concentrate *technique*, namely on the arrangement of his *sounds*, on the twenty-six letters of his alphabet, on the quality and duration of his syllables and on the varying weights of his accent, pillaging the Italian song books. I mean those of poems printed *with* the music rather than the pages of mere print alone.

The greatest technician, the true English writer of Epos, daring the disparate material of the Histories, again using his *mind*! It took the donkey-eared Milton to pass on that drivelling imbecility about woodnotes so dear to the Wordsworthian epiglottis.

To admire some of Blake's metric you have to forget Lewis Carroll.

That there was a fountain of poetry somewhere inside dippy William, I would be the last to refute, but that the furies and the surges gain by being presented in the dialect of

> Tiger, Tiger, catch 'em quick!
> All the little lambs are sick,

I am mildly inclined to deny. Mr Housman hereabouts is discussing how poetic the that which isn't intellect becomes when expressed in incommensurate language.

I seem to recall something of Herrick's which loses nothing by its author's having been lucid:

> Your dew drink offerings on my tomb

or something of that sort.

I suspect that Mr Housman suffers from a deficient curiosity. Such as he has seems hardly to have led him to consider any verse save that having good heavy swat on every alternate syllable, or at least formed predominantly on the system of *ti Tum ti Tum ti Tum*, sometimes up to ten syllables.

On page 47 our author goes down, deeply down, to that jocularity expected of men holding academic honours, and feeling a need to unbend, to meet, to mingle humanly with their audience. Rats, terriers, the 'bristling' of Mr Housman's skin under the razor, if a poetic thought darts through his memory, and last but not Keast, Fanny Brawne!

> Milton thou should'st be living at this hour![1]

[1] Meaning that he might have lectured at Cambridge.

DATE LINE[1]

I

Criticism has at least the following categories, differing greatly in the volume of their verbal manifestation, and not equally zoned.

1. Criticism by discussion, extending from mere yatter, logic-chopping, and description of tendencies up to the clearly defined record of procedures and an attempt to formulate more or less general principles.

Aristotle being neither poet nor complete imbecile contented himself with trying to formulate some of the general interior and exterior relations of work already extant.

He has presumably the largest bastard family of any philosopher. Ninkus, Pinkus and Swinky all try to say what the next writer must do.

Dante who was capable of executing the work and of holding general ideas, set down a partial record of procedures.

2. Criticism by translation.

3. Criticism by exercise in the style of a given period.

As you would not seriously consider a man's knowledge of tennis until he either could make or had made some sort of show in a tournament, so we can assume that until a man can actually control a given set of procedures there must be many elements in them of which he has but an imperfect knowledge.

This introduces almost a personal note, or at least a long-delayed reply to carpers who objected to my spending three days in trans-lating Fontenelle on the grounds that I should have been 'doing original work and not wasting my energies in translation'. They took the *Divagation* as a proof that I was merely gathering daisies.

4. Criticism via music, meaning definitely the setting of a poet's words; e.g. in *Le Testament*, Villon's words, and in *Cavalcanti*, I have set Guido's and Sordello's. In the famous caricature of Edward and Alfonso, seated on a bench in the Bois, the elder monarch

[1] 'Make It New,' 1934, London, Faber and Faber Ltd.; 1935, New Haven, Yale University Press.

remarks to the younger: 'A vôtre âge j'étais seulement Prince de
Galles, c'est le seul moyen de bien connaître Paris.'

This is the most intense form of criticism save:

5. Criticism in new composition.

For example the criticism of Seneca in Mr. Eliot's *Agon* is infinitely more alive, more vigorous than in his essay on Seneca.

Years ago I made the mistake of publishing a volume (*Instigations*)
without blatantly telling the reader that the book had a design.
Coming after an era of gross confusion and irrelevance, wherein
malicious camouflage is infinitely more general than any sort of
coherence whatsoever, such violent rupture with the general public
habit is perfectly useless, and may, for all I know, be unfair to those
readers who inhabit a middle zone between effulgent intellect and *les
cuistres*.

There would have been no point in asking indulgence as long as
the appearances were so greatly against one, I mean so long as the
appearance of mere haphazard gave ground for argument, and the
reader of ill-will had ample basis for hostile demonstration.

II

Criticism so far as I have discovered has two functions:

1. Theoretically it tries to forerun composition, to serve as gun-
sight, though there is, I believe, no recorded instance of the foresight having EVER been of the slightest use save to actual composers.
I mean the man who formulates any forward reach of co-ordinating
principle is the man who produces the demonstration.

The others who use the principle learn usually from the example,
and in most cases merely dim and dilute it.

I think it will usually be found that the work outruns the formulated or at any rate the published equation, or at most they proceed as
two feet of one biped.

2. Excernment. The general ordering and weeding out of what has
actually been performed. The elimination of repetitions. The work
analogous to that which a good hanging committee or a curator
would perform in a National Gallery or in a biological museum;

The ordering of knowledge so that the next man (or generation)
can most readily find the live part of it, and waste the least possible
time among obsolete issues.

'Admitted that it had nothing to do with life but said that it couldn't be changed, therefore I did not take the course.' (Letter from Cambridge student, Nov. 1933. The letter referred to economics and not to literature, but it is too good an example of the academic, of the, alas, 'university' spirit to leave unused.)

It is impossible to deal with the whole question of education, 'culture', *paideuma,* in one volume of literary criticism. What Mr Eliot calls 'Para something or other' need not for a few hundred pages concern us, save to say that University education during my time failed from lack of attention to its circle of reference:

(*a*) Society in general.

(*b*) The general intellectual life of the nation.

I take it this was equally true of England, the U.S.A. and several other nations with which I have had less painful experience.

We have passed from the time wherein it was possible to illude oneself by a 'glittering' or other generality. The contemporary philosopher on the Greek model with one profound (? if any) central (more or less) intuition and a lot of unverified hypotheses, analogies, uninspected detail, no longer inveigles serious attention. Philosophy since Leibnitz (at least since Leibnitz) has been a weak trailer after material science, engaging men of tertiary importance.

It is not to be expected that the knowledge of the human consciousness, or its most efficient registering material, language, can dispense with progress in method at least par with that of the particular sciences, nor that any one individual can escape all the limitations of his confrères. No biologist expects to formulate a WHOLE NEW biology. At best he expects to explore a limited field, to improve the knowledge of certain details and, if lucky, to clarify the relations of that field, both in regard to the field itself, and to its exterior reference.

You don't necessarily expect the bacilli in one test tube to 'lead to' those in another by a mere logical or syllogistic line. The good scientist now and then discovers similarities, he discovers family groups, similar behaviour in presence of like reagents, etc. Mark Carleton 'the great' improved American wheat by a series of searches. I see no reason why a similar seriousness should be alien to the critic of letters.

Language is not a mere cabinet curio or museum exhibit. It does definitely function in all human life from the tribal state onward. You cannot govern without it, you cannot make laws without it.

That is you make laws, and they become mere mare's nests for graft and discussion. 'The meaning has to be determined', etc.

There are other means of direct human communication but they are all narrowly zoned to their *specific* departments, plastic directness, mathematical relations (in music, or engineering), and in borderline territory where a little very clear language has to be used along with the 'technical' expression. (Even if it be only to label the photograph or the slide.) However much you accept of Frobenius's theory of *paideuma* as general and overreaching, overstretching the single man, whether you take this as literal fact, or as convenient modus of correlation, the spoken idiom is not only a prime factor, but certainly one of the most potent, progressively so as any modality of civilization ages. Printed word or drum telegraph are neither without bearing on the aggregate life of the folk. As language becomes the most powerful instrument of perfidy, so language alone can riddle and cut through the meshes. Used to conceal meaning, used to blur meaning, to produce the complete and utter inferno of the past century . . . discussion of which would lead me out of the bounds of this volume . . . against which, SOLELY a care for language, for accurate registration by language avails. And if men too long neglect it their children will find themselves begging and their offspring betrayed. Summaries of my conclusions after thirty years' search are now available (*How to Read, ABC of Reading*).

The present volume is a collection of reports (in the biologists' sense) on specific bodies of writing, undertaken in the hope, or with the aims, of criticism and in accordance with the ideogrammic method, approached in my very early *Serious Artist*, and there exemplified in at least one case; seriously indicated in Ernest Fenollosa's *The Chinese Written Character*, there dealt with narratively rather than formulated as a method *to be used*. This method is too necessary a conclusion from all the more intelligent activity of many decades for there to be the least question of its belonging to anyone in particular.

Fenollosa's work was given me in manuscript when I was ready for it. It saved me a great deal of time. It saved probably less time to a limited number of writers who noticed it promptly but who didn't live with it as closely as I did. Fenollosa died in 1908. I began an examination of comparative European literature in or about 1901; with the definite intention of finding out what had been written, and how. The motives I presumed to differ with the individual writers.

Rudolf Agricola had centuries before indicated at least three main groups of literary purpose:

> 'Ut doceat, ut moveat, ut delectet',

which divisions had, I suppose, come down from antiquity. Over and above any such great general zones, we now discern beyond and instead of simple process or 'technique' in the single work of a given time, the modalities, the general congeries of equations implied in 'style of a period'. That is a mode of writing which implies a very considerable basis of agreement between writer and reader, between writer and an order of existence, together with comparatively low percentage of difference.

'*Toutes mes choses datent de quinze ans*', says Brancusi. There is nothing very new in this section of preface, I am only trying to save the reader's time by condensing, instead of republishing, a considerable amount of printed matter, the initial purposes of which have already been served.

III

The Parable of the Horse and the Water

You can take a man to Perugia or to Borgo San Sepolcro but you can't make him prefer one kind of painting to another. All you can do is to prevent his supposing that there is only one kind of painting, or writing, or only two or three or a limited gamut.

When you broach such matters with a confrère, you listen to his account of things you yourself do not know from experience, you tell him what he doesn't know, and you discuss, or confer on things which both have seen.

In aiming at a new *paideuma*, whatever use my criticism may be found, in the long run, to have, it has been for some years the attempt to ascertain the relations of at least a certain number of literary phenomena (blocks of verbal manifestation) without which any opinion on writing as such, is bound to be incompetent, defective to a degree that will either cause 'pain' proportionate to the sensibility of the auditor, or excite his risible faculty.

English and American criticism of the generation preceding mine, and the completely contemptible and damnable activity of the literary bureaucracy in power (materially in power in the editorial offices, publishing houses, etc.) has been occupied chiefly with the inane assertion of the non-existence of the giraffe, and *magari* not of the giraffe alone, but of whole tribes of animals, the puma, the panther, the well-known Indian buffalo. Sheep and gelded oxen they had seen, but no W. H. Hudson was to be let back from the Andes with reports of birds 'antient upon the Earth', no Beebe was to go down with a patent appliance and get any more kinds of fish out of the sea depth. The largest of all beasts was the horned moose of the Dominion, and so forth. The concept of fauna was to be kept within bounds. And so forth.

That these *cuistres* have been shown up for fools time and again, has yet had almost no effect on the book trade. One piece of evidence against the whole cockeyed system is the signal incapacity of the 'ploot' to do anything for the enlivenment of letters. Seven blind men to pick the company's rifleshot. Sterile incompetents charged to spend the income of millions no longer even in monuments, where the facts are comparatively easy to discover, but *magari* in CHOOSING the paladins of tomorrow, in PICKING the rising talent, which is so subtle a process that even the best player attempts it with diffidence.

Demonstration has not availed. Capacity to pick the winner has, most signally, NOT affected these domains of material action. Men who have been wrong steadily decade after decade, who have persistently at intervals of five years, or ten years or even less than five, printed vast blurbs about authors now relegated to desuetude, still decree what books shall be printed, what books the vast congeries of American Carnegie libraries shall purchase. No 'regular and established publisher' has yet printed a new author's book or indeed any book on my recommendation (unless a couple of anthologies are to be counted). An analogous condition of affairs would doubtless be comic in the higher intellectual circles of pugilism or greyhound racing, but so is it gravely and solemnly on . . . well I suppose they aren't the slopes of Parnassus. . . . The mountain is still intact, the spring water still excellent. The Palux Laerna has always existed.

My present publishers or at least one member of the firm suggested including my early reviews of authors of my own generation. I don't see the use of it. This book ought to be printed to read, each page ought to convey at least a little to the reader. We are not here to pass a state examination. A board of auditors wanting to verify the accounts of past literary transactions can still find at least an adequate amount of the data in the British Museum, and there must be a few copies of out-of-print volumes of mine still unpurloined from the New York and Brooklyn public libraries.

Let it stand that the function of criticism is to efface itself when it has established its dissociations. Let it stand that from 1912 onward for a decade and more I was instrumental in forcing into print, and *secondarily* in commenting on, certain work now recognized as valid by all competent readers, the dates of various reviews, anthologies, etc., are ascertainable. René Taupin took the trouble to look up a good many that I had forgotten. Careless statement, due either to laziness (in fact more probably to general mental slovenliness than to any one cause) or to local pride and prejudice, or disposition to remain in comfortable inherited preconceptions invalidates a certain amount of writing in popular edition intended to be 'informative'.

I think there is only one largish current error of this sort, namely that in America, the stay-at-home, local congeries did ANYTHING toward the *stil 'nuovo* or the awakening. Robinson is still old style, Lindsey did have a rayon of his own, the rest trundled along AFTER the hypodermic injection had been effected via London. Even Frost the prize autochthonous specimen made his début in London, and was forced into the local New England bucolic recognition from Kensington, W.8. The *pièces justificatives* are the back files of *Poetry* and the *Egoist* from October 1912 onward. The *Little Review*, 1917-19, as monthly, with the later quarterly issues.

The gall and wormwood to the *tribus cimicium* was that but for the present execrated writer a number of troublesome fellows could have been left unnoticed, and that oblivion would have been much less disturbing to the lethargy, sloth, etc. All of which has (and always had) a humorous side, now increasingly apparent to the dispassionate regarder of human turmoil.

Emerging from cenacles; from scattered appearances in unknown periodicals, the following dates can function in place of more expensive reprint: *Catholic Anthology*, 1915, for the sake of printing sixteen pages of Eliot (poems later printed in *Prufrock*). Criticism of Joyce's *Dubliners*, in *Egoist*, 1916, and the series of notes on Joyce's work, from then on. Instrumentality in causing Joyce to be published serially and in volume form, *Egoist*, *Little Review*, culminating with the criticism of *Ulysses* in the *Mercure de France*, June 1922. This was, I believe, the first serious French criticism of Mr Joyce (that is to say it was in 'French' of a sort, but at any rate comprehensible).

It might here be noted that the *Mercure* was founded on decent principles, impersonal franco-centric but with the belief in facts, and in open discussion. Having been *the* great European review of letters for more decades than we can remember, the decline of the *Mercure* is merely the natural fatigue of men who have grown old, and out-lasted their strength. It is not a voluntary stultification or a refusal of information.

Valette's reply to my comment on the deficiencies of the *Mercure's* American notes, was to offer me the rubric ... at a time when I couldn't undertake it. Any contemporary English or American old-established literary review of his time would have tried to protect some form of ignorance or incompetence.

Perhaps my criticism of Mr Lewis was primarily for his power in organization of forms, but apart from Blast, and Gaudier's sculpture, *Tarr* was serialized in the *Egoist* and the foreign editorship of the *Little Review* was undertaken 'in order that the work of Joyce, Lewis, Eliot and myself might appear promptly and regularly and in one place, without inane and idiotic delay' (*Lit. Rev.* May 1917). As well as *Ulysses* (until publicly banned by 100 per cent subjects of Woodie Wilson the damned), and poems of Eliot's second phase, the review published a number of Mr Lewis's most active short stories. I think we were suppressed for *Cantleman's Spring Mate* before we were suppressed for *Bloom's* deshabille.

The decision against *Ulysses* has been revoked, as I suppose the world at large knows, but the baboon law is part of the American statute. The legal machinery for future imbecility on the lines of the suppression of *Ulysses* is still there and it would take only a slip back into the era of Andy Mellon to produce another and similar grin through the eternal horse collar of the Anglo-Saxon community.

The fact that certain authors now tempt the avarice of Tauchnitz and similars seems to me to eliminate the need of repairing or reinspecting the arguments used years ago to draw unwilling atten-tion.

In another thirty years perhaps the gross idiocy of two decades of publishers will also be more apparent. I mean their short-sighted-ness; and particularly their policy of debasing the literary coin to a point where it no longer deceives even the gulls. Trade bad save in

inferior imitations of Edgar Wallace, because greed of immediate
profit blinded them to the necessity of keeping alive just a wee bit of
inventiveness, of fostering just enough good seed corn for new crop,
of cherishing just that little bit of extra perception, just that bit of
unwanted honesty that divides say McAlmon from Sinclair Lewis,
and makes the latter so acceptable to the boob, whose recognized
limitations he portrays, without pulling the gaff on something that
affects personal vanity.

New York the eternal goat! Year after year, decade after decade
the same sort of obtuseness. America is now teeming with printed
books written by imitators of McAlmon, inferior to the original. So
far as I know no volume by McAlmon has yet been printed in his
own country.

Antheil once gave me a list of forgotten musical composers going
back to the 1860s who had, at successive intervals, been hailed as the
great real thing in America to the delay or detriment of remembered
composers.

It is not the *vox populi*. One is inclined to talk of popular taste,
when one should hunt for the chaps working the oracle.

It becomes at this point increasingly difficult to keep economic
discussion out of the narrative. Or say that lacking any decent
organization, lacking any sense of responsibility toward letters,
lacking men having any such sense and at the same time any power
or energy, the economic factors (trade control, etc.) became increasingly capable of forcing the degradation of books. Culmination perhaps in withdrawal of overdrafts of London publishers who didn't
behave.

At any rate from 1917 to 1919 the more active British product
appeared in New York. New York had the chance of taking over the
leadership in publishing and was too hog-stupid to grasp it. The
chance lay there unnoticed for a decade, and is, I should think, by
now lost.

For the post-war years up till 1924 or 1925 the activity of both
America and England was perhaps more apparent in Paris than anywhere else.

The new lot of American *émigrés* were anything but the Passionate
Pilgrims of James's day or the enquirers of my own. *We* came to
find something, to learn, possibly to conserve, but this new lot came
in disgust, harbingers, I think the term is, of an era of filth and

degradation at 'home' which will, I think, be increasingly apparent as just that. From Harding to Hoover, no clean thing in power. And heaven knows Wilson's stink was sufficient.

In 1933 we see the States with no contemporary daily news bulletin, the situation summed up by one experienced syndicate journalist: 'Of course the revolution has occurred but the press hasn't been told yet.'

IV

With the dawn of the year XII of the present era, the chronicler's old sap moves again; for the first time since we were that way ourselves, I am ready to take rash chances, to put my money on this year's colts.

That, however, is not yet chronicle and does not enter this book.

In the year XII where are we? We are in the epoch of Stalin, Gesell, C. H. Douglas and of Il Duce, with Mr Roosevelt still a more or less nebulous figure, a little here, a little there, a little to the fellow who's got the silver (without, however, 'ladling it out' to the owners of foreign idem), a little to the naval gun-smiths, a little discreet hope and family rumour that F. D. understands this and that, the great master of carom shot. (To-day January 28.)

What I wrote in last February he by March had admitted the half of, leaving the rest in the fog. *Und so weiter.* Mussolini a male of the species, and the author of this year's *consegna.*

'Gli uomini vivono in pochi.' Frobenius very much on the job, Cocteau 'fragile ma non debole'.

To come to my table of contents:

An examination

Of speech in relation to music. Sections I, II.

Of speech   III, IV, V.

VI. General summary of state of human consciousness in decades immediately before my own, the H. James and De Gourmont compendium.

VII. Cavalcanti, as bringing together all of these strands, the consciousness, depth of same almost untouched in writing between his time and that of Ibsen and James; meaning if you come at it not as platonic formulation of philosophy but as psychology.

VIII. A final segment, deferred to another volume, was retrospect to a more immediate past. After that section I have submitted to guidance. I had intended to provide the book derisively with an appendix, vermiform. Papa Flaubert compiled a *sottisier*, I also compiled a *sottisier*. I do not yield a jot in my belief that such compilations are useful, I concede that there may be no need of reprinting mine at this moment. At any rate the snippets are there on file. You can't know an era merely by knowing its best. Gourmont and James weren't the whole of the latter half of a century. There are all strata down to the bottom, the very.

You get the Middle Ages from Mussato, in a way you do not, I think, get them from Dante without Mussato; and Mussato is again a summit.

The contention that my *sottisier*, compiled fifteen years ago, could be equalled in the current press, doesn't seem to me relevant. But for a few lines by Milord Rochester one might think certain inanities were wholly Victorian and not *of* the laced Restoration.

I admit, without being asked, that the *sottisier* would have displayed nothing appertaining to the 'best that has been known and thought'. It might, *anʒi* help toward evaluation. However there is no hurry about it, the careful historian of the 1910's is not yet busy in numbers.

The rest of the items are I think either self-explanatory or better indicated in immediate notes.

J'Y TIENS

There is no use my moderator's suggesting that in my notes on Monro and Housman in the *Criterion* I have in a general way indicated the state of English culture in 1910-30 or 1933. I am not specifically concerned with the state of enlightenment among a few hundred very refined persons with an abnormal or super-medium interest in *belles lettres*. I distinctly assert that I made the *sottisier*, that I definitely examined symptoms which the visiting anthropologist or student of Kulturmorphologie would have noticed as 'customs of the tribus Britannicus', the material which the average man would have found easy to hand as printed matter in the city of London about 1918-19.

That constitutes a definite dimension, its examination a species of measurement of *mœurs contemporaines*. To be used as 'off set' against any other special conditions.

As to enlightened opinion: By 1920 or whatever date more precise, enlightened opinion had digested Fabre and Frazer, at least to the extent shown by the Gourmont citations.

By somewhere about 1750 'enlightened opinion' was digesting the disposition of Fontenelle toward the cosmos. The modality of such statement has an effect on the 'literal meaning'.

By 1934 Frazer is sufficiently digested for us to know that opposing systems of European morality go back to the opposed temperaments of those who thought copulation was good for the crops, and the opposed faction who thought it was bad for the crops (the scarcity economists of pre-history). That ought to simplify a good deal of argument. The Christian might at least decide whether he is for Adonis or Atys, or whether he is Mediterranean. The exact use of dyeing Europe with a mythology elucubrated to explain the thoroughly undesirable climate of Arabia Petraea is in some reaches obscure.

Further attempt to answer Mr Eliot's indirect query as to 'What Mr P. believes', would be perhaps out of place at this juncture. The peculiar frenzies of the Atys cult seem unadapted to the pleasanter parts of the Mediterranean basin. I have, I think, at no time attempted to conceal my beliefs from my so eminent colleague, but I have at all times desired to know the demarcation between what I know and what I do not know, as perhaps even the partial reprint of my *Cavalcanti* will help to convince the reader (if not, he can consult the Genova edition, with plates and further apparatus, if same be in the Museum Britannicum).

This difference between what is known, and what is merely faked or surmised has at all times seemed to me worth discovering. Obviously the more limited the field the more detailed can the demarcation become.

It is, I feel, obvious that only a limited number of authors are worth the attention there (*Rime*, Marsano edition) demonstrably given to Guido, it is I think arguable whether, even there, such attention would have been wisely spent *had I not* later set a good deal of him to music, or had I not wanted the edition to serve as a model for editions of a very limited number of authors.

(Again on the principle of getting the factors of main importance clearly detached from the rest . . . in this case very much a matter of photos and typography.)

It seems to me desirable to establish demarcation between the known and the unknown, in at least a few specimen areas.

Until one has taken the trouble to do so I don't see how one is to escape a certain gross clumsiness in the general Anschauung.

I mean for example, as I have said in a much shorter book (*à propos* Donne in the *ABC of Reading*) that it is perfectly ascertainable that a number of men in succeeding epochs have managed to be intelligible to each other concerning a gamut of perceptions which other bodies of men wholly deny.

It would seem to me rather unscientific to deny their existence at least as perceptions, at least as a correlatable congeries of communicable data, even though you quite obviously cannot discuss them profitably with nine-tenths of your acquaintance, though you occasionally can with quite simple unfeigning people.

As to what I believe:

I believe the *Ta Hio*

When a dozen people have convinced me that they understand that so lucid work, I may see reason for accepting a more elaborate exposition. Until then the case seems rather to resemble that of my last four pages on 'great bass', I don't know anyone save Antheil and Tibor Serly, and possibly two other composers who could make any use of those pages. The American composer John Becker tried vainly to get them printed in several musical periodicals, they serve just as well in carbon copies and in conversation as they could in print.

An epic is a poem including history. I don't see that anyone save a sap-head can now think he knows any history until he understands economics. Whether he propose to do anything, or to incite anyone else to action, he manifestly cannot understand Gibbon or Gatti's *Dazzi e Monti* or any other collection of data and documents touching the workings, without Ariadne's thread—the proof being that generations of so-called historians just haven't. Wherever you find a Medici you find a loan at low interest, often at half that of their contemporaries'.

I thought in my jactancy that I had performed a *tour de force* when I reduced a contemporary economic equation to what the benevolent consider verse; within 24 hours (twenty-four hours) I came on Dante inveighing against Philippe le Bel for debasing the currency (*Paradiso* XIX, 118).

I am leaving my remark on *anagke* in the H. James notes, but the Act of God alters with time. The wreck of a fifteenth-century vessel might be an Act of God, whereas disaster in storm of like dimensions would to-day be due to gross carelessness either in construction, navigation or in care of the machines. Some infamies in the year XII are as needless as death by thirst in the city of London. There is a TIME in these things.

It is quite obvious that we do not all of us inhabit the same time.

PART TWO
The Tradition

THE TRADITION[1]

Penitus enim tibi O Phoebe attributa est cantus.

The tradition is a beauty which we preserve and not a set of fetters to bind us. This tradition did not begin in A.D. 1870, nor in 1776, nor in 1632, nor in 1564. It did not begin even with Chaucer.

The two great lyric traditions which most concern us are that of the Melic poets and that of Provence. From the first arose practically all the poetry of the 'ancient world', from the second practically all that of the modern. Doubtless there existed before either of these traditions a Babylonian and a Hittite tradition whereof knowledge is for the most part lost. We know that men worshipped Mithra with an arrangement of pure vowel-sounds. We know that men made verses in Egypt and in China, we assume that they made them in Uruk. There is a Japanese metric which I do not yet understand, there is doubtless an agglutinative metric beyond my comprehension.

As it happens, the conditions of English and forces in the English tradition are traceable, for the most part, to the two traditions mentioned. It is not intelligent to ignore the fact that both in Greece and in Provence the poetry attained its highest rhythmic and metrical brilliance at times when the arts of verse and music were most closely knit together, when each thing done by the poet had some definite musical urge or necessity bound up within it. The Romans writing upon tablets did not match the cadences of those earlier makers who had composed to and for the Cÿthera and the Barbitos.

As touching the parallel development of the twin arts in the modern world, it may be noted that the *canzon* of Provence became the *canzone* of Italy, and that when Dante and his contemporaries began to compose philosophic treatises in verse the *son* or accompaniment went maying on its own account, and in music became the sonata; and, from the date of the divorce, poetry declined until such time as Baif and the Pléïade began to bring Greek and Latin and Italian renaissance fashions into France, and to experiment in music and 'quantity'.

Poetry, III, 3 (Dec. 1913).

The Italians of that century had renewed the art, they had written in Latin, and some little even in Greek, and had used the Hellenic meters. DuBellay translated Navgherius into French, and Spenser translated DuBellay's adaptations into English, and then as in Chaucer's time and times since then, *the English cribbed their technique from over the channel.* The Elizabethans 'made' to music, and they copied the experiments of Paris. Thus as always one wave of one of these traditions has caught and overflowed an earlier wave receding. The finest troubador had sung at the court of Coeur de Leon. Chaucer had brought in the 'making' of France and ended the Anglo-Saxon alliterative fashions. The *canzon* of Provence which had become the *canzone* and sonnet, had become *Minnesang;* it had become the ballade and it became many an 'Elizabethan' form. And at that age the next wave from Paris caught it, a wave part 'Romance' (in the linguistic sense) and part Latin. But Provence is itself Latin, in a way, for when the quantities of syllables had been lost through the barbarian invasions, rhyme had come in as courtly ornament. The first fragment of Provençal poetry is Latin with a Provençal refrain.

Dr Ker has put an end to much babble about folk song by showing us *Summer is ycummen in* written beneath the Latin words of a very old canon.

II

A return to origins invigorates because it is a return to nature and reason. The man who returns to origins does so because he wishes to behave in the eternally sensible manner. That is to say, naturally, reasonably, intuitively. He does not wish to do the right thing in the wrong place, to 'hang an ox with trappings', as Dante puts it. He wishes not pedagogy but harmony, the fitting thing.

This is not the place for an extensive discussion of technical detail. Of the uses and abuses of rhyme I would say nothing, save that it is neither a necessity nor a taboo.

As to quantity, it is foolish to suppose that we are incapable of distinguishing a long vowel from a short one, or that we are mentally debarred from ascertaining how many consonants intervene between one vowel and the next.

As to the tradition of *vers libre*: Jannaris in his study of the Melic poets comes to the conclusion that they composed to the feel of the thing, to the cadence, as have all good poets since. He is not inclined to believe that they were much influenced by discussions held in Alexandria some centuries after their deaths.

If the earnest upholder of conventional imbecility will turn at random to the works of Euripides, or in particular to such passages as *Hippolytus* 1268 *et Seq.*, or to *Alkestis* 266 *et seq.*, or idem 455 *et seq.*, or to *Phoenissae* 1030 *et circa*, or to almost any notable Greek chorus, it is vaguely possible that the light of *vers libre* might spread some faint aurora upon his cerebral tissues.

No one is so foolish as to suppose that a musician using 'four-four' time is compelled to use always four quarter notes in each bar, or in 'seven-eighths' time to use seven eighth notes uniformly in each bar. He may use one $\frac{1}{2}$, one $\frac{1}{4}$ and one $\frac{1}{8}$ rest, or any such combination as he may happen to choose or find fitting.

To apply this musical truism to verse is to employ *vers libre*.

To say that such and such combinations of sound and tempo are not proper, is as foolish as to say that a painter should not use red in the upper left hand corners of his pictures. The movement of poetry is limited only by the nature of syllables and of articulate sound, and by the laws of music, or melodic rhythm. Space forbids a complete treatise on melody at this point, and forbids equally a complete treatise on all the sorts of verse, alliterative, syllabic, accentual, and quantitative. And such treatises as the latter are for the most part useless, as no man can learn much of these things save by first-hand untrammeled, unprejudiced examination of the finest examples of all these sorts of verse, of the finest strophes and of the finest rhyme-schemes, and by a profound study of the art and history of music.

Neither is surface imitation of much avail, for imitation is, indeed, of use only in so far as it connotes a closer observation, or an attempt closely to study certain forces through their effects.

TROUBADOURS¹ – THEIR SORTS
AND CONDITIONS

The argument whether or no the troubadours are a subject worthy of study is an old and respectable one. If Guillaume, Count of Peiteus, grandfather of King Richard Cœur de Leon, had not been a man of many energies, there might have been little food for this discussion. He was, as the old book says of him, 'of the greatest counts in the world, and he had his way with women.' He made songs for either them or himself or for his more ribald companions. They say that his wife was Countess of Dia, 'fair lady and righteous', who fell in love with Raimbaut d'Aurenga and made him many a song. Count Guillaume brought composition in verse into court fashions, and gave it a social prestige which it held till the crusade of 1208 against the Albigenses. The mirth of Provençal song is at times anything but sunburnt, and the mood is often anything but idle. De Born advises the barons to pawn their castles before making war, thus if they won they could redeem them, if they lost the loss fell on the holder of the mortgage.

The forms of this poetry are highly artificial, and as artifice they have still for the serious craftsman an interest, less indeed than they had for Dante, but by no means inconsiderable. No student of the period can doubt that the involved forms, and the veiled meanings in the 'trobar clus', grew out of living conditions, and that these songs played a very real part in love intrigue and in the intrigue preceding warfare. The time had no press and no theatre. If you wish to make love to women in public, and out loud, you must resort to subterfuge; and Guillaume St Leider even went so far as to get the husband of his lady to do the seductive singing.

If a man of our time be so crotchety as to wish emotional, as well as intellectual, acquaintance with an age so out of fashion as the twelfth century, he may try in several ways to attain it. He may read the songs themselves from the old books—from the illuminated vellum—and he will learn what the troubadours meant to the folk of the century just after their own. He will learn a little about their

¹ The *Quarterly Review*, 1913.

costume from the illuminated capitals. Or he may try listening to the words with the music, for, thanks to Jean Beck and others,[1] it is now possible to hear the old tunes. They are perhaps a little Oriental in feeling, and it is likely that the spirit of Sufism is not wholly absent from their content. Or, again, a man may walk the hill roads and river roads from Limoges and Charente to Dordogne and Narbonne and learn a little, or more than a little, of what the country meant to the wandering singers, he may learn, or think he learns, why so many canzos open with speech of the weather; or why such a man made war on such and such castles. Or he may learn the outlines of these events from the 'razos', or prose paragraphs of introduction, which are sometimes called 'lives of the troubadours'. And, if he have mind for these latter, he will find in the Bibliothèque Nationale at Paris the manuscript of Miquel de la Tour, written perhaps in the author's own handwriting; at least we read 'I Miquel de la Tour, scryven, do ye to wit'.

Miquel gives us to know that such and such ladies were courted with greater or less good fortune by such and such minstrels of various degree, for one man was a poor vavassour, and another was King Amfos of Aragon; and another, Vidal, was son of a furrier, and sang better than any man in the world; and Raimon de Miraval was a poor knight that had but part of a castle; and Uc Brunecs was a clerk and he had an understanding with a *borgesa* who had no mind to love him or to keep him, and who became mistress to the Count of Rodez. 'Voila l'estat divers d'entre eulx.'

The monk, Gaubertz de Poicebot, 'was a man of birth; he was of the bishopric of Limozin, son of the castellan of Poicebot. And he was made monk when he was a child in a monastery, which is called Sain Leonart. And he knew well letters, and well to sing and well *trobar*.[2] And for desire of woman he went forth from the monastery. And he came thence to the man to whom came all who for courtesy wished honour and good deeds—to Sir Savaric de Mauleon—and this man gave him the harness of a joglar and a horse and clothing; and then he went through the courts and composed and made good canzos. And he set his heart upon a donzella gentle and fair and made his songs of her, and she did not wish to love him unless he should

---

[1] Walter Morse Rummel's *Neuf Chansons de Troubadours*, pub. Augener, Ltd., etc; also the settings by Aubry.

[2] Poetical composition, literally 'to find'.

get himself made a knight and take her to wife. And he told En Savaric how the girl had refused him, wherefore En Savaric made him a knight and gave him land and the income from it. And he married the girl and held her in great honour. And it happened that he went into Spain, leaving her behind him. And a knight out of England set his mind upon her and did so much and said so much that he led her with him, and he kept her long time his mistress and then let her go to the dogs (malamen anar). And En Gaubertz returned from Spain, and lodged himself one night in the city where she was. And he went out for desire of woman, and he entered the *alberc* of a poor woman; for they told him there was a fine woman within. And he found his wife. And when he saw her, and she him, great was the grief between them and great shame. And he stopped the night with her, and on the morrow he went forth with her to a nunnery where he had her enter. And for this grief he ceased to sing and to compose.' If you are minded, as Browning was in his *One Word More*, you may search out the song that En Gaubertz made, riding down the second time from Malleon, flushed with the unexpected knighthood.

> Per amor del belh temps suau
> E quar fin amor men somo.[1]

'For love of the sweet time and soft' he beseeches this 'lady in whom joy and worth have shut themselves and all good in its completeness' to give him grace and the kisses due to him a year since. And he ends in envoi to Savaric.

> Senher savaric larc e bo
> Vos troba hom tota fazo
> Quel vostre ric fag son prezan
> El dig cortes e benestan.[2]

La Tour has given us seed of drama in the passage above rendered. He has left us also an epic in his straightforward prose. 'Piere de Maensac was of Alverne (Auvergne) a poor knight, and he had a brother named Austors de Maensac, and they both were troubadours

---

[1] For love of the fair time and soft,
    And because fine love calls me to it.

[2] Milord Savaric, generous
    To thy last bond, men find thee thus,
    That thy rich acts are food for praise
    And courtly are thy words and days.

and they both were in concord that one should take the castle and the other the *trobar*.' And presumably they tossed up a *marabotin* or some such obsolete coin, for we read, 'And the castle went to Austors and the poetry to Piere, and he sang of the wife of Bernart de Tierci. So much he sang of her and so much he honoured her that it befell that the lady let herself go gay (*furar a del*). And he took her to the castle of the Dalfin of Auvergne, and the husband, in the manner of the golden Menelaus, demanded her much, with the church to back him and with the great war that they made. But the Dalfin maintained him (Piere) so that he never gave her up. He (Piere) was a straight man (*dreitz om*) and good company, and he made charming songs, tunes and the words, and good coblas of pleasure.' And among them is one beginning

> Longa saison ai estat vas amor
> Humils e francs, y ai faich son coman.[1]

Dante and Browning have created so much interest in Sordello that it may not be amiss to give the brief account of him as it stands in a manuscript in the Ambrosian library at Milan. 'Lo Sordels *si fo di Mantovana*. Sordello was of Mantuan territory of Sirier (this would hardly seem to be Goito), son of a poor cavalier who had name Sier Escort (Browning's El Corte), and he delighted himself in chançons, to learn and to make them. And he mingled with the good men of the court. And he learned all that he could and he made coblas and sirventes. And he came thence to the court of the Count of St Bonifaci, and the Count honoured him much. And he fell in love with the wife of the Count, in the form of pleasure (*a forma de solatz*), and she with him. (The Palma of Browning's poem and the Cunizza of Dante's.) And it befell that the Count stood ill with her brothers. And thus he estranged himself from her and from Sier Sceillme and Sier Albrics. Thus her brothers caused her to be stolen from the Count by Sier Sordello and the latter came to stop with them. And he (Sordello) stayed a long time with them in great happiness, and then he went into Proenssa where he received great honours from all the good men and from the Count and from the Countess who gave him a good castle and a wife of gentle birth.' (Browning with perfect right alters this ending to suit his own purpose.)

The luck of the troubadours was as different as their ranks, and

---

[1] For a long time have I stood toward Love
Humble and frank, and have done his commands.

they were drawn from all social orders. We are led far from polite and polished society when we come to take note of that Gringoire, Guillem Figiera, 'son of a tailor; and he was a tailor; and when the French got hold of Toulouse he departed into Lombardy. And he knew well *trobar* and to sing, and he made himself *joglar* among the townsfolk (*ciutadins*). He was not a man who knew how to carry himself among the barons or among the better class, but much he got himself welcomed among harlots and slatterns and by inn-keepers and taverners. And if he saw coming a good man of the court, there where he was, he was sorry and grieved at it, and he nearly split himself to take him down a peg (*et ades percussava de lui abaissar*).'

For one razo that shows an unusual character there are a dozen that say simply that such or such a man was of Manes, or of Cata-loigna by Rossilon, or of elsewhere, 'a poor cavalier.'[1] They made their way by favour at times, or by singing, or by some form of utility. Ademar of Gauvedan 'was of the castle Marvois, son of a poor knight. He was knighted by the lord of Marvois. He was a brave man but could not keep his estate as knight, and he became jongleur and was respected by all the best people. And later he went into orders at Gran Mon'. Elias Cairels 'was of Sarlat; ill he sang, ill he composed, ill he played the fiddle and worse he spoke, but he was good at writing out words and tunes. And he was a long time wander-ing, and when he quitted it, he returned to Sarlat and died there'. Perdigo was the son of a fisherman and made his fortune by his art. Peirol was a poor knight who was fitted out by the Dalfin of Auvergne and made love to Sail de Claustra; and all we know of Cercamon is that he made *vers* and *pastorelas* in the old way and that 'he went everywhere he could get to'. Pistoleta 'was a singer for Arnaut of Marvoil, and later he took to *trobar* and made songs with pleasing tunes and he was well received by the best people, although a man of little comfort and of poor endowment and of little stamina. And he took a wife at Marseilles and became a merchant and became rich and ceased going about the courts'. Guillems the skinny was a joglar of Manes, and the capital letter shows him throwing 3, 5, and 4, on a red dice board. 'Never had he on harness, and what he gained he lost *malamen*, to the taverns and the women. And he ended in a hospital in Spain.

---

[1] For example Piere Bermon and Palazol.

The razos have in them the seeds of literary criticism. The speech is, however, laconic. Aimar lo Ners was a gentleman. 'He made such songs as he knew how to.' Aimeric de Sarlat, a joglar, became a troubadour, 'and yet he made but one song.' Piere Guillem of Toulouse 'Made good coblas, but he made too many'. Daude of Pradas made canzos 'per sen de trobar', which I think we may translate 'from a mental grasp of the craft'. 'But they did not move from love, wherefore they had not favour among folk. They were not sung.' We find also that the labour and skill were divided. One man played the viol most excellently, and another sang, and another spoke his songs to music,[1] and another, Jaufre Rudel, Brebezieu's father-in-law, made 'good tunes with poor words to go with them'.

The troubadour's person comes in for as much free criticism as his performance. Elias fons Slada was a 'fair man verily, as to feature, a joglar, no good troubadour'.[2] But Faidit, a joglar of Uzerche, 'was exceedingly greedy both to drink and to eat, and he became fat beyond measure. And he took to wife a public woman; very fair and well taught she was, but she became as big and fat as he was. And she was from a rich town Alest of the Mark of Provenca from the seignory of En Bernart d'Andussa.'

One of the noblest figures of the time, if we are to believe the chronicle, was Savaric de Mauleon, the rich baron of Peiteu, mentioned above, son of Sir Reios de Malleon; 'lord was he of Malleon and of Talarnom and of Fontenai, and of castle Aillon and of Boetand of Benaon and of St Miquel en Letz and of the isles of Ners and of the isle of Mues and of Nestrine and of Engollius and of many other good places.' As one may read in the continuation of this notice and verify from the razos of the other troubadours, 'he was of the most open-handed men in the world.' He seems to have left little verse save the tenzon with Faidit.

'Behold divers estate between them all!' Yet, despite the difference in conditions of life between the twelfth century and our own, these few citations should be enough to prove that the people were much the same, and if the preceding notes do not do this, there is one tale left that should succeed.

'The Vicomte of St Antoni was of the bishopric of Caortz

[1] Richard of Brebezieu (disia sons).

[2] The 'joglar' was the player and singer, the 'troubadour' the 'finder' or composer of songs and words.

(Cahors), Lord and Vicomte of St Antoni; and he loved a noble lady who was wife of the seignor of Pena Dalbeges, of a rich castle and a strong. The lady was gentle and fair and valiant and highly prized and much honoured; and he very valiant and well trained and good at arms and charming, and a good trobaire, and had name Raimons Jordans; and the lady was called the Vicomtesse de Pena; and the love of these two was beyond all measure. And it befell that the Vicount went into a land of his enemies and was grievous wounded, so that report held him for dead. And at the news she in great grief went and gave candles at church for his recovery. And he recovered. And at this news also she had great grief.' And she fell a-moping, and that was the end of the affair with St Antoni, and 'thus was there more than one in deep distress'. 'Wherefore' Elis of Montfort, wife of William à-Gordon, daughter of the Viscount of Trozena, the glass of fashion and the mould of form, the pride of 'youth, beauty, courtesy', and presumably of justice, mercy, long-suffering, and so forth, made him overtures, and successfully. And the rest is a matter much as usual.

If humanity was much the same, it is equally certain that individuals were not any more like one another; and this may be better shown in the uncommunicative *canzoni* than in the razos. Thus we have a pastoral from the sensitive and little known Joios of Tolosa:

> Lautrier el dous temps de pascor
> En una ribeira,

which runs thus:

'The other day, in the sweet time of Easter, I went across a flat land of rivers hunting for new flowers, walking by the side of the path, and for delight in the greenness of things and because of the complete good faith and love which I bear for her who inspires me, I felt a melting about my heart and at the first flower I found, I burst into tears.

'And I wept until, in a shady place, my eyes fell upon a shepherdess. Fresh was her colour, and she was white as a snow-drift, and she had doves' eyes,' . . .

In very different key we find the sardonic Count of Foix, in a song which begins mildly enough for a spring song:

> Mas qui a flor si vol mesclar,

and turns swiftly enough to a livelier measure:

> Ben deu gardar lo sieu baston
> Car frances sabon grans colps dar
> Et albirar ab lor bordon
> E nous fizes in carcasses
> Ni en genes ni en gascon.

> Let no man lounge amid the flowers
> Without a stout club of some kind.
> Know ye the French are stiff in stour
> And sing not all they have in mind,
> So trust ye not in Carcason,
> In Genovese, nor in Gascon.

My purpose in all this is to suggest to the casual reader that the Middle Ages did not exist in the tapestry alone, nor in the fourteenth-century romances, but that there was a life like our own, no mere sequence of citherns and citoles, nor a continuous stalking about in sendal and diaspre. Men were pressed for money. There was unspeakable boredom in the castles. The chivalric singing was devised to lighten the boredom; and this very singing became itself in due time, in the manner of all things, an ennui.

There has been so much written about the poetry of the best Provençal period, to wit the end of the twelfth century, that I shall say nothing of it here, but shall confine the latter part of this essay to a mention of three efforts, or three sorts of effort which were made to keep poetry alive after the crusade of 1208.

Any study of European poetry is unsound if it does not commence with a study of that art in Provence. The art of quantitative verse had been lost. This loss was due more to ignorance than to actual changes of language, from Latin, that is, into the younger tongues. It is open to doubt whether the Aeolic singing was ever comprehended fully even in Rome. When men began to write on tablets and ceased singing to the *barbitos,* a loss of some sort was unavoidable. Propertius may be cited as an exception, but Propertius writes only one meter. In any case the classic culture of the Renaissance was grafted on to medieval culture, a process which is excellently illustrated by Andreas Divus Iustinopolitanus's translation of the *Odyssey* into Latin. It is true that each century after the Renaissance has tried in its own way to come nearer the classic, but, if we are to understand that part of our civilization which is the art of verse, we must begin at the root, and that root is medieval. The poetic art of Provence paved the way for the poetic art of Tuscany; and to this Dante bears sufficient witness in the *De Vulgari Eloquio*. The heritage of art is one thing to the public and quite another to the succeeding artists. The artist's inheritance from other artists can be little more than certain enthusiasms, which usually spoil his first work; and a definite knowledge of the modes of expression, which knowledge contributes to perfecting his more mature performance. This is a matter of technique.

After the compositions of Vidal, Rudel, Ventadour, of Bornelh and Bertrans de Born and Arnaut Daniel, there seemed little chance of doing distinctive work in the 'canzon de l'amour courtois'. There was no way, or at least there was no man in Provence capable of finding a new way of saying in six closely rhymed strophes that a certain girl, matron or widow was like a certain set of things, and that the troubadour's virtues were like another set, and that all this was very sorrowful or otherwise, and that there was but one obvious remedy. Richard of Brebezieu had done his best for tired ears; he had made similes of beasts and of stars which got him a passing favour. He had compared himself to the fallen elephant and to the self-piercing pelican, and no one could go any further. Novelty is reasonably rare even in modes of decadence and revival. The three devices tried for poetic restoration in the early thirteenth century were the three usual devices. Certain men turned to talking art and aesthetics and attempted to dress up the folk-song. Certain men tried to make verse more engaging by stuffing it with an intellectual and argumentative content. Certain men turned to social satire. Roughly, we may divide the interesting work of the later provençal period into these three divisions. As all of these men had progeny in Tuscany, they are, from the historical point of view, worth a few moments' attention.

The first school is best represented in the work of Giraut Riquier of Narbonne. His most notable feat was the revival of the *Pastorela*. The Pastorela is a poem in which a knight tells of having met with a shepherdess or some woman of that class, and of what fortune and conversation befell him. The form had been used long before by Marcabrun, and is familiar to us in such poems as Guido Cavalcanti's

In un boschetto trovai pastorella, or in Swinburne's *An Interlude*. Guido, who did all things well, whenever the fancy took him, has raised this form to a surpassing excellence in his poem *Era in pensier d'Amor, quand' io trovai*. Riquier is most amusing in his account of the inn-mistress at Sant Pos de Tomeiras, but even there he is less amusing than was Marcabrun when he sang of the shepherdess in *L'autrier iost' una sebissa*. Riquier has, however, his place in the apostolic succession; and there is no reason why Cavalcanti and Riquier should not have met while the former was on his journey to Campostella, although Riquier may as easily have not been in Spain at the time. At any rate the Florentine noble would have heard the *Pastorelas* of Giraut; and this may have set him to his *ballate*, which seem to date from the time of his meeting with Mandetta in Toulouse. Or it may have done nothing of the kind. The only more or less settled fact is that Riquier was then the best known living troubadour and near the end of his course.

The second, and to us the dullest of the schools, set to explaining the nature of love and its effects. The normal modern will probably slake all his curiosity for this sort of work in reading one such poem as the King of Navarre's *De Fine amour vient science e beautez*. 'Ingenium nobis ipsa puella fecit', as Propertius put it, or *anglice*:

> Knowledge and beauty from true love are wrought,
> And likewise love is born from this same pair;
> These three are one to whomso hath true thought, etc.

There might be less strain if one sang it. This peculiar variety of flame was carried to the altars of Bologna, whence Guinicello sang:

> Al cor gentil ripara sempre amore,
> Come l'augello in selva alla verdura

And Cavalcanti wrote: 'A lady asks me, wherefore I wish to speak of an accident[1] which is often cruel', and Dante, following in his elders' footsteps, the *Convito*.

The third school is the school of satire, and is the only one which gives us a contact with the normal life of the time. There had been Provençal satire before Piere Cardinal; but the sirventes of Sordello and De Born were directed for the most part against persons, while the Canon of Clermont drives rather against conditions. In so far as

---

[1] *Accidente*, used as a purely technical term of his scholastic philosophy.

Dante is critic of morals, Cardinal must be held as his forerunner. Miquel writes of him as follows:

'Piere Cardinal was of Veillac of the city Pui Ma Donna, and he was of honourable lineage, son of a knight and a lady. And when he was little his father put him for canon in the *canonica major* of Puy; and he learnt letters, and he knew well how to read and to sing; and when he was come to man's estate he had high knowledge of the vanity of this world, for he felt himself gay and fair and young. And he made many fair arguments and fair songs. And he made canzos, but he made only a few of these, and sirventes; and he did best in the said sirventes where he set forth many fine arguments and fair examples for those who understand them; for much he rebuked the folly of this world and much he reproved the false clerks, as his sirventes show. And he went through the courts of kings and of noble barons and took with him his joglar who sang the sirventes. And much was he honoured and welcomed by my lord the good king of Aragon and by honourable barons. And I, master Miquel de la Tour, escriuan (scribe), do ye to wit that N. Piere Cardinal when he passed from this life was nearly a hundred. And I, the aforesaid Miquel, have written these sirventes in the city of Nemze (Nîmes) and here are written some of his sirventes.'

If the Vicomtesse de Pena reminds us of certain ladies whom we have met, these sirventes of Cardinal may well remind us that thoughtful men have in every age found almost the same set of things or at least the same sort of things to protest against; if it be not a corrupt press or some monopoly, it is always some sort of equivalent, some conspiracy of ignorance and interest. And thus he says, 'Li clerc si fan pastor.' The clerks pretend to be shepherds, but they are wolfish at heart.

If he can find a straight man, it is truly matter for song; and so we hear him say of the Duke of Narbonne, who was apparently, making a fight for honest administration:

> Coms raymon duc de Narbona
> Marques de proensa
> Vostra valors es tan bona
> Que tot lo mon gensa,
> Quar de la mar de bayona
> En tro a valenca

Agra gent falsae fellona
Lai ab vil temensa,
Mas vos tenetz vil lor
Q'n frances bevedor
Plus qua perditz austor
No vos fan temensa.

'Now is come from France what one did not ask for'—he is addressing the man who is standing against the North—

Count Raymon, Duke of Narbonne,
Marquis of Provence,
Your valour is sound enough
To make up for the cowardice of
All the rest of the gentry.
For from the sea at Bayonne,
Even to Valence,
Folk would have given in (sold out),
But you hold them in scorn,
[Or, reading 'l'aur', 'scorn the gold'.]
So that the drunken French
Alarm you no more
Than a partridge frightens a hawk.

Cardinal is not content to spend himself in mere abuse, like the little tailor Figeira, who rhymes Christ's 'mortal pena' with

Car voletz totzjors portar la borsa plena,

which is one way of saying 'Judas!' to the priests. He, Cardinal, sees that the technique of honesty is not always utterly simple.

Li postilh, legat elh cardinal
La cordon tug, y an fag establir
Que qui nos pot de traisson esdir,

which may mean, 'The pope and the legate and the cardinal have twisted such a cord that they have brought things to such a pass that no one can escape committing treachery.' As for the rich:

Li ric home an pietat tan gran
Del autre gen quon ac caym da bel.
Que mais volon tolre q̄ lop no fan
E mais mentir que tozas de bordelh.

> The rich men have such pity
> For other folk—about as much as Cain had for Abel.
> For they would like to leave less than the wolves do,
> And to lie more than girls in a brothel.

Of the clergy, 'A tantas vey baylia', 'So much the more do I see clerks coming into power that all the world will be theirs, whoever objects. For they'll have it with taking or with giving' (i.e. by granting land, belonging to one man, to someone else who will pay allegiance for it, as in the case of De Montfort), 'or with pardon or with hypocrisy; or by assault or by drinking and eating; or by prayers or by praising the worse; or with God or with devilry.' We find him putting the age-long query about profit in the following:

> He may have enough harness
> And sorrel horses and bays;
> Tower, wall, and palace,
> May he have
> —the rich man denying his God.

The stanza runs very smoothly to the end

> Si mortz no fos
> Elh valgra per un cen

> A hundred men he would be worth
> Were there no death.

The modern Provençal enthusiast in raptures at the idea of chivalric love (a term which he usually misunderstands), and little concerned with the art of verse, has often failed to notice how finely the sound of Cardinal's poems is matched with their meaning. There is a lash and sting in his timbre and in his movement. Yet the old man is not always bitter; or, if he is bitter, it is with the bitterness of a torn heart and not a hard one. It is so we find him in the sirvente beginning:

> As a man weeps for his son or for his father,
> Or for his friend when death has taken him,
> So do I mourn for the living who do their own ill,
> False, disloyal, felon, and full of ill-fare,
> Deceitful, breakers-of-pact,
> Cowards, complainers,

Highwaymen, thieves-by-stealth, turn-coats,
Betrayers, and full of treachery,
Here where the devil reigns
And teaches them to act thus.

He is almost the only singer of his time to protest against the follies of war. As here:

Ready for war, as night is to follow the sun,
Readier for it than is the fool to be cuckold
When he has first plagued his wife!
And war is an ill thing to look upon,
And I know that there is not one man drawn into it
But his child, or his cousin or someone akin to him
Prays God that it be given over.

He says plainly, in another place, that the barons make war for their own profit, regardless of the peasants. 'Fai mal senher vas los sieu.' His sobriety is not to be fooled with sentiment either martial or otherwise. There is in him little of the fashion of feminolatry, and the gentle reader in search of trunk-hose and the light guitar had better go elsewhere. As for women: 'L'una fai drut.'

One turns leman for the sake of great possessions;
And another because poverty is killing her,
And one hasn't even a shift of coarse linen;
And another has two and does likewise.
And one gets an old man—and she is a young wench,
And the old woman gives the man an elixir.

As for justice, there is little now: 'If a rich man steal by chicanery, he will have right before Constantine (i.e. by legal circumambience) but the poor thief may go hang.' And after this there is a passage of pity and of irony fine-drawn as much of his work is, for he keeps the very formula that De Born had used in his praise of battle, 'Belh mes quan vey'; and, perhaps, in Sir Bertrans' time even the Provençal wars may have seemed more like a game, and may have appeared to have some element of sport and chance in them. But the twelfth century had gone, and the spirit of the people was weary, and the old canon's passage may well serve as a final epitaph on all that remained of silk thread and *cisclatons*, of viol and *gai saber*.

Never agin shall we see the Easter come in so fairly,
That was wont to come in with pleasure and with song,
No! but we see it arrayed with alarms and excursions,
Arrayed with war and dismay and fear,
Arrayed with troops and with cavalcades,
Oh, yes, it's a fine sight to see holder and shepherd
Going so wretched that they know not where they are

ARNAUT DANIEL[1]

RAZO

En Ar. Daniel was of Ribeyrac in Périgord, under Lemosi, near to Hautefort, and he was the best fashioner of songs in the Provençal, as Dante has said of him in his *Purgatorio* (XXVI, 142) and Tasso says it was he who wrote *Lancillotto*, but this is not known for certain, but Dante says only 'proze di romanzi'. Nor is it known if Benvenuto da Imola speaks for certain when he says En Arnaut went in his age to a monastery and sent a poem to the princes, nor if he wrote a satire on Boniface Castillane; but here are some of his canzos, the best that are left us; and he was very cunning in his imitation of birds, as in the poem *Autet*, where he stops in the middle of his singing, crying: 'Cadahus, en son us', as a bird cries, and rhyming on it cleverly, with no room to turn about on the words, 'Mas pel us, estauc clus', and in the other versets. And in *L'aura amara*, he cries as the birds in the autumn, and there is some of this also in his best poem, *Doutz brais e critz*.

And in *Breu brisaral*, he imitates, maybe, the rough singing of the joglar engles, from whom he learnt *Ac et no l'ac;* and though some read this *escomes*, not *engles*, it is likely enough that in the court of En Richart there might have been an English joglar, for En Bertrans calls Richart's brother 'joven re Engles', so why should there not be a joglar of the same, knowing alliterations? And he may, in the ending 'piula', have had in mind some sort of Arabic singing: for he knew well letters, in Langue d'Oc and in Latin, and he knew Ovid, of whom he takes Atalanta; and may be Virgil; and he talks of the Palux Laerna, though most copiers have writ this 'Uzerna', not knowing the place he spoke of. So it is as like as not he knew Arabic music, and perhaps had heard, if he understood not the meaning, some song in rough Saxon letters.

And by making song in *rimas escarsas* he let into Provençal poetry many words that are not found elsewhere and maybe some words half Latin, and he uses many more sounds on the rhyme, for, as Canello or Lavaud has written, he uses ninety-eight rhyme sounds in

[1] This essay appeared for the first time in *Instigations* (1920).

seventeen canzos, and Peire Vidal makes use of but fifty-eight in fifty-four canzos and Folquet of thirty-three in twenty-two poems, and Raimbaut Orenga uses 129 rhymes in thirty-four poems, a lower proportion than Arnaut's. And the songs of En Arnaut are in some versets wholly free and uneven the whole length of the verset, then the other five versets follow in the track of the first, for the same tune must be sung in them all, or sung with very slight or orderly changes. But after the earlier poems he does not rhyme often inside the stanza. And in all he is very cunning, and has many uneven and beautiful rhythms, so that if a man try to read him like English iambic he will very often go wrong; though En Arnaut made the first piece of 'blank verse' in the seven opening lines of the *Sols sui;* and he, maybe, in thinning out the rhymes and having but six repetitions to a canzone, made way for Dante who sang his long poem in threes. But this much is certain, he does not use the rhyme—*atage* and many other common rhymes of the provençal, whereby so many canzos are all made alike and monotonous on the sound or two sounds to the end from the beginning.

Nor is there much gap from *Lancan vei fueill'* or *D'autra guiza* to the form of the sonnet, or to the receipt for the Italian strophes of canzoni, for we have both the repetition and the unrepeating sound in the verset. And in two versets the rhymes run *abab cde abab cde;* in one, and in the other *abba cde abba cde;* while in sonnets the rhymes run *abab abab cde cde;* or *abba abba cde cde.* And this is no very great difference. A sonetto would be the third of a *son.*

And I do not give *Ac et no l'ac,* for it is plainly told us that he learned this song from a jongleur, and he says as much in his coda:

> Miells-de-ben ren
> Sit pren
> Chanssos grazida
> C'Arnautz non oblida.

'Give thanks my song, to Miells-de-ben that Arnaut has not forgotten thee.' And the matter went as a joke, and the song was given to Arnaut to sing in his repertoire 'E fo donatz lo cantar an Ar Daniel, qui et aysi trobaretz en sa obra'. And I do not give the tenzon with Trucs Malecs for reasons clear to all who have read it; nor do I translate the sestina, for it is a poor one, but maybe it is interesting to think if the music will not go through its permutation as the end words change their places in order, though the first line has only eight syllables.

And En Arnaut was the best artist among the Provençals, trying the speech in new fashions, and bringing new words into writing, and making new blendings of words, so that he taught much to Messire Dante Alighieri as you will see if you study En Arnaut and the *De Vulgari Eloquio;* and when Dante was older and had well thought the thing over he said simply, 'il miglior fabbro.' And long before Francesco Petrarca, he, Arnaut, had thought of the catch about '*Laura,* laura, l'aura', and the rest of it, which is no great thing to his credit. But no man in Provençal has written as he writes in *Doutz brais*: 'E quel remir' and the rest of it, though Ovid, where he recounts Atalanta's flight from Hippomenes in the tenth book, had written:

> cum super atria velum
> Candida purpureum simulatas inficit umbras.

And in Dante we have much in the style of:

> Que jes Rozers per aiga que l'engrois.

And Dante learned much from his rhyming, and follows him in *agro* and *Meleagro,* but more in a comprehension, and Dante has learned also of Ovid: 'in Metamorphoseos':

> Velut ales, ab alto
> Quae teneram prolem produxit in aera nido,

although he talks so much of Virgil.

I had thought once of the mantle of indigo as of a thing seen in a vision, but I have now only fancy to support this. It is like that men slandered Arnaut for Dante's putting him in his *Purgatorio,* but the Trucs Malecs poem is against this.

En Arnaut often ends a canzone with a verset in different tone from the rest, as markedly in *Si fos Amors.* In *Breu brisaral* the music is very curious, but is lost for us, for there are only two pieces of his music, and those in Milan, at the Ambrosiana (in R 71 superiore).

And at the end of *Doutz brais,* is a verset like the verset of a sirvente, and this is what he wrote as a message, not making a whole sirvente, nor, so far as we know, dabbling in politics or writing of it, as Bertrans de Born has; only in this one place in all that is left us. And he was a joglar, perhaps for his living, and only composed when he would, and could not to order, as is shown in the story of his remembering the joglar's canzone when he had laid a wager to make one of his own.

Can chai la fueilla is more like a sea song or an *estampida*, though the editors call it a canzone, and *Amors e jois*, and some others were so little thought of, that only two writers have copied them out in the manuscripts; and the songs are all different one from another, and their value nothing like even. Dante took note of the best ones, omitting *Doutz brais*, which is for us perhaps the finest of all, though having some lines out of strict pertinence. But *Can chai la fueilla* is very cleverly made with five, six and four and seven. And in *Sols sui* and in other canzos the verse is syllabic, and made on the number of syllables, not by stresses, and the making by syllables cannot be understood by those of Petramala, who imagine the language they speak was that spoken by Adam, and that one system of metric was made in the world's beginning, and has since existed without change. And some think if the stress fall not on every second beat, or the third, that they must have right before Constantine. And the art of En Ar. Daniel is not literature but the art of fitting words well with music, wellnigh a lost art, and if one will look to the music of *Chansson doil motz*, or to the movement of *Can chai la fueilla*, one will see part of that which I mean, and if one will look to the falling of the rhymes in other poems, and the blending and lengthening of the sounds, and their sequence, one will learn more of this. And En Arnaut wrote between 1180 and 1200 of the era, as nearly as we can make out, when the Provençal was growing weary, and it was to be seen if it could last, and he tried to make almost a new language, or at least to enlarge the Langue d'Oc, and make new things possible. And this scarcely happened till Guinicello, and Guido Cavalcanti and Dante; Piere Cardinal went to realism and made satirical poems. But the art of singing to music went wellnigh out of the words, for Metastasio has left a few catches, and so has Lorenzo di Medici, but in Bel Canto in the times of Durante, and Piccini, Paradeis, Vivaldi, Caldara and Benedetto Marcello, the music turns the words out of doors and strews them and distorts them to the tune, out of all recognition; and the philosophic canzoni of Dante and his timesmen are not understandable if they are sung, and in their time music and poetry parted company; the canzone's tune becoming a sonata without singing. And the ballad is a shorter form, and the Elizabethan

lyrics are but scraps and bits of canzoni much as in the 'nineties'
men wrote scraps of Swinburne.

Charles d'Orléans made good roundels and songs, as in *Dieu qui la
fait* and in *Quand j'oie la tambourine,* as did also Jean Froissart before
him in:

> Reviens, ami; trop longue est ta demeure:
> Elle me fait avoir peine et doulour.
> Mon esperit te demande à toute heure.
> Reviens, ami; trop longue est ta demeure.
>
> Car il n'est nul, fors toi, qui me sequerre,
> Ne secourra, jusques à ton retour.
> Reviens, ami; trop longue est ta demeure:
> Elle me fait avoir peine et doulour.

And in:

> Le corps s'en va, mais le cœur vous demeure.

And in:

> On doit le temps ainsi prendre qu'il vient:
> Tout dit que pas ne dure la fortune.
> Un temps se part, et puis l'autre revient:
> On doit le temps ainsi prendre qu'il vient.
>
> Je me comforte en ce qu'il me souvient
> Que tous les mois avons nouvelle lune:
> On doit le temps ainsi prendre qu'il vient:
> Tout dit que pas ne dure la fortune.

Which is much what Bernart de Ventadour has sung:

> Per dieu, dona, pauc esplecham d'amor
> Va sen lo temps e perdem lo melhor.

And Campion was the last, but in none of the later men is there the
care and thought of En Arnaut Daniel for the blending of words sung
out; and none of them all succeeded, as indeed he had not succeeded
in reviving and making permanent a poetry that could be sung. But
none of them all had thought so of the sound of the words with the
music, all in sequence and set together as had En Arnaut of Ribeyrac,
nor had, I think, even Dante Alighieri when he wrote *De Eloquio.*

And we find in Provence beautiful poems, as by Vidal when he
sings:

> Ab l'alen tir vas me l'aire.

And by the Viscount of St Antoni:

> Lo clar temps vei brunezir
> E'ls auzeletz esperdutz,
> Que'l fregz ten destregz e mutz
> E ses conort de jauzir.
> Donc eu que de cor sospir
> Per la gensor re qu'anc fos,
>   Tan joios
>   Son, qu'ades m'es vis
> Que folh'e flor s'espandis.
> D'amor son tug miei cossir. . . .

and by Bertrans de Born in *Dompna puois di me,* but these people sang not so many diverse kinds of music as En Arnaut, nor made so many good poems in different fashions, nor thought them so carefully, though En Bertrans sings with more vigour, it may be, and in the others, in Cercamon, Arnaut of Marvoil, in De Ventadour, there are beautiful passages. And if the art, now in France, of saying a song— *disia sons,* we find written of more than one troubadour—is like the art of En Arnaut, it has no such care for the words, nor such ear for hearing their consonance.

Nor among the Provençals was there any one, nor had Dante thought out an aesthetic of sound; of clear sounds and opaque sounds, such as in *Sols sui,* an opaque sound like Swinburne at his best; and in *Doutz brais* and in *L'aura amara* a clear sound, with staccato; and of heavy beats and of running and light beats, as very heavy in *Can chai la fueilla.* Nor do we enough notice how with his drollery he is in places nearer to Chaucer than to the Italians, and indeed the Provençal is usually nearer the English in sound and in feeling, than it is to the Italian, having a softer humour, not a bitter tongue, as have the Italians in ridicule.

Nor have any yet among students taken note enough of the terms, both of love terms, and of terms of the singing; though theology was precise in its terms, and we should see clearly enough in Dante's treatise when he uses such words as *pexa, hirsuta, lubrica,* combed, and shaggy and oily to put his words into categories, that he is thinking exactly. Would the Age of Aquinas have been content with anything less? And so with the love terms, and so, as I have said in my Guido, with metaphors and the exposition of passion. Cossir, solatz, plazers, have in them the beginning of the Italian philosophic precisions, and *amors qu'in҃ el cor me plou* is not a vague decoration. By the time of Petrarca the analysis had come to an end, only the vague decorations were left. And if Arnaut is long before Cavalcanti,

> Pensar de lieis m'es repaus
> E traigom ams los huoills crancs,
> S'a lieis vezer nols estuich,

leads toward *E gli occhi orbati fa vedere scorto,* though the music in Arnaut is not, in this place, quickly apprehended. And those who fear to take a bold line in their interpretation of *Cill de Doma,* might do worse than re-read:

> Una figura de la donna mia

and what follows it. And for the rest any man who would read Arnaut and the troubadours owes great thanks to Emil Levy of Freiburg i/B for his long work and his little dictionary (*Petit Dictionnaire Provençal-Français,* Karl Winter's Universitätsbuchhandlung, Heidelberg) and to U. A. Canello, the first editor of Arnaut, who has shown, I think, great profundity in his arrangement of the poems in their order, and has really hit upon their sequence of composition, and the developments of En Arnaut's trobar; and lastly to René Lavaud for his new Tolosan edition.

II

The twenty-three students of Provençal and the seven people seriously interested in the technic and aesthetic of verse may communicate with me in person. I give here only enough to illustrate the points of the razo, that is to say, as much as, and probably more than, the general reader can be bothered with. The translations are a makeshift; it is not to be expected that I can do in ten years what it took two hundred troubadours a century and a half to accomplish; for the full understanding of Arnaut's system of echoes and blending there is no substitute for the original; but in extenuation of the language of my verses, I would point out that the Provençals were not constrained by the modern literary sense. Their restraints were the tune and rhyme-scheme, they were not constrained by a need for certain qualities of writing, without which no modern poem is complete or satisfactory. They were not competing with De Maupassant's prose.

Their triumph is, as I have said, in an art between literature and music; if I have succeeded in indicating some of the properties of the latter I have also let the former go by the board. It is quite possible that if the troubadours had been bothered about 'style', they would not have brought their blend of word and tune to so elaborate a completion.

Can chai la fueilla is interesting for its rhythm, for the sea-chantey swing produced by the simple device of caesurae. The poem does not keep the same rhyme throughout, and the only reason for giving the whole of it in my English dither is that one can *not* get the effect of the thumping and iterate foot-beat from one or two strophes alone.

CAN CHAI LA FUEILLA

When sere leaf falleth
     from the high forkèd tips,
And cold appalleth
     dry osier, haws and hips,
Coppice he strips
     of bird, that now none calleth.
Fordel[1] my lips
     in love have, though he galleth.
Though all things freeze here,
     I can naught feel the cold,
For new love sees, here
     my heart's new leaf unfold;
So am I rolled
     and lapped against the breeze here:
Love who doth mould
     my force, force guarantees here.

Aye, life's a high thing,
     where joy's his maintenance,
Who cries 'tis wry thing
     hath danced never my dance,
I can advance
     no blame against fate's tithing
For lot and chance
     have deemed the best thing my thing.

[1] Pre-eminence.

Of love's wayfaring
        I know no part to blame,
All other pairing,
        compaired, is put to shame,
Man can acclaim
        no second for comparing
With her, no dame
        but hath the meaner bearing.

I'ld ne'er entangle
        my heart with other fere,
Although I mangle
        my joy by staying here
I have no fear
        that ever at Pontrangle
You'll find her peer
        or one that's worth a wrangle.

She'd ne'er destroy
        her man with cruelty
'Twixt here 'n' Savoy
        there feeds no fairer she,
Than pleaseth me
        till Paris had ne'er joy
In such degree
        from Helena in Troy.

She's so the rarest
        who holdeth me thus gay,
The thirty fairest
        can not contest her sway;
'Tis right, par fay,
        thou know, O song that wearest
Such bright array,
        whose quality thou sharest.

Chançon, nor stay
        till to her thou declarest:
'Arnaut would say
        me not, wert thou not fairest.'

CAN CHAI LA FUEILLA

Can chai la fueilla
 dels ausors entrecims,
El freitz s'ergueilla
 don sechal vais' el vims,
Dels dous refrims
 vei sordezir la brueilla;
Mas ieu soi prims
 d'amor, qui que s'en tueilla.

Tot quant es gela
 mas ieu non puesc frezir,
C'amors novela
 mi fal cor reverdir;
Non dei fremir
 c'Amors mi cuebr' em cela
Em fai tenir
 ma valor em cabdela.

Bona es vida
 pos joia la mante,
Que tals n'escrida
 cui ges no vai tan be;
No sai de re
 coreillar m'escarida,
Que per ma fe
 del miells ai ma partida.

De drudaria
 nom sai de re blasmar,
C'autrui paria
 torn ieu en reirazar;[1]
Ges ab sa par
 no sai doblar m'amia,
C'una non par
 que segonda noill sia

---

[1] Call for second throw of the dice

No vueill s'asemble
      mos cors ab autr' amor
Si qu'eu jail m'emble
      ni volva cap aillor;
Non ai paor
      que ja cel de Pontremble
N'aia gensor
      de lieis ni que la semble.

Ges non es croia
      cella cui soi amis;
De sai Savoia
      plus bella nos noiris;
Tals m'abelis
      don ieu plus ai de joia
Non ac Paris
      d'Elena, cel de Troia.

Tan pareis genta
      cella quem te joios
Las gensors trenta
      vens de belas faisos;
Ben es razos
      doncas que nos chans senta,
Quar es tan pros
      e de ric pretz manenta.

Vai t'en chansos
      denan lieis ti prezenta;
Que s'ill no fos
      noi meir[1] Arnautz s'ententa.

Lancan son passat shows the simple and presumably early style of
Arnaut, with the kind of reversal from more or less trochaic to more
or less iambic movement in fifth and eighth lines, a *kind* of rhythm
taken over by Elizabethan lyricists. Terms trochaic and iambic are,
however, utterly inaccurate when applied to syllabic metres set to a
particular melody.

[1] Lavaud: *metr'*.

LANCAN SON PASSAT LI GIURE

When the frosts are gone and over,
And are stripped from hill and hollow,
When in close the blossom blinketh
From the spray where the fruit cometh,
    The flower and song and the clarion
Of the gay season and merry
Bid me with high joy to bear me
    Through days while April's coming on.

Though joy's right hard to discover,
Such sly ways doth false Love follow,
Only sure he never drinketh
At the fount where true faith cometh;
    A thousand girls, but two or one
Of her falsehoods over chary,
Stabbing whom vows make unwary
    Their tenderness is vilely done.

The most wise runs drunkest lover,
Sans pint-pot or wine to swallow,
If a whim her locks unlinketh,
One stray hair his noose becometh.
    When evasion's fairest shown,
Then the sly puss purrs most near ye.
Innocents at heart beware ye,
    When she seems colder than a nun.

See, I thought so highly of her!
Trusted, but the game is hollow,
Not one won piece soundly clinketh,
All the cardinals that Rome hath,
    Yea, they all were put upon.
Her device is 'Slyly Wary'.
Cunning are the snares they carry,
    Yet while they watched they'd be undone.

Whom Love makes so mad a rover,
'Ll take a cuckoo for a swallow,

If she say so, sooth! he thinketh
There's a plain where Puy-de-Dôme is,
     Till his eyes and nails are gone,
He'll throw dice and follow fairly
—Sure as old tales never vary—
     For his fond heart he is foredone.

Well I know, sans writing's cover,
What a plain is, what's a hollow.
I know well whose honour sinketh,
And who 'tis that shame consumeth.
     They meet. I lose reception.
'Gainst this cheating I'd not parry
Nor amid such false speech tarry,
     But from her lordship will be gone.

Coda

Sir Bertran,[1] sure no pleasure's won
Like this freedom naught so merry
Twixt Nile 'n' where the suns miscarry
     To where the rain falls from the sun.

L'ANCAN SON PASSAT LI GIURE

Lancan son passat li giure
E noi reman puois ni comba,
Et el verdier la flors trembla
Sus el entrecim on poma,
     La flor e li chan eil clar quil
Ab la sazon doussa e coigna
M'enseignon c'ab joi m'apoigna,
     Sai el temps de l'intran d'april,

Ben greu trob' om joi desliure,
C'a tantas partz volv e tomba
Fals' Amors, que no s'asembla
Lai on leiautatz asoma;
     Qu'ieu non trob jes doas en mil
Ses falsa paraulla loigna,

[1] Presumably De Born.

E puois c'a travers non poigna
E no torne sa cartat vil.

Tuich li plus savi en vant hiure
Ses muiol e ses retomba,
Cui il gignosetz esclemba
La crin queil pend a la coma;
     E plus pres li brui de l'auzil
On plus gentet s'en desloigna;
Et fols cre miells d'una moigna
     Car a simple cor e gentil.

Ses fals' Amor cuidiei viure,
Mas ben vei c'um dat mi plomba
Quand ieu miells vei qu'il m'o embla
Car tuich li legat de Roma
     No son jes de sen tant sotil,
Que na devisa 'Messoigna',
Que tant soaument caloigna,
     Mens poira falsar un fil

Qui Amor sec, per tals liure:
Cogul tenga per colomba,
S'il l'o ditz ni ver li sembla
Fassaill plan del Puoi de Doma;
     Quan d'el plus prop es tant s'apil
Si col proverbis s'acoigna;
Sil trai l'uoill, el puois loil oigna,
     Sofra e sega ab cor humil.

Ben conosc ses art d'escriure
Que es plan o que es comba,
Qu'ieu sai drut que si assembla
Don blasm' a leis, el col groma;
     Qu'ieu n'ai ja perdut ric cortil
Car non vuoill gabs ab vergoigna
Ni blasme ab honor loigna
     Per que ieu loing son seignoril.

Bertran, non cre de sai lo Nil
Mais tant de fin joi m'apoigna
Tro lai on lo soleills poigna,
    Tro lai on lo soleills plovil.

The fifth poem in Canello's arrangement, *Lanquan vei fueill' e flor e frug*, has strophes in the form:

When I see leaf, and flower and fruit
    Come forth upon light lynd and bough,
And hear the frogs in rillet bruit,
    And birds quhitter in forest now,
Love inkirlie doth leaf and flower and bear,
And trick my night from me, and stealing waste it,
Whilst other wight in rest and sleep sojourneth.

Lanquan vei fueill' e flor e frug
    Parer dels albres eill ramel,
Et aug lo chan que faun el brug
    Ranas el riu, el bosc l'auzel,
Doncs mi fueilla em floris em fruch' Amors
El cor tan gen que la nueit me retsida
Quant autra gens dorm e pauz' e sojorna.

The sixth is in the following pattern, and the third strophe translates

Hath a man rights at love? No grain.
Yet gowks think they've some legal lien.
But she'll blame you with heart serene
That ships for Bari sink, mid-main,
Or 'cause the French don't come from Gascony
And for such crimes I am nigh in my shroud,
Since, by the Christ, I do such crimes or none.

Autet e bas is interesting for the way in which Arnaut breaks the flow of the poem to imitate the bird call in *Cadahus en son us*, and the repetitions of this sound in the succeeding strophes, highly treble, presumably, 'Neis Jhezus, Mas pel us', etc.

AUTET E BAS ENTRELS PRIMS FUOILLS

Now high and low, where leaves renew,
Come buds on bough and spalliard pleach
And no beak nor throat is muted;
Auzel each in tune contrasted
Letteth loose
Wriblis[1] spruce.
Joy for them and spring would set
Song on me, but Love assaileth
Me and sets my words t' his dancing.

I thank my God and mine eyes too,
Since through them the perceptions reach,
Porters of joys that have refuted
Every ache and shame I've tasted;
They reduce
Pains, and noose
Me in Amor's corded net.
Her beauty in me prevaileth
Till bonds seem but joy's advancing.

My thanks, Amor, that I win through;
Thy long delays I naught impeach;
Though flame's in my marrow rooted
I'd not quench it, well 't hath lasted,
Burns profuse,
Held recluse
Lest knaves know our hearts are met,
Murrain on the mouth that aileth,
So he finds her not entrancing.

He doth in Love's book misconstrue,
And from that book none can him teach,
Who saith ne'er's in speech recruited
Aught, whereby the heart is dasted,
Word's abuse
Doth traduce
Worth, but I run no such debt.

[1] Wriblis—warblings.

Right 'tis if man over-raileth
He tear tongue on tooth mischancing.[1]

That I love her, is pride, is true,
But my fast secret knows no breach.
Since Paul's writ was executed
Or the forty days first fasted,
Not Cristus
Could produce
Her similar, where one can get
Charms total, for no charm faileth
Her who's memory's enhancing.

Grace and valour, the keep of you
She is, who holds me, each to each,
She sole, I sole, so fast suited,
Other women's lures are wasted,
And no truce
But misuse
Have I for them, they're not let
To my heart, where she regaleth
Me with delights I'm not chancing.

Arnaut loves, and ne'er will fret
Love with o'er-speech, his throat quaileth,
Braggart voust's not to his fancying.

AUTET E BAS ENTRELS PRIMS FUOILLS

Autet e bas entrels prims fuoills
Son nou de flors li ram eil renc
E noi ten mut bec ni gola
Nuills auzels, anz braia e chanta
Cadahus
En son us;
Per joi qu'ai d'els e del tems
Chant, mas amors mi asauta
Quils motz ab lo son acorda.

[1] This is nearly as bad in the original.

Dieu o grazisc e a mos huoills,
Que per lor conoissensam venc.
Jois, qu'adreich auci e fola
L'ira qu'ieu n'agui e l'anta,
Er va sus
Qui qu'en mus,
D'Amor don sui fis e frems;
C'ab lieis c'al cor m'azauta
Sui liatz ab ferma corda.

Merces, Amors, c'aras m'acuoills!
Tart mi fo, mas en grat m'o prenc,
Car si m'art dinz la meola
Lo fuocs non vuoill que s'escanta;
Mas pel us
Estauc clus
Que d'autrui joi fant greus gems
E pustell ai' en sa gauta
Cel c'ab lieis si desacorda.

De bon' amor falsa l'escuoills,
E drutz es tornatz en fadenc,
Qui di qu'el parla noil cola
Nuilla res quel cor creanta
De pretz l'us;
Car enfrus
Es d'aco qu'eu mout ai crems;
E qui de parlar trassauta
Dreitz es qu'en la lengais morda.

Vers es qu'ieu l'am et es orguoills,
Mas ab jauzir cela loi tenc;
Qu'anc pos Sainz Pauls fetz pistola
Ni nuills hom dejus caranta,
Non poc plus,
Neis Jhesus,
Far de tals, car totz absems
Als bos aips don es plus auta
Cella c'om per pros recorda.

Pretz e Valors, vostre capduoills
Es la bella c'ab sim retenc,
Qui m'a sol et ieu liei sola,
C'autra el mon nom atalanta;
Anz sui brus
Et estrus
Als autras el cor teing prems,
Mas pel sieu joi trepa e sauta
No vuoill c' autra m'o comorda.

Arnautz ama e no di nems,
C'Amors l'afrena la gauta
Que fols gabs no laill comorda.

In the next poem we have the chatter of birds in autumn, the onomatopoeia obviously depends upon the *'utẓ, -etẓ, -encs* and *-ortẓ'* of the rhyme-scheme, seventeen of the sixty-eight syllables of each strophe therein included. I was able to keep the English in the same sound as the *Cadahus,* but I have not been able to make more than a map of the relative positions in this canzo.

L'AURA AMARA

The bitter air
Strips panoply
From trees
Where softer winds set leaves,
The glad
Beaks
Now in brakes are coy,
Scarce peep the wee
Mates
And un-mates,
    What gaud's the work?
    What good the glees?
What curse
I strive to shake!
Me hath she cast from high,
In fell disease
I lie, and deathly fearing.

So clear the flare
That first lit me
To seize
Her whom my soul believes;
If cad
Sneaks,
Blabs, slanders, my joy
Counts little fee
Baits
And their hates.
   I scorn their perk
    And preen, at ease.
Disburse
Can she, and wake
Such firm delights, that I
Am hers, froth, lees
Bigod! from toe to earring.

Amor, look yare!
Know certainly
The keys;
How she thy suit receives;
Nor add
Piques,
'Twere folly to annoy.
I'm true, so dree
Fates;
No debates
   Shake me, nor jerk.
    My verities
Turn terse,
And yet I ache.
Her lips, not snows that fly
Have potencies
To slake, to cool my searing.

Behold my prayer,
(Or company
Of these)
Seeks whom such height achieves,

Well clad
Seeks
Her, and would not cloy.
Heart apertly
States
Thought. Hope waits
   'Gainst death to irk:
   False brevities
And worse!
To her I raik.[1]
Sole her; all others' dry
Felicities
I count not worth the leering.

Ah, fair face, where
Each quality
But frees
One pride-shaft more, that cleaves
Me; mad frieks
(O' they beck) destroy,
And mockery
Baits
Me, and rates.
   Yet I not shirk
   Thy velleities,
Averse
Me not, nor slake
Desire, God draws not nigh
To Dome,[2] with pleas
Wherein's so little veering.

Now chant prepare,
And melody
To please
The king, who'll judge thy sheaves,
Worth, sad,

[1] Raik—haste precipitate.

[2] Our Lady of Puy-de-Dôme? No definite solution of the reference yet found.

Sneaks
Here; double employ
Hath there. Get thee
Plates
Full, and cates,
  Gifts, go! Nor lurk
  Here till decrees
Reverse,
And ring thou take.
Straight t' Arago I'd ply
Cross the wide seas
But 'Rome' disturbs my hearing.

Coda

At midnight mirk,
In secrecies
I nurse
My served make[1]
In heart; nor try
My melodies
At other's door nor mearing.[2]

L'AURA AMARA

L'aura amara
Fals bruoills brancutz
Clarzir
Quel doutz espeissa ab fuoills,
Els letz
Becs
Dels auzels ramencs
Ten balps e mutz,
Pars
E non-pars;
Per qu'eu m'esfortz

---

[1] Make—mate, fere, companion.
[2] Dante cites this poem in the second book of *De Vulgari Eloquio* with poems of his own, De Born's, and Cino Pistoija's.

De far e dir
Plazers
A mains per liei
Que m'a virat bas d'aut,
Don tem morir
Sils afans no m'asoma.

Tant fo clara
Ma prima lutz
D'eslir
Lieis don crel cors los huoills,
Non pretz
Necs
Mans dos aigonencs[1];
D'autra s'esdutz
Rars
Mos preiars,
Pero deportz
M'es adauzir
Volers,
Bos motz ses grei
De liei don tant m'azaut
Qu'al sieu servir
Sui del pe tro c'al coma

Amors, gara,
Sui ben vengutz
C'auzir
Tem far sim desacuoills
Tals detz
Pecs
Que t'es miells quet trencs;
Qu'ieu soi fis drutz
Cars
E non vars,
Mal cors ferms fortz
Mi fai cobrir

---

[1] Lavaud: *angovencs*. Most probable meaning an angevin, small coin of Anjou, with argot diminutive ending.

Mains vers;
Cab tot lo nei
M'agr' ops us bais al chaut
Cor refrezir
Que noi val autra goma.

Si m'ampara
Cill cuim trahutz
D'aizir,
Si qu'es de pretz capduoills,
Dels quetz
Precs
C'ai dedinz a rencs,
L'er fors rendutz
Clars
Mos pensars;
Qu'eu fora mortz
Mas fam sofrir
L'espers
Queill prec quem brei,
C'aisson ten let e baut;
Que d'als jauzir
Nom val jois una poma.

Doussa car', a
Totz aips volgutz,
Sofrir
M'er per vos mainz orguoills,
Car etz
Decs
De totz mos fadencs,

Don ai mainz brutz
Pars
E gabars;
De vos nom tortz,
Nim fai partir
Avers,
C'anc non amei
Ren tan ab meins d'ufaut,
Anz vos desir
Plus que Dieus cill de Doma

Erat para
Chans e condutz,
Formir
Al rei qui t'er escuoills;
Car pretz
Secs
Sai, lai es doblencs,
E mantengutz
Dars
E manjars:
De joi lat portz,
Son anel mir,
Sil ders,
C'anc non estei
Jorn d'Aragon quel saut
Noi volgues ir,
Mas sai m'an clamat Roma.

Coda
Faitz es l'acortz
Qu'el cor remir
Totz sers
Lieis cui domnei
Ses parsonier Arnaut;
Qu'en autr' albir
N'es fort m'ententa soma.

The eleventh canzo is mainly interesting for the opening bass onomatopoeia of the wind rowting in the autumn branches. Arnaut may have caught his alliteration from the *joglar engles,* a possible hrimm-hramm-hruffer, though the device dates at least from Naevius.

En breu brisaral temps braus,
Eill bisa busina els brancs
Qui s'entreseignon trastuich
De sobreclaus rams de fuoilla;
Car noi chanta auzels ni piula
M' enseign' Amors qu'ieu fassa adonc
Chan que non er segons ni tertz
Ans prims d'afrancar cor agre.

The rhythm is too tricky to be caught at the first reading, or even at the fifth reading; there is only part of it in my copy.

> Briefly bursteth season brisk,
> Blasty north breeze racketh branch,
> Branches rasp each branch on each
> Tearing twig and tearing leafage,
>   Chirms now no bird nor cries querulous;
> So Love demands I make outright
> A song that no song shall surpass
>   For freeing the heart of sorrow.
>
> Love is glory's garden close,
> And is a pool of prowess staunch
> Whence get ye many a goodly fruit
> If true man come but to gather.
>   Dies none frost bit nor yet snowily,
> For true sap keepeth off the blight
> Unless knave or dolt there pass . . .

The second point of interest is the lengthening out of the rhyme in *piula*, *niula*, etc. In the fourth strophe we find:

> The gracious thinking and the frank
> Clear and quick perceiving heart
> Have led me to the fort of love.
> Finer she is, and I more loyal
> Than were Atalanta and Meleager.

Then the quiet conclusion, after the noise of the opening, 'Pensar de lieis m'es repaus':

> To think of her is my rest
> And both of my eyes are strained wry
> When she stands not in their sight,
> Believe not the heart turns from her,
>   For nor prayers nor games nor violing
> Can move me from her a reed's-breadth.

The most beautiful passages of Arnaut are in the canzo beginning:
'Doutz brais e critz.'

GLAMOUR AND INDIGO

Sweet cries and cracks
           and lays and chants inflected
By auzels who, in their Latin belikes,
Chirm each to each, even as you and I
Pipe toward those girls on whom our thoughts attract;
Are but more cause that I, whose overweening
Search is toward the Noblest, set in cluster
Lines where no word pulls wry, no rhyme breaks gauges.

No cul de sacs
           nor false ways me deflected
When first I pierced her fort within its dykes,
Hers, for whom my hungry insistency
Passes the gnaw whereby was Vivien wracked;[1]
Day-long I stretch, all times, like a bird preening,
And yawn for her, who hath o'er others thrust her
As high as true joy is o'er ire and rages.

Welcome not lax,
           and my words were protected
Not blabbed to other, when I set my likes
On her. Not brass but gold was 'neath the die.
That day we kissed, and after it she flacked
O'er me her cloak of indigo, for screening
Me from all culvertz' eyes, whose blathered bluster
Can set such spites abroad; win jibes for wages.

God, who did tax
           not Longus' sin,[2] respected

[1] Vivien, strophe 2, nebotz Sain Guillem, an allusion to the romance *Enfances Vivien*.

[2] Longus, centurion in the crucifixion legend.

That blind centurion beneath the spikes
And him forgave, grant that we two shall lie
Within one room, and seal therein our pact,

Yes, that she kiss me in the half-light, leaning
To me, and laugh and strip and stand forth in the lustre
Where lamp-light with light limb but half engages.

The flowers wax

              with buds but half perfected;
Tremble on twig that shakes where the bird strikes—
But not more fresh than she! No empery,
Though Rome and Palestine were one compact,
Would lure me from her; and with hands convening
I give me to her. But if kings could muster
In homage similar, you'd count them sages.

Mouth, now what knacks!

              What folly hath infected
Thee? Gifts, that th' Emperor of the Salonikes
Or Lord of Rome were greatly honoured by,
Or Syria's lord, thou dost from me distract;
O fool I am! to hope for intervening
From Love that shields not love! Yea, it were juster
To call him mad, who 'gainst his joy engages.

Political Postscript

The slimy jacks

              with adders' tongues bisected,
I fear no whit, nor have; and if these tykes
Have led Galicia's king to villeiny—[1]
His cousin in pilgrimage hath he attacked—
We know—Raimon the Count's son[2] —my meaning
Stands without screen. The royal filibuster
Redeems not honour till he unbar the cages.

[1] King of the Galicians, Ferdinand II, King of Galicia, 1157-88, son of Berangere, sister of Raimon Berenger IV ('quattro figlie ebbe', etc.) of Aragon, Count of Barcelona.

[2] His second son, Lieutenant of Provence, 1168.

Coda

I should have seen it, but I was on such affair.
Seeing the true king crown'd here in Estampa.[1]

DOUTZ BRAIS E CRITZ

Doutz brais e critz,
Lais e cantars e voutas
Aug del auzels qu'en lor latins fant precs
Quecs ab so par, atressi cum nos fam
A las amigas en cui entendem;
E doncas ieu qu'en la genssor entendi
Dei far chansson sobre totz de bell' obra
Que noi aia mot fals ni rima estrampa.

Non fui marritz
Ni non presi destoutas
Al prim qu'intriei el chastel dinz lo decs,
Lai on estai midonz, don ai gran fam
C'anc non l'ac tal lo nebotz Sain Guillem;
Mil vetz lo jorn en badaill em n'estendi
Per la bella que totas autras sobra
Tant cant val mais fis gaugz qu'ira ni rampa.

Ben fui grazitz
E mas paraulas coutas,
Per so que jes al chausir no fui pecs,
Anz volgui mais prendre fin aur que ram,
Lo jorn quez ieu e midonz nos baizem
Em fetz escut de son bel mantel endi
Que lausengier fals, lenga de colobra,
Non o visson, don tan mals motz escampa.

Dieus lo chauzitz
Per cui foron assoutas

<hr/>

[1] King crowned at Etampes, Philippe Auguste, crowned May 29, 1180, at age
of sixteen. This poem might date Arnaut's birth as early as 1150.

Las faillidas que fetz Longis lo cecs,
Voilla, sil platz, qu'ieu e midonz jassam
En la chambra on amdui nos mandem
Uns rics convens don tan gran joi atendi,
Quel seu bel cors baisan rizen descobra
E quel remir contral lum de la lampa

Ges rams floritz
De floretas envoutas
Cui fan tremblar auzelhon ab lurs becs
Non es plus frescs, per qu'ieu no volh Roam
Aver ses lieis ni tot Jherusalem;
Pero totz fis mas juntas a lim rendi,
Qu'en liei amar, agr' ondral reis de Dobra
O celh cui es l'Estel e Luna-pampa.

Bocca, que ditz?
Qu'en crei quem auras toutas
Tals promessas don l'emperaire grecs
En for' onratz ol senher de Roam
Ol reis que ten Sur e Jherusalem;
Doncs ben sui fols que queir tan quem rependi
Ni eu d'Amor non ai poder quem cobra,
Ni saveis es nuls om que joi acampa.

Los deschauzitz
Ab las lengas esmoutas
Non dubt' ieu jes, sil seignor dels Galecs
An fag faillir, perqu'es dreitz s'o blasmam,
Que son paren pres romieu, so sabem,
Raimon lo filh al comte, et aprendi
Que greu faral reis Ferrans de pretz cobra
Si mantenen nol solv e nol escampa

Eu l'agra vist, mas estei per tal obra,
C'al coronar fui del bon rei d'estampa.

(Mos sobrecors, si tot grans sens lo sobra,
Tenga que ten, si non gaire nois ampa.)

Arnaut's tendency to lengthen the latter lines of the strophe after the diesis shows in: *Er vei vermeils, vertz, blaus, blancs, gruocs,* the strophe form being:

> Er vei vermeils, vertz, blaus, blancs, gruocs
>   Vergiers, plans, plais, tertres e vaus;
> Eil votz del auzels sona e tint
>   Ab doutz acort maitin e tart.
> Som met en cor qu'ien colore mon chan
> D'un' aital flor don lo friutz sia amors,
> E jois lo grans, e l'olors d'enoi gandres.

> Vermeil, green, blue, peirs, white, cobalt,
> Close orchards, hewis, holts, hows, vales,
> And the bird-song that whirls and turns
> Morning and late with sweet accord,
> Bestir my heart to put my song in sheen
> T'equal that flower which hath such properties,
> It seeds in joy, bears love, and pain ameises.

The last cryptic allusion is to the quasi-allegorical descriptions of the tree of love in some long poem like the *Romaunt of the Rose*.

Dante takes the next poem as a model of canzo construction; and he learned much from its melody. We note the soft suave sound as against the staccato of *L'aura amara*.

CANZON

> I only, and who elrische pain support,
> Know out love's heart o'er borne by overlove,
> For my desire that is so firm and straight
> And unchanged since I found her in my sight
> And unturned since she came within my glance,
> That far from her my speech springs up aflame;
> Near her comes not. So press the words to arrest it.

> I am blind to others, and their retort
> I hear not. In her alone, I see, move,
> Wonder . . . And jest not. And the words dilate

Not truth; but mouth speaks not the heart outright:
I could not walk roads, flats, dales, hills, by chance,
To find charm's sum within one single frame
As God hath set in her t'assay and test it.

And I have passed in many a goodly court
To find in hers more charm than rumour thereof . . .
In solely hers. Measure and sense to mate,
Youth and beauty learnèd in all delight,
Gentrice did nurse her up, and so advance
Her fair beyond all reach of evil name,
To clear her worth, no shadow hath oppresst it.

Her contact flats not out, falls not off short . . .
Let her, I pray, guess out the sense hereof
For never will it stand in open prate
Until my inner heart stand in daylight,
So that heart pools him when her eyes entrance,
As never doth the Rhone, fulled and untame,
Pool, where the freshets tumult hurl to crest it.

Flimsy another's joy, false and distort,
No paregale that she springs not above . . .
Her love-touch by none other mensurate.
To have it not? Alas! Though the pains bite
Deep, torture is but galzeardy and dance,
For in my thought my lust hath touched his aim.
God! Shall I get no more! No fact to best it!

No delight I, from now, in dance or sport,
Nor will these toys a tinkle of pleasure prove,
Compared to her, whom no loud profligate
Shall leak abroad how much she makes my right.
Is this too much? If she count not mischance
What I have said, then no. But if she blame,
Then tear ye out the tongue that hath expresst it.

The song begs you: Count not this speech ill chance,
But if you count the song worth your acclaim
Arnaut cares lyt who praise or who contest it.

SOLS SUI

Sols sui qui sai lo sobrafan quem sortz
Al cor d'amor sofren per sobramar,
Car mos volers es tant ferms et entiers
C'anc no s'esduis de celliei ni s'estors
Cui encubric al prim vezer e puois:
Qu'ades ses lieis dic a lieis cochos motz
Pois quan la vei non sai, tant l'ai, que dire.

D'autras vezer sui secs e d'auzir sortz
Qu'en sola lieis vei et aug et esgar;
E jes d'aisso noill sui fals plazentiers
Que mais la vol non ditz la bocal cors;
Qu'eu no vau tant chams, vauz ni plans ni puois
Qu'en un sol cors trob aissi bos aips totz:
Qu'en lieis los volc Dieus triar et assire.

Ben ai estat a maintas bonas cortz,
Mas sai ab lieis trob pro mais que lauzar
Mesura e sen et autres bos mestiers,
Beutat, joven, bos faitz e bels demors.
Gen l'enseignet Cortesia e la duois,
Tant a de si totz faitz desplazens rotz
De lieis no cre rens de ben si' a dire.

Nuills jauzimens nom fora breus ni cortz
De lieis cui prec qu'o vuoilla devinar,
Que ja per mi non o sabra estiers
Sil cors ses dirs nos presenta de fors;
Que jes Rozers per aiga que l'engrois
Non a tal briu c'al cor plus larga dotz
Nom fassa estanc d'amor, quand la remire.

Jois e solatz d'autram par fals e bortz,
C'una de pretz ab lieis nois pot egar,
Quel sieus solatz es dels autres sobriers.
Ai si no l'ai! las! Tant mal m'a comors!
Pero l'afans m'es deportz, ris e jois

Car en pensan sui de lieis lecs e glotz:
Ai Dieus, si ja'n serai estiers jauzire!

Anc mais, sous pliu, nom plac tant treps ni bortz
Ni res al cor tant de joi nom poc dar
Cum fetz aquel don anc feinz lausengiers
No s'esbrugic qu'a mi solses tresors ...
Dic trop? Eu non, sol lieis non sia enois.
Bella, per dieu, lo parlar e la votz
Vuoill perdre enans que diga ren queus tire.

Ma chansos prec que nous sia enois
Car si voletz grazir lo son els motz
Pauc preza Arnautz cui que plassa o que tire.

The XVIth canto goes on with the much discussed and much too
emphasized cryptogram of the ox and the hare. I am content with
the reading which gives us a classic allusion in the Palux Laerna.
The lengthening of the verse in the last three lines of the strophe is,
I think, typically Arnaut's. I leave the translation solely for the sake
of one strophe.

ERE THE WINTER

Ere the winter recommences
And from bough the leaf be wrested,
On Love's mandate will I render
A brief end to long prolusion:
So well have I been taught his steps and paces
That I can stop the tidal-sea's inflowing.
My stot outruns the hare; his speed amazes.

Me he bade without pretences
That I go not, though requested;
That I make no whit surrender
Nor abandon our seclusion:
'Differ from violets, whose fear effaces
Their hue ere winter; behold the glowing
Laurel stays, stay thou. Year long the genet blazes.'

You who commit no offences
'Gainst constancy; have not quested;
Assent not! Though a maid send her
Suit to thee. Think you confusion
Will come to her who shall track out your traces?
And give your enemies a chance for boasts and crowing?
No! After God, see that she have your praises.

Coward, shall I trust not defences!
Faint ere the suit be tested?
Follow! till she extend her
Favour. Keep on, try conclusion
For if I get in this naught but disgraces,
Then must I pilgrimage past Ebro's flowing
And seek for luck amid the Laernian mazes.

If I've passed bridge-rails and fences,
Think you then that I am bested?
No, for with no food or slender
Ration, I'd have joy's profusion
To hold her kissed, and there are never spaces
Wide to keep me from her, but she'd be showing
In my heart, and stand forth before his gazes.

Lovelier maid from Nile to Sences
Neither robed is, nor divested,
So great is her body's splendour
That you would think it illusion.
Amor, if she but hold me in her embraces,
I should not feel hail's cold, nor winter's blowing,
Nor break for all the pain in fever's dazes.

Arnaut hers from foot to face is,
He would not have Lucerne, without her, owing
Him, nor lord the land whereon the Ebro grazes.

ERE THE WINTER

Ans quel cim reston de branchas
Sec ni despoillat de fuoilla

Farai, c'Amors m'o comanda,
Breu chansson de razon loigna.
Que gen m'a duoich de las artz de s'escola;
Tant sai quel cors fatz restar de suberna
E mos bous es pro correns que lebres.

Ab razos coindas e franchas
M'a mandat qu'ieu no m'en tuoilla
Ni non serva autra ni'n blanda
Puois tant fai c'ab si m'acoigna;
Em di que flors noil semble de viola
Quis camja leu sitot nonca s'inverna,
Ans per s'amor sia laurs o genebres.

Dis: tu, c'aillors non t'estranchas
Per autra quit deing nit vuoilla,
Totz plaitz esquiva e desmanda
Sai e lai qui quet somoigna;
Gran son dan fai qui se meteus afola,
E tu no far failla don hom t'esquerna,
Mas apres Dieu lieis honors e celebres.

E tu, coartz, non t'afranchas
Per respeich c'amar not vuoilla;
Sec, s'il te fuig nit fai ganda,
Que greu er c'om noi apoigna
Qui s'afortis de preiar e no cola.
Qu'ieu passera part la palutz de Lerna
Com peregrins o lai per on cor Ebres.

S'ieu n'ai passatz pons ni planchas
Per lieis, cuidatz qu'ieu m'en duoilla?
Non eu, c'ab joi ses vianda
M'en sap far meizina coigna
Baisan tenen; el cors, sitot si vola,
Nois part de lieis quel capdella el governa.
Cors, on qu'ieu an, de lieis not loinz ni sebres!

De part Nil entro c'a Sanchas
Gensser nois viest nis despuoilla,

Car sa beutatz es tant granda
Que semblariaus messoigna.
Bem vai d'amor, qu'elam baisa e m'acola,
E nom frezis freitz ni gels ni buerna,
Num fai dolor mals ni gota ni febres.

Sieus es Arnautz del cim tro en la sola
E senes lieis no vol aver Lucerna
Nil senhoriu del reion que cor Ebres.

The feminine rhyming throughout and the shorter opening lines
keep the strophe much lighter and more melodic than that of the
canzo which Canello prints last of all.

SIM FOS AMORS DE JOI DONAR TANT LARGA

Ingenium nobis ipsa puella fecit;

PROPERTIUS II, I.

Had Love as little need to be exhorted
To give me joy, as I to keep a frank
And ready heart toward her, never he'd blast
My hope, whose very height hath high exalted,
And cast me down . . . to think on my default,
And her great worth; yet thinking what I dare,
More love myself, and know my heart and sense
Shall lead me to high conquest, unmolested.

I am, spite long delay, pooled and contorted
And whirled with all my streams 'neath such a bank
Of promise, that her fair words hold me fast
In joy, and will, until in tomb I am halted.
As I'm not one to change hard gold for spalt,
And no alloy's in her, that debonaire
Shall hold my faith and mine obedience
Till, by her accolade, I am invested.

Long waiting hath brought in and hath extorted
The fragrance of desire; throat and flank
The longing takes me . . . and with pain surpassed
By her great beauty. Seemeth it hath vaulted

O'er all the rest . . . them doth it set in fault
So that whoever sees her anywhere
Must see how charm and every excellence
Hold sway in her, untaint, and uncontested.

Since she is such: longing no wise detorted
Is in me . . . and plays not the mountebank,
For all my sense is her, and is compassed
Solely in her; and no man is assaulted
(By God his dove!) by such desires as vault
In me, to have great excellence. My care
On her so stark, I can show tolerance
To jacks whose joy's to see fine loves uncrested.

Miels-de-Ben, have not your heart distorted
Against me now; your love has left me blank,
Void, empty of power or will to turn or cast
Desire from me . . . not brittle,[1] nor defaulted.

Asleep, awake, to thee do I exalt
And offer me. No less, when I lie bare
Or wake, my will to thee, think not turns thence,
For breast and throat and head hath it attested.

Pouch-mouthed blubberers, culrouns and aborted,
May flame bite in your gullets, sore eyes and rank
T' the lot of you, you've got my horse, my last
Shilling, too; and you'd see love dried and salted.
God blast you all that you can't call a halt!
God's itch to you, chit-cracks that overbear
And spoil good men, ill luck your impotence!!
More told, the more you've wits smeared and congested.

Coda

Arnaut has borne delay and long defence
And will wait long to see his hopes well nested.

[1] 'Brighter than glass, and yet as glass is, brittle.' The comparisons to glass
went out of poetry when glass ceased to be a rare, precious substance. (Cf.
Passionate Pilgrim, III.)

SIM FOS AMORS

Sim fos Amors de joi donar tant larga
Cum ieu vas lieis d'aver fin cor e franc,
Ja per gran ben nom calgra far embarc,
Qu'er am tant aut quel pes mi poia em plomba;
Mas quand m'albir cum es de pretz al som
Mout m'en am mais car anc l'ausiei voler,
C'aras sai ieu que mos cors e mos sens
Mi farant far, lor grat, rica conquesta.

Pero s'ieu fatz lonc esper no m'embarga,
Qu'en tant ric luoc me sui mes e m'estanc
C'ab sos bels digz mi tengra de joi larc,
E segrai tant qu'om mi port a la tomba,
Qu'ieu non sui ges cel que lais or per plom;
E pois en lieis nos taing c'om ren esmer
Tant li serai fis et obediens
Tro de s'amor, s'il platz, baisan m'envesta.

Us bons respietz mi reven em descarga
D'un doutz desir don mi dolen li flanc,
Car en patz prenc l'atan el sofr' el parc
Pois de beutat son las autras en comba,
Que le genser par c'aia pres un tom
Plus bas de liei, qui la ve, et es ver;
Que tuig bon aip, pretz e sabers e sens
Reingnon ab liei, c'us non es meins ni'n resta.

E pois tant val, nous cujetz que s'esparga
Mos ferms volers ni qu'eisforc ni qu'eisbranc,
Car eu no sui sieus ni mieus si m'en parc,
Per cel Seignor queis mostret en colomba:
Qu'el mon non ha home de negun nom
Tant desires gran benanansa aver
Cum ieu fatz lieis, e tenc a noncalens
Los enoios cui dans d'Amor es festa.

Na Miells-de-ben, ja nom siatz avarga
Qu'en vostr' amor me trobaretz tot blanc,[1]
Qu'ieu non ai cor ni poder quem descarc
Del ferm voler que non hieis de retomba;
Que quand m'esveill ni clau lo huoills de som
A vos m'autrei, quan leu ni vau jazer;
E nous cujetz queis merme mos talens,
Non fara jes, qu'aral sent en la testa.

Fals lausengier, fuocs las lengas vos arga
E que perdatz ams los huoill de mal cranc,
Que per vos son estraich caval e marc,
Amor toletz c'ab pauc del tot non tomba;
Confondaus Dieus que ja non sapchatz com,
Queus fatz als drutz maldire e vil tener;
Malastres es queus ten, desconoissens,
Que peior etz qui plus vos amonesta.

Arnautz a faitz e fara loncs atens,
Qu'atenden fai pros hom rica conquesta.

In *De Vulgari Eloquio*, II, 13, Dante calls for freedom in the rhyme order within the strophe, and cites this canzo of Arnaut's as an example of poem where there is no rhyme within the single strophe. Dante's 'Rithimorum quoque relationi vacemus' implies no carelessness concerning the blending of rhyme sounds, for we find him at the end of the chapter 'et tertio rithimorum asperitas, nisi forte sit lenitati permista: nam lenium asperorumque rithimorum mixtura ipsa tragoedia nitescit', as he had before demanded a mixture of shaggy and harsh words with the softer words of a poem. 'Nimo scilicet eiusdem rithimi repercussio, nisi forte novum aliquid atque intentatum artis hoc sibi praeroget.' The *De Eloquio* is ever excellent testimony of the way in which a great artist approaches the detail of métier.

[1] Cf. *Donna mi prega*, strophe v, 1. 8.

CAVALCANTI[1]

MEDIEVALISM

I

Safe may'st thou go my canzon whither thee pleaseth
Thou art so fair attired'

Apart from the welcome given to or withheld from a fine performance, it seems to me that the vogue of Guido's canzone,
Donna mi Prega, was due to causes not instantly apparent to
the modern reader. I mean that it shows traces of a tone of thought
no longer considered dangerous, but that may have appeared about
as soothing to the Florentine of A.D. 1290 as conversation about Tom
Paine, Marx, Lenin and Bucharin would to-day in a Methodist
bankers' board meeting in Memphis, Tenn.

The teaching of Aristotle had been banned in the University of
Paris in 1213. This prejudice had been worn down during the century,
but Guido shows, I think, no regard for anyone's prejudice. We may
trace his ideas to Averroes, Avicenna; he does not definitely proclaim
any heresy, but he shows leanings toward not only the proof by
reason, but toward the proof by experiment. I do not think that he
swallowed Aquinas. It may be impossible to prove that he had heard
of Roger Bacon, but the whole canzone is easier to understand if we
suppose, or at least one finds, a considerable interest in the speculation,
that he had read Grosseteste on the Generation of Light.

In all of which he shows himself much more 'modern' than his
young friend Dante Alighieri, *qui était diablement dans les idées reçues,*
and whose shock is probably recorded in the passage of *Inferno* X
where he finds Guido's father and father-in-law paying for their
mental exertions. In general, one may conclude that the conversation
in the Cavalcanti-Uberti family was more stimulating than that in
Tuscan bourgeois and ecclesiastical circles of the period.

My conclusions are based on the whole text of Guido, or at least
the serious part of the text, excluding rhymed letters, skits and simple

[1] As published in *Make It New* (1934), but the essay as a whole must be
dated 1910-1931.

pastorals; the canzone by itself does not conclusively prove my
assertions.

II

The medieval Italian poets brought into poetry something which had
not been or not been in any so marked and developed degree in the
poetry of the troubadours. It is still more important for anyone wishing to have well-balanced critical appreciation of poetry in general to
understand that this quality, or this assertion of value, has not been
in poetry *since;* and that the English 'philosophical' and other
'philosophical' poets have not produced a comparable *Ersatz*.

The Greek aesthetic would seem to consist wholly in plastic, or in
plastic moving toward coitus, and limited by incest, which is the sole
Greek taboo. This new thing in medieval work that concerns us has
nothing to do with Christianity, which people both praise and blame
for utterly irrelevant and unhistorical reasons. Erotic sentimentality
we can find in Greek and Roman poets, and one may observe that the
main trend of Provençal and Tuscan poets is not toward erotic
sentimentality.

But they are not pagans, they are called pagans, and the troubadours
are also accused of being Manichaeans, obviously because of a muddle
somewhere. They are opposed to a form of stupidity not limited to
Europe, that is, idiotic asceticism and a belief that the body is evil.
This more or less masochistic and hell-breeding belief is always
accompanied by bad and niggled sculpture (Angoulême or Bengal);
Gandhi[1] to-day is incapable of making the dissociation that it is not
the body but its diseases and infirmities which are evil. The same
statement is true of mind: the infections of mind being no less
hideous than those of physique. In fact, a man's toothache annoys
himself, but a fool annoys the whole company. Even for epidemics, a
few cranks may spread a wider malefaction than anything short of
plague universal. This invention of hells for one's enemies, and mess,
confusion in sculpture, is always symptomatic of supineness, bad
hygiene, bad physique (possibly envy); even the diseases of mind,
they do not try to cure as such, but devise hells to punish, not to
heal, the individual sufferer.

Against these European Hindoos we find the 'medieval clean line',
as distinct from medieval niggle. Byzantium gives us perhaps the
best architecture, or at least the best inner structure, that we know, I

[1] Possibly false attribution, i.e. in so far as it applied to Gandhi.

mean for proportions, for ornament flat on the walls, and not bulging and bumping and indulging in bulbous excrescence. The lines for example of the Byzantine heritage in Sicily, from which the best 'Romanesque', developing to St Hilaire in Poictiers; or if the term Romanesque has become too ambiguous through loose usage, let me say that there are medieval churches such as the cathedral at San Leo, or San Zeno in Verona, and others of similar form which are simply the Byzantine minus riches. It is the bare wall that the Constantinopolitan would have had money enough to cover with gold mosaic.

Perhaps out of a sand-swept country, the need of interior harmony. That is conjecture. Against this clean architecture, we find the niggly Angoulême, the architectural ornament of bigotry, superstition, and mess.

What is the difference between Provence and Hellas? There is, let us grant, a line in Propertius about *ingenium nobis fecit*. But the subject is not greatly developed. I mean that Propertius remains mostly inside the classic world and the classic aesthetic, plastic to coitus. Plastic plus immediate satisfaction.

The whole break of Provence with this world, and indeed the central theme of the troubadours, is the dogma that there is some proportion between the fine thing held in the mind, and the inferior thing ready for instant consumption.

Their freedom is not an attack on Christian prudery, because prudery is not a peculiarly Christian excrescence. There is plenty of prudery in Virgil, and also in Ovid, where rumour would less lead one to expect it.

I am labouring all this because I want to establish a disjunction as to the Tuscan aesthetic. The term metaphysic might be used if it were not so appallingly associated in people's minds with unsupportable conjecture and devastated terms of abstraction.

The Tuscan demands harmony in something more than the plastic. He declines to limit his aesthetic to the impact of light on the eye. It would be misleading to reduce his aesthetic to terms of music, or to distort the analysis of it by analogies to the art of sonority. Man shares plastic with the statue, sound does not require a human being to produce it. The bird, the phonograph, sing. Sound can be exteriorized as completely as plastic. There is the residue of perception, perception of something which requires a human being to produce it. Which even may require a certain individual to produce it.

This really complicates the aesthetic. You deal with an interactive force: the *virtu* in short.

And dealing with it is not anti-life. It is not maiming, it is not curtailment. The senses at first seem to project for a few yards beyond the body. Effect of a decent climate where a man leaves his nerve-set open, or allows it to tune in to its ambience, rather than struggling, as a northern race has to for self-preservation, to guard the body from assaults of weather.

He declines, after a time, to limit reception to his solar plexus. The whole thing has nothing to do with taboos and bigotries. It is more than the simple athleticism of the *mens sana in corpore sano*. The conception of the body as perfect instrument of the increasing intelligence pervades. The lack of this concept invalidates the whole of monastic thought. Dogmatic asceticism is obviously not essential to the perceptions of Guido's ballate.

Whether it is necessary to modernize or nordicize our terminology and call this 'the aesthetic or interactive vasomotor magnetism in relation to the consciousness', I leave to the reader's own taste and sense of proportion. I am inclined to think that a habit of mind which insists upon, or even tends toward, such terminology somewhat takes the bloom off the peach.

Out of these fine perceptions, or subsequent to them, people say that the Quattrocento, or the sculpture of the Quattrocento, discovered 'personality'. All of which is perhaps rather vague. We might say: The best Egyptian sculpture is magnificent plastic; but its force comes from a non-plastic idea, i.e. the god is inside the statue.

I am not considering the merits of the matter, much less those merits as seen by a modern aesthetic purist. I am using historic method. The god is inside the stone, *vacuos exercet aera morsus*. The force is arrested, but there is never any question about its latency, about the force being the essential, and the rest 'accidental' in the philosophic technical sense. The shape occurs.

There is hardly any debate about the Greek classical sculpture, to them it is the plastic that matters. In the case of the statue of the Etruscan Apollo at Villa Giulia (Rome) the 'god is inside', but the psychology is merely that of an Hallowe'en pumpkin. It is a weak derivation of fear motive, strong in Mexican masks, but here reduced to the simple briskness of small boy amused at startling his grandma.

This is a long way from Greek statues, in which 'the face don't matter'.

This sculpture with something inside, revives in the Quattrocento portrait bust. But the antecedents are in verbal manifestation.

Nobody can absorb the *poeti dei primi secoli* and then the paintings of the Uffizi without seeing the relation between them, Daniel, Ventadour, Guido, Sellaio, Botticelli, Ambrogio Praedis, Nic. del Cossa.

All these are clean, all without hell-obsession.

Certain virtues are established, and the neglect of them by later writers and artists is an impoverishment of their art. The stupidity of Rubens, the asinine nature of French court life from Henry IV to the end of it, the insistence on two dimensional treatment of life by certain modernists, do not constitute a progress. A dogma builds on vacuum, and is ultimately killed or modified by, or accommodated to knowledge, but values stay, and ignorant neglect of them answers no purpose.

Loss of values is due usually to lumping and to lack of dissociation. The disproved is thrown out, and the associated, or contemporarily established, goes temporarily with it.

'Durch Rafael ist das Madonnenideal Fleisch geworden', says Herr Springer, with perhaps an unintentional rhyme. Certainly the metamorphosis into carnal tissue becomes frequent and general somewhere about 1527. The people are corpus, corpuscular, but not in the strict sense 'animate', it is no longer the body of air clothed in the body of fire; it no longer radiates, light no longer moves from the eye, there is a great deal of meat, shock absorbing, perhaps—at any rate absorbent. It has not even Greek marmoreal plastic to restrain it. The dinner scene is more frequently introduced, we have the characters in definite act of absorption; later they will be but stuffing for expensive upholsteries.

Long before that a change had begun in the poetry. The difference between Guido and Petrarch is not a mere difference in degree, it is a difference in kind.

There are certain things Petrarch does not know, cannot know. I am not postulating him as 'to blame' for anything, or even finding analogy for his tone in post-Peruginian painting.

Leave all question of any art save poetry. In that art the gulf between Petrarch's capacity and Guido's is the great gulf, not of degree, but of kind. In Guido the 'figure', the strong metamorphic or 'picturesque' expression is there with purpose to convey or to interpret a definite meaning. In Petrarch it is ornament, the prettiest ornament he could find, but not an irreplaceable ornament, or one that he couldn't have used just about as well somewhere else. In fact he very often does use it, and them, somewhere, and nearly everywhere, else, all over the place.

We appear to have lost the radiant world where one thought cuts through another with clean edge, a world of moving energies '*mezzo oscuro rade*', '*risplende in sè perpetuale effecto*', magnetisms that take form, that are seen, or that border the visible, the matter of Dante's *paradiso,* the glass under water, the form that seems a form seen in a mirror, these realities perceptible to the sense, interacting, '*a lui si tiri*' untouched by the two maladies, the Hebrew disease, the Hindoo disease, fanaticisms and excess that produce Savonarola, asceticisms that produce fakirs, St Clement of Alexandria, with his prohibition of bathing by women. The envy of dullards who, not having '*intelletto*', blame the lack of it on innocent muscles. For after asceticism, that is anti-flesh, we get the asceticism that is anti-intelligence, that praises stupidity as 'simplicity', the cult of *naïveté*. To many people the term 'medieval' connotes only the two diseases. We must avoid these unnecessary idea-clots. Between those diseases, existed the Mediterranean sanity. The '*section d'or*', if that is what it meant, that gave the churches like St Hilaire, San Zeno, the Duomo di Modena, the clear lines and proportions. Not the pagan worship of strength, nor the Greek perception of visual non-animate plastic, or plastic in which the being animate was not the main and principal quality, but this 'harmony in the sentience' or harmony *of* the sentient, where the thought has its demarcation, the substance its *virtu,* where stupid men have not reduced all 'energy' to unbounded undistinguished abstraction.

For the modern scientist energy has no borders, it is a shapeless 'mass' of force; even his capacity to differentiate it to a degree never dreamed by the ancients has not led him to think of its shape or even its loci. The rose that his magnet makes in the iron filings, does not lead him to think of the force in botanic terms, or wish to visualize that force as floral and extant (*ex stare*).

A medieval 'natural philosopher' would find this modern world full of enchantments, not only the light in the electric bulb, but the thought of the current hidden in air and in wire would give him a mind full of forms, *'Fuor di color'* or having their hyper-colours. The medieval philosopher would probably have been unable to think the electric world, and *not* think of it as a world of forms. Perhaps algebra has queered our geometry. Even Bose with his plant experiments seems intent on the plant's capacity to feel—not on the plant idea, for the plant brain is obviously filled with, or is one idea, an *idée fixe,* a persistent notion of pattern from which only cataclysm or a Burbank can shake it. Or possibly this will fall under the eye of a contemporary scientist of genius who will answer: But, damn you, that is exactly what we do feel; or under the eye of a painter who will answer: Confound you, you *ought* to find just that in my painting.

DONNA MI PREGA

(*Dedicace*—To Thomas Campion his ghost, and to the ghost of Henry Lawes, as prayer for the revival of music)

Because a lady asks me, I would tell
Of an affect that comes often and is fell
And is so overweening: Love by name,
E'en its deniers can now hear the truth,
I for the nonce to them that know it call,
Having no hope at all
    that man who is base in heart
Can bear his part of wit
    into the light of it,
And save they know't aright from nature's source
I have no will to prove Love's course
    or say
Where he takes rest; who maketh him to be;
Or what his active *virtu* is, or what his force;
Nay, nor his very essence or his mode;
What his placation; why he is in verb,
Or if a man have might
    To show him visible to men's sight.

In memory's locus taketh he his state   *Place*
Formed there in manner as a mist of light   *La ove*
Upon a dusk that is come from Mars and stays.   *e*

Love is created, hath a sensate name,   *chi lo*
His modus takes from soul, from heart his will;   *fa*
From form seen doth he start, that, understood,   *creare*
Taketh in latent intellect—
As in a subject ready—
      place and abode,
Yet in that place it ever is unstill,
Spreading its rays, it tendeth never down
By quality, but is its own effect unendingly
Not to delight, but in an ardour of thought
That the base likeness of it kindleth not.

It is not *virtu*, but perfection's source   *Virtú*
Lying within perfection postulate   *e*
Not by the reason, but 'tis felt, I say.   *potenza*
Beyond salvation, holdeth its judging force,
Maintains intention reason's peer and mate;
Poor in discernment, being thus weakness' friend,
Often his power meeteth with death in the end
Be he withstayed
    or from true course
       bewrayed
E'en though he meet not with hate
       or villeiny
Save that perfection fails, be it but a little;
Nor can man say he hath his life by chance
Or that he hath not stablished seigniory
Or loseth power, e'en lost to memory.

He comes to be and is when will's so great   *Essenza*
It twists itself from out all natural measure;   *e*
Leisure's adornment puts he then never on,   *movimento*
Never thereafter, but moves changing state,
Moves changing colour, or to laugh or weep
Or wries the face with fear and little stays,
Yea, resteth little
      yet is found the most
Where folk of worth be host.
And his strange property sets sighs to move

And wills man look into unformèd space
Rousing there thirst
                    that breaketh into flame.
None can imagine love
                    that knows not love;
Love doth not move, but draweth all to him;
Nor doth he turn
                    for a whim
                              to find delight
Nor to seek out, surely, great knowledge or slight.

Look drawn from like,   *Piacimento*
                    delight maketh certain in seeming
Not can in covert cower,
                    beauty so near,
Not yet wild-cruel as darts,
So hath man craft from fear
                              in such his desire
To follow a noble spirit,
                    edge, that is, and point to the dart,
Though from her face indiscernible;
He, caught, falleth
                    plumb on to the spike of the targe.
Who well proceedeth, form not seeth,
                              following his own emanation.
There, beyond colour, essence set apart,
In midst of darkness light light giveth forth
Beyond all falsity, worthy of faith, alone
That in him solely is compassion born.

Safe may'st thou go my canzon whither thee pleaseth
Thou art so fair attired that every man and each
Shall praise thy speech
So he have sense or glow with reason's fire,
To stand with other
                    hast thou no desire.

PARTIAL EXPLANATION

A commentary is a piece of writing in which we expose and seek to
excuse our ignorance of the subject. The less we know, the longer
our explanations.

The following canzone was known as 'the philosophic canzone';
the stir that it caused, over and above the stir aroused by any beautiful work, may be attributed in part to the state of philosophic
opinion in and about A.D. 1290. Guido is called a 'natural philosopher',
I think an 'atheist', and certainly an 'Epicurean', not that anyone
had then any clear idea or has now any very definite notion of what
Epicurus taught. But a natural philosopher was a much less safe
person than a 'moral philosopher'.

It is not so much what Guido says in the poem, as the familiarity
that he shows with dangerous thinking; *natural demonstration* and
the proof by experience or (?) experiment. If after-dinner talk of the
Uberti and Cavalcanti was any warrant for Guido's tone it is small
wonder that Dante who was, as a young man, *bien pensant*, and probably quite content with the orthodoxy of Guinicello, thought it
necessary to lodge the tough-minded seniors of these tribes in the
Tenth Canto of his *Inferno*, where indeed, the elder Cavalcanti
might seem to be expecting his son.

My own sympathies extend even to the disrespect for Virgilio, but
that point may seem irrelevant.

From this poem and from passages elsewhere it would seem that
Guido had derived certain notions from the Aristotelian commentators, the *'filosofica famiglia'*, Ibn Sina, for the *spiriti, spiriti* of the
eyes, of the senses; Ibn Rachd, *che il gran comento feo*, for the demand
for intelligence on the part of the recipient; Albertus Magnus, for the
proof by experience; and possibly Grosseteste, *De Luce et de
Incòhatione Formarum*, although this will need proving.

At any rate for any serious thought in Guido's time we must
suppose the Arabian background: the concentric spheres of the
heavens, Ibn Baja's itinerary of the soul going to God, Averroes's
specifications for the degrees of comprehension; and we may perhaps
consider Guido as one of that 'tenuous line who from Albertus
Magnus to the renaissance' meant the freedom of thought, the contempt, or at least a moderated respect, for stupid authority.

He is possibly against Sigier and for Albertus, he wants no proof that contradicts the 'rationes naturales', he is not jamming down a dogma unsupported by nature. His truth is not against 'natural dimostramento' or based on authority. It is a truth for elect recipients, not a truth universally spreadable or acceptable. The 'dove sta memoria' is Platonism. The 'non razionale ma che si sente' is for experiment, it is against the tyranny of the syllogism, blinding and obscurantist. The tone of his mind is infinitely more 'modern' than Dante's 'Fuor di salute, giudichar mantiene', his position, here as on the rest of these cardinal points, shows him to be 'very dangerous' to the peace of the medieval mind, if immobility may be considered as 'peace'.

And all this is done with the suavity of a song, with the neatness of scalpel-cut. Guido is eclectic, he swallows none of his authors whole. There is no open 'atheism', indeed no direct attack on any church dogma, but there is probably a sense of briskness; I mean it would not have been comforting to lovers of quiet.

If part of this is conjecture, I think one can, at any rate, scarcely exaggerate the gulf between Guido's state of mind and that of Dante in the same epoch, or between it and Dante's willingness to take on any sort of holy and orthodox furniture. Dante's 'heresies' are due to feeling, annoyance with Popes and so forth, rather than to intellectual hunger, or to his feeling cramped in the Aquinian universe.

I may be wrong, but I cannot believe that Guido 'swallowed' Aquinas. It is perhaps by merest accident, but we find nowhere in his poem any implication of a belief in a geocentric or theocentric material universe.

'BUT THE POEM IS VERY OBSCURE.'

The poem is extremely clear in a number of places, the philosophic terms are used with a complete precision of technique. I am aware that I have distorted 'accidente' into 'affect' but I have done so in order not to lose the tone of my opening line by introducing an English word of double entente.

For the rest, there are certain enigmas, and the celebrated commentators have done nothing to solve them. These which face us today are precisely the same ones which faced Del Garbo in 1302 or 1320 or Di Giunta in 1527.

Considering the clarity and precision of the text where it is clear, I am loth to think that these obscure points indicate merely a loose usage or remplissage, on the part of the author.

Textual research brings us to a definite limit of knowledge about certain MS. readings. The earliest known copyists found certain passages either illegible or incomprehensible: as for example, *la gire*, *largir*, or *laire simiglglianza*.

Frate Egidio (Colonna, Romano, il beato, degli Agostiniani) goes round it. He begins his commentary with a graceful description of a notable lady, who must have begun life 'of Paphos and the Isles' but has attained a safe anonymity. She is seated on an anonymous mountain, by an anonymous fountain, whence she sends forth her ministers: Solomon and Ovidius Naso. However, *il beato* casts no satisfactory light on the phrase '*laire simiglglianza*'. Dino del Garbo is, in the modern sense, a much more serious character. He quotes a good deal of Aristotle, explains the preceding line as if it read: '*E si non ha diletto*' or '*quando non ha diletto*' but slurs over the *la gir* or *largir*. The manuscripts do not help us.

La gire means 'turn there', and *largir* is 'to give away freely', 'to give likeness freely'? Or is *simiglglianza* the subject?

For purpose of translation one has, as Rossetti remarks, to cut through various knots, and make arbitrary decisions. I have perforce, here as elsewhere, selected one of the possible meanings, or at least attempted to do so, but without any wish to insist upon it, or to conceal either the depths of my ignorance, or my width of uncertainty. Gilson[1] summarizes Grosseteste's ideas on light as follows:

'*La lumière est une substance corporelle très subtile et qui se rapproche de l'incorporel. Ses propriétés caractéristiques sont de s'engendrer elle-même perpetuellement et de se diffuser sphériquement autour d'un point d'une manière instantanée. Donnons-nous un point lumineux, il s'engendre instantanément autour de ce point comme centre une sphère lumineuse immense. La diffusion de la lumière ne peut être contrariée que par deux raisons; ou bien elle rencontre une obscurité qui l'arrête, ou bien elle finit par atteindre la limite extrême de sa raréfaction, et la propagation de la lumière prend fin par là même. Cette substance extremement ténue est aussie l'étoffe dont toutes choses sont faites; elle est la première forme corporelle et ce que certains nomment la corporéité.*'

This French summary is most able, and most lucid. It is far more suggestive of the canzone, Donna mi Prega, than the original Latin

[1] Etienne Gilson, *Philosophie du Moyen Age*, Payot, Paris, 1925.

of Grosseteste,[1] but my suggestion is not that Guido is a mere dilettante poetaster dragging in philosophic terms or caught by a verbal similarity (e.g. as Lorenzo Medici, dabbling in Platonism in his rhymed account of talk with Ficino). For 'risplende in sè perpetuale effecto' we find the Latin approximation (*De Luce*, the Baur edition):

p. 51. *Lux enim per se in omnem partem se ipsam diffundit* ...
.... *a puncto lucis sphaera lucis quamvis magna* ... *generetur* ...

p. 52, *Lux prima forma in materia creata, seipsam seipsam* ...
multiplicans (? *multiplicans = largir*).

p. 56, *aer quoque ex se corpus spirituale vel spiritum corporalem generans.*

p. 58, *Forma autem, ut pote simplicissima unitatis obtinet locum,* as bearing on the '*formato*' or '*non formato loco*'.

p. 73, *aut transitus radii ad rem visam est rectus per medium diaphani unius generis* ... *aut transitus* ... *modi spiritualis, per quam ipsum est speculum* ... *transitus* ... *per* .. *plura diaphana* ...

p. 91, reference to Plato ... *anima substantia seipsam movens.*

p. 345, *formam lucis in aere vel in corpore* ... *transparente* .. *nec lucis essentiam ibi esse* ... *conceditur* ... *nomine formae habitus consentitur* ...

p. 347, *aeternae rationes rerum causatarum*, from Timaeus.

Grosseteste derives from Arabic treatises on perspective. It is too much to say that Guido had, perforce, read the Bishop of Lincoln, but certainly that is the *sort* of thing he had read.

His definition of '*l'accidente*', i.e. the whole poem, is a scholastic definition in form, it is as clear and definite as the prose treatises of the period, it shows an equal acuteness of thought. It seems to me quite possible that the whole of it is a sort of metaphor on the generation of light, or that at any rate greater familiarity with the philosophy of the period would elucidate the remaining tangles, particularly if one search for the part of philosophy that was in a state of activity in the years 1270-1290. One cannot absolutely rule out the possibility of Guido's having seen some scraps of MS. by Roger Bacon, although that is, perhaps, unlikely.

[1] L. Baur, *Die philosophischen Werke des Robert Grosseteste,* Münster, 1912, *Beiträge z. Gesch. Phil. d. Mittelalt.* Latin text and German Commentary, vols. IX and XVIII, 4-6.

Considering the quality of Guido's mind as manifest in indisputable passages it would, I think, be the greatest possible error to imagine that any part of the poem is decoration or stuffing. '*Talento de voler*' looks weak, but may not even that be due to an *idée fixe* on our part—'*di voler provare*' meaning, perhaps, technically, 'try to prove', and the whole phrase, 'I have no inclination to attempt proof' rather than 'wish to will to prove'? If not, the *talento* is dragged in for the rhyme, and we must count it a blemish.

It may not be amiss, as illustrating the contemporary situation of philosophic thought in the British desert, and the recognition of one serious mind by another, to recall an incident of fifteen years past. When the late T. E. Hulme was trying to be a philosopher in that milieu, and fussing about Sorel and Bergson and getting them translated into English, I spoke to him one day of the difference between Guido's precise interpretive metaphor, and the Petrarchan fustian and ornament, pointing out that Guido thought in accurate terms; that the phrases correspond to definite sensations undergone; in fact very much what I had said in my early preface to the Sonnets and Ballate.

Hulme took some time over it in silence, and then finally said: 'That is very interesting'; and after a pause: 'That is more interesting than anything I ever read in a book.'

I was talking of certain passages in the Sonnets and Ballate, and not of this canzone, but the point should hold as well for the canzone.

What we need now is not so much a commentator as a lexicon. It is the precise sense of certain terms *as understood at that particular epoch* that one would like to have set before one.

For example does '*intenzion*' mean intention (a matter of will)? does it mean intuition, intuitive perception, or does the line hold the same meaning as that in Yeats's Countess Cathleen, *intenzion* being intention, and *ragione* meaning not reason, but 'being right'?

At such points the commentators either branch off and give their own theories about the cosmos in general, or they restate with vague verbosity what Guido has said with greater pre- and con- cision.

As the philosophy of the time has been completely scrapped, there are very few specialists who can help us. I should be glad to hear from anyone who has more definite knowledge. Up to the present I have found out what I have found out by concentration on the text, and not by reading commentators, and I strongly suspect that is the road the next man will have to follow.

There are certain definite impasses, for definite palaeographical reasons. The copyists simply did not know, and we are unlikely to find any more anterior manuscripts.

The other dimension of the poem is its lyricism, in the strictest sense of the term. It is made for song not for rhetorical declamation; on which count Dante twice mentions it in *De Vulgari Eloquio*, II, 12. First in connection with his own: '*Donne ch' avete intelletto d' amore*'; and secondly in comparison with his '*Poscia ch' Amor del tutto m' ha lasciato*'.

THE CANZONE

As it appears in the manuscript 'Ld', Laurenziano 46-40, folio 32 verso, with a few errors corrected. Accents added from the Giuntine edition.

Edizione Guinta 1527.

DONNA mi priegha
               perch' i volglio dire   *io*
                              uno
D'un accidente
        che sovente
               é fero
Ed é sí altero
        ch'é chiamato amore   *Amore*

SICCHE chi l negha   *Si chì lo*
          possa il ver sentire   *Ed a'l*
Ond a 'l presente
        chonoscente
            chero   *io nò*
Perch i no spero
        ch om di basso chore   *c' huom*

                       raggio ne
ATAL ragione portj chonoscenza
Chè senza
        natural dimostramento   *hó*
Non o talento   *Ld. most rare*
        di voler provare   *Ld dove ei*
Laove nascie e chì lo fá criare   *posa, è*

E QUAL è sua virtu e sua potenza

L'essenza

        e poi ciaschun suo movimento

E 'l piacimento

        che 'l fá dire amare

E se hom per veder lo puó mostrare:—

    sia . . ver-
    tute,
    e potenza
    MS. *per*

    huomo

IN quella parte

        dove sta memoria

Prende suo stato

        sí formato

        chome

Diafan dal lume

        d' una schuritade

    Edizione
    Giuntina
    1527
    memora
    MS. *su*

    oscurltate

LA qual da Marte

        viene e fa dimora

Elgli é creato

        e a sensato

        nome

D'alma chostume

        di chor volontade

    Loqual

    ed há

    è di cor

VIEN da veduta forma ches s' intende

Che 'l prende

        nel possibile intelletto

Chome in subgetto

        locho e dimoranza

E in quella parte mai non a possanza

PERCHÉ de qualitatde non disciende

Risplende

        in sé perpetuale effecto

Non a diletto

        mà consideranza

Perche non pote laire simiglglianza:—

    ch ès'
    Giuntine
    and Ld
    Chè prende

    há posanza
    MS. *Ca*
    pesança
    MS.
    risprende
    Edizione
    Giuntina
    1527
    há

NON é virtute

        mà da questa vene

    Si, ch' ei
    non puote
    largir
    simigli-
    anza

Perfezione   *dà quella*
                    ches si pone   *Perchè*
                                        tale   *perfettion*
                                                              si
Non razionale
                    mà che si sente dicho

FUOR di salute   *omits si*
                        giudichar mantene
E l antenzione   *Chè là in-*
                        per ragione   *tenzion*
                                        vale   *per ragion*
Discerne male   MS.
                        in chui é vizio amicho   *Diserue*

DI sua virtu seghue ispesso morte   *sua*
Se forte   *potenza . . .*
            la virtú fosse impedita   *spesso*
La quale aita
                la contrara via   *contraria*
Nonche opposito natural sia

MÀ quanto che da ben perfett e torte   *non perchè*
Per sorte   *opposta*
            non po dir om ch abbi vita   *naturale*
                                                             buon
Che stabilita   *perfetto*
            non a singnioria   *tort' é*
                                                             MS. *forte*
A simil puó valer quant uom l obblia:—   *può . . . c'*
                                                             haggia
                                                             hà
                                                             valor
                                                             quando
                                                             s' oblia

LESSER é quando   MS. omits
                    lo volere a tanto   *é*
                                                             é
Ch oltre   *oltra*
            di natura
                        torna   *s' adorna*
Poi non si addorna
                        di riposo maj

MOVE changiando cholr riso in pianto   *core, è riso*
E lla fighura   *è pianto*

con paura
                    storna
Pocho soggiorna
                    anchor di lui vedraj

CHE n gente di valore il piu si trova
La nova
                    qualità move a sospirj   *i sospiri*
E vol ch om mirj   MS. Ld
                    in un formato locho   *Destando-*
Destandos' ira la qual manda focho   *sitj*
                                                            loqual
INMAGINAR nol puo hom che nol prova   *puote*
E non si mova
MS. Ca *Ne mova già* perch' a llui si tirj   *Già non*
E non si aggirj   Edizione
                    per trovarvi giocho   Giuntina
E certamente gran saver nè pocho:—   1527.
                                                            giri

DA ssimil tragge   *Nè certa-*
                    complessione e sghuardj   *mente*
Che fá parere   *Di*
                    lo piacere   MS. *com-*
                                                            prenssione
                    piu certo   *sguardo.*
Non puó choverto   omits *e*
                    star quand é si giunto   omits *piu*

NON giá selvagge
                    la biltá son dardj   *le . . dardo*
Ch a tal volere   *Chè tal*
                    per temere
                    sperto   *esperto*
Hom seghue merto   *Consegue*
                    spirito che punto   *ch' é*

E NON si puó chonosciere per lo viso
Chompriso   *, bianco,*
                    biancho in tale obbietto chade   *vade*
E chi ben aude

forma non si vede   *Cao*
Perchè lo mena chi dallui procede   *informa*

                                                     dà lei

FUOR di cholore essere diviso   *d'essere*
Asciso   *Assiso*
            mezzo schuro luce rade   *in mezzo*
Fuor d'ongni fraude   *oscuro luci*
                    dice dengno in fede
Chè solo da chostui nasce merzede:—   *di*

TU puoj sichuramente gir chanzone
Dove ti piace ch i t o sí ornata   *ch' io t' hó*
Ch assa lodata   *si adornata*
            sará tua ragione   *assai*
Dalle persone
ch anno intendimento
Di star con l' altre tu non aj talento:—

THE OTHER DIMENSION

The danger of a canzone composed entirely in hendeca-syllabics is that of going heavy. Dante avoids it in *Donne ch' Avete* without using inner rhymes. Here Guido employs them.

The canzone of Guido's which Dante takes as a model of 'construction' is not the *Donna mi Prega* but *Poiche di Doglia*, of which only the first strophe is preserved, and this strophe for some obscure reason (or from simple habits of imitation) all editors insist on printing as a ballata, beginning with Di Giunta and ending, curiously enough, with Rivalta. Apart from Dante's clear reference to it, one should be able to observe its formation.

The reader will not arrive at a just appreciate of the canzone unless he be aware that there are three kinds of melopœia, that is to say, poems made to speak, to chant and to sing. This canzone, Guido's poetry in general, and the poems of medieval Provence and Tuscany in general, were all made to be sung. Relative estimates of value inside these periods must take count of the cantabile values.

Modern professors with lifted eyebrows patronizing Dante's judgments in such matters appear to me rather like hypothetical persons who having taken an elementary course in phonetics or physics and having heard their wives' sisters play Chaminade, bring out: 'Bach's opinions on the fugue which our later criticism has superseded. . . .'

The canzone was to poets of this period what the fugue was to musicians in Bach's time. It is a highly specialized form, having its own self-imposed limits. I trust I have managed to print the *Donna mi Prega* is such a way that its articulations strike the eye without need of a rhyme table. The strophe is here seen to consist of four parts, the second lobe equal to the first as required by the rules of the canzone; and the fourth happening to equal the third, which is not required by the rules as Dante explains them.

Each strophe is articulated by 14 terminal and 12 inner rhyme sounds, which means that 52 out of every 154 syllables are bound into pattern. The strophe reverses the proportions of the sonnet, as the short lobes precede the longer. This reversal is obviously of advantage to the strophe *as part of* a longer composition.

At this point we divagate for fuller ultimate reference. The prestige of the sonnet in English is a relic of insular ignorance. The sonnet was not a great poetic *invention*. The sonnet occurred automatically when some chap got stuck in the effort to make a canzone. His 'genius' consisted in the recognition of the fact that he had come to the end of his subject matter.

It should not be necessary for me to quote the whole of the *De Vulgari Eloquio*. That notable opusculum is available in many and cheap editions. My own brief study of Arnaut Daniel may throw a further light on earlier phases of the canzone in the *lingua materna*.

As to the use of canzoni in English, whether for composition or in translation: it is not that there aren't rhymes in English; or enough rhymes or even enough two-syllable rhymes, but that the English two-syllable rhymes are of the wrong timbre and weight. They have extra consonants at the end, as in *flowing* and *going;* or they go squashy; or they fluff up as in *snowy* and *goeth*. They are not *rime agute;* they do not offer readily the qualities and contrasts that Dante has discussed so ably in *De Eloquio*.

Even so, it is not that one 'cannot' use them but that they demand at times, sacrifice of values that had not come into being and were therefore not missed in Limoges, A.D. 1200. Against which we have our concealed rhymes and our semi-submerged alliteration. (*En passant*, the alliteration in Guido's canzone is almost as marked as the rhyming though it enters as free component.)

It is not that one language cannot be made to do what another has done, but that it is not always expeditious to approach the same goal by the same alley. I do not think rhyme-aesthetic, *any* rhyme-aesthetic, can ever do as much damage to English verse as that done by latinization, in Milton's time and before. The rhyme pattern is, after all, a matter of chiselling, and a question of the *lima amorosa*, whereas latinization is a matter or compost, and in the very substance of the speech. By latinization I mean here the attempt to use an uninflected language as if it were an inflected one, i.e. as if each word had a little label or postscript telling the reader at once what part it takes in the sentence, and specifying its several relations. Not only does such usage—with remnants of Latin order—ruin the word order in English, but it shows a fundamental mis-comprehension of the organism of the language, and fundamental stupidity of this kind is bound to spread its effects through the whole fibre of a man's writing.

HENDECASYLLABLES

Another prevalent error is that of dealing with Italian hendeca-syllables as if they were English 'iambic pentameter'. One is told in college that Italian verse is not accentual but syllabic but I can't remember anyone's having ever presented the Anglo-American reader with a lucid discrimination between the two systems of measurement.

Some day I shall erect a monument to the books one reads in country hotels. Their titles and their authors evade one. One is not there 'on business', one does not take notes and make excerpts. Let me, however, record here, that once in Sicily I came upon a century-old Italian school-book containing intelligent remarks upon metric. It was probably G. Biagioli's *Tractato d'Armonia di Verso Italiano* (Palermo, 1836), with reference to the *Elementi de Poesia* of G. Gherardini. The author did not 'lay down rules', he merely observed that Dante's hendecasyllables were composed of combinations of rhythm units of various shapes and sizes and that these pieces were put together in lines so as to make, roughly, eleven syllables in all. I say 'roughly' because of the liberties allowed in elision. I had discovered this fact for myself in Indiana twenty years before and in my own work and made use of the knowledge continually, but I wish to salute Messrs Biagioli and Gherardini.

This system represented versification when it was in a healthy state, when *motz* had not been divorced from *son* and before the sonnet had got in its dirty work.

Historically the sonnet, the 'little tune', had already in Guido's day become a danger to composition. It marks an ending or at least a decline of metric invention. It marks the beginning of the divorce of words and music. Sonnets with good musical setting are rare. The spur to the musician is slight. The monotony of the 14 even lines as compared to the constantly varying strophes of Ventadour or of Arnaut; the vocal heaviness of the hendecasyllable unrelieved by a shorter turn are all blanketing impediments for the music. This is not to say that the unrelieved hendecasyllable is impossible, and Dante, seeking the difficult, is quite right to set the canzone in unrelieved hendecasyllables as the grand bogey of technical mastery.

Guido, as we here observe, and as Dante had observed before us:

rithimorum repercussionem frequenter videtur assumptum.

He keeps the sound sharp and light in the throat by the rhymes inside the long line. Even some of the best Provençals, using a strophe of half his length, are unable to keep this cantabile virtue. All of which is probably a matter of specialists who will not be content with any general statement but will want to compare sound by sound the actual examples of mastersong that *totam artem comprehendunt.*

But one owes it to the general reader to jab his curiosity as to the degree of sonorous art, one might almost say of concrete or material sonority, required in this exposition of a general theme in the case of the *Donna mi Prega;* and of its relativity to the sonnet.

Of the great songs one remembers, that is songs with music, from *Ierusalem Mirabilis* to *Le Pauvre Laboureur,* and from that to Debussy's settings of Charles d'Orléans, does one remember a sonnet? And if so, how many?

The canzone, any canzone, is obviously in intention a *capolavoro,* a consummation of métier. Perhaps no poet has left half a dozen, or shall we say that Dante and Arnaut Daniel alone have left a half dozen each, that anyone can remember? If I exaggerate, I do not exaggerate very greatly.

Of Guido this one survives undisputed. There is one inferior canzone ascribed to him; there is a strophe of another (*Poiche di Doglia*); and there is, I should be inclined to sustain, an approximate certainty of his having written the canzone to Fortune.[1]

Apart from *Donna mi Prega*, Guido's reputation rests largely on the ballate, more or less his own field. That is to say, for purposes of song he chose a lighter and freer form, *not* the sonnet. In the ballata the first lobe is not immediately re-echoed. Tradition is that the ballata is made from popular dance-song, a scrap of folk-song caught up for the beauty of its tune, or for some felicity, and then made into an art-form more emotional and more emotive than the form of the Italian canzone.

Note that by A.D. 1290 the sonnet is already ceasing to be lyric, it is already the epistle without a tune, it is in a state of becoming, and tends already to oratorical *pronunciamento*.

The strophes of canzoni are perforce symmetrical as the musical composition is only one-fifth or one-sixth the length of the verbal composition and has to be repeated. I don't believe we can prove complete absence of modulation; or that in case of canzon in tenzone one should assume impossibility of answer to tonic from dominant. Neither do we know what happened to the tune of the sestina while the recurrence scheme was performing its evolution; the six units of the tune may, and in the case of Arnaut's *Oncle ed Ongla* could very well, have followed some permutation of modes or key. The aesthetic of the carry-through of one rhyme scheme from strophe to strophe is of Provençal not of Tuscan composition.

We know something of twelfth-century music, or have at least some grounds for particular conjecture, graphs, that is, of pitch sequence for some two hundred melodies; we are without any such comparable guide for 'Dante and his Circle'. I know of no manuscript containing music of that particular period; the one 'item' in the Siena *Archivio* is not a fragment of melody, but two lines of police record: Casella jugged for being out after curfew.

But considering the finesse of some of the Limousin melodies there is nothing to prevent our conjecture that the decadence of verbal mastery in Italian poetry may have paced a parallel decline in the

[1] 1934. Whole question of authenticity of the other canzoni thrown wide open again by examination of manuscript I. ix. 18 in Comunale di Siena. For further details, see my *Guido Cavalcanti: Rime*, Genova, Anno X. Vide: *Tre Canzoni*. Quaderni dell' Accademia Chigiana, Siena, 1949, certainly authentic.

melodic component. This would apply to the perfection of the single line or the 'snatch' of song; to the close fit of word and melody, but not, presumably, to the whole form of the music. One may summarize the phases of development of the canzon as follows:

1. Strophe with few terminal sounds, no more than four sounds, repeated throughout the poem, meaning that the same rhyme would occur 18 or 24 times in the poem, or even more. After a century or so this grew monotonous, and we have

2. Use of *rimas escarsas* which may mean either the hunting up of less usual terminal sounds, or the spacing out of the rhymes. In Arnaut's *L'Aura Amara*, we have 14 different rhyme sounds only 3 of which repeat inside the strophe, 11 of them repeat only from one strophe to the rest, that is occur only 6 or 7 times in the poem.

3. Abandonment of the carry-through in *Can Chai la Fueilla*. Here in Guido's canzone eight different sounds form the pattern inside the strophe; five occur four times, and three twice.

To be well done this patterning must lighten, not clog the movement, either of sense or sound.

As to the atrocities of my translation, all that can be said in excuse is that they are, I hope, for the most part intentional, and committed with the aim of driving the reader's perception further into the original than it would without them have penetrated. The melodic structure is properly indicated—and for the first time—by my disposition of the Italian text, but even that firm indication of the rhyme and the articulation of the strophe does not stress *all* the properties of Guido's triumph in sheer musicality.

One must strive almost at any cost to avoid a sort of mealy mumbling almost universally tolerated in English. If English verse undulates the average ear tolerates it, or even welcomes it, though the undulation be but as a wobble of bread-dough, utterly noncantabile, even when not wholly unspeakable.

I have not given an English 'equivalent' for the *Donna mi Prega;* at the utmost I have provided the reader, unfamiliar with old Italian, an instrument that may assist him in gauging *some* of the qualities of the original.

All this is not so unconnected with our own time as it might seem. Those writers to whom *vers libre* was a mere 'runnin' dahn th' road', videlicet escape, and who were impelled thereto by no inner need of, or curiosity concerning, the quantitative element in metric, having come to the end of that lurch, lurch back not into experiment with the canzone or any other unexplored form, but into the stock and trade sonnet.

THE VOCABULARY

In accordance with the views exposed in the preceding pages, and recognizing the justness of Karl Vossler's remarks about our 'schwankenden Kenntnis', but being dubious of the sense in which he applies the term, or the justness of applying it to the 'nicht weniger schwankenden psychologischen Terminologie Cavalcantis' I have spent a certain amount of time trying to deal with the vocabulary used in the canzone, and elsewhere in Guido.

The following pages have appeared or may appear elsewhere in discussion of Luigi Valli's theories *re* secret conspiracies, mystic brotherhoods, widely distributed (and uniform) cipher in 'all' or some poems of the period, etc. I do not believe that much, if anything, that Valli says can be applied to the *Donna mi Prega*. Some of it, perhaps a good deal of it, may possibly apply to the sonnets; at any rate Valli deserves thanks for disturbing a too facile acceptance of cut and dried acceptances. In one or two cases where I think him wrong, I certainly owe him a quickened curiosity, and a better guess than I should have made without the irritant of his volume.[1]

I now set down simply citations and passages from works accessible to Cavalcanti (or contemporaneous or slightly later), where technical philosophical terms occur in a sense compatible with, or casting light on the usage of the same or similar terms in his writing. In the case of the canzone itself the reader may, if still interested, compare the clarity and profundity of the literal sense of the poem, with the, to me at least, far less satisfactory and coherent exposition by Signor Valli.

If he have a long memory he may even recall that I cited Avicenna and Averroes as, probably, the main origins of Guido's philosophical location, and indicated his possible acquaintance with Grosseteste. As to my further digging:

1. Where various MSS. and most editions read *destando s' ira*, I had left the reading of MS. Ld, *destandositj* in order to indicate the uncertainty of the reading. I was looking for some possible equivalent of the Latin *sitis*. This is not necessary, as *Ira* makes sense, but it

[1] Luigi Valli, 'Il Linguaggio Segreto di Dante'. Roma, 'Optima', 1928.

does not mean Wrath. It is a very good illustration of the way words
shift in meaning through careless usage. Dr Walther Echstein of
Vienna having given me a clue, a list of more or less forgotten
technical and theological lexicons, I find in that of Johannes Tytz
(pub. 1619) that *Ire, Ira* 'according to Aristotle' (by which Tytz
obviously means some Latin translation of Aristotle) is *accensio
sanguinis circum cor;* which can be translated with the varying
shades: 'enflaming, inflammation, or enkindling of the blood about
the heart'. Tytz continues citing other writers by abbreviation:
'Ioan. Damas. vaporatione fellis, vel perturbatione fiens (? splenis).
Hugo. irrationabilis perturbatio mentis. Aug. ulciscendi libido.
Casid. immoderatus animi motus, concitatus ad poenam seu vindic-
tam. Gers. ira est duplex, non est peccatum imo magis poena.' That
is to say that in the norm of use *Ire* meant the commotion. It is only
its excesses that meant 'Wrath'. 'Species Irae excesse effectu nom-
inatae sunt, furor, insania, rancor. Non puram passionem, imo
quamdam actionem qua deordinatur homo, et quantum ad Deum et
quantum ad proximum.'

The six daughters of Ire are: 'rixa, timor mentis, contumelia,
clamor, indignatio, blasphemia.' This also lights a line in one of the
sonnets. 'Che ciascun' altra in ver di lei chiamo ira.' I made a dull
translation of it eighteen years ago, because I was interested in the
other lines of the sonnet and that one seemed merely a blank. The
Ira is, as we see, not wrath. And the line means: 'So that by comparison with her, any other woman means merely a senseless confusion.'

2. *Chiamo* and *Dico* appear in Guido's Canzone and the Sonnets.
They look at first, second and third sight like padding. A plunge into
the prose philosophers of the period shows that they are used as
'*I define*', or '*for this I should use the term*'. And that they thus in verse
give an air of leisure and precision; are not cotton wool but an
elegance.

3. I guessed right in stressing the difference between *Amore* (noun)
and *Amare* (verb) in the first strophe. The philosophical difference is
that a noun is a significant sound which makes no discrimination as to
time. 'Nomen est vox significativa, ad placitum, sine tempore, cuius
nulla pars est significativa separate.' The verb locates in time.
'Verbum logice consideratum est quod consignificat tempus'
(Albertus Magnus).

The reader will see that the English version of St John loses this philosophical or metaphysical shade in reading: 'the word became flesh', for 'verbum caro', etc.

4. Perhaps the strongest justification of collateral research is to be found when we came to the passage which the best editors have up to now read (with various spellings):

> 'che prende—nel possibile intelletto
> come 'n subietto.'

There is no metrical or palaeographic objection to this reading which occurs in several very early codices. But I find in Avicenna's *Metaphysices Compendium* (trad, Nematallah Carame; pub. Pont. Inst. Orient. Stud. 1926) that when one thing enters or exists in another as a wooden peg in a wall this thing is not *accidens* in a 'subject'. Therefore if the phrase reads *che prende* Guido is either using very careless language or means that his image of the seen form busts up or melts when it enters the possible (or receptive) intellect.

Lib. 1, Cap. 3, III. ' Quando autem etc. non sicut palus et murus, sed utraque in altera diffusa secundum totam suam essentiam ... etc. Omnis autem essentia cuius subsistentia est in subiecto est accidens.'

So that turning to Codex Ce, Chigiana L. V. 176 which contains the Del Garbo exegesis of the canzone we find *che 'l prende;* it is slightly rougher metrically, but it is presumably the correct reading as neither from the character of the excellent old MSS. nor from Del Garbo's prose have we any reason to think that either he or the scribe inserted the extra pronoun. The single letter would show both that Guido read Avicenna (or someone who agreed with that dissociation of ideas) and more important for our literary purpose that his language is speech of precision.

The MSS. Ce, Mm, Rh, Lh, Lb and La

Michele Barbi suspects that Ce shows the writing of Boccaccio 'in his old age when his hand was no longer steady'. This might well be. Boccaccio was a friend of the Garbo family as we know by his sonnet on the death of Dino's son. Dino had a wide reputation as a physician, he attended Mussato and we have record of the bracing effect of his presence in the sick room.

The reading *che 'l* persists in MSS. Mm, Rh, Lh, in the text given with Garbo's commentary in Lb and finally in La from which we can calculate the probable duration of the medieval tradition or at least the interest in, and knowledge of, Avicenna, etc. The Medicean scholar who transcribed La was presumably the last copyist to understand the text placed before him. This single detail gives much greater authority to La than one would otherwise have accorded it.

Avicenna is, *en passant*, one of the most attractive authors of the period, I recommend to Signor Valli's attention the *seicento* edition of the *De Almahad* which contains the paragraph beginning 'Amplius in coitu phantasia'.

5. The rashness of hasty conclusion is again indicatable from another line where the change of a single letter would shift our whole series of guesses concerning Guido's philosophical leanings. There is absolutely no certainty whatsoever in the present state of our knowledge, and I think 'scientific' certainty will probably remain out of the question. The importance of the matter will never outweigh the difficulties or the value of living men's time.

In my text I gave *laire simiglglianʒa;* other writers gave *largir* or some variant, there are more than a dozen readings of this passage, which indicates that the copyists were puzzled, and in the end had to put down something whether they understood it or not. Reading *'largir'* one can at a pinch cast out guesses regarding Grosseteste or about some treatise on light and maximum of diffusion. But supposing that the illegible or incomprehensible word were not the *largir* or *la ire* or *la gire,* but that the copyist had dropped an *r* from the *pote* that precedes it; we should have *porte l'aire.* The reading does not occur in any MSS. But the single letter would throw the passage into 'pneumatic philosophy'. There is plenty of pneumatism in Guido's sonnets.

The study of terms of abuse has been neglected. For centuries if you disliked a man you called him a Manichaean, as in some circles to-day you call him a Bolshevic to damage his earning capacity. But suppose the term Epicurean in 1290 had not become merely a term of abuse, a pejorative likely to damage the slandered object. Suppose that some germ of the admittedly uncertain sense of Epicureanism still existed, and that tradition is correct and has even a shade of precise meaning when it calls Guido-Epicurean, one is within one's rights in wondering whether the pneumatism comes *via* Epicurus.

Salvador says that the doctrine comes originally out of Egypt, and Fr. Fiorentino that it comes *via* Democritus; it exists in both Stoic and Epicurean forms.

One cannot insist on the reading *porte,* but it does indicate the kind of possibility one must consider before plumping it down that Guido belonged to such or such gang of mystics.

With the general precision of terminology in an age when highbrows had very little save terminology to occupy their attention, we have no right to suppose that the meaning of Epicureanism had been filed down to mean merely 'exaggerated and lazy hedonism'.

According to the pneumatici the likeness of things, or a sort of emanation of them was carried upon the pneuma, or special air, and entered the hearts, etc. If Guido's sonnet:

'Per gli occhi fiere un spirito sottile'

is not as thoroughgoing a bit of pneumatism as one could desire, it is at any rate a more complete exposition of its modus than I am likely to get into a couple of lines. If I muddle the question it is at least one that has to be considered. As is also the then opinion, or ten dozen opinions regarding hypostasis; 'lumen est colorum hypostasis' says one writer out of agreement, it would appear, with subsequent science.

The serious author (I was about to write: Confound it, the serious author) must really look into these details before blandly, or energumenically, assuring us that the canzone expresses some one particular dogma, let alone that dogma in cipher.

I don't think I began translating it with any preconceived notion of what I should find: but if ever poem seemed to me a struggle for clear definition, that poem is the *Donna mi Prega.* Nor do I see where a code cipher could be slipped into it. Valli would indubitably leap on the first word, *Donna,* but there is nothing to prove the contention that even if Guido is writing to a fellow lodge member he is writing in cipher. There is the *bianco* in the last strophe, which Valli might connect with his Augustinian 'dealbatio'. But we are still far from heresy, let alone such an one as he postulates, a violent and dangerous heresy which would land the lot of them 'nel rogo', indeed the odour of roast heretic is far more prevalent in Valli's conjecture than in the pages of contemporary chronicle.

Taking the analysis from another angle. Or let us say, looking for its Christian affiliation: of Augustine I find nothing but the agreement with Augustine's sequence of

'esse, species rei, et ordo'

corresponding to Persons of the Trinity, and, in the human spirit to

'memory, intelligence and will'.

This sequence is followed in the *Donna mi Prega*. But it is probably too general to serve as indication of anything in particular. One can merely observe that there is in this connection no contradiction between the two authors.

There is certainly more meat for us in Avicenna's passage, already noticed.

'Deinceps, si recipiens in sui constitutivo non indiget eo quod in ipso recipitur, tunc hoc vocamus recepti subjectum; si autem eo indiget, tunc non subjectum ipsum vocaremus sed forsitan hylen (῞ΥΛΗ) vocabimus. Omnis essentia quae non sit in subiecto est substantia. Omnis autem essentia cuius subsistentia est in subiecto est accidens' (*Metaphysices Compendium*, Tr. I, Cap. III, 3. p. 6; Bishop Carame's translation, Pont. Inst. Orient. Stud. 1926).

Albertus Magnus also offers: 'Secundum autem accidens memorabilia sunt quaecumque sunt cum phantasia, sicut sunt intellecta intellectus possibilis quae ex phantasmatibus iterum applicantur, quando ex intellectis anima reflectitur in rem prius per sensum acceptam'. But his tone of mind is not quite in keeping with Guido's thought.

There is, as I had indicated, a mare's nest in *'intenzione'*; in some theologians it is a matter of will, with the meaning 'intention'. But from Alfarabi into Averroes, and from them into Albertus there is a first and a second *intentio*, which are modes of perception. Duns Scotus's 'voluntas super intellectu' seems to have no bearing on the poem. The whole poem is alive with Eriugenian vigour.

Occam, after Guido's death, has written: 'terminus conceptus est intentio seu passio animae aliquid naturaliter significans vel consignificans, nata esse pars propositionibus mentalis.' That is no use as 'source' but it might serve as determining verbal usage *circa* 1328.

At times and with some texts before me, 'natural dimostramento', would seem to imply almost biological proof. In postulating Guido as 'the great logician', which Boccaccio says that he was, I do not want to exaggerate, or cast him in the fifteenth century in place of the thirteenth.

However, if Guido and his correspondents are a gang (secret) of Nonconformists, aching to reform mother church, plotting and corresponding in hyper-heretical cipher, the most indigestible morsel for Signor Valli is Egidio Colonna, il beato. Colonna is a very dead author, possibly no Anglo-Saxon has seen his name save in some brief passage or footnote to the effect that he wrote a comment on Guido, and seen it but to be bored. Some old geezer has written a commentary. He is indeed a very dead author, my sincere commiseration goes out to anyone who has to read his appallingly prolix work on the education of princes. (Dante in *Convito*, IV, 24, 1. 97 disposed of an Egidio Eremita.) The researcher's first jolt comes, or at least my first jolt came in discovering how many editions of his work were printed between the years 1500 and 1600; my second in finding (Fr. Fiorentino's *Manual of Philosophy*) that the Frate Egidio was chief among the immediate disciples of Aquinas. 'Tra i seguaci di questa prima età spetta il primo luogo ad Egidio Colonna.' So that when the editor of the *Parnaso* mentions Egidio's commentary in evidence of Guido's position, it was for that age very much what it would be if we found to-day a commentary by William James on some lyrist whose work had filled less than a hundred pages.

Are we to conclude that the eminent Thomist was gulled, or that he was a heretic ramping in secret and concealing the poet's meaning?

In either case Signor Valli should look at Egidio's exegesis. It begins aptly for his purpose with the secret fountain, obviously the source or font of tradition, the lady sends out her messengers, the first of whom is King Solomon, excellent for the mystic theory, but the second is Ovidius Naso, and while you and I, gentle reader, might grant that Ovid had in him more divine wisdom than all the Fathers of the Church put together, would Signor Valli at this point join our party?

Of course if Valli can seriously find his ascetic cipher in the ballata beginning:

'In un boschetto trovai pastorella'

he might even find it in Ovid's Eclogue that begins with the words: 'Aestus erat'. But would the Frate Egidio? Would the eminent Aristotelian have chosen just these three men, Solomon, Ovid and Guido, as messengers from our lady of Paphos, or from the Divina Sapienza? Was Ovid also singing the yearning of the passive intellect for the active, and if so did he suspect it?

There are still other difficulties before Signor Valli, but perhaps I have mentioned enough. And perhaps Guido was enamoured as Dante has remarked of a certain Madonna Primavera, who, as Dante does not remark, had set the dance in Langue d'Oc and in Lemosi.

And even if Dante's admiration for Virgil's 'style' is a cryptogram meaning not Virgil's style but his 'maniera di simboleggiare' (Valli); might not Guido's disrespect of Virgil free him from charge of simboligization?

By all of which I do not mean Valli is necessarily wrong in his main contention. He is merely a very bad advocate, trusting to conviction rather than to clear-headed observation and logic. If he will throw out his suppositions, and his inept evidence and stick to the unsolved enigmas one can give him many passages on which the, by him, hated positivisti could gain no foothold whatever.

Arnaut would be perhaps better ground for him than Guido. What for example is 'Mantle of Indigo'? Is 'doma', in 'cils di doma', an equivalent to the Italian word *domma*, meaning dogma?

If Arnaut says 'I love her more than god does her of the dogma', does he speak of a secret doctrine more precious to its followers than the orthodox? Does the illegible 'di noigandres' boggle a Greek 'ennoia' or 'dianoia'? At least it is open ground, and if Valli chose to assert these things no one could bring proof against him. Coming to Guido, he could find various inexplicable passages: 'Morte' would indeed fit his cipher in several places; as in

> 'che Morte 'l porta in man tagliato in croce'.

The

> 'beyond life's compass thrown,
>
> .   .   .   .   .   .
>
> melted of bronze or carven in tree or stone',
> 'Fatto di pietra o di rame o di legno',

would serve him. What is the magic river 'filled full of lamias' that Guido sends to Pinella in return for her caravan? Who is 'del tondo sesto' and why the 'sixth round'?

It would be as myopic to reject Valli's theory as impossible, as it would be to think Valli had proved his case, or even approached a proof, or considered the limits and definition of what he says he is proving.

There are places where attempted application of his code would turn a good poem into a mere piece of priggishness and vain theory, in no way accounting for its manifest lyric impulse, or for the emotional force in its cadence. Here the code theory will, naturally, be as unwelcome and annoying, as it is welcome when he tries to turn a bad poem into a subject of historic interest, or to at least an amusing riddle. Valli must try to imagine what sort of mysticism his adepts and neophytes practised, and what its effect would have been, for certainly neither Frederick II nor Cavalcanti were openly famed as ascetics. Frederick has been accused of nearly everything, even, recently, of orthodoxy (to the great distress of his admirers), but never yet of timidity.

If Guido is concealing anything it is certainly not the spirit of complete personal independence, nor yet of open defiance of piety— for whoever be the heroine of the sonnet 'Una figura . . .' its blasphemous intention is open to the simplest capacity. If sect existed, Guido's pastorellas, as distinct from donne, may as well imply contempt for the sect as for anything else in the neighbourhood.

A really good mind throws out not only the *idées reçues* of its time, but the fancy snobbism of the 'elect'; Rabelais was no more bluffed by the pagan authors so modish in his day, than he was by the ecclesiastics.

In sum, Valli cannot offer us merely two alternatives, he must offer us something like thirty. He can take the *Convito*, and play with it as he likes, but he must leave the *De Vulgari Eloquio*, which, if not an aesthetic treatise in modern mode, is most certainly a technical treatise, on the way to hammer sounds into lines, and as such still valid. Whatever Dante's symboligating propensities, he was positivist on his craft, in this he was a *fabbro*, and one respecting the craft and the worker. Italian poetry would have gained by following his traces, and our own would be less a mess if Chaucer had so closely considered technique instead of uselessly treating the Astrolabe.

In no case can the answer be simple, and in any case the learned Valli might do well to recognize the still extant folk-ways of the Latins; having offered him so many subjects for meditation I offer him still another though he may not see the connection: I was once engaged in trying to get a Northumbrian intellectual out of jail *emprès Ponthoise*, and in so doing I fell into converse with the Corsican cop on duty, and at the end of eight or ten minutes he drew from

his pocket two poems written in Anagram, so that the letters beginning the lines in the one read 'PIERRE ET MARIE', and in the other
'LUCILE ET PIERRE', and after I read through them he added, as excuse,
or as explanation, 'Ça plaît beaucoup aux dames.'

There is still perfectly solid ground for arguing that the language
of Guido is secret only as the language of any technical science is
secret for those who have not the necessary preparation. The 'tondo
sesto' may be the 'tondo di Sesto' ('Empirico').

THE CANZONE: FURTHER NOTES

It is 'impossible' to argue every opinion on every passage of the
canzone, or in any case it would conduce to an endless volume.
Without disputing Valli's opinion or anyone else's opinion, I shall
now simply tabulate some few bits of information or tradition that,
as I see it, should be considered before coming to a conclusion,
regardless as to whether they confirm my own views or anyone's
views. In none of the immediately following notes do I mean to
imply anything, or to lead the reader to think that, say Del Garbo's
opinion, or anyone else's opinion is conclusive.

Strophe I
(I give the words, and omit line numbers)

Donna

Del Garbo, egregio medicine doctor and as such presumably
acquainted with Averroes. (MS. Ce, Chig. L, 176.) *Sic*: 'Causa aût
(ait or aiunt) movês (the circumflex means *n*) ad hoc ē mulier ut dn̄a
(donna) que i pm̄ rogavit... attribuit nom̄ donna... mulieri
digne... e in etate puerile iq̄ua cognitio nô perfecta nô attribuit. hc
nom̄ donna. Iterum et attribuit muliere digne', etc. Del Garbo is not
looking for or admitting any cryptogram, he is concerned with its
being a woman old enough to possess knowledge, and of good
family. The question noble blood, etc., was then, as we know from
Dante, a subject of interest and debate.

Accidente

(See quotation from Avicenna on p. 378.)
For Del Garbo it is 'passio' (affect) distinct from the extrinsic, an
'accidente'. And the dogmas are mainly concerned with substances,
original creations, the Trinity, etc., also with original sin.

From the rest of the list it would seem that the time spirit among the students in Paris, 1279, was drifting much more to general *non curanza* and scepticism than to mystic conjurations. Something that Renan translates as 'raison naturelle' had appeared in one of Gregory IX's denunciations of Frederick II.

Natural dimostramento

After the repeated, somewhat frenetic attacks on Averroism, by Albert, Aquinas, etc., and repeated condemnations, Etienne Tempier, in 1277, condemns among other propositions: 'Quod *naturalis* philosophus simpliciter debet negare mundi novitatem, quia nititur causis et rationibus naturalibus: *fidelis* autem potest negare mundi æternitatem quia nititur causis supernaturalibus'.

The bishop *versus* the quarter; Aquinas foams at the mouth about people who discuss these things with kids, instead of publishing formal answers to him; there is question whether the accursed by Gm. de Tocco are Goliardiae, 'qui Averrois erant communiter sectantes', or whether it ought to read Garlandiae (data in Renan's *Averroès*).

In any case the poet is obstreperous. His work is no guarantee of tranquillity and mental sleep.

I do not want to lengthen the list of commentators who restate Guido's propositions less accurately than he has. Still if one is to speculate on where his propositions lead, I should say he even exceeds the last remark in this paragraph of condemnation of Tempier's, which is: 'philosophus debet captivare intellectum in obsequim fidei'. Guido certainly in 'non razionale, ma che si sente' allows more importance to feeling than the bishop would have approved.

But I doubt if it can be proved that Guido has emitted a provably heretical proposition, i.e. one definite bashing in any specific dogma. He defines.

Del Garbo (Ce) sic: 'et ĉ -i- sine nâli dem̂ostratiôe q̄i velit dicere q/ eo q̄ dicet extræt ex prîcipi^s faĉ naturaĺ et nô solû extract ex principij faĉ nâl (illegible word . . .? uno) ex principi^o faĉ moraĺ et astrologie et ô (audieret huic) sermonis dz ēc îteligês.' The interesting contribution, despite the illegibility, is the 'astrologie'. And the main contention would seem to be that he 'extracts', sets apart the natural fact from 'principles', i.e. dogma. And 'not only the natural fact, but the moral and astrological fact'. Del Garbo died, I believe, Sept. 30th, A.D. 1327. The passage would seem to back up what I have already said regarding Guido's general attitude. Del Garbo would seem to have noticed the same implications that I did. (The MS. Ce reads erroneously 'posa' for 'nasce', l. 10, and 'amore' for 'amare', l. 13, with later correction above the line. Garbo is misled by these readings in his comment.) I think we might consider Del Garbo's comment as that of the objective critic, Averroist, natural philosopher, really looking at Guido's words (i.e. the MS. as it lay before him even in its one or two textual errors); and that we might consider Egidio as seeking the theological rather than philosophical verity, i.e. lecturing on what Guido 'ought to have meant'. I do not want to force this view. *Vide infra,* end of note on 'intelletto'.

Amare

In distinction to *amore, vide* p. 377.

Strophe II

Memoria. Vide p. 381.
Diafan. Vide pp. 359-60. Cf. *Paradiso* X, 69.
Marte

Da Marte: I suppose as 'impulse'. At any rate there is a Neo-platonic gradation of the assumption of faculties as the mind descends into matter through the seven spheres, *via* the gate of Cancer: in Saturn, reason; in Jupiter, practical and moral; in Mars, the 'spirited'; in Venus, the sensuous. Cf. Dante's *voi ch' intendendo il terzo ciel movete.* Macrobius, *In Somnium Scipionis;* and Plotinus, *Ennead.*

Del Garbo animadverts on the 'luxurious' nature of those in whose horoscope Mars is in the house of Venus, Taurus, Libra, etc.

S' intende

Cf. Spinoza: The intellectual love of a thing consists in the under-standing of its perfections. The *forma s'intende* so that the *amore* (accidens) takes *state.*

Che'l prende. Vide p. 378

Possibile intelletto and *Come in subjecto. Vide* p. 378.

There is no safety: until several specialists have been on this topic for a decade each, no one has any right to present opinions as if they were proved.

Albertus says memory. Renan has a note (*Averroès et l' Aver-oïsme,* p. 126) on Denis, combating Averroes regarding 'intellect

passif'. *Sic*: 'L'intellect passif n'est alors que la faculté de recevoir les
PHANTASMATA.' This is exactly what I think is NOT in Guido
Cavalcanti. The terms *intellectus possibilis*, POSSIBLE, and the
Passive intellect belong to two different schools, two different sets
of terminology. In dealing with Guido Cavalcanti we should stick
to such authors as use 'possible intelletto'. Or if the 'passif' equals the
'possible' then the *l* before *prende* goes out.

Unless a term is left meaning one particular thing, and unless all
attempt to unify different things, however small the difference, is
clearly abandoned, all metaphysical thought degenerates into a
soup. A soft terminology is merely an endless series of indefinite
middles.

Del Garbo explains: 'et sic dyaphani qñ lumine îformat ita inform-
at^v memoria ex spc^ rei ex$_q^a$catur amor.' In addition to which I note
the following in Renan, speaking of Zimara on Averroes: 'L'intellect
actif n'est ni Dieu lui-même . . . ni une simple faculté de l'âme . . .
mais une substance supérieure à l'âme, séparable, incorruptible'
(Renan, *Averroès*, p. 376). Cf. debate of Guido Cavalcanti with
Orlandi, Sonnet XVI and Orlandi's reply.

Guido is, I think, 'safe' in confining himself to a discussion of an
'accidens', which probably lay outside the scope of the dogma. I
mean that he can remain scientific without treading on the toes of
theology (save of course by implication and general frame of mind).
And the 'che si sente' would even justify my use of the term 'affect'
in translation.

Cf. also Carlini's translation of Aristotle's *Metaphysics* (XI (K) I.
1059 a, 29): 'Che se diversa è la scienza che studia le sostanze e . . .
quella che studia gli accidenti? E quale delle due è la sapienza?
Poiché una di esse procederà dimostrativamente, quella intorno agli
accidenti; l'altra, quella delle sostanze, riguarderà, invece, i primi
principii.'

Locho, dimoranʒa.
('Proprio loco', in Orlandi's sonnet.)

Risplende in sé. Vide p. 360

Largir simiglianʒa: simiglianʒa. (p. 379)
The pseudo Dionysius mentions that the order of angels called
Dominions is 'elevated above dissimilarity'.

Largir simiglianza: Largir.

Renan (*averroès et l'Averroïsme*) cites a passage of Albertus (*De apprehensione*, pars V, vol. 21 of the works): '*Possibilis speculativa recipiens cum eis lumen suscipit agentis, cui de die in diem fit similior; et quum acceperit possibilis omnia speculata seu intellecta, habet lumen agentis ut formam sibi adhaerentem ... Ex possibili et agente compositus est intellectus adeptus, et divinus dicitur, et tunc homo perfectus est. Et fit per hunc intellectum homo Deo quodam modo similis, eo quod potest sic operari divina, et LARGIRI sibi et aliis intellectus divinos, et accipere omnia intellecta quodam modo, et est hoc illud scire quod omnes appetunt, in quo felicitas consistit contemplativa.*'

I do not think this indicates that Guido was in any way taking Albertus as model. Renan prefaces the citation with a phrase that would suit Signor Valli: 'L'intellect agent s'unit au possible', it continues 'si comme la lumière au diaphane.'

I do not, in the canzone, smell 'ittisâl', Sufi doctrine of union.

In one receipt for 'contemplation' I find that it properly should imply contemplation of divine things, from which *Amore* is omitted. It seems possible that Guido is claiming rank for *Amor*. In any case my thesis would be that he, familiar with the most lively philosophic thought of the time, is treating his topic rather more efficiently than the contemporary prose lecturers. Using the citation from Albertus solely as lexicography, the meaning of the passage enclosing 'largir simiglianza' would yield: Radiates splendour in itself, itself's perpetual effect, as it cannot confer its likeness (on anything else).

Or, one might interpret: glows throughout the possible intellect, which it has completely transfused, but does not penetrate into lower strata.

Pesanza for *Possanza* seems to me simply the duller, even stupider word, a dead instead of an active word: simpliste reading. Ld and Ce both clearly read *possanza*. Di Giunta: *posanza*. The ignorant connection of weight and descent would easily account for ignorant changing to *pesanza* as precursor of *discende*. Colonna reads *posanza* and comments on *inquietudine*. Frachetta makes out a sort of case for *pesanza*, less poetical to our sense. He was perhaps more anxious to display his 'knowledge' of Aristotle than an understanding of Guido. However, the intellectual concept was not supposed to be subject to whatever the Middle Ages called what we now call gravity.

The error *chei* in the last line of the strophe would, however, naturally occur from someone *understanding* 'largir simiglianza', and looking, too hastily, for an object upon which the simiglianza was to be conferred. ('Si chei non puote.')

Ld and Ce *ought* to be independent if the dissimilarity of 'Perche non pote' (Ld) and 'Si che non puote' (Ce, Del Garbo) is any indication. Rivalta in fact derives them from Mart. and Ba of his main middle group. His reasons for preferring *pesanza* are not clear to me.

Strophe III

Virtute.

Del Garbo in discussing the opening lines of this strophe formulates the alternative: 'ut virtus, aut procedens ex virtute.'

Antenzione. Vide p. 361

Discerne male.

The interpreter with too great a thirst for metaphysics, and metaphysical interpretations, must not rush over this phrase. It blocks several too abstract, too deadly intellectual decodings. If the *Amor* is limited to *amor sapientiae* why drag in this phrase and why also drag in the *che si sente?*

Opposito natural.

Merely to note the repetition of *natural* at this point and refer it to anything that has been said regarding *natural dimostramento* (Strophe I).

Strophe IV

L'esser é quando.

Time relation established. If the *'possibil' intelletto* is merely faculty for receiving phantasmata, the *amor* here should presumably pass from latent possibility into 'being' (? active existence). Cf. also the lines in Orlandi's sonnet:

> Sustanza, o accidente, o ei memora?
> E cagion d' occhi, o è voler di core?'

Formato locho.

In my translation I followed the reading 'non formato'. I do not think it can be held as the correct one. Rivalta chooses 'non fermato' which I distinctly disbelieve in, despite the emendation above the lines in the Roman, Del Garbo MS. (Ce). Rivalta argues from his favourite 'Mart'. Ba, with the Colonna comment, gives very visibly 'un formato'.

This occurs also in the highly respectable Mb and in Ld. Di Giunta's editing of the canzone was extremely careful, as may be indicated still further by the list of variants known to him.

The point would also dispose of the canard that MS. Ma was in any way connected with Di Giunta's edition despite certain similarities in its other readings. Neither can I believe that its calligraphy indicates any such antiquity. If it represents any state of Di Giunta's opinion, even copied by a later hand, it does not represent his final opinion whereby the *non fermato* is relegated to rejected variants. 'Non formato' is useful for immediate effect, i.e. of the single line, but does not cohere in the general exposition. The 'formato locho' is the tract or locus marked out in the 'possibile intelletto', and is buttressed by the rest of Orlandi's line 'ov' ei dimora'. I do not think Egidio is sound in thinking the 'formato *locho*' is a single image. Determined locus or habitat would be nearer the mark. This is not absolutely what Egidio Colonna specifies when he says: 'riguardar l' imagine . . . laquale è nella fantasia . . laquale è formata e figurata di diverse figure . . . e diverse imagine.'

Colonna has read 'che prende' not 'che 'l prende' and obscured our Avicennian 'accident' diffused throughout the 'subject'. To keep all the distinctions the 'formato *locho*' would have, I should say, to be the 'fantasia' itself, already pervaded by the *accidente*, which *comes from* the seen form.

As to 'form'; you may here add the whole of medieval philosophy by way of footnote. Form, Gestalt, 'every spiritual form sets in movement the bodies in which (or among which) it finds itself'. Aquinas's attack on Averroes in which he has to twist the meaning of the term almost 180 degrees off its course, etc. 'Veduta forma' must, however, be extrinsic and perceived, if we are to leave any shred of verbal meaning in any term whatsoever.

As parallel to the 'qual è suo *proprio* luongo?' in the second line of Orlandi's sonnet of enquiry, Albertus Magnus (I think it is the *Sex principiis*) has:'non omnis situs est proprie et principaliter dicta positio.'

Destandosi ira.

I think we can accept this reading as correct, for *ira*, *vide* p. 376. We have Ba, Ma, Rivalta against a dispersed set of readings.

Immaginar.

Still meaning at that time, I should think, to form an image. Taking this line by itself, perhaps a rash procedure, you can isolate a general negation of image-making faculty in those not 'chonoscenti'.

Strophe V

Da simil.

Possibly far-fetched to drag in supposedly Epicurean attraction of likes, or to say that this widely held doctrine is here any special indication of Guido Cavalcanti's position, save in so far as it would rule out certain forms of mysticisms which teach attraction of opposites. A very slight flimsy aid in any sort of discussion.

Non già selvagge.

Ce gives: 'Mon gia selnagg$_i^o$ la belta suo dardo.'

Mb: 'Non go (or ga) selvagge, la (or lo) bilta $\overline{\text{faq}}$. dardi' with several dots around whatever I take or mistake for the *q*.

In Ce the *o* over the terminal *i* of *selnaggi* may also be intended for an *e*. At any rate I do not pretend to understand this strophe, or to know whether *punto* is noun or verb, or whether *selvaggie* or *o* is the verb in that line, or whether the verb is *son* supposing that word is not *suo*.

The reading of Ld is clearly: 'Non gia selvagge la bilta son dardj.'

Rivalta: 'selvaggio le beltà son dardo.'

Di Giunta: 'selvagge le bilta son dardo.'

La: 'suo dardo' (followed, I think, by Lc).

Le: seems to have: 'suo tardo'.

Lm: 'son dardo'.

Ba is clearly: 'la bilta son dardo' (or else I cannot read my own hand writing in my copy of Ba).

With which, as the general meaning is fairly clear, whichever phrase is correct, I cheerfully abandon the line to that ultimate judge, Tom Tiddler.

Punto.

Colonna, reading *che punto*, takes it to mean *stimulo*.

Bianco.

I think my translation is forced. I doubt very much if *bianco* can here have the highly particularized meaning of the 'bull's eye' or centre of the target. The reader must choose for himself among medieval doctrines of colour, of diaphana, of all colours united in the white, of (I think less likely) ideas of katharsis, and balance this or bring it into relation with the 'ultra-violet' or whatever interpretation one is to give to the 'outside of colour' three lines further on; 'colores fiant ex complexione ignis cum corpore dyaphano.' My final opinion is that *compriso bianco* means understood as a whole. Cf. *Paradiso* VIII, 112, 42 and X.

Franchetta and the 'Aldine'.

Franchetta was a cultivated man who made a serious attempt to understand the canzone *via* Aristotle, we may take him as indicative of the state of aesthetics in 1585. There is nothing to indicate that he tried to place himself in 1290. His general interpretation of this passage (*cade*, etc.) is that it is simple negation of the question asked in 1. 14: 'Et se huom per veder lo puo mostrare?' The visual sense perceives colour, the mind perceives the proportion; Love is not colour, nor an object having colour.

The idea that Franchetta mistook the Giuntine edition for an Aldine could not have been put forward by anyone who had read F. with care. Thanks to Mr Adrian Stokes I have been able to locate the Aldine text: not of Guido's complete poems but of this canzone. Aldus printed it at the end of his second or third edition of Petrarch with the canzoni of Dante and Cino cited by Petrarch in 'Lasso me, ch'io non so in qual parte pieghi'.

Pico's remarks on Guido in the commentary on G. Benivieni, end of cap. 2, add nothing to our esteem of Pico. ...

Aude.

With the well-known alternative *vade*, Cd gives yet another turn with 'Et che bene *ha di*forma nô se vede'. Here, as in the case of the *dardo*, all one can say is that no one has yet improved on Di Giunta during the four disposable centuries.

Asciso.

I have no doubt regarding this reading. It means cut off. Contrast this with the 'forman adhaerentem' of Albertus (*vide* note on *largir*) and connect with note on *rade*.

Rade.

The fifth meaning given to *radere* in the *Vocabolario della Crusca* is *andar resente*, and the example 'Quella torre è dritta, e perpendicolare, e ci mostra (il senso) quella pietra nel cadere venirla radendo senza piegar pur un capello da questa o da quella parte'. I take it that the *Amor* moves with the light in darkness, never touching it and never a hair's breadth from it.

Franchetta takes *radere* to mean merely cut off or blot out. This would let one in for the dark night of the soul, instead of leaving us the clean though highly complicated image. I think both Guido and Arnaut exploit Latin. Guido was not slave to use of the article, which has now become such a bore in French and Italian. 'Quoi! paroles en liberté!' exclaims a disgusted state examiner. I also think Guido is avoiding *radiare* and the 'delle tenebre radiare luce'. In Dante the 'Primum mobile' might be said *radere* the fixed heaven (*abscissum*).

Envoi. There is a diverting parallel to the coda in the 1602 edition of Colonna's commentary:

> 'Va spositione mia sicuramente
> A gente di valor, a cui ti mando,
> Di star con nessun' huomo ti comando
> Il qual vuol usar l' occhio per la mente.'

This is very possibly Thomism, in extreme gibe at observing Averroists and Roger-Baconians? Or perhaps it is only exuberance at getting to the end of his job (not necessarily scribbled down by the learned commentator in person).

GUIDO'S RELATIONS

The critic, normally a bore and a nuisance, can justify his existence in one or more minor and subordinate ways: he may dig out and focus attention upon matter of interest that would otherwise have passed without notice; he may, in the rare cases when he has any really general knowledge or 'perception of relations' (swift or other) locate his finds with regard to other literary inventions; he may, thirdly, or as you might say, conversely and as part and supplement of his activity, construct cloacae to carry off the waste matter, which stagnates about the real work, and which is continuously being heaped up and caused to stagnate by academic bodies, obese publishing houses, and combinations of both, such as the Oxford Press. (We note their particular infamy in a recent re-issue of Palgrave.)

Since Dante's unfinished brochure on the common tongue, Italy may have had no general literary criticism, the brochure is somewhat 'special' and of interest mainly to practitioners of the art of writing. Lorenzo Valla somewhat altered the course of history by his close inspection of Latin usage. His prefaces have here and there a burst of magnificence, and the spirit of the Elegantiae should benefit any writer's lungs. As he wrote about an ancient idiom, Italian and English writers alike have, when they have heard his name at all, supposed that he had no 'message' and, in the case of the Britons, they returned, we may suppose, to Pater's remarks on Pico. (Based on what the weary peruser of some few other parts of Pico's output, might pettishly denounce as Pico's one remarkable paragraph.)

The study called 'comparative literature' was invented in Germany but has seldom if ever aspired to the study of 'comparative values in letters'.

The literature of the Mediterranean races continued in a steady descending curve of renaissance-ism. There are minor upward fluctuations. The best period of Italian poetry ends in the year 1321. So far as I know one excellent Italian tennis-player and no known Italian writer has thought of considering the local literature in relation to rest of the world.

Leopardi read, and imitated Shakespeare. The Prince of Monte Nevoso has been able to build his unique contemporary position because of barbarian contacts, whether consciously, and *via* visual stimulus from any printed pages, or simply because he was aware of, let us say, the existence of Wagner and Browning. If Nostro Gabriele started something new in Italian. Hating barbarism, teutonism, never mentioning the existence of the ultimate Britons, unsurrounded by any sort of society or milieu, he ends as a solitary, superficially eccentric, but with a surprisingly sound standard of values, values, that is, as to the relative worth of a few perfect lines of writing, as contrasted to a great deal of flub-dub and 'action'.

The only living author who has ever taken a city or held up the diplomatic crapule at the point of machine-guns, he is in a position to speak with more authority than a batch of neurasthenic incompetents or of writers who never having swerved from their jobs, might be, or are, supposed by the scientists and the populace to be incapable of action. Like other serious characters who have taken seventy years to live and to learn to live, he has passed through periods wherein he lived (or wrote) we should not quite say 'less ably', but with less immediately demonstrable result.

This period 'nel mezzo', this passage of the 'selva oscura' takes men in different ways, so different indeed that comparison is more likely to bring ridicule on the comparer than to focus attention on the analogy—often admittedly far-fetched.

In many cases the complete man makes a 'very promising start', and then flounders or appears to flounder for ten years, or for twenty or thirty (cf. Henry James's middle period) to end, if he survive, with some sort of demonstration, discovery, or other justification of his having gone by the route he has (apparently) stumbled on.

When I 'translated' Guido eighteen years ago I did *not* see Guido at all. I saw that Rossetti had made a remarkable translation of the *Vita Nuova*, in some places improving (or at least enriching) the original; that he was indubitably the man 'sent', or 'chosen' for that particular job, and that there was something in Guido that escaped him or that was, at any rate, absent from his translations. A *robustezza*, a masculinity. I had a great enthusiasm (perfectly justified), but I did not clearly see exterior demarcations—Euclid inside his cube, with no premonition of Cartesian axes.

My perception was not obfuscated by Guido's Italian, difficult as it then was for me to read. I was obfuscated by the Victorian language.

If I hadn't been, I very possibly couldn't have done the job at all. I should have seen the too great multiplicity of problems contained in the one problem before me.

I don't mean that I didn't see dull spots in the sonnets. I saw that Rossetti had taken most of the best sonnets, that one couldn't make a complete edition of Guido simply by taking Rossetti's translations and filling in the gaps, it would have been too dreary a job. Even though I saw that Rossetti had made better English poems than I was likely to make by (in intention) sticking closer to the direction of the original. I began by meaning merely to give prose translation so that the reader ignorant of Italian could see what the melodic original meant. It is, however, an illusion to suppose that more than one person in every 300,000 has the patience or the intelligence to read a foreign tongue for its sound, or even to read what are known to be the masterworks of foreign melody, in order to learn the qualities of that melody, or to see where one's own falls short.

What obfuscated me was not the Italian but the crust of dead English, the sediment present in my own available vocabulary—which I, let us hope, got rid of a few years later. You can't go round this sort of thing. It takes six or eight years to get educated in one's art, and another ten to get rid of that education.

Neither can anyone learn English, one can only learn a series of Englishes. Rossetti made his own language. I hadn't in 1910 made a language, I don't mean a language to use, but even a language to think in.

It is stupid to overlook the lingual inventions of precurrent authors, even when they are fools or flapdoodles or Tennysons. It is sometimes advisable to sort out these languages and inventions, and to know what and why they are.

Keats, out of Elizabethans, Swinburne out of a larger set of Elizabethans and a mixed bag (Greeks, *und so weiter*), Rossetti out of Sheets, Kelly, and Co. plus early Italians (written and painted); and so forth, including *King Wenceslas*, ballads and carols.

Let me not discourage a possible reader, or spoil anyone's naïve enjoyment, by saying that my early versions of Guido are bogged in Dante Gabriel and in Algernon. It is true, but let us pass by it in silence. Where both Rossetti and I went off the rails was in taking an English sonnet as the equivalent for a sonnet in Italian. I don't mean in overlooking the mild difference in the rhyme scheme. The mistake is 'quite natural', very few mistakes are 'unnatural'. Rime looks very important. Take the rimes off a good sonnet, and there is a vacuum. And besides the movement of *some* Italian sonnets *is* very like that in some sonnets in English. The feminine rhyme goes by the board . . . again for obvious reasons. It had gone by the board, quite often, in Provençal. The French made an ecclesiastical law about using it 50/50.

As a bad analogy, imagine a Giotto or Simone Martini fresco, 'translated' into oils by 'Sir Joshua', or Sir Frederick Leighton. Something is lost, something is somewhat denatured.

Suppose, however, we have a Cimabue done in oil, not by Holbein, but by some contemporary of Holbein who can't paint as well as Cimabue.

There are about seven reasons why the analogy is incorrect, and six more to suppose it inverted, but it may serve to free the reader's mind from preconceived notions about the English of 'Elizabeth' and her British garden of song-birds. —And to consider language as a medium of expression.

(Breton forgives Flaubert on hearing that Father Gustave was trying only to give 'l'impression de la couleur jaune' (*Nadja*, p. 12).)

Dr Schelling has lectured about the Italianate Englishman of
Shakespeare's day. I find two Shakespeare plots within ten pages of
each other in a forgotten history of Bologna, printed in 1596. We
have heard of the effects of the travelling Italian theatre companies,
commedia dell' arte, etc. What happens when you idly attempt to
translate early Italian into English, unclogged by the Victorian era,
freed from sonnet obsession, but trying merely to sing and to leave
out the dull bits in the Italian, or the bits you don't understand?

I offer you a poem that 'don't matter', it is attributed to Guido in
Codex Barberiniano Lat. 3953. Alacci prints it as Guido's; Simone
Occhi in 1740 says that Alacci is a fool or words to that effect and
a careless man without principles, and proceeds to print the poem
with those of Cino Pistoia. Whoever wrote it, it is, indubitably, not
a *capo lavoro.*

> 'Madonna la vostra belta enfolio
> Si li mei ochi che menan lo core   MS. *oghi*
> A la bataglia ove l' ancise amore
> Che del vostro placer armato uscio;   *usio*
>
> Si che nel primo asalto che asalio
> Passo dentro la mente e fa signore,
> E prese l' alma che fuzia di fore
> Planzendo di dolor che vi sentio.
>
> Però vedete che vostra beltate
> Mosse la folia und e il cor morto
> Et a me ne convien clamar pietate,
>
> Non per campar, ma per aver conforto
> Ne la morte crudel che far min fate
> Et o rason sel non vinzesse il torto.'

Is it worth an editor's while to include it among dubious attributions?
It is not very attractive: until one starts playing with the simplest
English equivalent.

> 'Lady thy beauty doth so mad mine eyes,
> Driving my heart to strife wherein he dies.'

Sing it of course, don't try to speak it. It thoroughly falsifies the
movement of the Italian, it is an opening quite good enough for

Herrick or Campion. It will help you to understand just why
Herrick, and Campion, and possibly Donne are still with us.

The next line is rather a cliché; the line after more or less lacking
in interest. We pull up on:

> 'Whereby thou seest how fair thy beauty is
> To compass doom'.

That would be very nice, but it is hardly translation.

Take these scraps, and the almost impossible conclusion, a tag of
Provençal rhythm, and make them into a plenum. It will help you to
understand some of M. de Schloezer's remarks about Stravinsky's
trend toward melody. And you will also see what the best Elizabethan lyricists did, as well as what they didn't.

My two lines take the opening and two and a half of the Italian,
English more concise; and the octave gets too light for the sestet.
Lighten the sestet.

> 'So unto Pity must I cry
> Not for safety, but to die.
> Cruel Death is now mine ease
> If that he thine envoy is.'

We are preserving one value of early Italian work, the cantabile;
and we are losing another, that is the specific weight. And if we
notice it we fall on a root difference between early Italian, 'The
philosophic school coming out of Bologna', and the Elizabethan
lyric. For in these two couplets, and in attacking this sonnet, I have
let go the fervour and the intensity, which were all I, rather blindly,
had to carry through my attempt of twenty years gone.

And I think that if anyone now lay, or if we assume that they
mostly *then* (in the expansive days) laid, aside care for specific statement of emotion, a dogmatic statement, made with the seriousness of
someone to whom it mattered whether he had three souls, one in the
head, one in the heart, one possibly in his abdomen, or lungs, or
wherever Plato, or Galen, had located it; if the anima is still breath,
if the stopped heart is a dead heart, and if it is all serious, much more
serious than it would have been to Herrick, the imaginary investigator
will see more or less how the Elizabethan modes came into being.

Let him try it for himself, on any Tuscan author of that time,
taking the words, not thinking greatly of their significance, not

balking at clichés, but being greatly intent on the melody, on the single uninterrupted flow of syllables—as open as possible, that can be sung prettily, that are not very interesting if spoken, that don't even work into a period or an even metre if spoken.

And the mastery, a minor mastery, will lie in keeping this line unbroken, as unbroken in sound as a line in one of Miro's latest drawings is on paper; and giving it perfect balance, with no breaks, no bits sticking ineptly out, and no losses to the force of individual phrases.

> 'Whereby thou seest how fair thy beauty is
> To compass doom.'

Very possibly too regularly 'iambic' to fit in the finished poem.

There is opposition, not only between what M. de Schloezer distinguishes as musical and poetic lyricism, but in the writing itself there is a distinction between poetic lyricism, the emotional force of the verbal movement, and melopœic lyricism, the letting the words flow on a melodic current, realized or not, realizable or not, if the line is supposed to be sung on a sequence of notes of different pitch.

But by taking these Italian sonnets, which are not metrically the equivalent of the English sonnet, by sacrificing, or losing, or simply not feeling and understanding their cogency, their sobriety, and by seeking simply that far from quickly or so-easily-as-it-looks attainable thing, the perfect melody, careless of exactitude of idea, or careless as to which profound and fundamental idea you, at that moment, utter, perhaps in precise enough phrases, by cutting away the apparently non-functioning phrases (whose appearance deceives) you find yourself in the English *seicento* song-books.

Death has become melodious; sorrow is as serious as the nightingale's, tombstones are shelves for the reception of rose-leaves. And there is, quite often, a Mozartian perfection of melody, a wisdom, almost perhaps an ultimate wisdom, deplorably lacking in guts. My phrase is, shall we say, vulgar. Exactly, because it fails in precision. Guts in surgery refers to a very limited range of internal furnishings. A thirteenth-century exactitude in search for the exact organ best illustrating the lack, would have saved me that plunge. We must turn again to the Latins. When the late T. Roosevelt was interviewed in France on his return from the jungle, he used a phrase which was translated (the publication of the interview rather annoyed him).

The French at the point I mention ran: 'Ils ont voulu me briser les *reins* mais je les ai solides.'

And now the reader may, if he like, return to the problem of the 'eyes that lead the heart to battle where him love kills'. This was not felt as an inversion. It was 1280, Italian was still in the state that German is to-day. How can you have 'PROSE' in a country where the chambermaid comes into your room and exclaims: 'Schön ist das Hemd!'

Continue: who is armed with thy delight, is come forth so that at the first assault he assails, he passes inward to the mind, and lords it there, and catches the breath (soul) that was fleeing, lamenting the grief I feel.

'Whereby thou seest how thy beauty moves the madness, whence is the heart dead (stopped) and I must cry on Pity, not to be saved but to have ease of the cruel death thou puttest on me. And I am right (?) save the wrong him conquereth.'

Whether the reader will accept this little problem in melopœia as substitute for the cross-word puzzle I am unable to predict. I leave it on the supposition that the philosopher should try almost everything once.

As second exercise, we may try the sonnet by Guido Orlando which is supposed to have invited Cavalcanti's *Donna mi Prega*.

> 'Say what is Love, whence doth he start   ?
> Through what be his courses bent   ?
> Memory, substance, accident   ?
> A chance of eye or will of heart   ?
>
> Whence he state or madness leadeth   ?
> Burns he with consuming pain   ?
> Tell me, friend, on what he feedeth   ?
> How, where, and o'er whom doth he reign   ?
>
> Say what is Love, hath he a face   ?
> True form or vain similitude   ?
> Is the Love life, or is he death   ?
>
> Thou shouldst know for rumour saith:
> Servant should know his master's mood—
> Oft art thou ta'en in his dwelling-place.'

I give the Italian to show that there is no deception, I have invented nothing, I have given a *verbal* weight about equal to that of the original, and arrived at this equality by dropping a couple of syllables per line. The great past-master of pastiche has, it would seem, passed this way before me. A line or two of this, a few more from Lorenzo Medici, and he has concocted one of the finest gems in our language.

> 'Onde si move e donde nasce Amore
> qual è suo proprio luogo, ov' ei dimora
> Sustanza, o accidente, o ei memora?
> E cagion d' occhi, o è voler di cuore?
>
> Da che procede suo stato o furore?
> Come fuoco si sente che divora?
> Di che si nutre domand' io ancora,
> Come, e quando, e di cui si fa signore?
>
> Che cosa è, dico, amor? ae figura?
> A per se forma o pur somiglia altrui?
> E vita questo amore ovvero e morte?
>
> Ch 'l serve dee saver di sua natura:
> Io ne domando voi, Guido, di lui:
> Odo che molto usate in la sua corte.'

We are not in a realm of proofs, I suggest, simply, the way in which early Italian poetry has been utilized in England. The Italian of Petrarch and his successors is of no interest to the practising writer or to the student of comparative dynamics in language, the collectors of bric-à-brac are outside our domain.

There is no question of giving Guido in an English contemporary to himself, the ultimate Britons were at that date unbreeched, painted in woad, and grunting in an idiom far more difficult for us to master than the Langue d'Oc of the Plantagenets or the Lingua di Si.

If, however, we reach back to pre-Elizabethan English, of a period when the writers were still intent on clarity and explicitness, still preferring them to magniloquence and the thundering phrase, our trial, or mine at least, results in:

> 'Who is she that comes, makying turn every man's eye
> And makying the air to tremble with a bright clearenesse

That leadeth with her Love, in such nearness
No man may proffer of speech more than a sigh?

Ah God, what she is like when her owne eye turneth, is
Fit for Amor to speake, for I cannot at all;
Such is her modesty, I would call
Every woman else but an useless uneasiness.

No one could ever tell all of her pleasauntness
In that every high noble vertu leaneth to herward,
So Beauty sheweth her forth as her Godhede;

Never before so high was our mind led,
Nor have we so much of heal as will afford
That our mind may take her immediate in its embrace.'

The objections to such a method are: the doubt as to whether one has the right to take a serious poem and turn it into a mere exercise in quaintness; the 'misrepresentation' not of the poem's antiquity, but of the proportionate feel of that antiquity, by which I mean that Guido's thirteenth-century language is to twentieth-century Italian sense much less archaic than any fourteenth-, fifteenth-, or early sixteenth-century English is for us. It is even doubtful whether my bungling version of twenty years back isn't more 'faithful', in the sense at least that it tried to preserve the fervour of the original. And as this fervour simply does not occur in English poetry in those centuries there is no ready-made verbal pigment for its objectification.

In the long run the translator is in all probability impotent to do *all* of the work for the linguistically lazy reader. He can show where the treasure lies, he can guide the reader in choice of what tongue is to be studied, and he can very materially assist the hurried student who has a smattering of a language and the energy to read the original text alongside the metrical gloze.

This refers to 'interpretative translation'. The 'other sort'. I mean in cases where the 'translater' is definitely making a new poem, falls simply in the domain of original writing, or if it does not it must be censured according to equal standards, and praised with some sort of just deduction, assessable only in the particular case.

HELL[1]

I have always mistrusted Ronsard's boast of having read the *Iliad* in three days, though he might have scuttered through Salel in that time. As a stunt I also might possibly have burrowed through Binyon's version[2] in similar period had it been printed in type decently large.

I state that I have read the work, that for thirty years it never would have occurred to me that it would be possible to read a translation of the *Inferno* from cover to cover, and that this translation has therefore one DEMONSTRATED dimension, whatever may be left to personal taste of the reader or conjecture of acrid critics.

Fools have their uses, and had it not been for the professional pomp of Mr Wubb or whatever his name is, I might not have found the volume. Mr Wubb leapt upon Binyon's opening triad of lines and managed to display such complete ignorance of the nature of Dantescan verse, and at the same time so thoroughly indicated at least one virtue of Binyon's work that I was aroused to wonder if the venerable Binyon had been able to keep on at that pace.

The venerable Binyon has, I am glad to say, produced the most interesting English version of Dante that I have seen or expect to see, though I remain in a considerable obscurity as to how far he knows what he has done, and how far he intended the specific results perceptible to the present examiner.

The younger generation may have forgotten Binyon's sad youth, poisoned in the cradle by the abominable dogbiscuit of Milton's rhetoric. I found our translator in 1908 among very leaden Greeks, and in youthful eagerness I descended on the British Museum and perused, it now seems, in retrospect, for days the tales of . . . demme if I remember anything but a word, one name, Penthesilea, and that not from reading it, but from hearing it spoken by a precocious Binyonian offspring. MR. BINYON'S ODE, poster of, was it THE EVENING STANDARD 'Milton Thou should'st', or whatever it was. 'Of Virtuous sire egregious offspring great!'

[1] *The Criterion*, April 1934.
[2] *Dante's Inferno translated into English Triple Rhyme*, by Laurence Binyon (Macmillan).

At any rate Dante has cured him. If ever demonstration be needed of the virtues of having a good model instead of a rhetorical bustuous rumpus, the life in Binyon's translation can prove it to next century's schoolboys.

· Mr B. says in preface that he wanted to produce a poem that could be read with pleasure in English. He has carefully preserved all the faults of his original.

This in the circumstances is the most useful thing he could have done. There are already 400 translations of Dante carefully presenting the English reader with a set of faults alien to the original, and therefore of no possible use to the serious reader who wants to understand Dante.

Ninety per cent of the extant versions erect (as Eliot has remarked of G. Murray) 'between the reader and the original a barrier more impassable than the Greek language'.

First: Mr Binyon has not offered us a pre-Raphaelite version of Dante.

Note that even Shadwell in his delicate renderings of cantos 26 to 33 of the *Purgatorio* has given us something not Dante, he has given us something that might almost have started from *Aucassin and Nicolette,* so far as the actual feel and texture of the work is concerned. He has taken the most fragile frosting and filigree, to begin on, he started, if my memory serves me, with that particular part of the *Commedia,* and gradually went on to the rest, or at least first to the *Purgatorio* and then to the *Paradiso,* with great delicacy of expression.

I propose to deal with our present translator very severely. He is himself a dour man, with all the marginalia of the Commonwealth. You could dress him and pass him off for one of Noll's troopers, and though he be my elder in years, I am, if his preface means what I think it does, his senior in the struggle with early Italian verse.

I cannot imagine any serious writer being satisfied with his own work in this field, or indeed any serious writer being satisfied with his own produce in this field or in any other.

If Binyon has been on this job for twelve years, I have been on it or in its environs for three and twenty or longer. Twenty-eight might be more exact. However drastically I hack at the present translation, I warn the rash novice that I can probably make a fool of any other critic who rushes in without similar preparation.

Irritated by Binyon's writing his lines hind side before, with the verbs stuck out of place on the tail syllable, and with multiple relative clauses, I (somewhere along about canto VI) wondered if it was worth while showing up the defects in Dante, especially as it seems probable that no one since Savage Landor would have been capable of weighing them. Weighing them, that is, justly, and in proportion to the specific force of the WHOLE POEM.

Heaven knows critical sense has not abounded in Italy.

Dante's Inferno Part One
'Culture and Refinement'
(*Kensington cinema billboard,* A.D. 1915)

The devil of translating medieval poetry into English is that it is very hard to decide HOW you are to render work done with one set of criteria in a language NOW subject to different criteria.

Translate the church of St Hilaire of Poitiers into Barocco?

You can't, as anyone knows, translate it into English of the period. The Plantagenet Kings' Provençal was Langue d'Oc.

Latin word order obeyed the laws for dynamics of inflected language, but in 1190 and in 1300, the language of the highbrows was still very greatly Latin. The concept of word order in uninflected or very little inflected language had not developed to anything like twentieth-century straightness. Binyon makes a very courageous statement, and a sound one: 'melodious smoothness is not the characteristic of Dante's verse.'

Despite Sordello's mastery and the ingenuity of Ar. Daniel, despite Dante's Provençal studies and the melody of his own lyrics, and despite the tremendous music of the *Commedia,* Dante, in taking up narrative, chucked out a number of MINOR criteria, as any writer of a long poem must in favour of a main virtue, and that main virtue Binyon (willing or not meaning to) has possibly exaggerated. At any rate it is now possible to READ the 34 Canti . . . *as a continuity.*

There is no danger that the reader will be intoxicated at any point, and lulled into delight with the sound, as he may quite well be even with the original.

Binyon is in the fortunate position of not having to introduce his poet, he doesn't have to resurrect him, or gain attention for him. Here he is with one of the three greatest reputations in all literature. Anyone who don't know the *Commedia* is thereby ignoramus. It is not to be expected that I can honestly care very much how it strikes the new reader.

If, after all these years, I have read straight through the *Inferno,* and if, after all my previous voyages over that text, and even efforts to help the less trained, I have now a clearer conception of the *Inferno as a whole* than I had the week before last, that is a debt, and not one that I mean to be tardy in paying.

'The love of a thing consists in the understanding of its perfections' (Spinoza).

Spinoza's statement distinctly includes knowing what they (the perfections) are NOT. Mr Binyon has not offered a lollypop, neither did Dante. *Pensi lettor!*

The habit of a degraded criticism is to criticize all, or most books, as if all books were written with the same aim. The old teachers of dialectic knew better (*Ut moveat, ut doceat ut delectet*).

Dante wrote his poems to MAKE PEOPLE THINK, just as definitely as Swinburne wrote a good deal of his poetry to tear the pants off the Victorian era and to replace the Albert Memorial by Lampascus.

The style for a poem written to that end, or in translation of same, differs from the style suited to a 3000 dollar magazine story in the wake of de Maupassant.

Prosody

I have never seen but one intelligent essay on Dante's 'metre', and that was in an out-of-print school-book found in a Sicilian hotel, the author cited an author who had examined Dante's actual practice and found that the 'eleven syllable' line was composed of various different syllable-groups, totalling roughly eleven syllables, and not running, so far as I can remember, to more than seventeen. Any pedant can verify the top limit, and it doesn't greatly matter so long as the student does not confuse the so-called 'syllabic' system with 'English pentameter', meaning a swat at syllables, 2, 4, 6, 8, 10 in each line, mitigated by 'irregularities' and 'inverted feet'.

Mr Wubb had apparently *not* heard of the difference, at the time of his objection to Binyon. There is nothing in Binyon's own preface to indicate that he himself had it clearly in mind as a 'concept'. He does not refer to the *De Vulgari Eloquio.* It wouldn't surprise me if he had read it and forgotten it (more or less), but a man can't be immured for forty years with Koyets' and Sotatz' without developing some

sort of sensibility to outline and demarcation, and without learning
to distinguish muddy from clear; neither can he go on reading Dante
for twelve years with the serious intention of finding an English
equivalent without perceiving at least SOME of the qualities of the
SOUND of the original, whether or no he invent a 'system' or theory
for explaining that sound.

SHIFT:

I remember Yeats wanting me to speak some verse aloud in the old
out-of-door Greek theatre at Siracusa, and being annoyed when I
bellowed the

ποικιλόθρον’, ἀθάνατ’ ’Αφρόδιτα

and refused to spout English poesy. I don't know how far I succeeded
in convincing him that English verse wasn't CUT. Yeats himself in
his early work produced marvellous rhythmic effects 'legato', verse,
that is, very fine to murmur and that may be understood if whispered
in a drawing-room, even though the better readers may gradually
pull the words out of shape (by excessive lengthening of the vowel
sounds).

The musical terms 'staccato' and 'legato' apply to verse. The
common verse of Britain from 1890 to 1910 was a horrible agglom-
erate compost, not minted, most of it not even baked, all legato, a
doughy mess of third-hand Keats, Wordsworth, heaven knows what,
fourth-hand Elizabethan sonority blunted, half melted, lumpy. The
Elizabethan 'iambic' verse was largely made to bawl in theatres, and
had considerable affinity with barocco.

Working on a decent basis, Binyon has got rid of pseudo-
magniloquence, of puffed words, I don't remember a single decorative or rhetorical word in his first ten cantos. There are vast
numbers of mono-syllables, little words. Here a hint from the *De
Eloquio* may have put him on the trail.

In the matter of rhyme, nearly everyone knows that Dante's
rhymes are 'feminine', i.e. accent on the penultimate, *crucciata,
aguzza, volge, maligno*. There are feminine rhymes in English, there
are ENOUGH, possibly, to fill the needs of an almost literal version of
the *Divina Commedia*, but they are of the wrong quality; *bloweth,
knowing, waiteth*.

Binyon has very intelligently avoided a mere pseudo or obvious
similarity, in favour of a fundamental, namely the sharp clear quality

of the original SOUND as a whole. His *past, admits, checked, kings,* all masculine endings, but all leaving a residue of vowel sound in state of potential, or latent, as considered by Dante himself in his remarks on troubadour verse.

I do not expect to see another version as good as Binyon's, I can to a great extent risk being unjust to forty translators whose work I haven't seen. Few men of Binyon's position and experience have tried or will try the experiment. You cannot counterfeit forty years' honest work, or get the same result by being a clever young man who prefers vanilla to orange or heliotrope to lavender perfume.

> 'La sculpture n'est pas pour les jeunes hommes'
> (Brancusi.)

A younger generation, or at least a younger American generation, has been brought up on a list of acid tests, invented to get rid of the boiled oatmeal consistency of the bad verse of 1900, and there is no doubt that many young readers seeing Binyon's inversions, etc., will be likely to throw down the translation under the impression that it is incompetent.

The fact that this idiom, which was never spoken on sea or land, is NOT fit for use in the new poetry of 1933-4 does not mean that it is unfit for use in a translation of a poem finished in 1321.

Before flying to the conclusion that certain things are 'against the rules' (heaven save us, procedures are already erected into RULES!) let the neophyte consider that a man cannot be in New York and Pekin at the same moment. Certain qualities are in OPPOSITION to others, water cannot exist as water and as ice at the same time.

It WOULD be quite possible to conserve the natural word order, without giving up the rhymes used by Binyon, IF one used run-on instead of end-stopped verses. BUT Dante's Verses are mostly end-stopped. Various alternatives are offered at every juncture, but let the neophyte try half a dozen before deciding that Binyon has sacrificed the greater virtue for the less in a given case.

He has not made such sacrifices in his refusal to bother with feminine rhyme. Specific passages must be judged line by line. And this process I propose to illustrate by particular cases before falling into general statement.

In a poem 200 pages long, or more exactly in a poem the first third of which is 200 pages long, the FIRST requirement is that the reader be able to proceed. You can't do this with Chapman's *Homer*. You plunge into adjectival magnificence and get stuck. You have two or more pages of admiration, and then wait to regather your energies, or you acquire a definite impression of Chapman's language, and very little of Ilion. There are even, and this is more pertinent, a great number of persons familiar with the Paolo and Francesca incident, and very muzzy about the *Commedia* as a Whole.

Literature belongs to no one man, and translations of great works ought perhaps to be made by a committee. We are cut off (by idiotic economic system), etc. from the old habit of commentary printed WITH a text. Up to canto VIII or IX I was torn between wanting Binyon to spend the next ten years revising his *Inferno*, and the wish he should go on to the end of the *Commedia*, and then, if he had time, turn back for revision. I now think he has earned his right to the pleasures of the *Purgatorio* and the third section of the poem. Some, perhaps most of the strictures made on particular passages, might better be made privately to the translator were there such opportunity or any likelihood that my opinion would be well received. It is nearly impossible to make the RIGHT suggestion for emending another man's work. Even if you do, he never quite thinks it remains his own. This ulcerated sense of property might disappear in an ideal republic. At most, one can put one's finger on the fault and hope the man himself will receive inspiration from the depths of his own personal Helicon.

> *Dante's Inferno Part Two*
> 'Not a Dull Moment'.
> (*Kensington billboard*)

If any of the following citations seem trifling or carping let the reader think how few contemporary works merit *in any degree* this sort of attention.

For most translation one would merely say, take it away and start again. There is nothing in the following list that couldn't be dealt with in a second or third edition.

An imaginary opponent might argue that Binyon had given us 'penny plain' for 'twopence coloured'. Sargent used to do coloured impressions of Velasquez, but so far as I know he didn't try the process on Dürer. If Binyon has given us an engraving, he has put the original in its own colour on the opposite page.

If the opponent think Binyon somewhat naif not to try to hide the defects of Dante, this also has its use and its interest, at least as preparation for understanding subsequent Italy. At last one sees what Petrarch was trying to get away from, and why the Italians have put up with Petrarch.

Minor triumph, in 1932: I drove an Italian critic, author of a seven volume history of Italian literature, to his last ditch, whence he finally defended Petrarch on the sole ground that 'one occasionally likes a chocolate cream'. A literary decadence can proceed not only from a bad colossal author, but from a small man's trying to avoid the defects in the work of a great man.

Returning from relative to intrinsic value: We owe Binyon a great debt for having shown (let us hope once and for all) how little Dante needs NOTES. The general lay reader has been hypnotized for centuries by the critical apparatus of the *Commedia*. An edition like Moore's with no notes, especially if approached by a young student, is too difficult. One was thankful in 1906 to Dent for the Temple bilingual edition, it saved one from consulting Witte, Toynbee, God knows whom, but at any rate from painfully digging in with a dictionary, a Dante dictionary, etc . . . . and one (I believe MORE— I cannot believe my experience unique) never got through to the essential fact that it is really THERE ON THE PAGE.

One got interested in the wealth of heteroclite material, incident, heteroclite anecdote, museum of medieval history, etc. Whenever there was an immediate difficulty one looked at a note, instead of reading on for ten lines and waiting for Dante to tell one.

Binyon's canto headings average about half a page. Up to canto XIII I can think of only one item necessary, or at least that one wanted, for the understanding of the text, which he hasn't included in his summaries.

This is really an enormous benefit, a very great work of clearance and drainage. And it ought not to pass without gratitude. It is partly due to this clearance that the version leaves one so clear headed as to the general line of the Cantico.

At the start the constant syntactical inversions annoy one. Later one gets used to the idiom and forgets to notice them. In any case there is nothing worse than Dante's own:

> 'già mai non vada,
> di là più che de qua essere aspetta.'

There are however during the first dozen cantos a number of alterations from singular to plural, or vice versa, which do no good whatever.

In the main Binyon's having his eye on the word and not the thing makes for the honesty of the version, or transparency in the sense that one sees through TO the original. Later the translator gets his eye on the object without losing grip on the verbal manifestation.

MINUTIA: Canto I, *freckled* not very good for *gaetta*.

III. Not having worked into the idiom one is annoyed by inversions and extra words. Shadwell, if I remember rightly, tried an eight syllable line to get a weight equal to the Italian. I don't know that anyone has thought of attempting the poem in terza rima, but with fewer English lines than the Italian. It would breed, probably, considerable confusion, it might cause a denseness that would defeat the main end: penetrability.

III. 134, *crimson* for *vermiglia*, given the context this is Binyon's worst oversight, or in strict sense *lack* of sight.

Canto V. *Inspects*, good. *I mean* for *dico*, excellent. *Scrutinize*, excellent; *row on row* excellent and not literal, *Desire* and *Reason*, with caps, a little out of style; *rapt in air*, excellent.

And comest journeying through the black air, good. *Caina* is Cain's hell, rather than *place*.

VI, line 3, *which* (printer's error), 1.28, faint Miltonism. *Muddy* for *tinta*, good.

For thou wast made before I was unmade, good.

VII, *from class to class*, modern and not trecento, But very interesting as lyric insertion from the translator. Certain glints or side lights, have value as comment.

IX. I don't know that it is necessary to assume that Dante's Medusa is the strictly classical female. Bunting has perhaps pierced deeper with his 'Come, we'll enamel him'. Enamel is both stone and fusing heat. Frogs don't *run* through water. Not quite sure re *spaldi*, it is a *gallery;* I dare say it might be a closed gallery under *battlements* (as at Assisi).

X. I don't think *slaughterhouse* helps; *nato* has gender, and would allow *son* as equivalent.

XI. *Of all malice*, passage, rather modern in attitude, not quite the *odio in cielo acquista*.

XII. Excellent example Binyon's understanding of the difference between the Dantescan line and English 'pentameter':

Running as in the world once they were wont.

There is an excellent slight distortion making for greater vividness and forcing the reader to think more about the exact meaning of the original in:

Who live by violence and on other's fear.

On the next page, a very clear example of quality of motion in the original

che morì per la bella Deianira.

Figliastro, usually *step* son (printer's error?).

XIII, *fosco,* dark, and *schietto* not so much smooth as *clean* or *straightish; polsi,* both *wrists* and *vigour; becomes the grain,* excellent and the kind of thing Dante liked.

XIV, *tames* for *maturi,* not so felicitous.

1. 92. Dante's metaphor (*pasto*) about all the traffic will stand, but to *seek light,* as well as to have *taste vouchedsafe* is 'uno di piu'.

XV, *avventa?* sea forced in by the wind; *nervi,* a word one could wrangle over; *fiera,* possibly more *proud* than *fierce.*

This minor contentiousness is not impertinent if it emphasize the progressive tightening of poet's attention from Homer to Ovid, to Dante. Dürer's grasshopper in the foreground will serve for visual comparison. Dürer is about the most helpful source for optical suggestion that I can think of. One might also note the almost uninterrupted decadence of writers' attention for centuries after Dante, until the gradual struggle back toward it in Crabbe, Stendhal, Browning and Flaubert.

XVIII. Coming back again to the rhyming, not only are we without strict English feminine equivalents for terminal sounds like *ferrigno, rintoppa, argento, tronca, stagna, feruto,* but any attempt at ornamental rhyme would be out of place, any attempt at explosive rhyme à la Hudibras, or slick epigrammatic rhyme à la Pope or trick rhyme à la Hood, or in fact any kind of rhyming excrescence or ornament would be out of place in the *Commedia,* where Dante's rhyme is but a stiffer thread in the texture, to keep the whole from sprawling and pulling out of trim shape (cf. weave of any high grade trouser material).

One advantage of having the book in penetrable idiom is that we (one, I) see more clearly the grading of Dante's values, and especially how the whole hell reeks with money. The usurers are there as against nature, against the natural increase of agriculture or of any productive work.

Deep hell is reached via Geryon (fraud) of the marvellous patterned hide, and for ten cantos thereafter the damned are all of them damned for money.

The filth heaped upon Thais seems excessive, and Binyon here might have given us a note indicating the gulf between Francesca, or Rahab, and the female who persuaded Alexander to burn the Palace of Persepolis. The allusive bit of conversation doesn't explain this, though I suppose it occurs in whatever account Dante knew.

Dante's morals are almost sovietic in his location of the grafters who are lower down than even the simonists. The English term barrator has been, I think, reserved for translations of Dante and occurs nowhere else outside the dictionary, the present legal sense being either different or specialized. *Baro* is a cheater at cards, in Italian, and *grafter* is the exact equivalent of *barattier*, and if grafter is now a neologism, there are, despite Dante's theorizing about aulic speech, several unparliamentary and uncurial terms in this section of the *Inferno*. Meaning betrayer of public trust, the term is more exact than one used explicitly of appropriation of vessels at sea. The word has applied to so many members of the social register, so many multi-millionaires, American presidents, French cabinet ministers, that it will probably have social if not literary status henceforward.

XX. Whether anyone has noted the Spanish sound at the end of this canto, I don't know, it is possibly a parallel for Arnaut's passage in Provençal in the *Purgatorio* (Sobilia, ? Sibilia, nocque, introcque).

XXV. These low circles are not for simple carnality, the damned here have always a strong stain of meanness, cheating though not, I admit, brought into strong relief: *fraudulent* homicide, Cacus for 'furto *frodolente*'. It begins with the usurers in canto XI. We have lost the medieval discrimination between productive and destructive investment, as we have lost the idea of decay of intelligence re/*ben del intelletto*.

Though Dante's sense of main construction is perhaps rudimentary in comparison with Flaubert's, one might note definite parallels, or stays, tending toward general shape, apart from the diagrammatic or cartographic scheme, e.g. the Spanish suggestion, Ciampolo (XXII) against the honest Romeo, Agnel in the Ovidian metamorphosis (*due e nessun*) vs. Bertrand (*ed uno in due*).

The punishment of prophets and soothsayers seems overdone, but 'wax image witchcraft' is the clue, or at any rate the link between Dante's attitude and our own, a common basis for revulsion. (XX, 123.) 'Fecer malie con erbe e con imago' (XXV, 97.)

> 'Nor Ovid more of Arethusa sing,
> To water turned, or Cadmus to a snake.'

I give this alternative to show how easy it is to get a couple of word for word lines of smooth and liquid versification that are utterly un-Dantescan and translate much less than Binyon's contortion.

After a comparatively dull stretch, canto XXV imposes Dante's adjunct, the profounder metamorphosis of the nature (soul), agglutinous fluidity, and he calls specific attention to it, and to the fact that he is adding something not in Lucan and Ovid. In fact after Guido and Dante, whatever there may have been in human mind and perception, literature does not again make any very serious attempt to enter these regions of consciousness till almost our own day, in the struggles of Henry James and of Ibsen (who has passed out of fad and not yet come back into due currency). (Even Donne and Co. were engaged in something rather different.)

XXVI, moment of inattention '*winging the heavenly vault*' is nonsense, not in the original, out of place.

Re punishment of Ulysses, no one seems to note the perfectly useless, trifling, unprovoked sack of the Cicones in the *Odyssey*. Troy was one thing, they were inveigled.

Helen's father was trying to dodge destiny by a clever combination, etc., but for the sack of the Ciconian town there was no excuse handy, it is pure devilment, and Ulysses and Co. deserved all they got thereafter (not that there is any certainty that Dante had this in mind).

It gives a crime and punishment motif to the *Odyssey*, which is frequently overlooked, and is promptly and (?) properly snowed under by the human interest in Odysseus himself, the live man among duds. Dante definitely accents the theft of the Palladium, whereon one could turn out a volume of comment. It binds through from Homer to Virgil to Dante.

XXVI. Supposing this to be the first segment the translator attempted, his later work shows very considerable progress, and a much more vigorous grasp on his matter.

From here on there are one or two slack passages a matter of a line or two, there are a few extra words and there are compensations as in XXVIII, *plow still disinters* being more specific than *accoglie*, *camminata* is *corridor* rather than *chamber*, and *burella* a *pit-shaft*. One ends with gratitude for demonstration that forty years' honest work do, after all, count for something; that some qualities of writing cannot be attained simply by clever faking, young muscles or a desire to get somewhere in a hurry.

The lines move to their end, that is, draw along the eye of the reader, instead of cradling him in a hammock. The main import is not sacrificed to detail. Simple as this appears in bald statement, it takes time to learn how to achieve it.

THE RENAISSANCE[1]

'All criticism is an attempt to define the classic.'

I

THE PALETTE

No one wants the native American poet to be *au courant* with the literary affairs of Paris and London in order that he may make imitations of Paris and London models, but precisely in order that he shall not waste his lifetime making unconscious, or semi-conscious, imitations of French and English models thirty or forty or an hundred years old.

Chaucer is better than Crestien de Troyes, and the Elizabethan playwrights are more interesting than the Pléïade, because they went beyond their models.

The value of a capital or metropolis is that if a man in a capital cribs, quotes or imitates, someone else immediately lets the cat out of the bag and says what he is cribbing, quoting or imitating.

America has as yet no capital. The study of 'comparative literature' received that label about eighty years ago. It has existed for at least two thousand years. The best Latin poets knew Greek. The troubadours knew several jargons. Dante wrote in Italian, Latin and Provençal, and knew presumably other tongues, including a possible smattering of Hebrew.

I once met a very ancient Oxford 'head,' and in the middle of dinner he turned to me, saying: 'Ah—um, ah—poet. Ah, some one showed me a new poem the other day, the—ah—the *Hound of Heaven*.'

I said, 'Well, what did you think of it?' and he answered, 'Couldn't be bothered to stop for every adjective!'

That enlightened opinion was based on a form of comparative literature called 'the classic education'.

The first step of a renaissance, or awakening, is the importation of models for painting, sculpture or writing. We have had many 'movements', movements stimulated by 'comparison'. Flaminius and

[1] *Poetry*. Chicago, 1914.

Amaltheus and the latinists of the quattrocentro and cinquecento began a movement for enrichment which culminated in the Elizabethan stage, and which produced the French Pléïade. There was wastage and servile imitation. The first effect of the Greek learning was possibly bad. There was a deal of verbalism. We find the decadence of this movement in Tasso and Ariosto and Milton.

The romantic awakening dates from the production of *Ossian*. The last century rediscovered the middle ages. It is possible that this century may find a new Greece in China. In the meantime we have come upon a new table of values. I can only compare this endeavour of criticism to the contemporary search for pure color in painting. We have come to some recognition of the fact that poets like Villon, Sappho and Catullus differ from poets like Milton, Tasso and Camoens, and that size is no more a criterion of writing than it is of painting.

I suppose no two men will agree absolutely respecting 'pure color' or 'good color', but the modern painter recognizes the importance of the palette. One can but make out one's own spectrum or table. Let us choose: Homer, Sappho, Ibycus, Theocritus' idyl of the woman spinning with charmed wheel: Catullus, especially the *Collis O Heliconii*. Not Virgil, especially not the Æneid, where he has no story worth telling, no sense of personality. His hero is a stick who would have contributed to *The New Statesman*. He has a nice verbalism. Dante was right to respect him, for Dante had no Greek, and the Æneid would have stood out nobly against such literature as was available in the year 1300.

I should wish, for myself at least, a few *sirventes* of Bertran de Born, and a few strophes of Arnaut Daniel, though one might learn from Dante himself all that one could learn from Arnaut: precision of statement, particularization. Still there is no tongue like the Provençal wherein to study the subsidiary arts of rhyme and rhyme-blending.

I should want also some further medieval song-book, containing a few more troubadour poems, especially one or two by Vidal and Marueil, six poems of Guido's, German songs out of Will Vesper's song book, and especially some by Walter von der Vogelweide.

I should want Dante of course, and the *Poema del Cid*, and the *Sea-farer* and one passage out of *The Wanderer*. In fact, some knowledge of the Anglo-Saxon fragments—not particularly the Beowulf

—would prevent a man's sinking into contentment with a lot of wish-wash that passes for classic or 'standard' poetry.

So far as the palette of sheer color is concerned, one could, at a pinch, do without nearly all the French poets save Villon. If a man knew Villon and the *Sea-farer* and Dante, and that one scrap of Ibycus, he would, I think, never be able to be content with a sort of pretentious and decorated verse which receives praise from those who have been instructed to like it, or with a certain sort of formal verbalism which is supposed to be good writing by those who have never read any French prose.

What one learns from other French poets, one might as readily learn from Voltaire and Stendhal and Flaubert. One is a fool, of course, if one forego the pleasure of Gautier, and Corbière and the Pléïade, but whether reading them will more discontent you with bad writing than would the reading of Mérimée, I do not know.

A sound poetic training is nothing more than the science of being discontented.

After Villon, the next poet for an absolutely clear palette, is Heine. It takes only a small amount of reading to disgust one, not with English poets, but with English standards. I can not make it too clear that this is not a destructive article. Let anyone drink any sort of liqueur that suits him. Let him enjoy the aroma as a unity, let him forget all that he has heard of technic, but let him not confuse enjoyment with criticism, constructive criticism, or preparation for writing. There is nothing like futurist abolition of past glories in this brief article. It does not preclude an enjoyment of Charles d'Orleans or Mark Alexander Boyd. 'Fra bank to bank, fra wood to wood I rin.'

Since Lamb and his contemporary critics everything has been based, and absurdly based, on the Elizabethans, who are a pastiche. They are 'neither very intense nor very accomplished.' (I leave Shakespeare out of this discussion and also the Greek dramatists.) Or let us say that Keats very probably made the last profitable rehash of Elizabethanism. Or let us query the use of a twentieth century poet's trying to dig up what Sidney himself called 'Petrarch's long deceasèd woes'.

Chaucer should be on every man's shelf. Milton is the worst sort of poison. He is a thorough-going decadent in the worst sense of the term. If he had stopped after writing the short poems one might respect him. The definite contribution in his later work consists in his developing the sonority of the English blank-verse paragraph. If poetry consisted in derivation from the Greek anthology one could not much improve on Drummond of Hawthornden's *Phoebus, Arise*. Milton is certainly no better than Drummond. He makes his pastiche out of more people. He is bombast, of perhaps a very high order, but he is the worst possible food for a growing poet, save possibly Francis Thompson and Tasso.

Goethe is perhaps the only one of the poets who tried to be colossi unsuccessfully, who does not breed noxious contentments. His lyrics are so fine, so unapproachable—I mean they are as good as Heine's and Von der Vogelweide's—but outside his lyrics he never comes off his perch. We are tired of men upon perches.[1]

Virgil is a man on a perch. All these writers of pseudo *épopée* are people on perches. Homer and the author of the *Poema del Cid* are keen on their stories. Milton and Virgil are concerned with decorations and trappings, and they muck about with a moral. Dante is concerned with a *senso morale*, which is totally different matter. He breeds discontentments. Milton does not breed discontentments, he only sets the neophyte trying to pile up noise and adjectives, as in these lines:

> Thus th' ichthyosaurus was dubbed combative . . .
> Captive he led with him Geography . . .
> Whom to encompass in th' exiguous bonds . . .

There is no end to this leonine ramping.

It is possible that only Cavalcanti and Leopardi can lift rhetoric into the realm of poetry. With them one never knows the border line. In Leopardi there is such sincerity, such fire of sombre pessimism, that one can not carp or much question his manner. I do not mean that one should copy the great poets whom I have named above—one does not copy colors on a palette. There is a difference between what one enjoys and what one takes as proof color.

I dare say it is, in this century, inexpicable how or why a man should try to hold up a standard of excellence to which he himself can not constantly attain. An acquaintance of mine deliberately says that mediocre poetry is worth writing. If mediocrities want immortality they must of course keep up some sort of cult of mediocrity; they must develop the habit of preserving Lewis Morris and Co.

[1] Revision: Goethe did attempt to do an honest job of work *in his time*. E.P.

The same crime is perpetrated in American schools by courses in
'American literature'. You might as well give courses in 'American
chemistry', neglecting all foreign discoveries. This is not patriotism.

No American poetry is of any use for the palette. Whitman is the
best of it, but he never pretended to have reached the goal. He knew
himself, and proclaimed himself 'a start in the right direction'. He
never said, 'American poetry is to stay where I left it'; he said it was
to go on from where he started it.

The cult of Poe is an exotic introduced via Mallarmé and Arthur
Symons. Poe's glory as an inventor of macabre subjects has been
shifted into a reputation for verse. The absurdity of the cult is well
gauged by Mallarmé's French translation—*Et le corbeau dit jamais
plus*.

A care for American letters does not consist in breeding a contentment with what has been produced, but in setting a standard for
ambition. A decent artist weeps over a failure; a rotten artist tries to
palm it off as a masterpiece.

NOTE—I have not in this paper set out to give a whole history of
poetry. I have tried in a way to set forth a color-sense. I have said,
as it were, 'Such poets are pure red . . . pure green.' Knowledge of
them is of as much use to a poet as the finding of good color is to a
painter.

Undoubtedly pure color is to be found in Chinese poetry, when
we begin to know enough about it; indeed, a shadow of this perfection is already at hand in translations. Liu Ch'e, Chu Yuan, Chia
I, and the great *vers libre* writers before the Petrarchan age of Li Po,
are a treasury to which the next century may look for as great a
stimulus as the renaissance had from the Greeks.

II

Whether from habit, or from profound intuition, or from sheer
national conceit, one is always looking to America for signs of a
'renaissance'. One is open-eyed to defects. I have heard passionate
nonentities rave about America's literary and artistic barrenness. I
have heard the greatest living American saying, with the measured
tones of deliberate curiosity, 'Strange how all taint of art or letters
seems to shun that continent . . . ah . . . ah, God knows there's little
enough here . . . ah . . .'

And yet we look to the dawn, we count up our symptoms; year

in and year out we say we have this and that, we have so much, and so
much. Our best asset is a thing of the spirit. I have the ring of it in a
letter, now on my desk, from a good but little known poet, complaining of desperate loneliness, envying Synge his material, to-wit,
the Arran Islands and people, wishing me well with my exotics, and
ending with a sort of defiance: 'For me nothing exists, *really exists,*
outside America.'

That writer is not alone in his feeling, nor is he alone in his belief
in tomorrow. That emotion and belief are our motive forces, and as
to their application we can perhaps best serve it by taking stock of
what we have, and devising practical measures. And we must do this
without pride, and without parochialism; we have no one to cheat
save ourselves. It is not a question of scaring someone else, but of
making ourselves efficient. We must learn what we can from the
past, we must learn what other nations have done successfully under
similar circumstances, we must think how they did it.

We have, to begin with, architecture, the first of the arts to arrive,
the most material, the least dependent on the inner need of the poor
—for the arts are noble only as they meet the inner need of the poor.
Bach is given to all men, Homer is given to all men: you need only
the faculty of music or of patience to read or to hear. Painting and
sculpture are given to all men in a particular place, to all who have
money for travel.

And architecture comes first, being the finest branch of advertisement, advertisement of some god who has been successful, or of
some emperor or of some business man—a material need, plus
display. At any rate we have architecture, the only architecture of our
time. I do not mean our copies of old buildings, lovely and lovable
as they are; I mean our own creations, our office buildings like
greater *campanili,* and so on.

And we have, or we are beginning to have, collections. We have
had at least one scholar in Ernest Fenollosa, and one patron in Mr
Freer. I mean that these two men at least have worked as the great
Italian researchers and collectors of the quattrocento worked and
collected. But mostly America, from the White House to the gutter,
is still dominated by a 'puritanical' hatred to what is beyond its
understanding.

So it is to the fighting minority that I speak, to a minority that has
been until now gradually forced out of the country. We have looked

to the wrong powers. We have not sufficiently looked to ourselves. We have not defined the hostility or inertia that is against us. We have not recognized with any Voltairian clearness the nature of this opposition, and we have not realized to what an extent a renaissance is a thing made—a thing made by conscious propaganda.

The scholars of the quattrocento had just as stiff a stupidity and contentment and ignorance to contend with. It is in the biographies of Erasmus and Lorenzo Valla that we must find consolation. They were willing to work at foundations. They did not give the crowd what it wanted. The middle ages had been a jumble. There may have been a charming diversity, but there was also the darkness of decentralization. There had been minute vortices at such castles as that of Savairic de Maleon, and later at the universities. But the *rinascimento* began when Valla wrote in the preface of the *Elegantiae*:

Linguam Latinam distribuisse minus erit, optimam frugem, et vere divinam nec corporis, sed animi cibum? Haec enim gentes populosque omnes, omnibus artibus, quae liberales vocantur, instituit: haec optimas leges edocuit: haec viam ad omnem sapientiam munivit, haec denique praestitit, ne barbari amplius dici possent. . . . In qua lingua disciplinae cunctae libero homine dignae continetur. . . . Linguam Romanam vivere plus, quam urbem.

'*Magnum ergo Latini sermonis sacramentum est.*' '*Ibi namque Romanum imperium est, ubicunque Romana lingua dominatur.*'

That is not 'the revival of classicism'. It is not a worship of corpses. It is an appreciation of the great Roman vortex, an understanding of, and an awakening to, the value of a capital, the value of centralization, in matters of knowledge and art, and of the interaction and stimulus of genius foregathered. *Ubicunque Romana lingua dominatur!*

That sense, that reawakening to the sense of the capital, resulted not in a single great vortex, such as Dante had dreamed of in his propaganda for a great central court, a peace tribunal, and in all his ghibelline speculations; but it did result in the numerous vortices of the Italian cities, striving against each other not only in commerce but in the arts as well.

America has no natural capital. Washington is a political machine, I dare say a good enough one. If we are to have an art capital it also must be made by conscious effort. No city will make such effort on behalf of any other city. The city that plays for this glory will have to plot, deliberately to plot, for the gathering in of great artists, not merely as incidental lecturers but as residents. She will have to plot for the centralization of young artists. She will have to give them living conditions as comfortable as Paris has given since the days of Abelard.

The universities can no longer remain divorced from contemporary intellectual activity. The press cannot longer remain divorced from the vitality and precision of an awakened university scholarship. Art and scholarship need not be wholly at loggerheads.

But above all there must be living conditions for artists; not merely for illustrators and magazine writers, not merely for commercial producers, catering to what they think 'the public' or 'their readers' desire.

Great art does not depend on the support of riches, but without such aid it will be individual, separate, and spasmodic; it will not group and become a great period. The individual artist will do fine work in corners, to be discovered after his death. Some good enough poet will be spoiled by trying to write stuff as vendible as bath-tubs; or another because, not willing or able to rely on his creative work, he had to make his mind didactic by preparing to be a professor of literature, or abstract by trying to be a professor of philosophy, or had to participate in some other fiasco. But for all that you will not be able to stop the great art, the true art, of the man of genius.

Great art does not depend upon comfort, it does not depend upon the support of riches. But a great age is brought about only with the aid of wealth, because a great age means the deliberate fostering of genius, the gathering-in and grouping and encouragement of artists.

In my final paper of this series, I shall put forth certain plans for improvement.

III

No, I am not such a fool as to believe that a man writes better for being well fed, or that he writes better for being hungry either. Hunger—some experience of it—is doubtless good for a man; it puts an edge on his style, and so does hard common sense. In the end I believe in hunger, because it is an experience, and no artist can have too many experiences. Prolonged hunger, intermittent hunger and anxiety, will of course break down a man's constitution, render him fussy and over-irritable, and in the end ruin his work or prevent its full development.

That nation is profoundly foolish which does not get the maximum of best work out of its artists. The artist is one of the few producers. He, the farmer and the artisan create wealth; the rest shift and consume it. The net value of good art to its place of residence has been computed in logarithms; I shall not go into the decimals. When there was talk of selling Holbein's *Duchess of Milan* to an American, England bought the picture for three hundred and fifty thousand dollars. They figured that people came to London to see the picture, that the receipts of the community were worth more per annum than the interest on the money. People go where there are good works of art. Pictures and sculpture and architecture pay. Even literature and poetry pay, for where there is enough intelligence to produce and maintain good writing, there society is pleasant and the real estate values increase. Mr F. M. Hueffer has said that the difference between London and other places is that 'No one lives in London merely for the sake of making money enough to live somewhere else.'

The real estate values, even in Newark, New Jersey, would go up if Newark were capable of producing art, literature or the drama. In the quattrocento men went from one Italian city to another for reasons that were not solely commercial.

The question is not: Shall we try to keep up the arts?— but: How can we maintain the arts most efficiently? Paris can survive 1870 and 1914 because she is an intellectual and artistic vortex. She is that vortex not because she had a university in the middle ages—Cordova and Padua had also medieval universities. France recognizes the cash value of artists. They do not have to pay taxes save when covenient; they have a ministry of fine arts doing its semi-efficient best. Literary but inartistic England moves with a slow paw pushing occasional chunks of meat towards the favoured. England does as well as can be expected, considering that the management of such affairs is entrusted to men whose interests are wholly political and who have no sort of intuition or taste. That is to say, in England, if someone of good social position says that your work is 'really literary', and that you are not likely to attack the hereditary interests or criticise the Albert Memorial, you can be reasonably sure of a pension. If your sales have suddenly slumped, you can also have 'royal bounty', provided that you respect the senile and decrepit and say a good word for Watts's pictures.

The result is that France gets Rodin's work when he is fifty instead of the day he began doing good work. England gets Rodin's work after it has gone to seed, and rejects the best work of Epstein in his full vigor. England let half her last generation of poets die off, and pensioned such survivors as hadn't gone into something 'practical'.

But even this is enough to show that bourgeois France and stolid England recognize the cash value of art. I don't imagine that these sordid material considerations will weigh with my compatriots. America is a nation of idealists, as we all know; and they are going to support art for art's sake, because they love it, because they 'want the best', even in art. They want beauty; they can't get along without it. They are already tired of spurious literature.

They recognize that all great art, all good art, goes against the grain of contemporary taste. They want men who can stand out against it. They want to back such men and women to the limit. How are they to go about it? Subsidy? Oh, no. They don't want to pauperize artists!

Of course Swinburne was subsidized by his immediate forebears, and Shelley also; and Browning, the robust, the virile, was subsidized by his wife; and even Dante and Villon did not escape the stigma of having received charities. Nevertheless it is undemocratic to believe that a man with money should give—horrible word!—*give* it, even though not all of it, to painters and poets.

They give it to sterile professors; to vacuous preachers of a sterilized form of Christianity; they support magazines whose set and avowed purpose is either to degrade letters or to prevent their natural development. Why in heaven's name shouldn't they back creators, as well as students of Quinet? Why shouldn't they endow men whose studies are independent, put them on an equal footing with men whose scholarship is merely a pasteurized, Bostonized imitation of Leipzig?

How are they to go about it? Committees are notably stupid; they vote for mediocrity, their mind is the least common denominator. Even if there are a few intelligent members, the unintelligent members will be the ones with spare time, and they will get about trying to 'run the committee', trying to get in new members who will vote for their kind of inanity. *Et cetera, ad infinitum.*

There is one obvious way, which does not compel individuals to wait for an organization:

Private people can give stipends to individual artists. That is to say, you, Mr Rockefeller, you, Laird Andy of Skibo, and the rest of you (I am not leaving you out, reader, because you have only one million or half of one); you can endow individuals for life just as you endow chairs in pedagogy and callisthenics. More than that, you can endow them with the right to name their successors. If they don't need the money they can pass it on, before their deaths, to younger artists in whom they believe.

For instance, you may begin by endowing Mr James Whitcomb Riley, Mr George Santayana, Mr Theodore Roosevelt, Mr Jack London, or anybody else you believe in. And any artist will applaud you. Any artist would rather have a benefice conferred upon him by *one* of these men as an individual than by a committee of the 'forty leading luminaries of literature'. I take a hard case; I don't suppose for a moment that Mr Riley or Mr Roosevelt, Mr Santayana or Mr London wants money—in all probability they would one and all refuse it if offered; but none of them would refuse the right of allotting an income, sufficient to cover the bare necessities of life, to some active artist whom they believe in.

If you endow enough men, individuals of vivid and different personality, and make the endowment perpetual, to be handed down from artist to artist, you will have put the arts in a position to defy the subversive pressure of commercial advantage, and of the mediocre spirit which is the bane and hidden terror of democracy.

Democracies have fallen, they have always fallen, because humanity craves the outstanding personality. And hitherto no democracy has provided sufficient place for such an individuality. If you so endow sculptors and writers you will begin for America an age of awakening which will over-shadow the quattrocento; because our opportunity is greater than Leonardo's: we have more aliment, we have not one classic tradition to revivify, we have China and Egypt, and the unknown lands lying upon the roof of the world—Khotan, Kara-shar and Kan-su.

So much for the individual opportunity—now for the civic. Any city which cares for its future can perfectly well start its vortex. It can found something between a graduate seminar and the usual

'Arts Club' made up of business men and of a few 'rather more than middle-aged artists who can afford to belong'.

I have set the individually endowed artist against the endowed professor or editor. I would set the endowment of such grouping of young artists parallel with the endowment, for one year or three, of scholars and fellows by our universities. Some hundreds of budding professors are so endowed, to say nothing of students of divinity.

There is no reason why students of the arts—not merely of painting but of all the arts—should not be so endowed, and so grouped: that is, as artists, not merely as followers of one segregated art. Such endowment would get them over the worst two or three years of their career, the years when their work can't possibly pay.

Scientists are so endowed. It is as futile to expect a poet to get the right words, or any sort of artists to do real work, with one eye on the public, as it would be to expect the experimenter in a chemical laboratory to advance the borders of science, if he have constantly to consider whether his atomic combinations are going to flatter popular belief, or suit the holders of monopolies in some over-expensive compound. The arts and sciences hang together. Any conception which does not see them in their interrelation belittles both. What is good for one is good for the other.

Has any one yet answered the query: why is it that in other times artists went on getting more and more powerful as they grew older, whereas now they decline after the first outburst, or at least after the first successes? Compare this with the steady growth of scientists.

The three main lines of attack, then, which I have proposed in this little series of articles, are as follows:

First, that we should develop a criticism of poetry based on world-poetry, on the work of maximum excellence. (It does not in the least matter whether this standard be that of my own predilections, or crochets or excesses. It matter very much that it be decided by men who have made a first-hand study of world-poetry, and who 'have had the tools in their hands'.)

Second, that there be definite subsidy of individual artists, writers, etc., such as will enable them to follow their highest ambitions without needing to conciliate the ignorant *en route*. (Even some of our stock-size magazine poets might produce something worth while if they could afford occasionally to keep quiet for six months or a year at a stretch.)

Third, there should be a foundation of such centres as I have described. There should be in America the 'gloire de cénacle'. Tariff laws should favor the creative author rather than the printer, but that matter is too long to be gone into.

In conclusion, the first of these matters must be fought out among the artists themselves. The second matter concerns not only the excessively rich, but the normally and moderately rich, who contribute to all sorts of less useful affairs: redundant universities, parsons, Y.M.C.A.'s, and the general encouragement of drab mediocrity. The third matter concerns millionaires, multimillionaires and municipalities.

When a civilization is vivid it preserves and fosters all sorts of artists—painters, poets, sculptors, musicians, architects. When a civilization is dull and anemic it preserves a rabble of priests, sterile instructors, and repeaters of things second-hand. If literature is to reappear in America it must come through, but in spite of, the present commercial system of publication.

NOTES ON
ELIZABETHAN CLASSICISTS[1]

I

The reactions and 'movements' of literature are scarcely, if ever, movements against good work or good custom. Dryden and the precursors of Dryden did not react against *Hamlet*. If the eighteenth-century movement toward regularity is among those least sympathetic to the public of our moment, it is 'historically justifiable', even though the katachrestical vigours of Marlowe's *Hero and Leander* may not be enough to 'explain' the existence of Pope. A single faulty work showing great powers would hardly be enough to start a 'reaction'; only the mediocrity of a given time can drive the more intelligent men of that time to 'break with tradition'.

I take it that the phrase 'break with tradition' is currently used to mean 'desert the more obvious imbecilities of one's immediate elders'; at least, it has had that meaning in the periodical mouth for some years. Only the careful and critical mind will seek to know how much tradition inhered in the immediate elders.

Vaguely in some course of literature we heard of 'the old fourteeners', vulgariter, the metre of the *Battle of Ivry*. *Hamlet* could not have been written in this pleasing and popular measure. The 'classics', however, appeared in it. For Court ladies and cosmopolitan heroes it is perhaps a little bewildering, but in the mouth of Oenone:

The Heroycal Epistles of the learned Poet Publius Ovidius Naso. In English verse: set out and translated by George Tuberuile. 1567. London: Henry Denham.

OENONE TO PARIS

To Paris that was once her owne
   though now it be not so,
From Ida, Oenon greeting sendes
   as these hir letters show,

[1] Originally appeared as "Elizabethan Classicists" in *The Egoist*: IV, 8 (Sept. 1917) 120–22; 9 (Oct. 1917) 135–36; 10 (Nov. 1917) 154–56; 11 (Dec. 1917) 168–69; and V, 1 (Jan. 1918) 8–9.

May not the nouel wife endure
    that thou my Pissle reade.
That they with Grecian fist were wrought
    thou needste not stand in dreade.

Pegasian nymph renounde in Troie,
    Oenone hight by name,
Of thee (of thee that were mine owne), complaine
    if thou permit the same,
What froward god doth seeke to barre
    Oenone to be thine?
Or by what guilt have I deserude
    that Paris should decline?
Take paciently deserude woe
    and never grutch at all:
But undeserued wrongs will grieve
    a woman at the gall.

Scarce were thou of so noble fame,
    as plainly doth appeare:
When I (the offspring of a floud)
    did choose thee for my feere.
And thou, who now art Priams sonne
    (all reuerence layde apart)
Were tho a Hyard to beholde
    when first thou wanste my heart.
How oft have we in shaddow laine
    whylst hungrie flocks have fedde?
How oft have we of grasse and greanes
    preparde a homely bedde?
How oft on simple stacks of strawe
    and bennet did we rest?
How oft the dew and foggie mist
    our lodging hath opprest?
Who first discouerde thee the holtes
    And lawndes of lurcking game?
Who first displaid thee where the whelps
    lay sucking of their Dame?
I sundrie tymes have holpe to pitch
    thy toyles for want of ayde:

And forst thy Hounds to climbe the hilles
    that gladly would have stayde.

One boysterous Beech Oenone's name
    in outward barke doth beare:
And with thy caruing knife is cut
    OENON, every wheare.
And as the trees in tyme doe ware
    so doth encrease my name:
Go to, grow on, erect your selves
    helpe to aduance my fame.

There growes (I minde it uerie well)
    upon a banck, a tree
Whereon ther doth a fresh recorde
    and will remaine of mee,
Live long thou happie tree, I say,
    that on the brinck doth stande;
And hast ingraued in thy barke
    these wordes, with Paris hande:

'When Pastor Paris shall reuolte,
    and Oenon's love forgoe:
Then Xanthus waters shall recoyle,
    and to their Fountaines floe.'
Now Ryuer backward bend thy course,
    let Xanthus streame retier:
For Paris hath renounst the Nymph
    and prooude himself a lier.
That cursed day bred all my doole,
    the winter of my joy,
With cloudes of froward fortune fraught
    procurde me this annoy;
When cankred craftie Iuno came
    with Venus (Nurce of Love)
And Pallas eke, that warlike wench,
    their beauties pride to proue.

The pastoral note is at least not unpleasing, and the story more
real than in the mouths of the later poets, who enliven us with the
couplet to the tune:

> 'Or Paris, who, to steal that daintie piece,
> Traveled as far as 'twas 'twixt Troy and Greece.'

The old versions of Ovid are worth more than a week's random reading. Turning from the *Heroides* I find this in a little booklet said to have been 'printed abroad'. It is undated, and bears 'C. Marlow' on the title-page.

AMORUM[1]

> Now on the sea from her olde loue comes shee
> That drawes the day from heaven's cold axle-tree,
> Aurora whither slidest thou down againe,
> And byrdes from Memnon yearly shall be slaine.
>
> Now in her tender arms I sweetlie bide,
> If euer, now well lies she by my side,
> The ayre is colde, and sleep is sweetest now,
> And byrdes send foorth shril notes from every bow.
>
> Whither runst thou, that men and women loue not,
> Holde in thy rosie horses that they moue not.
> Ere thou rise stars teach seamen where to saile,
> But when thou comest, they of their course faile.
> Poore trauailers though tired, rise at thy sight,
> The painful Hinde by thee to fild is sent,
> Slow oxen early in the yoke are pent.
> Thou cousnest boyes of sleep, and dost betray them
> To Pedants that with cruel lashes pay them.

Any fault is more pleasing than the current fault of the many. One should read a few bad poets of every era, as one should read a little trash of every contemporary nation, if one would know the worth of the good in either.

Turning from translation, for a moment, to *The Shepherdes Starre* (1591), for the abandonment of syntax and sense, for an interesting experiment in metric, for beautiful lines astray in a maze of unsense, I find the incoherent conclusion of much incoherence, where Amaryllis says: 'In the meane while let this my Roundilay end my follie'; and tilts at the age-old bogie of 'Sapphics', Aeolium Carmen, which perhaps Catullus alone of imitators has imitated with success.

---

[1] *Amorum*, lib. 1, elegia 13.

THE SHEPHERDES STARRE, 1591

Amaryllis. In the mean while let this my Roundilay end my follie:

Sith the nymphs are thought to be happier creatures,
For that is faier *Helicon* a Fountaine,
Where all use like white Ritch iuorie foreheads
    Daily to sprinckle,

Sith the quire of Muses atend *Diana*,
Ever use to bathe heauie thoughts refyning,
With the Silver skinne, Civet and Mir using
    For their adornment,

Sith my sacred Nymphs priuiledge abateth,
Cause *Dianas* grace did elect the *Myrtle*,
To be pride of every branch in order
    last of her handmaides;

Should then I thus liue to behold euerted
Skies, with impure eyes in a fountaine harboured
Where *Titans* honour seated is as under
    All the beholders?

Helpe wofull *Ecco*, reabound relenting,
That *Dianas* grace on her helpe recalling,
May well heare thy voice to bewaile, reanswere
    Faire *Amaryllis*.

Fairer in deede then *Galatea*, fairest
Of *Dianas* troope to bewitch the wisest,
With amasing eye to abandon humours
    of any gallants,

Shee *Thetis* faier, *Galataea modest*,
—Albeit some say in a Chrystal often,
Tis a rule, there lurketh a deadly poyson,
    Tis but a false rule.

For what Yse is hid in a Diamond Ring,
Where the wise beholder hath eyes refusing,

Allabasters vaines to no workman hidden,
    Gold to no Touchstone.

There bedeckes fairest *Rosamond* the fountaine,
Where resorts those greene *Driades* the waterie
Nimphs, of olive plants recreat by *Phaebus*
    Till they be maried.

So beginning ends the report of her fame,
Whose report passing my pennes relation,
Doth entreat her loue, by reinspiration
To dull heads yeelding faer eies reflection,
    Still to be present.

Surely among poems containing a considerable amount of beauty, this is one of the worst ever written. Patient endeavour will reveal to the reader a little more coherence and syntax than is at first glance apparent, but from this I draw no moral conclusion.

For all half-forgotten writing there is, to my mind, little criticism save selection. 'Those greene *Driades*'; Oenone, 'offspring of a floud'; the music of the Elegy must make their own argument.

II

A great age of literature is perhaps always a great age of translations; or follows it. The Victorians in lesser degree had FitzGerald, and Swinburne's Villon, and Rossetti. One is at first a little surprised at the importance which historians of Spanish poetry give to Boscan, but our histories give our own translators too little. And worse, we have long since fallen under the blight of the Miltonic or noise tradition, to a stilted dialect in translating the classics, a dialect which imitates the idiom of the ancients rather than seeking their meaning, a state of mind which aims at 'teaching the boy his Latin' or Greek or whatever it may be, but has long since ceased to care for the beauty of the original; or which perhaps thinks 'appreciation' obligatory, and the meaning and content mere accessories.

Golding was no inconsiderable poet, and the Marlow of the translations has beauties no whit inferior to the Marlow of original composition. In fact, the skill of the translations forbids one to balk at the terminal *e*. We conclude the identity without seeking through works of reference.

Compare (pardon the professional tone whereof I seem unable to divest myself in discussing these matters), compare the anonymous rather unskilled work in the translation of *Sixe Idillia*, with Marlow's version of *Amorum*, lib. III, 13.

THE XVIII JDILLION

HELLENS EPITHALAMION[1]

In Sparta long agoe, where Menelaus wore the crowne,
Twelve noble Virgins, daughters to the greatest in the towne,
All dight upon their haire in Crowtoe garlands fresh and greene,
Danst at the chamber doore of Helena the Queene,
What time this Menelay, the younger Sonne of Atreus,
Did marry with this louely daughter of Prince Tyndarus.
And therewithal at eue, a wedding song they jointly sung,
With such a shuffling of their feete, that all the Pallace rung.

THE IX JDILLION

CYCLOPS TO GALATEA THE WATER-NYMPH

O Apple, sweet, of thee, and of myself I use to sing,
And that at midnight oft, for thee, aleavne faunes up I bring,
All great with young, and four beares whelps, I nourish up for thee.
But come thou hither first, and thou shalt have them all of me.
And let the blewish colorde Sea beat on the shore so nie.
The night with me in cave, thou shalt consume more pleasantlie.
There are the shadie Baies, and there tall Cypres-trees doe sprout,
And there is Ivie blacke, and fertill Vines are al about.
Coole water there I haue, distilled of the whitest snowe,
A drinke divine, which out of woody Aetna mount doth flowe.
In these respects, who in the Sea and waues would rather be?
But if I seem as yet, too rough and sauage unto thee,
Great store of Oken woode I have, and never quenched fire;
And I can well endure my soul to burn with thy desire,
With this my onely eie, then which I nothing think more trimme,
Now woe is me, my mother bore not me with finns to swimme,
That I might dive to thee.

---

[1] *Sixe Idillia,* published by Joseph Barnes, Oxford, 1588; one hundred copies reprinted by H. Daniel, Oxford, 1883.

The 'shuffling of their feete' is pleasing, but the Cyclops speaks perhaps too much in his own vein. Marlow is much more dexterous.

AMORUM[1]

Ac amicam si pecatura est, ut occulte peccat

Seeing thou art faire, I bar not thy false playing,
But let not me poore soule wit of thy straying.
Nor do I give thee counsaile to liue chast
But that thou wouldst dissemble when 'tis past.
She hath not trod awry that doth deny it,
Such as confesse haue lost their good names by it.
What madness ist to tell night sports by day,
Or hidden secrets openly to bewray,
The strumpet with the stranger will not do,
Before the room be cleare, and dore put too.
Will you make shipwracke of your honest name
And let the world be witness of the same?
Be more aduisde, walke as a puritaine,
And I shall think you chast do what you can.
Slippe still, onely deny it when tis done,
And before people immodest speeches shun,
The bed is for lasciuious toyings meete,
There use all toyes, and treade shame under feete,
When you are up and drest, be sage and graue,
And in the bed hide all the faults you haue.
Be not ashamed to strippe you being there
And mingle thighes, mine ever yours to beare,
There in your rosie lips my tongue intomb,
Practice a thousand sports when there you come,
Forbare no wanton words you there would speake,
And with your pastime let the bedsted creake.
But with your robes, put on an honest face,
And blush and seeme as you were full of grace.
Deceiue all, let me erre, and think I am right
And like a wittal, thinke thee uoide of slight.

[1] *Amorum*, lib. III, elegia 13. These translations are reprinted in the Clarendon Press edition of Marlowe's Works, 1910.

The reader, if he can divert his thought from matter to manner, may well wonder how much the eighteenth-century authors have added, or if they added anything save a sort of faculty for systematization of product, a power to repeat certain effects regularly and at will.

But Golding's book published before all these others will give us more matter for reverie. One wonders, in reading it, how much more of the Middle Ages was Ovid. We know well enough that they read him and loved him more than the more Tennysonian Virgil.

Yet how great was Chaucer's debt to the Doctor Amoris? That we will never know. Was Chaucer's delectable style simply the first Ovid in English? Or, as likely, is Golding's Ovid a mirror of Chaucer? Or is a fine poet ever translated until another his equal invents a new style in a later language? Can we, for our part, know our Ovid until we find him in Golding? Is there one of us so good at his Latin, and so ready in imagination that Golding will not throw upon his mind shades and glamours inherent in the original text which had for all that escaped him? Is any foreign speech ever our own, ever so full of beauty as our *lingua materna* (whatever *lingua materna* that may be)? Or is not a new beauty created, an old beauty doubled when the overchange is well done?

Will

> '. . . . cum super atria velum
> Candida purpureum simulatas inficit umbras'

quite give us the 'scarlet curtain' of the simile in the *Flight from Hippomenes?* Perhaps all these things are personal matters, and not matter for criticism or discussion. But it is certain that 'we' have forgotten our Ovid, 'we' being the reading public, the readers of English poetry, have forgotten our Ovid since Golding went out of print.

METAMORPHOSES[1]

While in this garden Proserpine was taking hir pastime,
In gathering eyther Violets blew, or Lillies white as Lime,
And while of Maidenly desire she fillde hir Haund and Lap,
Endeauoring to outgather hir companions there. By hap
Dis spide her: lovde her: caught her up: and all at once well nere.
So hastie, hote, and swift a thing is Loue as may appeare.

[1] *Metamorphoses*, by Arthur Golding, 1567. The Fyft booke. Reprint of 300 copies by De la More Press, in folio.

The Ladie with a wailing voyce afright did often call
Hir mother and hir waiting Maides, but Mother most of all.

ATALANTA[1]

And from the Cities of Tegea there came the Paragone
Of Lycey forrest, Atalant, a goodly Ladie, one
Of Schoenyes daughters, then a Maide. The garment she did weare
A brayded button fastned at hir gorget. All hir heare
Untrimmed in one only knot was trussed. From hir left
Side hanging on hir shoulder was an Ivorie quiuer deft:
Which being full of arrowes, made a clattering as she went.
And in hir right hand she did beare a bow already bent.
Hir furniture was such as this. Hir countnance and hir grace
Was such as in a Boy might well be cald a Wenches face.

THE HUNTING

Assoone as that the men came there, some pitched the toyles,
Some tooke the couples from the Dogs, and some pursude the foyles
In places where the swine had tract: desiring for to spie
Their owne destruction. Now there was a hollow bottom by,
To which the watershots of raine from all the high grounds drew.
Within the compasse of this pond great store of Oysyers grew;
And Sallowes lithe, and flackring flags, and moorish Rushes eke,
And lazie Reedes on little shankes, and other baggage like.
From hence the Bore was rowzed out, and fiersly forth he flies
Among the thickest of his foes as thunder from the Skies.

FLIGHT FROM HIPPOMENES

.... Now while Hippomenes
Debates theis things within himself and other like to these,
The Damzell ronnes as if her feete were wings. And though that shee
Did fly as swift as arrow from a Turkye bowe: yit hee
More woondred at hir beawtye than at swiftnesse of her pace,
Her ronning greatly did augment her beawtye and her grace.
The wynd ay whisking from her feete the labells of her socks
Uppon her back as whyght as snowe did tosse her golden locks,

---

[1] *Atalanta*. The Eight booke.

And eke thembroydred garters that were tyde beneathe her ham.
A redness mixt with whyght uppon her tender body cam,
As when a scarlet curtaine streynd ageinst a playstred wall
Dooth cast like shadowe, making it seeme ruddye therewith all.

Reality and particularization! The Elizabethans themselves began
the long series of sins against them. In Ovid at least they are not
divorced from sweeping imagination as in the *Fasti* (v. 222):

'Unius tellus ante coloris erat';

or in the opening of the *Metamorphoses*, as by Golding:
'Which Chaos hight, a huge rude heape and nothing else but even
A heavie lump and clottred clod of seedes.

Nor yet the earth amiddes the ayre did hang by wondrous slight
Just peysed by hir proper weight. Nor winding in and out
Did Amphitrytee with her armes embrace the earth about,
For where was earth, was sea and ayre, so was the earth unstable.
The ayre all darke, the sea likewise to beare a ship unable.

The suttle ayre to flickring fowles and birdes he hath assignde'.

I throw in the last line for the quality of one adjective, and close
this section of excerpts with a bit of fun anent Bacchus.

ADDRESS TO BACCHUS. IV

Thou into Sea didst send
The Tyrrhene shipmen. Thou with bittes the sturdy neckes dost bend
Of spotted Lynxes: throngs of Fownes and Satyres on thee tend,
And that old Hag that with a staff his staggering limmes doth stay
Scarce able on his Asse to sit for reeling every way.
Thou comest not in any place but that is hearde the noyse
Of gagling womens tatling tongues and showting out of boyes.
With sound of Timbrels, Tabors, Pipes, and Brazen pannes and pots
Confusedly among the rout that in thine Orgies trots.

III

The sin or error of Milton—let me leave off vague expressions of a
personal active dislike, and make my yearlong diatribes more coherent.
Honour where it is due! Milton undoubtedly built up the sonority of
the blank verse paragraph in our language. But he did this at the cost

of his idiom. He tried to turn English into Latin; to use an unin-flected language as if it were an inflected one, neglecting the genius of English, distorting its fibrous manner, making schoolboy trans-lations of Latin phrases: 'Him who disobeys me disobeys'.

I am leaving apart all my disgust with what he has to say, his asinine bigotry, his beastly hebraism, the coarseness of his mentality, I am dealing with a technical matter. All this clause structure modelled on Latin rhetoric, borrowed and thrust into sonorities which are sometimes most enviable.

The sin of vague pompous words is neither his own sin nor original. Euphues and Gongora were before him. The Elizabethan audience was interested in large speech. 'Multitudinous seas incarna-dine' caused as much thrill as any epigram in *Lady Windermere's Fan* or *The Importance of Being Earnest*. The dramatists had started this manner, Milton but continued in their wake, adding to their high-soundingness his passion for latinization, the latinization of a lang-uage peculiarly unfitted for his sort of latinization. Golding in the ninth year of Elizabeth can talk of 'Charles his wane' in translating Ovid, but Milton's fields are 'irriguous', and worse, and much more notably displeasing, his clause structure is a matter of 'quem's', 'cui's', and 'quomodo's'.

Another point in defence of Golding: his constant use of 'did go', 'did say', etc., is not fustian and mannerism; it was contemporary speech, though in a present-day poet it is impotent affectation and definite lack of technique. I am not saying 'Golding is a greater poet than Milton'; these quantitative comparisons are in odium.[1] Milton is the most unpleasant of English poets,and he has certain definite and analysable defects. His unpleasantness is a matter of personal taste. His faults of language are subject to argument just as are the faults of any other poet's language. His popularity has been largely due to his bigotry, but there is no reason why that popular quality should be for ever a shield against criticism. His real place is nearer to Drum-mond of Hawthornden than to 'Shakespear and Dante' whereto the stupidity of our forebears tried to exalt him.

His short poems are his defenders' best stronghold, and it will take some effort to show that they are better than Drummond's *Phoebus Arise*. In all this I am not insisting on 'Charles his wane' as

[1] 1929. His *Metamorphoses* form possibly the most beautiful book in our language.

the sole mode of translation. I point out that Golding was endeavouring to convey the sense of the original to his readers. He names the thing of his original author, by the name most germane, familiar, homely, to his hearers. He is intent on conveying a meaning, and not on bemusing them with a rumble. And I hold that the real poet is sufficiently absorbed in his content to care more for the content than the rumble; and also that Chaucer and Golding are more likely to find the *mot juste* (whether or no they held any theories there-anent) than were for some centuries their successors, saving the author of *Hamlet*.

Beside the fustian tradition, the tradition of cliché phrases, copies of Greek and Latin clause structure and phrase structure, two causes have removed the classics from us. On one hand we have ceased to read Greek with the aid of Latin cribs, and Latin is the only language into which any great amount of Greek can be in a lively fashion set over; secondly, there is no discrimination in classical studies. The student is told that all the classics are excellent and that it is a crime to think about what he reads. There is no use pretending that these literatures are read as literature. An apostolic succession of school teachers has become the medium of distribution.

The critical faculty is discouraged, the poets are made an exercise, a means of teaching the language. Even in this there is a great deal of buncome. It is much better that a man should use a crib, and know the content of his authors than that he should be able to recite all the rules in Allen and Greenough's *Grammar*. Even the teaching by rules is largely a hoax. The Latin had certain *case feelings*. For the genitive he felt source, for the dative indirect action upon, for the accusative direct action upon, for the ablative all other peripheric sensation, i.e. it is less definitely or directly the source than the genitive, it is contributory circumstance; lump the locative with it, and one might call it the 'circumstantial'. Where it and the dative have the same form, we may conclude that there was simply a general indirect case.

The humanizing influence of the classics depends more on a wide knowledge, a reading knowledge, than on an ability to write exercises in Latin; it is ridiculous to pretend that a reading knowledge need imply more than a general intelligence of the minutiae of grammar. I am not assuming the position of those who objected to Erasmus's 'tittle-tattles',[1] but there is a sane order of importance.

[1] Greek accents.

When the classics were a new beauty and ecstasy people cared a damn sight more about the meaning of the authors, and a damn sight less about their grammar and philology.

We await, *vei jauʒen lo jorn*, the time when the student will be encouraged to say which poems bore him to tears, and which he thinks rubbish, and whether there is any beauty in 'Maecenas sprung from a line of kings'. It is bad enough that so much of the finest poetry in the world should be distributed almost wholly through class-rooms, but if the first question to be asked were: 'Gentlemen, are these verses worth reading?' instead of 'What is the mood of 'manet'?' if, in short, the professor were put on his mettle to find poems worth reading instead of given the *facilem descensum*, the shoot, the supine shoot, of grammatical discussion, he might more dig out the vital spots in his authors, and meet from his class a less persistent undercurrent of conviction that all Latin authors are a trial.

The uncritical scholarly attitude has so spread, that hardly a living man can tell you at what points the Latin authors surpass the Greek, yet the comparison of their differences is full of all fascinations. Because Homer is better than Virgil, and Aeschylus, presumably, than Seneca, there has spread a superstition that the mere fact of a text being in Greek makes it of necessity better than a text written in Latin—which is buncombe.

Ovid indubitably added and invented much that is not in Greek, and the Greeks might be hard put to it to find a better poet among themselves than is their disciple Catullus. Is not Sappho, in comparison, a little, just a little Swinburnian?

I do not state this as dogma, but one should be open to such speculation.

I know that all classic authors have been authoritatively edited and printed by Teubner, and their wording ultimately settled at Leipzig, but all questions concerning 'the classics' are not definitely settled, cold-storaged, and shelved.

I may have been an ensanguined fool to spend so much time on medieval literature, or the time so 'wasted' may help me to read Ovid with greater insight. I may have been right or wrong to read renaissance latinists, instead of following the professional caution that 'after all if one confined oneself to the accepted authors one was sure of reading good stuff, whereas there was a risk in hunting about among the unknown'.

I am much more grateful for the five minutes during which a certain lecturer emphasized young Icarus begorming himself with Daedalus' wax than for all the dead hours he spent in trying to make me a scholar.

> '.... modo quas vaga moverat aura,
> Captabat plumas: flavam modo pollice ceram
> Mollibat; lusuque suo mirabile patris
> Impediebat opus.'

'Getting in both of their ways.' My plagiarism was from the life and not from Ovid, the difference is perhaps unimportant.

Yet if after sixteen years a professor's words came back to one, it is perhaps important that the classics should be humanly, rather than philologically taught, even in class-rooms. A barbaric age given over to *education* agitates for their exclusion and desuetude. Education is an onanism of the soul. Philology will be ascribed to De la Sade.

And there is perhaps more hope for the débutante who drawls in the last fashionable and outwearied die-away cadence 'Ayh! Trois Contes? THAT's a good buk', than for the connoisseur stuffed full of catalogues; able to date any author and enumerate all the ranges of 'influences'.

IV

Meditation after further reading during which I found nothing of interest:

1

Beauty is a brief gasp between one cliché and another. In this case, between the 'fourteeners' and the rhymed couplet of 'pentameter'.

2

'C. M.' was a poet, likewise Golding, both facts already known to all 'students of the period'. Turbeyville or Turberuile is not a discovery.

Horace would seem to confer no boons upon his translators. With the exception of Chapman, the early translators of Homer seem less happy than the translators of Ovid. Horace's *Satires* are, we believe, the basis of much eighteenth-century satire. The earliest English version of any Horace that I have found is headed:

'A Medicinable Morall, that is 2 bookes of Horace his Satyres, Englyshed according to the prescription of saint Hierome (Episto. ad Ruffin.) Quod malum est, muta, Quod bonum est, prode. The Wailyngs of the Prophet Hieremiah done into Englyshe verse also Epigrammes, by T. Drant. Perused and allowed according to the Queen Madiesties Iniunctions, London 1566.'

The mutation of the satire is not inviting. The *Ars Poetica* opens as follows:

> 'A Paynter if he shoulde adioyne
>   unto a womans heade
> A long maires necke and overspread
>   the corpse in everye steade
> With sondry feathers of straunge huie,
>   the whole proportioned so
> Without all good congruitye
>   the nether parts do goe
> Into a fishe, on hye a freshe
>   welfavord womans face:
> My frinds let in to see this sighte
>   could you not laugh a pace?'

By 1625 the Miltonic cliché is already formed. It is perhaps not particularly Milton's. Sir T. Hawkins is greeted by John Beaumont, but I do not find his translations very readable. I turn back, indeed, gratefully to Corinna (*Amores* 1, 5) in a long loose gown

> 'Her white neck hid with trellis hanging downe
> Resembling fair Semiramis going to bed
> Or Layis of a thousand lovers spread.'

'C. M.' gets quality even in the hackneyed topic:

> 'What age of Varroes name shall not be told,
> And Iasons Argos, and the fleece of golde,
> Lofty Lucresius shall live that houre
> That Nature shall dissolve this earthly bowre.
> Eneas warre, and Titerius shall be read
> While Rome of all the conquering world is head.
> Till Cupid's bow and fierie shafts be broken,
> Thy verses, sweete Tibullus, shal be spoken.'

As late as 1633 Saltonstall keeps some trace of good cadence, though it is manifestly departing.

> 'Now Zephyrus warmes the ayre, the yeare is runne
> And the long seeming winter now is done,
> The Ramme which bore faire Hellen once away,
> Hath made the darke night equall to the day.
> Now boyes and girles do sweet Violets get,
> Which in the country often grow unset,
> Faire coloured flowers in the Meddowes spring,
> And now the Birds their untaught notes do sing.'
>   (*Tristia* XII.)

Tuberuile in the 1567 edition of the *Heroides* does not confine himself to one measure, nor to rhyme. I think I have seen a misstatement about the date of the earliest blank verse in English. These eight lines should prevent its being set too late. The movement is, to me at least, of interest, apart from any question of scholastic preciosity.

> 'Aemonian Laodamie sendeth health,
> And greeting to Protesilaus hir spouse:
> And wisheth it, where he soiourns, to stay.
> Report hath spread in Aulide that you lie
> In rode, by meane of fierce and froward gale.
> Ah when thou me forsookste, where was the winde,
> Then broiling seas thine Oares should have withstood,
> That was a fitting time for wrathful waves.'

His *Phaedra* has the 'fourteener' measure.

> 'My pleasure is to haughtie hills
>   and bushie brakes to hie:
> To pitch my hay, or with my Houndes
>   to rayse a lustie crie.'

But there is an infinite monotony of fourteeners, and there is subsequently an infinite plethora of rhymed ten-syllable couplets. And they are all 'exactly alike'. Whether they translate Horace or Homer they are all exactly alike. Beauty is a gasp between clichés.

For every 'great age' a few poets have written a few beautiful lines, or found a few exquisite melodies, and ten thousand people have copied them, until each strand of music is planed down to a dullness. The Sapphic stanza appears an exception, and yet, . . . Greece and Alexandria may have been embedded knee-deep in bad Sapphics, and it is easy to turn it to ridicule, comical, thumping.

v

There is a certain resonance in *Certain Bokes of Virgiles Aenaeis by Henry Earl of Surrey* (apud Ricardum Tottel 1557).

> They whisted all, with fixed face attent
> When prince Aenas from the royal seat
> Thus gan to speak, O Queene, it is thy will,
> I should renew a woe can not be told:
> How that the Grekes did spoile and overthrow
> The Phrygian wealth, and wailful realm of Troy,
> Those ruthful things that I myself beheld,
> And whereof no small part fel to my share,
> Which to expresse, who could refraine from teres,
> What Myrmidon, or yet what Dolopes?
> What stern Ulysses waged soldiar?
>
> And loe moist night now from the welkin falles
> And sterres declining counsel us to rest.'

Still there is hardly enough here to persuade one to re-read or to read the *Aeneid*. Besides it is 'so Miltonic'. 'Tho. Phaer, Docteur of Phisike' in 1562, published a version in older mould, whereof this tenebrous sample:

> 'Even in ye porche, and first in Limbo iawes done wailings dwell
> And Cares on couches lyen, and Settled Mindes on vengeans fell
> Disease leane and pale and combrous Age of dompishe yeres
> As Scillas and Centaurus, man before and beast behind
> In every doore they stampe, and Lyons sad with gnashing sound
> And Bugges with hundryd heades as Briary, and armid round
> Chimera fightes with flames and gastly Gorgon grim to see
> Eneas sodenly for feare his glistering sword out toke.'

He uses inner rhyme, and alliteration apparently without any design, merely because they happen. Such lines as 'For as at sterne I stood, and steering strongly held my helme' do not compare favourably with the relatively free Saxon fragments. But when we come to

'The XII BUKES OF ENEADOS of the famose Poete Virgill, traslatet out of Latyne verses into Scottish metir by the Reverend Father in God Mayster Gawin Douglas Bishop of Dunkel, unkil to the Erle of Angus, every book having hys particular prologue (printed in 1553)'[1]

we have to deal with a highly different matter.

> 'The battellis and the man I will discrive
> Fra Troyis boundis, first that fugitive
> By fate to Italie, came and coist lauyne
> Ouer land and se, cachit with meikill pyne
> By force of goddis above, fra every stede
> Of cruel Juno, throw auld remembrit feid
> Grete payne in battelles, suffered he also
> Or he his goddis, brocht in Latio
> And belt the ciete, fra quham of nobil fame
> The Latyne peopil, taken has thare name.'

His commas are not punctuation, but indicate his caesurae.

Approaching the passage concerning the 'hundryd headed Bugges' of Dr Phaer, Douglas translates as follows:

> 'Fra thine strekis the way profound anone
> Deep unto hellis flude, of Acherone
> With holebisme, and hidduous swelth unrude
> Drumly of mude, and skaldand as it war wode.
>
> Thir riueris and thir watteris kepit war
> Be ane Charon, ane grisly ferrear
> Terribyl of schape, and sluggard of array
> Apoun his chin feill, chanos haris gray.'

I am inclined to think that he gets more poetry out of Virgil than any other translator. At least he gives one a clue to Dante's respect for the Mantuan. In the first book Aeneas with the 'traist Achates' is walking by the sea-board:

> 'Amid the wod, his mother met them tuay
> Semand ane made, in vissage and array

---

[1] Written about 1512, i.e. early in the reign of Henry VIII, and by no means 'Elizabethan'.

With wappinnis, like the Virgins of Spartha
Or the stowt wensche, of Trace Harpalita
Haistand the hors, her fadder to reskewe
Spediar than Hebroun, the swift flude did persew.
For Venus efter the gys, and manor there
Ane active bow, apoun her schulder bare
As sche had bene, ane wilde huntreis
With wind waffing, hir haris lowsit of trace.'

This is not spoiled by one's memory of Chaucer's allusion.

'Goyng in a queynt array
As she hadde ben an hunteresse,
With wynd blowynge upon hir tresse';

Douglas continues:

'Hir skirt kiltit, till her bare knee
And first of uther, unto them, thus speike sche.'

From Aenas answer, these lines:

'Quhidder thou be Diane, Phebus sister brycht
Or than sum goddes, of thyr Nymphyis kynd
Maistres of woddis beis to, us happy and kynd
Relief our lang travell, quhat ever thow be.'

And after her prophecy:

Vera incessu patuit dea.

'Thus sayd sche, and turnand incontinent
Hir nek schane, like unto the Rose in May
Hir heuinly haris, glitterand bricht and gay
Kest from her forehead, ane smell glorious and sueit
Hir habit fell doune, couering to her feit
And in hir passage, ane verray god did her kyith
And fra that he knew, his moder alswith.

Bot Venus with ane sop, of myst baith tway
And with ane dirk cloud closit round about
That na man sul tham se . . . .

Hir self uplyft, to Paphum past swyith
To vesy her resting place, joly and blyith

There is hir tempill, in Cipirland
Quharin thare dois ane hundreth altaris stand
Hait burning full of Saba, sence all houris
Ane smelland swete, with fresch garland and flouris.'

Gawine Douglas was a great poet, and Golding has never had due praise since his own contemporaries bestowed it upon him. Caxton's *Virgil* (1490) is a prose redaction of a French version. The eclogue beginning

'Tityrus, happilie thou lyste, tumbling under a beech tree'

is too familiar to quote here.

The celebrated distych:

'All trauellers doo gladlie report great praise of Vlysses
For that he knewe manie mens manners, and saw many citties'

is quoted by Wm. Webbe, in 1586, as a perfect example of English quantity and ascribed to 'Master Watson, fellow of S. John's', forty years earlier. If Master Watson continued his Odyssey there is alas no further trace of it.

Conclusions after this reading:

1. The quality of translations declined in measure as the translators ceased to be absorbed in the subject matter of their original. They ended in the 'Miltonian' cliché; in the stock and stilted phraseology of the usual English verse as it has come down to us.

2. This 'Miltonian' cliché is much less Milton's invention than is usually supposed.

3. His visualization is probably better than I had thought. The credit due him for developing the resonance of the English blank verse paragraph is probably much less than most other people have until now supposed.

4. Gawine Douglas his works, should be made accessible by reprinting.

5. This will probably be done by some dull dog, who will thereby receive cash and great scholastic distinction. I, however, shall die in the gutter because I have not observed that commandment which

says 'Thou shalt respect the imbecilities of thine elders in order that thy belly shall be made fat from the jobs which lie in their charge'.

6. That editors, publishers, and universities loathe the inquisitive spirit.

(1916 circa)

TRANSLATORS OF GREEK:[1]
EARLY TRANSLATORS OF HOMER

I. HUGUES SALEL

The dilection of Greek poets has waned during the last pestilent century, and this decline has, I think, kept pace with a decline in the use of Latin cribs to Greek authors. The classics have more and more become a baton exclusively for the cudgelling of schoolboys, and less and less a diversion for the mature.

I do not imagine I am the sole creature who has been well taught his Latin and very ill-taught his Greek (beginning at the age, say, of twelve, when one is unready to discriminate matters of style, and when the economy of the adjective cannot be wholly absorbing). A child may be bulldozed into learning almost anything, but man accustomed to some degree of freedom is loath to approach a masterpiece through five hundred pages of grammar. Even a scholar like Porson may confer with former translators.

We have drifted out of touch with the Latin authors as well, and we have mislaid the fine English versions: Golding's *Metamorphoses;* Gavin Douglas's *Æneids;* · Marlowe's *Eclogues* from Ovid, in each of which books a great poet has compensated, by his own skill, any loss in transition; a new beauty has in each case been created. Greek in English remains almost wholly unsuccessful, or rather, there are glorious passages but no long or whole satisfaction. Chapman remains the best English 'Homer', marred though he may be by excess of added ornament, and rather more marred by parentheses and inversions, to the point of being hard to read in many places.

And if one turn to Chapman for almost any favourite passage one is almost sure to be disappointed; on the other hand I think no one will excel him in the plainer passages of narrative, as of Priam's going to Achilles in the XXIVth Iliad. Yet he breaks down in Priam's

---

[1] Taken from *Instigations* (1920), and is composed of parts of an earlier series. 'Hugues Salel' appeared in *The Egoist*, V, 7 (August 1918); 'Andreas Divus' in *The Egoist*, V, 8 (September 1918) and 9 (October 1918); 'Aeschylus' in *The Egoist*, VI, 1 (Jan.-Feb. 1919) and 2 (March-April 1919).

prayer at just the point where the language should be the simplest and austerest.

Pope is easier reading, and, out of fashion though he is, he has at least the merit of translating Homer into *something*. The nadir of Homeric translation is reached by the Leaf-Lang prose; Victorian faddism having persuaded these gentlemen to a belief in King James fustian; their alleged prose has neither the concision of verse nor the virtues of direct motion. In their preface they grumble about Chapman's 'mannerisms', yet their version is full of 'Now behold I' and 'yea even as' and 'even as when' tushery possible only to an affected age bent on propaganda. For, having, despite the exclusion of the *Dictionnaire Philosophique* from the island, finally found that the Bible couldn't be retained either as history or as private Reuter from J'hvh's Hebrew Press Bureau, the Victorians tried to boom it, and even its wilfully bowdlerized translations, as literature.

'So spake he, and roused Athene that already was set thereon. . . . Even as the son of . . . even in such guise. . . .'

perhaps no worse than

'With hollow shriek the steep of Delphos leaving'[1]

but bad enough anyway.

Of Homer two qualities remain untranslated: the magnificent onomatopœia, as of the rush of the waves on the sea-beach and their recession in:

$$\pi\alpha\rho\grave{\alpha} \ \theta\widetilde{\imath}\nu\alpha \ \pi\text{o}\lambda\upsilon\phi\lambda\text{o}\acute{\imath}\sigma\beta\text{o}\text{io} \ \theta\alpha\lambda\acute{\alpha}\sigma\sigma\eta\varsigma$$

untranslated and untranslatable; and, secondly, the authentic cadence of speech; the absolute conviction that the words used, let us say by Achilles to the 'dog-faced' chicken-hearted Agamemnon, are in the actual swing of words spoken. This quality of actual speaking is *not* untranslatable. Note how Pope fails to translate it:

> 'There sat the seniors of the Trojan race
> (Old Priam's chiefs, and most in Priam's grace):
> The king, the first; Thymœtes at his side;
> Lampus and Clytius, long in counsel try'd;

[1] Milton, of course, whom my detractors say I condemn without due circumspection.

Panthus and Hicetaon, once the strong;
And next, the wisest of the reverend throng,
Antenor grave, and sage Ucalegon,
Lean'd on the walls, and bask'd before the sun.
Chiefs, who no more in bloody fights engage,
But wise through time, and narrative with age,
In summer days like grasshoppers rejoice,
A bloodless race, that send a feeble voice.

These, when the Spartan queen approach'd the tower,
In secret own'd resistless beauty's power:
They cried, No wonder, such celestial charms
For nine long years have set the world in arms!
What winning graces! What majestic mien!
She moves a goddess, and she looks a queen!
Yet hence, oh Heaven, convey that fatal face,
And from destruction save the Trojan race.'

This is anything but the 'surge and thunder', but it is, on the other
hand, a definite idiom, within the limits of the rhymed pentameter
couplet it is even musical in parts; there is imbecility in the antithesis,
and bathos in 'she looks a queen', but there is fine accomplishment in:
   'Wise through time, and narrative with age',
Mr Pope's own invention, and excellent. What we definitely can *not*
hear is the voice of the old men speaking. The simile of the grasshoppers is well rendered, but the old voices do not ring in the ear.
   Homer (III, 156-60) reports their conversation:

Οὐ νέμεσις Τρῶας καὶ ἐυκνήμιδας Ἀχαιοὺς
Τοιῇδ' ἀμφὶ γυναικὶ πολὺν χρόνον ἄλγεα πάσχειν ·
Αἰνῶς ἀθανάτῃσι θεῇς εἰς ὦπα ἔοικεν ·
Ἀλλὰ καὶ ὣς τοίη περ ἐοῦσ' ἐν ἤῃυσὶ νεέσθω,
Μηδ' ἡμῖν τεκέεσσί τ' ὀπίσσω πῆμα λίποιτο.

Which is given in Sam. Clark's *ad verbum* translation:

'Non *est* indigne ferendum, Trojanos et bene-ocreatos Archivos
Tali de muliere longum tempus dolores pati:
Omnino immortalibus deabus ad vultum redeat,
Neque nobis liberisque in posterum detrimentum relinquatur.'

Mr Pope has given six short lines for five long ones, but he has
added 'fatal' to face (or perhaps only lifted it from νέμεσις), he has

added 'winning graces', and 'majestic', 'looks a queen'. As for own-
ing beauty's resistless power secretly or in the open, the Greek is:

Τοῖοι ἄρα Τρώων ἡγήτορες ἧντ᾿ ἐπὶ πύργῳ.
Οἱ δ᾿ ὡς οὖν εἴδονθ᾿ Ἑλένην ἐπὶ πύργον ἰοῦσαν,
Ἦκα πρὸς ἀλλήλους ἔπεα πτερόεντ᾿ ἀγόρευον·

and Sam. Clark as follows:

'Tales utique Trojanorum proceres sedebant in turri.
Hi autem ut viderunt Helenam ad turrim venientem,
Submisse inter se verbis alatis dixerunt';

Ἦκα is an adjective of sound, it is purely objective, even *submisse*[1]
is an addition; though Ἦκα might, by a slight strain, be taken to
mean that the speech of the old men came little by little, a phrase from
each of the elders. Still it would be purely objective. It does not even
say they spoke humbly or with resignation.

Chapman is no closer than his successor. He is so *galant* in fact,
that I thought I had found his description in Rochefort. The passage
is splendid, but splendidly unhomeric:

'All grave old men, and soldiers they had been, but for age
Now left the wars; yet counsellors they were exceedingly sage.
And as in well-grown woods, on trees, cold spiny grasshoppers
Sit chirping, and send voices out, that scarce can pierce our ears
For softness, and their weak faint sounds ; so, talking on the tow'r,
These seniors of the people sat; who when they saw the pow'r
Of beauty, in the queen, ascend, ev'n those cold-spirited peers,
Those wise and almost wither'd men, found this heat in their years,
That they were forc'd (though whispering) to say: 'What man can
        blame
The Greeks and Trojans to endure, for so admir'd a dame,
So many mis'ries, and so long? In her sweet count'nance shine
Looks like the Goddesses. And yet (though never so divine)
Before we boast, unjustly still, of her enforced prise,
And justly suffer for her sake, with all our progenies,
Labour and ruin, let her go; the profit of our land
Must pass the beauty'. Thus, though these could bear so fit a hand

---

[1] I. e. Clark is 'correct', but the words shade differently. Ἦκα means low,
quiet, with a secondary meaning of 'little by little'. *Submisse* means low, quiet,
with a secondary meaning of modesty, humbly.

On their affections, yet, when all their gravest powers were us'd,
They could not choose but welcome her, and rather they accus'd
The Gods than beauty; for thus spake the most-fam'd king of
    Troy':

The last sentence representing mostly Ὥς ἄρ' ἔφαν in the line :

Ὥς ἄρ' ἔφαν' Πρίαμος δ' Ἑλένην ἐκαλέσσατο φωνῇ.

'Sic dixerunt: Priamus autem Helenam vocavit voce'.

Chapman is nearer Swinburne's ballad with:

        'But those three following men', etc

than to his alleged original.

Rochefort is as follows (*Iliade*, Livre III, M. de Rochefort, 1772):

> 'Hélène à ce discours sentit naître en son âme
> Un doux ressouvenir de sa première flamme;
> Le désir de revoir les lieux qu'elle a quittés
> Jette un trouble inconnu dans ses sens agités.
> Tremblante elle se lève et les yeux pleins de larmes,
> D'un voile éblouissant elle couvre ses charmes;
> De deux femmes suivie elle vole aux remparts.
> Là s'étaient assemblés ces illustres vieillards
> Qui courbés sous le faix des travaux et de l'âge
> N'alloient plus au combat signaler leur courage,
> Mais qui, près de leur Roi, par de sages avis,
> Mieux qu'en leurs jeunes ans défendoient leur païs.
>
>   Dans leurs doux entretiens, leur voix toujours égale
> Ressembloit aux accents que forme la cigale,
> Lorsqu'aux longs jours d'été cachée en un buisson,
> Elle vient dans les champs annoncer la moisson.
> Une tendre surprise enflamma leurs visages;
> Frappés de ses appas, ils se disoient entre eux:
> 'Qui pourroit s'étonner que tant de Rois fameux,
> Depuis neuf ans entiers aient combattu pour elle?
> Sur le trône des cieux Vénus n'est pas plus belle.
> Mais quel que soit l'amour qu'inspirent ses attraits,
> Puisse Ilion enfin la perdre pour jamais,
> Puisse-t-elle bientôt à son époux rendue,
> Conjurer l'infortune en ces lieux attendue.''

Hugues Salel (1545), praised by Ronsard, is more pleasing:

> 'Le Roi Priam, et auec luy bon nombre
> De grandz Seigneurs estoient à l'ombre
> Sur les Crenaulx, Tymoetes et Panthus,
> Lampus, Clytus, excellentz en vertus,
> Hictaon renomme en bataille,
> Ucalegon iadis de fort taille,
> Et Antenor aux armes nompareil
> Mais pour alors ne seruantz qu'en conseil.
>
> Là, ces Vieillards assis de peur du Hasle
> Causoyent ensemble ainsi que la Cigale
> Ou deux ou trois, entre les vertes fueilles,
> En temps d'Esté gazouillant à merveilles;
> Lesquelz voyans la diuine Gregeoise,
> Disoient entre eux que si la grande noise
> De ces deux camps duroit longe saison,
> Certainement ce n'estoit sans raison:
> Veu la Beaulté, et plus que humain ouvrage,
> Qui reluysoit en son diuin visaige.
> Ce neantmoins il vauldrait mieulx la rendre,
> (Ce disoyent ilz) sans guères plus attendre.
> Pour éviter le mal qui peult venir,
> Qui la voudra encores retenir.'

Salel is a most delightful approach to the Iliads; he is still absorbed in the subject-matter, as Douglas and Golding were absorbed in their subject-matter. Note how exact he is in the rendering of the old men's mental attitude. Note also that he is right in his era. I mean simply that Homer *is* a little *rustre*, a little, or perhaps a good deal, mediaeval, he has not the dovetailing of Ovid. He has onomatopœia, as of poetry sung out; he has authenticity of conversation as would be demanded by an intelligent audience not yet laminated with aesthetics; capable of recognizing reality. He has the repetitions of the *chanson de geste*. Of all the French and English versions I think Salel alone gives any hint of some of these characteristics. Too obviously he is not onomatopœic, no. But he is charming, and readable, and 'Briseis Fleur des Demoiselles' has her reality.

Nicolo Valla is, for him whom runs, closer:

'Consili virtus, summis de rebus habebant
Sermones, et multa inter se et magna loquentes,
Arboribus quales gracili stridere cicadae
Saepe solent cantu, postquam sub moenibus altis
Tyndarida aspiciunt, procerum tum quisque fremebat,
Mutuasque exorsi, Decuit tot funera Teucros
Argolicasque pati, longique in tempore bellum
Tantus in ore decor cui non mortalis in artus
Est honor et vultu divina efflagrat imago.
Diva licet facies, Danaum cum classe recedat
Longius excido ne nos aut nostra fatiget
Pignora sic illi tantis de rebus agebant.'

This hexameter is rather heavily accented. It shows, perhaps, the source of various 'ornaments' in later English and French translations. It has indubitable sonority even though monotonous.

It is the earliest Latin verse rendering I have yet come upon, and is bound in with Raphael of Volterra's first two Iliads, and some further renderings by Obsopeo.

Odyssea (Liber primus)

Dic mihi musa uirum captae post tempora Troiae
Qui mores hominum multorum uidit et urbes
Multa quoque et ponto passus dum naufragus errat
Ut sibi tum sociis uitam seruaret in alto
Non tamen hos cupiens fato deprompsit acerbo
Ob scelus admissum extinctos ausumque malignum
Qui fame compulsu solis rapuere iuvencos
Stulti ex quo reditum ad patrias deus abstulit oras.
Horum itaque exitium memora mihi musa canenti.'

Odyssea (Liber secundus)

'Cum primum effulsit roseis aurora quadrigis
Continuo e stratis proles consurgit Ulyxis
Induit et uestes humerosque adcomodat ensem
Molia denin pedibus formosis uincula nectit
Parque deo egrediens thalamo praeconibus omnis
Concilio cogunt extemplo mandat Achaeos
Ipse quoque ingentem properabat aedibus hastam
Corripiens: geminique canes comitantur euntem

Quumque illi mirum Pallas veneranda decorem
Preberet populus venientem suspicit omnis
Inque throno patrio ueteres cessere sedenti.'

The charm of Salel is continued in the following excerpts. They do not cry out for comment. I leave Ogilby's English and the lines of Latin to serve as contrast or cross-light.

Iliade (Livre I), Hugues Salel (1545):[1]

The Ire

Ie te supply Déesse gracieuse,
Vouloir chanter l'Ire pernicieuse,
Dont Achilles fut tellement espris,
Que par icelle, ung grand nombre d'espritz
Des Princes Grecs, par dangereux encombres,
Feit lors descente aux infernales Umbres.
Et leurs beaulx Corps privéz de Sépulture
Furent aux chiens et aux oiseaulx pasture.

Iliade (Lib. m) John Ogilby (1660):

Helen

Who in this chamber, sumptuously adornd
Sits on your ivory bed, nor could you say,
By his rich habit, he had fought to-day:
A reveller or masker so comes drest,
From splendid sports returning to his rest.
Thus did love's Queen warmer desires prepare.
But when she saw her neck so heavenly faire.
Her lovely bosome and celestial eyes,
Amazed, to the Goddess, she replies:
Why wilt thou happless me once more betray,
And to another wealthy town convey,
Where some new favourite must, as now at Troy
With utter loss of honour me enjoy.

Iliade (Livre VI), Salel:

Glaucus Respond À Diomède

Adonc Glaucus, auec grace et audace,

---

[1] Abbé de St Chéron.

Luy respondit: 'T'enquiers tu de ma race?
Le genre humain est fragile et muable
Comme la fueille et aussi peu durable.
Car tout ainsi qu'on uoit les branches uertes
Sur le printemps de fueilles bien couuertes
Qui par les uents d'automne et la froidure
Tombent de l'arbre et perdent leur uerdure
Puis de rechef la gelée passée,
Il en reuient à la place laissée:
Ne plus ne moins est du lignage humain:
Tel est huy uif qui sera mort demain.
S'il en meurt ung, ung autre reuint naistre.
Voylà comment se conserue leur estre.'

Iliade (Lib. VI), as in Virgil, Dante, and others:

'Quasim gente rogas? Quibus et natalibus ortus?
Persimile est foliis hominum genus omne caducis
Quae nunc nata uides pulchrisque, uirescere sylvis
Autumno ueniente cadunt, simul illa perurens
Incubuit Boreas: quaedam sub uerna renasci
Tempora, sic uice perpetua succrescere lapsis,
Semper item noua, sic aliis obeuntibus, ultro
Succedunt alii iuuenes aetate grauatis.
Quod si forte iuvat te qua sit quisque suorum
Stirpe satus, si natales cognoscere quaeris
Forte meos, referam, quae sunt notissima multis.'

Iliade (Libre IX), Salel:

Calydon
En Calydon règnoit
Oenéus, ung bon Roy qui donnoit
De ses beaulx Fruictz chascun an les Primices
Aux Immortelz, leur faisant Sacrifices.
Or il aduint (ou bien par son uouloir.
Ou par oubly) qu'il meit à nonchalloir
Diane chaste, et ne luy feit offrande,
Dont elle print Indignation grande
Encontre luy, et pour bien le punir
Feit ung Sanglier dedans ses Champs uenir

Horrible et fier qui luy feit grand dommage
Tuant les Gens et gastant le Fruictage.
Maintz beaulx Pomiers, maintz Arbres reuestuz
De Fleur et Fruict, en furent abattuz,
Et de la Dent aguisée et poinctue,
Le Bléd gasté et la Vigne tortue.
Méléager, le Filz de ce bon Roy,
Voyant ainsi le piteux Désarroy
De son Pays et de sa Gent troublée
Proposa lors de faire une Assemblée
De bons Veneurs et Leutiers pour chasser
L'horrible Beste et sa Mort pourchasser.
Ce qui fut faict. Maintes Gens l'y trouvèrent
Qui contre luy ses Forces éprouvèrent;
Mais à la fin le Sanglier inhumain
Receut la Mort de sa Royale Main.
Estant occis, deux grandes Nations
Pour la Dépouille eurent Contentions
Les Curetois disoient la mériter,
Ceulx d'Etolie en uouloient hériter.

Iliade (Livre X), Salel:

Quand Ulysses fut en la riche tente
Du compaignon, alors il diligente
De bien lier ses cheuaulx et les loge
Soigneusement dedans la même loge
Et au rang même où la belle monture
Du fort Gregeois mangeoit pain et pasture
Quand aux habitz de Dolon, il les pose
Dedans la nef, sur la poupe et propose
En faire ung jour à Pallas sacrifice,
Et luy offrir à jamais son seruice.
Bien tost après, ces deux Grecs de ualeur
Se cognoissant oppresséz de chaleur,
Et de sueur, dedans la mer entrèrent
Pour se lauer, et très bien se frotèrent
Le col, le dos, les jambes et les cuisses,
Ostant du corps toutes les immondices,
Estans ainsi refreichiz et bien netz,

Dedans des baingz souefs bien ordonnez,
S'en sont entréz, et quand leurs corps
Ont esté oinctz d'huyle par le dehors
Puis sont allez manger, prians Minerue
Qu'en tous leurs faictz les dirige et conserue
En respandant du uin à pleine tasse,
(pour sacrifice) au milieu de la place.

II. ANDREAS DIVUS

In the year of grace 1906, 1908, or 1910 I picked from the Paris quais a Latin version of the *Odyssey* by Andreas Divus Justinopolitanus (Parisiis, In officina Christiani Wecheli, MDXXXVIII), the volume containing also the *Batrachomyomachia,* by Aldus Manutius, and the *Hymni Deorum* rendered by Georgius Dartona Cretensis. I lost a Latin *Iliads* for the economy of four francs, these coins being at that time scarcer with me than they ever should be with any man of my tastes and abilities.

In 1911 the Italian savant, Signore E. Teza, published his note, 'Quale fosse la Casata di Andreas Divus Justinopolitanus?' This question I am unable to answer, nor do I greatly care by what name Andreas was known in the privacy of his life: Signore Dio, Signore Divino, or even Mijnheer van Gott may have served him as patronymic. Sannazaro, author of *De Partu Virginis,* and also of the epigram ending *hanc et sugere,* translated himself as Sanctus Nazarenus; I am myself known as Signore Sterlina to James Joyce's children, while the phonetic translation of my name into the Japanese tongue is so indecorous that I am seriously advised not to use it, lest it do me harm in Nippon. (Rendered back *ad verbum* into our maternal speech it gives for its meaning, 'This picture of a phallus costs ten yen.' There is no surety in shifting personal names from one idiom to another.)

Justinopolis is identified as Capodistria; what matters is Divus' text. We find for the 'Nekuia' (*Odys.* XI):

'At postquam ad navem descendimus, et mare,
Nauem quidem primum deduximus in mare diuum.
Et malum posuimus et vela in navi nigra:
Intrò autem oues accipientes ire fecimus, intrò et ipsi

Iuimus dolentes, huberes lachrymas fundentes:
Nobis autem a tergo navis nigrae prorae
Prosperum ventum imisit pandentem velum bonum amicum
Circe benecomata gravis Dea altiloqua.
Nos autem arma singula expendientes in navi
Sedebamus: hanc autem ventusque gubernatorque dirigebat:
Huius āt per totum diem extensa sunt vela pontum transientis:
Occidit tunc Sol, obumbratae sunt omnes viae:
Haec autem in fines pervenit profundi Oceani:
Illic autem Cimmeriorum virorum populusque civitasque,
Caligine et nebula cooperti, neque unquam ipsos
Sol lucidus aspicit radiis,
Neque quando tendit ad coelum stellatum,
Neque quando retro in terram a coelo vertitur:
Sed nox pernitiosa extenditur miseris hominibus:
Navem quidem illuc venientes traximus, extra autem oves
Accepimus: ipsi autem rursus apud fluxum Oceani
Iuimus, ut in locum perveniremus quem dixit Circe:
Hic sacra quidem Perimedes Eurylochusque
Faciebant: ego autem ensem acutum trahens a foemore,
Foveam fodi quantum cubiti mensura hinc et inde:
Circum ipsam autem libamina fundimus omnibus mortuis;
Primum mulso, postea autem dulci vino:
Tertio rursus aqua, et farinas albas miscui:
Multum autem oravi mortuorum infirma capita:
Profectus in Ithacam, sterilem bovem, quae optima esset,
Sacrificare in domibus, pyramque implere bonis:
Tiresiae autem seorsum ovem sacrificare vovi
Totam nigram, quae ovibus antecellat nostris:
Has autem postquam votis precationibusque gentes mortuorum
Precatus sum, oves autem accipiens obtruncavi:
In fossam fluebat autem sanguis niger, congregataeque sunt
Animae ex Erebo cadaverum mortuorum,
Nymphaeque iuvenesque et multa passi senes,
Virginesque tenerae, nuper flebilem animum habentes,
Multi autem vulnerati aereis lanceis
Viri in bello necati, cruenta arma habentes,
Qui multi circum foveam veniebant aliunde alius
Magno clamore, me autem pallidus timor cepit.

Iam postea socios hortans iussi
Pecora, quae iam iacebant iugulata saevo aere,
Excoriantes comburere: supplicare autem Diis,
Fortique Plutoni, et laudatae Proserpinae.
At ego ensem acutum trahens a foemore,
Sedi, neque permisi mortuorum impotentia capita
Sanguinem prope ire, antequam Tiresiam audirem:
Prima autem anima Elpenoris venit socii:
Nondum enim sepultus erat sub terra lata,
Corpus enim in domo Circes reliquimus nos
Infletum et insepultum, quoniam labor alius urgebat:
Hunc quidem ego lachrymatus sum videns, misertusque sum
    animo,
Et ipsum clamando verba velocia allocutus sum:
    Elpenor, quomodo venisti sub caliginem obscuram:
Praevenisti pedes existens quam ego in navi nigra?
    Sic dixi: hic autem mihi lugens respondit verbo:
Nobilis Laertiade, prudens Ulysse,
Nocuit mihi dei fatum malum, et multum vinum:
Circes autem in domo dormiens, non animadverti
Me retrogradum descendere eundo per scalam longam,
Sed contra murum cecidi: ast autem mihi cervix
Nervorum fracta est, anima autem infernum descendit:
Nunc autem his qui venturi sunt postea precor non praesentibus
Per uxorem et patrem, qui educavit parvum existentem,
Telemachumque quem solum in domibus reliquisti.
Scio enim quod hinc iens domo ex inferni
Insulam in Aeaeam impellens benefabricatam navim:
Tunc te postea Rex iubeo recordari mei
Ne me infletum, insepultum, abiens retro, relinquas
Separatus, ne deorum ira fiam
Sed me combure cum armis quaecunque mihi sunt,
Sepulchrumque mihi accumula cani litore maris,
Viri infelicis, et cuius apud posteros fama sit:
Haecque mihi perfice, figeque in sepulchro remum,
Quo et vivus remigabam existens cum meis sociis.
    Sic dixit: at ego ipsum, respondens, allocutus sum:
Haec tibi infelix perficiamque et faciam:
Nos quidem sic verbis respondentes molestis

Sedebamus: ego quidem separatim supra sanguinem ensem tene-
    bam:
Idolum autem ex altera parte socii multa loquebatur:
Venit autem insuper anima matris mortuae
Autolyci filia magnanimi Anticlea,
Quam vivam dereliqui iens ad Ilium sacrum,
Hanc quidem ego lachrymatus sum videns miseratusque sum
    animo:
Sed neque sic sivi priorem licet valde dolens
Sanguinem prope ire, antequam Tiresiam audirem:
Venit autem insuper anima Thebani Tiresiae,
Aureum sceptrum tenens, me autem novit et allocuta est:
Cur iterum o infelix linquens lumen Solis
Venisti, ut videas mortuos, et iniucundam regionem?
Sed recede a fossa, remove autem ensem acutum,
Sanguinem ut bibam, et tibi vera dicam.
    Sic dixit: ego autem retrocedens, ensem argenteum
Vagina inclusi: hic autem postquam bibit sanguinem nigrum,
Et tunc iam me verbis allocutus est vates verus:
    Reditum quaeris dulcem illustris Ulysse:
Hunc autem tibi difficilem faciet Deus, non enim puto
Latere Neptunum, quam iram imposuit animo
Iratus, quod ei filium dilectum excaecasti:
    Sed tamen et sic mala licet passi pervenietis,
    Si volueris tuum animum continere et sociorum.'

The meaning of the passage is, with a few abbreviations, as I have
interpolated it in my Third Canto:

'And then went down to the ship, set keel to breakers,
Forth on the godly sea,
We set up mast and sail on the swart ship,
Sheep bore we aboard her, and our bodies also,
Heavy with weeping; and winds from sternward
Bore us out onward with bellying canvas,
Circe's this craft, the trim-coifed goddess.
Then sat we amidships—wind jamming the tiller—
Thus with stretched sail we went over sea till day's end.
Sun to his slumber, shadows o'er all the ocean,
Came we then to the bounds of deepest water,

To the Kimmerian lands and peopled cities
Covered with close-webbed mist, unpierced ever
With glitter of sun-rays,
Nor with stars stretched, nor looking back from heaven,
Swartest night stretched over wretched men there,
The ocean flowing backward, came we then to the place
Aforesaid by Circe.
Here did they rites, Perimedes and Eurylochus,
And drawing sword from my hip
I dug the ell-square pitkin,
Poured we libations unto each the dead,
First mead and then sweet wine, water mixed with white flour,
Then prayed I many a prayer to the sickly death's-heads,
As set in Ithaca, sterile bulls of the best
For sacrifice, heaping the pyre with goods.
Sheep, to Tiresias only; black and a bell sheep.
Dark blood flowed in the fosse,
Souls out of Erebus, cadaverous dead,
Of brides, of youths, and of much-bearing old;
Virgins tender, souls stained with recent tears,
Many men mauled with bronze lance-heads,
Battle spoil, bearing yet dreary arms,
These many crowded about me,
With shouting, pallor upon me, cried to my men for more beasts.
Slaughtered the herds, sheep slain of bronze,
Poured ointment, cried to the gods,
To Pluto the strong, and praised Proserpine,
Unsheathed the narrow sword,
I sat to keep off the impetuous, impotent dead
Till I should hear Tiresias.
But first Elpenor came, our friend Elpenor,
Unburied, cast on the wide earth,
Limbs that we left in the house of Circe,
Unwept, unwrapped in sepulchre, since toils urged other.
Pitiful spirit, and I cried in hurried speech:
'Elpenor, how art thou come to this dark coast?
Cam'st thou a-foot, outstripping seamen?
                    And he in heavy speech:
'Ill fate and abundant wine! I slept in Circe's ingle,

Going down the long ladder unguarded, I fell against the buttress,
Shattered the nape-nerve, the soul sought Avernus.
But thou, O King, I bid remember me, unwept, unburied,
Heap up mine arms, be tomb by sea-board, and inscribed:
'*A man of no fortune and with a name to come.*'
And set my oar up, that I swung mid fellows'.
Came then another ghost, whom I beat off, Anticlea,
And then Tiresias, Theban,
Holding his golden wand, knew me and spoke first:
'Man of ill hour, why come a second time,
Leaving the sunlight, facing the sunless dead, and this joyless
    region?
Stand from the fosse, move back, leave me my bloody bever,
And I will speak you true speeches'.
                                          And I stepped back,
Sheathing the yellow sword. Dark blood he drank then,
And spoke: 'Lustrous Odysseus
Shalt return through spiteful Neptune, over dark seas,
Lose all companions'. Foretold me the ways and the signs.
Came then Anticlea, to whom I answered:
'Fate drives me on through these deeps. I sought Tiresias',
Told her the news of Troy. And thrice her shadow
Faded in my embrace.'

It takes no more Latin than I have to know that Divus' Latin is not
the Latin of Catullus and Ovid; that it is *illepidus* to chuck Latin
nominative participles about in such profusion; that Romans did not
use *habentes* as the Greeks used ἔχοντες, etc. And *nos* in line 53 is
unnecessary. Divus' Latin has, despite these wems, its quality; it is
even singable, there are constant suggestions of the poetic motion;
it is very simple Latin, after all, and a crib of this sort may make just
the difference of permitting a man to read fast enough to get the
swing and mood of the subject, instead of losing both in a dictionary.

Even *habentes* when one has made up one's mind to it, together
with less obvious exoticisms, does not upset one as

'the steep of Delphos leaving'.

One is, of necessity, more sensitive to botches in one's own tongue
than to botches in another, however carefully learned.

For all the fuss about Divus' errors of elegance, Samuelis Clarkius and Jo. Augustus Ernestus do not seem to have gone him much better—with two hundred years extra Hellenic scholarship at their disposal.

The first Aldine Greek Iliads appeared I think in 1504, Odyssey possibly later.[1] My edition of Divus is of 1538, and as it contains Aldus' own translation of the Frog-fight, it may indicate that Divus was in touch with Aldus in Italy, or quite possibly the French edition is pirated from an earlier Italian printing. A Latin Odyssey in some sort of verse was at that time infinitely worth doing.

Raphael of Volterra had done his prose Odyssey with the opening lines of several books and a few other brief passages in verse. This was printed with Laurenzo Valla's prose Iliads as early as 1502. He begins:

'Dic mihi musa virum captae post tempora Troiae
Qui mores hominum multorum vidit et urbes
Multa quoque et ponto passus dum naufragus errat
Ut sibi tum sotiis (sociis) vitam servaret in alto
Non tamen hos cupiens deprompsit acerbo.'

Probably the source of 'Master Watson's' English quantitative couplet, but obviously not copied by Divus:

'Virum mihi dic musa multiscium qui valde multum
Erravit, ex quo Troiae sacram urbem depopulatus est:
Multorum autem virorum vidit urbes et mentem cognovit:
Multos autem hic in mare passus est dolores, suo in animo,
Liberans suamque animam et reditum sociorum.'

On the other hand, it is nearly impossible to believe that Clark and Ernestus were unfamiliar with Divus. Clark calls his Latin crib a composite 'non elegantem utique et venustam, sed ita Romanam, ut verbis verba'. A good deal of Divus' *venustas* has departed. Clark's hyphenated compounds are, I think, no more Roman than are some of Divus' coinage; they may be a trifle more explanatory, but if we read a shade more of colour into ἀθέσφατος οἶνος than we can into *multum vinum*, it is not restored to us in Clark's *copiosum*

[1] My impression is that I saw an *Iliad* by Andreas Divus on the Quais in Paris, at the time I found his version of the *Odyssey*, but an impression of this sort is, after eight years, untrustworthy, it may have been only a Latin *Iliad* in similar binding.

vinum, nor does *terra spatiosa* improve upon *terra lata*, εὐρυοδείης being (if anything more than *lata*): 'with wide ways of streets', the wide ways of the world, traversable, open to wanderers. The participles remain in Clark-Ernestus, many of the coined words remain unchanged. Georgius Dartona gives, in the opening of the second hymn to Aphrodite:

'Venerandam auream coronam habentem pulchram Venerem
Canam, quae totius Cypri munimenta sortita est
Maritimae ubi illam zephyri vis molliter spirantis
Suscitavit per undam multisoni maris,
Spuma in molli: hanc autem auricurae Horae
Susceperunt hilariter, immortales autem vestes induere:
Capite vero super immortali coronam bene constructam posuere
Pulchram, auream: tribus autem ansis
Donum orichalchi aurique honorabilis:
Collum autem molle, ac pectora argentea
Monilibus aureis ornabant. . . .' etc.

Ernestus, adding by himself the appendices to the Epics, gives us:

'Venerandam auream coronam habentem pulchram Venerem
Canam, quae totius Cypri munimenta sortita est
Maritimae, ubi illam zephyri vis molliter spirantis
Tulit per undam multisoni maris
Spuma in molli: hanc autem auro comam religatae Horae
Susceperunt hilariter, immortales autem vestes induere:
Caput autem super immortale coronam bene constructam posuere
Pulchram, auream, perforatis autem auriculis
Donum orichalchi preciosi:
Collum autem molle ac pectora candida[1]
Monilibus aureis ornabant . . . . .', etc.

'Which things since they are so' lead us to feel that we would have had no less respect for Messrs Clarkius and Ernestus if they had deigned to mention the name of their predecessors. They have not done this in their prefaces, and if any mention is made of the sixteenth-century scholars, it is very effectually buried somewhere in the

---

[1] Reading ἀργυφέοισιν variant ἀργυρέοισιν offered in footnote. In any case *argentea* is closer than *candida*.

voluminous Latin notes, which I have not gone through *in toto*. Their edition (Glasgow, 1814) is, however, most serviceable.

Translation of Aeschylus

A search for Aeschylus in English is deadly, accursed, mind-rending. Browning has 'done' the Agamemnon, or 'done the Agamemnon in the eye' as the critic may choose to consider. He has written a modest and an apparently intelligent preface.

'I should hardly look for an impossible transmission of the reputed magniloquence and sonority of the Greek; and this with the less regret, inasmuch as there is abundant musicality elsewhere, but nowhere else than in his poem the ideas of the poet'.

He quotes Matthew Arnold on the Greeks: 'their expression is so excellent, because it is so simple and so well subordinated, because it draws its force directly from the pregnancy of the matter which it conveys . . . not a word wasted, not a sentiment capriciously thrown in, stroke on stroke.'

He is reasonable about the Greek spelling. He points out that γόνον ἰδὼν κάλλιστον ἀνδρῶν sounds very poorly as 'Seeing her son the fairest of men' but is outshouted in 'Remirando il figliuolo bellissimo degli uomini', and protests his fidelity to the meaning of Aeschylus.

His weakness in this work is where it essentially lay in all of his expression, it rests in the term 'ideas'.—'Thought' as Browning understood it—'ideas' as the term is current, are poor two-dimensional stuff, a scant, scratch covering. 'Damn ideas, anyhow.' An idea is only an imperfect induction from fact.

The solid, the 'last atom of force verging off into the first atom of matter' is the force, the emotion, the objective sight of the poet. In the *Agamemnon* it is the whole rush of the action, the whole wildness of Kassandra's continual shrieking, the flash of the beacon fires burning unstinted wood, the outburst of

Τροίαν 'Αχαιῶν οὖσαν,

or the later   Τροίαν 'Αχαιοὶ τῇδ' ἔχουσ' ἐν ἡμέρᾳ.

'Troy is the Greeks'.' Even Rossetti has it better than Browning: 'Troy's down, tall Troy's on fire', anything, literally anything that can be shouted, that can be shouted uncontrolledly and hysterically.

'Troy is the Greeks' . . .' is an ambiguity for the ear. 'Know that our men are in Ilion.'

Anything but a stilted unsayable jargon. Yet with Browning we have
> 'Troia the Achaioi hold',

and later,
> 'Troia do the Achaioi hold',

followed by:
> 'this same day
> I think a noise—no mixture—reigns i' the city
> Sour wine and unguent pour thou in one vessel——'

And it does not end here. In fact it reached the nadir of its bathos in a later speech of Klutaimnestra in the line

> 'The perfect man his home perambulating!'

We may add several exclamation points to the one which Mr Browning has provided. But then all translation is a thankless, or is at least most apt to be a thankless and desolate undertaking.

What Browning had not got into his sometimes excellent top-knot was the patent, or what should be the patent fact that inversions of sentence order in an uninflected language like English are not, simply and utterly *are not* any sort of equivalent for inversions and perturbations of order in a language inflected as Greek and Latin are inflected. That is the chief source of his error. In these inflected languages order has other currents than simple sequence of subject, predicate, object; and all sorts of departures from this Franco-English natural position are in Greek and Latin neither confusing nor delaying; they may be both simple and emphatic, they do not obstruct one's apperception of the verbal relations.

Obscurities *not inherent in* the matter, obscurities due not to the thing but to the wording, are a botch, and are *not* worth preserving in a translation. The work lives not by them but despite them.

Rossetti is in this matter sounder than Browning, when he says that the only thing worth bringing over is the beauty of the original; and despite Rossetti's purple plush and molasses trimmings he meant by 'beauty' something fairly near what we mean by the 'emotional intensity' of his original.

Obscurities inherent in the thing occur when the author is piercing, or trying to pierce into, uncharted regions; when he is trying to express things not yet current, not yet worn into phrase; when he is ahead of the emotional, or philosophic sense (as a painter might be ahead of the colour-sense) of his contemporaries.

As for the word-sense and phrase-sense, we still hear workmen and peasants and metropolitan bus-riders repeating the simplest sentences three and four times, back and forth between interlocutors: trying to get the sense 'I sez to Bill, I'm goin' to 'Arrow' or some other such subtlety from one occiput into another.

'You sez to Bill, etc.'

'Yus, I sez . . . . etc.'

'O!'

The first day's search at the Museum reveals 'Aeschylus' printed by Aldus in 1518; by Stephanus in 1557; no English translation before 1777, a couple in the 1820's, more in the middle of the century, since 1880 past counting, and no promising names in the list. Sophocles falls to Jebb and does not appear satisfactory.

From which welter one returns thankfully to the Thomas Stanley Greek and Latin edition, with Saml. Butler's notes, Cambridge, 'typis ac sumptibus academicis', 1811—once a guinea or half-a-guinea per volume, half leather, but now mercifully, since people no longer read Latin, picked up at 2s. for the set (eight volumes in all) rather less than the price of their postage. Quartos in excellent type.

Browning shows himself poet in such phrases as 'dust, mud's thirsty brother', which is easy, perhaps, but is English, even Browning's own particular English, as 'dust, of mud brother thirsty', would not be English at all; and if I have been extremely harsh in dealing with the first passage quoted it is still undisputable that I have read Browning off and on for seventeen years with no small pleasure and admiration, and am one of the few people who know anything about his *Sordello,* and have never read his *Agamemnon,* have not even now when it falls into a special study been able to get through his *Agamemnon.*

Take another test passage:

Οὗτός ἐστιν 'Αγαμέμνων, ἐμὸς
Πόσις, νεκρὸς δὲ τῆσδε δεξιᾶς χερός,
῎Εργον δικαίας τέκτονος. Τάδ ὧδ' ἔχει.

> 'Hicce est Agamemnon, maritus
> Meus, hac dextra mortuus,
> Facinus justae artificis. Haec ita se habent.'

We turn to Browning and find:

> '——this man is Agamemnon,
> My husband, dead, the work of this right hand here,
> Aye, of a just artificer: so things are'.

To the infinite advantage of the Latin, and the complete explanation of why Browning's Aeschylus, to say nothing of forty other translations of Aeschylus, is unreadable.

Any bungling translation:

> 'This is Agamemnon,
> My husband,
> Dead by this hand,
> And a good job. These, gentlemen, are the facts'.

No, that is extreme, but the point is that any natural wording, anything which keeps the mind off theatricals and on Klutaimnestra actual, dealing with an actual situation, and not pestering the reader with frills and festoons of language, is worth all the convoluted tushery that the Victorians can heap together.[1]

I can conceive no improvement on the Latin, it saves by *dextra* for δεξιᾶς χερός, it loses a few letters in 'se habent' but it has the same drive as the Greek.

The Latin can be a whole commentary on the Greek, or at least it can give one the whole parsing and order, and let one proceed at a comfortable rate with but the most rudimentary knowledge of the original language. And I do not think this a trifle; it would be an ill day if men again let the classics go by the board; we should fall into something worse than, or as bad as, the counter-reformation: a welter of gum-shoes, and cocoa, and Y.M.C.A. and Webbs, and social theorizing committees, and the general hell of a groggy doctrinaire obfuscation; and the very disagreeablizing of the classics, every pedagogy which puts the masterwork further from us, either by obstructing the schoolboy, or breeding affectation in dilettante

[1] In 1934, one would emend the last lines to:
> 'I did it. That's how it is.'

readers, works toward such a detestable end. I do not know that strict logic will cover all of the matter, or that I can formulate anything beyond a belief that we test a translation by the feel, and particularly by the feel of being in contact with the force of a great original, and it does not seem to me that one can open this Latin text of the Agamemnon without getting such sense of contact:

'Mox sciemus lampadum luciferarum   498
Signorumque per faces et ignis vices,
An vere sint, an, somniorum instar,
Gratum veniens illud lumen eluserit animum nostrum.
Praeconem hunc a littore video obumbratum
Ramis olivae:testatur autem haec mihi frater
Luti socius aridus pulvis,
Quod neque mutus, neque accendens facem
Materiae montanae signa dabit per fumum ignis.'

Or

'Apollo, Apollo!   1095
Agyieu Apollo mi!
Ah! quo me tandem duxisti? ad qualem domum?

.   .   .   .   .

Heu, heu, ecce, ecce, cohibe a vacca   1134
Taurum: vestibus involvens
Nigricornem machina
Percutit; cadit vero in aequali vase.
Insidiosi lebetis casum ut intelligas velim.

.   .   .   .   .

'Heu, heu, argutae lusciniae fatum *mihi tribuis*:

.   .   .   .   .

'Heu nuptiae, nupitae Paridis extiliales   1165
Amicis! eheu Scamandri patria unda!'

All this howling of Kassandra comes at one from the page, and the grimness also :

'Ohime! lethali intus percussus sum vulnere.'   1352
'Tace: quis clamat vulnus lethaliter vulneratus?'
'Ohime! iterum secundo ictu sauciatus.'
'Patrari facinus mihi videtur regis ex ejulatu.'   1355
'At tuta communicemus consilia.'
'Ego quidem vobis meam dico sententiam', etc.

Here or in the opening of the play, or where you like in this Latin,
we are at once in contact with the action, something real is going on,
we are keen and curious on the instant, but I cannot get any such
impact from any part of the Browning.

> 'In bellum nuptam
> Autricemque contentionum, Helenam?   695
> Quippe quae congruenter
> Perditrix navium, perditrix virorum, perditrix urbium,
> E delicatis
> Thalami ornamentis navigavit
> Zephyri terrigenae aura.
>
> Et numerosi scutiferi,
> Venatores secundum vestigia,
> Remorum inapparentia
> Appulerunt ad Simoentis ripas
> Foliis abundantes
> Ob jurgiu cruentum.'
>
> 'War-wed, author of strife,
> Fitly Helen, destroyer of ships, of men,
> Destroyer of cities,
> From delicate-curtained room
> Sped by land breezes.
>
> Swift the shields on your track,
> Oars on the unseen traces,
> And leafy Simois
> Gone red with blood.'[1]
> Contested Helen, ᾿Αμφινεικῇ.
>
> 'War-wed, contested,
> (Fitly) Helen, destroyer of ships; of men;
> Destroyer of cities,
>
> From the delicate-curtained room
> Sped by land breezes.
> Swift the shields on your track,
> Oars on the unseen traces.

---

[1] For note on 'H. D.'s' translations from Euripides, *vide* '*Instigations*'.

Red leaves in Simois!'
'Rank flower of love, for Troy.'

'Quippe leonem educavit . . .
Mansuetum, pueris amabilem . . .
. . . divinitus sacerdos Ates (i.e. Paris)
In aedibus enutritus est.'

'Statim igitur venit   746
Ad urbem Ilii,
Ut ita dicam, animus
Tranquillae serenitatis, placidum
Divitiarum ornamentum
Blandum oculorum telum,
Animum pungens flos amoris,
(*Helena*) accubitura. Perfecit autem
Nuptiarum acerbos exitus,
Mala vicina, malaque socia,
Irruens in Priamidas,
Ductu Jovis Hospitalis,
Erinnys luctuosa sponsis.'

It seems to me that English translators have gone wide in two ways, first in trying to keep every adjective, when obviously many adjectives in the original have only melodic value, secondly they have been deaved with syntax; have wasted time, involved their English, trying first to evolve a definite logical structure for the Greek and secondly to preserve it, *and all its grammatical relations,* in English.

One might almost say that Aeschylus' Greek is agglutinative, that his general drive, especially in choruses, is merely to remind the audience of the events of the Trojan war; that syntax is subordinate, and duly subordinated, left out, that he is not austere, but often even verbose after a fashion (not Euripides' fashion).

A reading version might omit various things which would be of true service only if the English were actually to be sung on a stage, or chanted to the movements of the choric dance or procession.

Above suggestions should *not* be followed with intemperance. But certainly more sense and less syntax (good or bad) in translations of Aeschylus might be a relief.

Chor. Anapest:

'O iniquam, Helenam, una quae multas,   1464
Multas admodum animas
Perdidisti ad Trojam!
Nunc vero nobilem memorabilem (*Agam. animam*),
Deflorasti per caedem inexpiabilem.
Talis erat tunc in aedibus
Eris viri domitrix aerumna.'

Clytemnestra:

'Nequaquam mortis sortem exopta   1470
Hisce gravatus;
Neque in Helenam iram convertas,
Tanquam viriperdam, ac si una multorum
Virorum animas Graecorum perdens,
Intolerabilem dolorem effecerit.'

.   .   .   .   .   .

Clytemnestra:

'Mortem haud indignam arbitror   130
Huic contigisse:
Neque enim ille insidiosam cladem
Aedibus intulit; sed meum ex ipso
Germen sublatum, multum defletam
Iphigeniam cum indigne affecerit,
Digna passus est, nihil in inferno
Glorietur, gladio inflicta
Morte luens quae prior perpetravit.'
'Death not unearned, nor yet a novelty in this house;
Let him make talk in hell concerning Iphigenia.'

(If we allow the last as ironic equivalent of the literal 'let him not
boast in hell'.)

'He gets but a thrust once given (by him)
Back-pay, for Iphigenia.'

One can further condense the English but at the cost of obscurity.
Morshead is bearable in Clytemnestra's description of the beacons:

'From Ida's top Hephaestos, Lord of fire,
Sent forth his sign, and on, and ever on,

Beacon to beacon sped the courier-flame
From Ida to the crag, that Hermes loves
On Lemnos; thence into the steep sublime
Of Athos, throne of Zeus, the broad blaze flared.
Thence, raised aloft to shoot across the sea
The moving light, rejoicing in its strength
Sped from the pyre of pine, and urged its way,
In golden glory, like some strange new sun,
Onward and reached Macistus' watching heights.'

P.S. I leave these notes, rough as they are, to indicate a block of matter needing examination, the indication being necessary if a reader is to gauge the proportions and relations of other subjects here outlined.

THE REV. G. CRABBE, LL.B.[1]

'Since the death of Laurence Sterne or thereabouts, there has been neither in England nor America any sufficient sense of the value of realism in literature, of the value of writing words that conform precisely with fact, of free speech without evasions and circumlocutions.'

I had forgotten, when I wrote this, the Rev. Crabbe, LL.B.

Think of the slobber that Wordsworth would have made over the illegitimate infant whom Crabbe dismisses with: '*There smiles your Bride, there sprawls your new-born Son.*'

Byron liked him, but the British Public did not. The British public liked, has liked, likes and always will like all art, music, poetry, literature, glass engraving, sculpture, etc. in just such measure as it approaches the Tennysonian tone. It likes Shakespear, or at least accepts him in just so far as he is 'Tennysonian'. It has published the bard of Avon expurgated and even emended. There has never been an edition of 'Purified Tennyson'.

'Is it credible that his (Tennyson's) whole mind should be made up of fine sentiments,' says Bagehot. Of course it wasn't. It was that lady-like attitude toward the printed page that did it—that something, that ineffable 'something', which kept Tennyson out of his works. When he began to write for Viccy's ignorant ear, he immediately ceased to be the 'Tennyson so muzzy that he tried to go out through the fireplace', the Tennyson with the broad North accent, the old man with the worst manners in England (except Carlyle's), the Tennyson whom 'it kept the whole combined efforts of his family and his publishers to keep respectable'. He became the Tate Gallery among poets.

The afflatus which has driven great artists to blurt out the facts of life with directness or with cold irony, or with passion, and with always precision; which impels Villon to write—

'Necessity makes men run wry,
And hunger drives the wolf from wood';

[1] 'The Future,' 1917.

which impels Homer to show Hermes replying to Calypso—

> 'You, a goddess, ask of me who am a god,
> Nevertheless I will tell you the truth';

which in contact with Turgenev builds a whole novel into the enforcement of some one or two speeches, so that we have, as the gaunt culmination, some phrase about the 'heart of another' or the wide pardon in Maria Timofevna's 'Nothing but death is irrevocable'; this urge, this impulse (or perhaps it is a different urge and impulse) leads Tennyson into pretty embroideries.

He refined the metric of England, at least he improved on some of Shelley's but did not reach the Elizabethans. Whereas Shakespear has never been refined enough for his compatriots. The eighteenth century set itself to mending his metres, and the nineteenth to mending his morals.

The cult of the innocuous has debouched into the adoration of Wordsworth. He was a silly old sheep with a genius, an unquestionable genius, for imagisme, for a presentation of natural detail, wildfowl bathing in a hole in the ice, etc., and this talent, or the fruits of this talent, he buried in a desert of bleatings.

Blake denounced him as an atheist, but for all that he has been deemed so innocuous that he has become, if not the backbone, at least one of the ribs of British kultur. And Crabbe?

The worst that should be said of him is that he still clings to a few of Pope's tricks, and that he is not utterly free from the habit of moralizing. What is, in actuality, usually said of him is that he is 'unpoetic', or, patronizingly, 'that you can't call this really great poetry'.

Pope is sometimes an excellent writer, Crabbe is never absolute slush, nonsense or bombast. That admission should satisfy the multitudinous reader, but it will not.

If the nineteenth century had built itself on Crabbe? Ah, if! But no; they wanted confections.

Crabbe has no variety of metric, but he shows no inconsiderable skill in the use of his one habitual metre, to save the same from monotony.

I admit that he makes vague generalities about 'Vice', 'Villainy and Crime', etc., but these paragraphs are hardly more than short cuts between one passage of poetry and another.

He does not bore you, he does not disgust you, he does not bring on that feeling of nausea which we have when we realize that we are listening to an idiot who occasionally makes beautiful (or ornamental) verses.

Browning at his best went on with Crabbe's method. He expressed an adoration of Shelley, and he might have learned more from Crabbe, but he was nevertheless the soundest of all the Victorians. Crabbe will perhaps keep better than Browning, he will have a savour of freshness; of course he is *not* 'the greater poet' of the two, but then he gives us such sound satisfaction in his best moments. And those moments are precisely the moments when he draws his 'Borough' with greatest exactness, and when he refrains from commenting. They are the moments 'when he lets himself go', when he is neither 'The Rev.' nor the 'LL.B.' but just good, sensible Crabbe, as at the end of 'Inns', or reporting conversations in 'Amusements', 'Blaney', 'Clelia', and the people remembered by 'Benbow'. If Englishmen had known how to select the best out of Crabbe they would have less need of consulting French stylists. Et pourtant—

'Then liv'd the good Squire Asquill—what a change
Has Death and Fashion shown us at the Grange?
He bravely thought it best became his rank,
That all his Tennants and his Tradesmen drank;

He was delighted from his favourite Room
To see them 'cross the Park go daily home,
Praising aloud the Liquor and the Host,
And striving who should venerate him most

. . . .

Along his valleys in the Evening-Hours
The Borough Damsels stray'd to gather Flowers
Or by the Brakes and Brushwood of the Park
To take their pleasant rambles in the dark.

Some Prudes, of rigid kind, forbore to call
On the kind Females—Favourites at the Hall;
But better natures saw, with much delight,
The different orders of mankind unite;
'Twas schooling Pride to see the Footman wait,
Smile on his sister and receive her plate.

Or Sir Denys admitting Clelia to the alms-house—

> 'With all her faults,' he said, 'the woman knew
> How to distinguish—had a manner too;
> And, as they say, she is allied to some
> In decent station—let the creature come.'

Oh, well! Byron enjoyed him. And the people liked Byron. They liked him for being 'romantic'. They adored Mrs Hemans. And some day when Arthur's tomb is no longer an object for metrical research, and when the Albert Memorial is no longer regilded, Crabbe's people will still remain vivid. People will read Miss Austen because of her knowledge of the human heart, and not solely for her refinement.

His, Crabbe's, realism is not the hurried realism of ignorance, he describes an inn called 'The Boar'; in his day there was no 'Maison Tellier' to serve for a paradigm:

> 'There dwells a kind old aunt, and there you'll see
> Some kind young nieces in her company:
>
> .   .   .   .
>
> What though it may some cool observers strike,
> That such fair sisters should be so unlike;
> And still another and another comes,
> And at the Matron's table smiles and blooms;
>
> .   .   .   .
>
> A pious friend who with the ancient Dame
> At sober cribbage takes an Evening-Game;
> His cup beside him, through their play he quaffs
>
> .   .   .   .
>
> Or growing serious to the Text resorts,
> And from the Sunday-Sermon makes reports, . . .

IRONY, LAFORGUE, AND
SOME SATIRE[1]

As Lewis has written, 'Matter which has not intelligence enough to permeate it grows, as you know, gangrenous and rotten'—to prevent quibble, let us say animal matter. Criticism is the fruit of maturity, *flair* is a faculty of the rarest. In most countries the only people who know enough of literature to appreciate—i.e. to determine the value of—new productions are professors and students, who confine their attention to the old. It is the mark of the artist that he, and he almost alone, is indifferent to oldness or newness. Staleness he will not abide; jade may be ancient, flowers should be reasonably fresh, but mutton cooked the week before last is, for the most part, unpalatable.

The unripe critic is constantly falling into such pitfalls. 'Originality', when it is most actual, is often sheer lineage, is often a closeness of grain. The innovator most damned for eccentricity, is often most centrally in the track or orbit of tradition, and his detractors are merely ignorant. The artist is in sane equilibrium, indifferent utterly to oldness or newness, so the thing be apposite to his want.

The scholar, often selfish, will as a rule have little to do with contemporary letters. He plays it safe. He confines himself to what many have already approved. The journalist is left as our jury. He is often an excellent fellow, and, in that case, a scoffer at his chosen or enforced position. He says, 'It is this that makes banderlog of us all.' I quote his phrase quite correctly; he was speaking of journalists. He talked intelligently on many other matters, and he did not look in the least like banderlog. He looked in fact rather like the frontispiece to my edition of Leopardi. Within three weeks as many journalists—all successful and one of them, at least, at the 'top of the tree'—have all said the same thing to me in slightly varying words. The journalist and his papers exists by reason of their 'protective coloring'. It is their job to think as their readers think at a given moment.

· · · · · · · · · ·

[1] Reprinted from *Poetry*, XI, 2 (Nov. 1917).

It is impossible that Jules Laforgue should have written his poems in America in 'the eighties'. He was born in 1860, died in 1887 of *la misère*, of consumption and abject poverty in Paris. The vaunted sensitiveness of French perception, and the fact that he knew a reasonable number of wealthy and influential people, did nothing to prevent this. He had published two small volumes, one edition of each. The seventh edition of his collected poems is dated 1913, and doubtless they have been reprinted since then with increasing celerity.

He is perhaps the most sophisticated of all the French poets, so it is not to be supposed that any wide public has welcomed or will welcome him in England or America. The seven hundred people in both those countries, who have read him with exquisite pleasure, will arise to combat this estimate, but no matter. His name is as well known as Mallarmé's, his writings perhaps are as widely distributed. The anthology of Van Bever and Leautaud has gone into, I suppose, its fiftieth thousand.

> Un couchant des Cosmogonies!
> Ah! que la Vie est quotidienne . . .
> Et, du plus vrai qu'on se souvienne,
> Comme on fut piètre et sans génie. . . .

What in heaven's name is the man in the street to make of this, or of the *Complainte des Bons Ménages!*

> L'Art sans poitrine m'a trop longtemps bercé dupe.
> Si ses labours sont fiers, que ses blés décevants!
> Tiens, laisse-moi bêler tout aux plis de ta jupe
> Qui fleure le couvent.

The red-blood has turned away, like the soldier in one of Plato's dialogues. Delicate irony, the citadel of the intelligent, has a curious effect on these people. They wish always to be exhorted, at all times no matter how incongruous and unsuitable, to do those things which almost anyone will and does do whenever suitable opportunity is presented. As Henry James has said, 'It was a period when writers besought the deep blue sea "to roll".'

The ironist is one who suggests that the reader should think, and this process being unnatural to the majority of mankind, the way of the ironical is beset with snares and with furze-bushes.

Laforgue was a purge and a critic. He laughed out the errors of Flaubert, i.e., the clogging and cumbrous historical detail. He left *Coeur Simple*, *L'Education*, *Madame Bovary*, *Bouvard*. His, Laforgue's, *Salome* makes game of the rest. The short story has become vapid because sixty thousand story writers have all set themselves to imitating De Maupassant, perhaps a thousand from the original.

I think Laforgue implies definitely that certain things in prose were at an end. I think also that he marks the next phase after Gautier in French poetry. It seems to me that without a familiarity with Laforgue one can not appreciate—i.e., determine the value of— certain positives and certain negatives in French poetry since 1890.

He is an incomparable artist. He is, nine-tenths of him, critic— dealing for the most part with literary poses and *clichés*, taking them as his subject matter; and—and this is the important thing when we think of him as a poet—he makes them a vehicle for the expression of his own very personal emotions, of his own unperturbed sincerity.

> Je ne suis pas 'ce gaillard-là!' ni Le Superbe!
> Mais mon âme, qu'un cri un peu cru exacerbe,
> Est au fond distinguée et franche comme une herbe.

This is not the strident and satiric voice of Corbière, calling Hugo '*Garde Nationale épique*', and Lamartine '*Lacrimatoire des abonnés*'. It is not Tailhade drawing with rough strokes the people he sees daily in Paris, and bursting with guffaws over the Japanese in their mackintoshes, the West Indian mulatto behind the bar in the Quartier. It is not Georges Fourest burlesquing in a café; Fourest's guffaw is magnificent, he is hardly satirical. Tailhade draws from life and indulges in occasional squabbles. Corbière is hard-bitten, perhaps the most poignant poet since Villon, in very much Villon's manner.

Laforgue was a better artist than any of these men save Corbière. He was not in the least of their sort. Corbière lived from 1842 to 1875. Tailhade was born in 1854, and is still living. During the eighties he seems to have been writing Swinburnian verse, and his satires *Au Pays du Mufle*, now part of *Poèmes Aristophanesques*, appeared in 1891. Corbière's poems, first printed in 1873, were hardly obtainable until the reprint of 1891. Thus, so far as the public is concerned, these poets are almost contemporary with each other.

They 'reached' England in the nineties. Beardsley's *Under the Hill* was until recently the only successful attempt to produce 'anything like Laforgue' in our tongue. *Under the Hill* was issued in a limited edition. Laforgue's *Moralités Légendaires* was issued in England by the Ricketts and Hacon press in a limited edition, and there the thing has remained. Laforgue can never become a popular cult because tyros can not imitate him. Recent translations of his prose are held up because of copyright laws.

I do not think one can too carefully discriminate between Laforgue's tone and that of his contemporary French satirists. He is the finest wrought; he is most 'verbalist'. Bad verbalism is rhetoric, or the use of *cliché* unconsciously, or a mere playing with phrases. But there is good verbalism, distinct from lyricism or imagism, and in this Laforgue is a master. He writes not the popular language of any country but an international tongue common to the excessively cultivated, and to those more or less familiar with French literature of the first three-fourths of the nineteenth century.

He has done, sketchily and brilliantly, for French literature a work not incomparable to what Flaubert was doing for 'France' in *Bouvard and Pécuchet,* if one may compare the flight of the butterfly with the progress of an ox, both proceeding toward the same point of the compass. He has dipped his wings in the dye of scientific terminology. Pierrot *imberbe* has

Un air d'hydrocephale asperge.

The tyro can not play about with such things, the game is too dangerous. Verbalism demands a set form used with irreproachable skill. Satire needs, usually, the form of cutting rhymes to drive it home.

Chautauquas, Mrs. Eddys, Dr. Dowies, Comstocks, societies for the prevention of all human activities are impossible in the wake of Laforgue. And he is therefore an exquisite poet, a deliverer of the nations, a Numa Pompilius, a father of light. And to the crowd this mystery, the mystery why such force should reside in so fragile a book, why such power should coincide with so great a nonchalance of manner, will remain forever a mystery.

Que loin l'âme type
Qui m'a dit adieu

> Parce que mes yeux
> Manquaient de principes!
>
> Elle, en ce moment,
> Elle, si pain tendre,
> Oh! peut-être engendre
> Quelque garnement.
>
> Car on l'a unie
> Avec un monsieur,
> Ce qu'il y a de mieux,
> Mais pauvre en génie.

Laforgue is perhaps incontrovertible. John B. Yeats has written of the relation of art and 'certitude' and we are perhaps too prone to connect 'certitude' only with the 'strong silent man' of the kinema. There are, however, various species.

THE HARD AND SOFT IN
FRENCH POETRY[1]

I apologize for using the semetaphorical terms 'hard' and 'soft' in this essay, but after puzzling over the matter for some time I can see no other way of setting about it. By 'hardness' I mean a quality which is in poetry nearly always a virtue—I can think of no case where it is not. By softness I mean an opposite quality which is not always a fault. Anyone who dislikes these textural terms may lay the blame on Théophile Gautier, who certainly suggests them in *Emaux et Camées;* it is his hardness that I had first in mind. He exhorts us to cut in hard substance, the shell and the Parian.

We may take it that Gautier achieved hardness in *Emaux et Camées;* his earlier work did in France very much what remained for the men of 'the nineties' to accomplish in England. An examination of what Gautier wrote in 'the thirties' will show a similar beauty, a similar sort of technique. If the Parnassians were following Gautier they fell short of his merit. Heredia is perhaps the best of them. He tries to make his individual statements more 'poetic'; his whole, for all this, becomes frigid. Samain follows him and begins to go 'soft', there is just a suggestion of muzziness. Heredia is 'hard', but there or thereabouts he ends. It is perhaps that Gautier is intent on being 'hard'; is intent on conveying a certain verity of feeling, and he ends by being truly poetic. Heredia wants to be poetic *and* hard; the hardness appears to him as a virtue in the poetic. And one tends to conclude that all attempts to be poetic in some manner or other defeat their own end; whereas an intentness on the quality of the emotion to be conveyed makes for poetry.

Another possible corollary is that the subject matter will very nearly make the poem. Subject matter will, of course, not make the poem; e.g., compare Mangan's *Kathleen ni Houlihan,* with Yeats' *Song that Red Hanrahan made about Ireland,* where the content is almost identical.

On the other hand the man who first decides that certain things are poetry has great advantage over all who follow him, and who

[1] Reprinted from *Poetry*, XI, 5 (Feb. 1918).

accede in his opinion. Gautier did decide that certain things were
worth making into poems, whereas the Parnassians only acceded in
other men's opinions about subject matter, and accepted Gautier's
advice to cut, metaphorically, in hard stone, etc.

Gautier is individual and original even in such poems as the *Poem
of Woman,* and the *Symphony in White Major,* which seem but variants on old themes. I have found what might be a germ of the
Symphony in Renaissance Latin, and there is an Elizabethan lyric
about *Swan's down ever.* Nevertheless Gautier's way of thinking
about these things was at bottom his own.

His originality is not in his form, his hard, close-cut lines and
stanzas. Bernard, a poet praised by Voltaire, and at one time Rameau's
librettist, wrote French in clear hard little stanzas:

> J'ai vu Daphné, Terpsichore légère,
> Sur un tapis de rose et de fougère,
> S'abandonner à des bonds pleins d'appas,
> Voler, languir. . . . . .

This is not from a stanza but it shows Bernard's perfectly orderly
method.

Gautier writing in opposition to, or in rejection of, the swash of
Hugo, De Musset & Co. came undoubtedly as a contrast, but he can
scarcely have seemed so 'different' to Frenchmen versed in their own
earlier poetry as he does to the English reader coming upon him with
slight prelude save English.

We have however some hardness in English, and in Landor we
have a hardness which is not of necessity 'rugged'; as in 'Past ruin'd
Ilion Helen lives'. Indeed, Gautier might well be the logical
successor to Landor, were he not in all probability the logical co-heir
with Landor of certain traditions.

Landor is, from poem to poem, extremely uneven. Our feeling of
him must in part rest on our admiration of his prose. Lionel Johnson
had a certain hardness and smoothness, but was more critic than poet,
and not a very great poet. There is definite statement in George
Herbert, and likewise in Christina Rossetti, but I do not feel that they
have much part in this essay. I do not feel that their quality is really
the quality I am seeking here to define.

We have in English a certain gamut of styles: we have the good
Chaucerian, almost the only style in English where 'softness' is

tolerable; we have the good Elizabethan; which is not wholly un-Chaucerian: and the bad, or muzzy, Elizabethan; and the Miltonic, which is a bombastic and rhetorical Elizabethan coming from an attempt to write English with Latin syntax. Its other mark is that the rich words have gone: *i.e.*, words like *preluciand*, which have a folk tradition and are, in feeling, germane to all Europe: *Leuchend, luisant, lucente;* these words are absent in Miltonism, and purely pedantic words, like *irriguous*, have succeeded them.

We have Pope, who is really the Elizabethan satiric style, more or less born out of Horace, and a little improved or at least regularized. And we have Landor—that is, Landor at his best. And after that we have 'isms' and 'eses': the pseudo-Elizabethanism—*i.e.*, bad Keats; the romantics, Swinburnese, Browningese, neo-celticism. And how the devil a poet writing English manages to find or make a language for poems is a mystery.

It is approximately true, or at least it is a formulation worth talking over: that French prose is good in proportion as it reaches a sort of norm; English prose is good in proportion as a man makes it an individual language, one which he alone uses. This statement must not be swallowed whole. And we must also remember that when Italians were writing excellent and clear prose—in the time of Henry VIII—Englishmen could scarcely make a clear prose formulation even in documents of state and instructions to envoys; so backward were things in this island, so rude in prose the language which had been exquisite in the lyrics of Chaucer.[1]

French 'clarity' can be talked to death, and there are various kinds of French prose—the Voltaire-Anatole-France kind, the Stendhal roughness and directness, the Flaubertian art, and also the 'soft' prose. Flaubert and Anatole France are both 'softer' than Voltaire and Stendhal. Remy de Gourmont is almost the only writer who seems to me good in a French prose which must, I think, be called 'soft'. It is with him a peculiar and personal medium.

If this seem an over-long prologue, think how little discussion there is of these things. Only a few professors and their favourite students seem to have read enough to be able to consider a matter of style with any data at their disposal—these and a few poets of the better sort; and professors are not paid to spread heresies and bring uncertainties into accepted opinion; and poets of the worse sort seem

[1] Moderate this statement by consideration of Mallory. E.P.

seldom to have any reading. So a prologue is needed even for a brief attempt to find out where French verse has got to; or where it had arrived a few years ago, seeing that since the war, *faute de combattants,* no one has had time to go forward, or even to continue the work of 1912-1914—since undigested war is no better for poetry than undigested anything else.

Since Gautier, Corbière has been hard, not with a glaze or parian finish, but hard like weather-bit granite. And Heredia and Samain have been hard decreasingly, giving gradually smoothness for hardness. And Jammes has been 'soft', in his earlier poems with a pleasurable softness. And De Regnier seems to verge out of Parnassianism into an undefined sort of poetry. Tailhade is hard in his satire.

Romains, Vildrac, Spire, Arcos, are not hard, any one of them, though Spire can be acid. These men have left the ambitions of Gautier; they have done so deliberately, or at least they have, in the quest of something well worth seeking, made a new kind of French poetry. I first wrote of *Unanimisme* in the *New Age* something over four years ago. Romains is the centre of it. A recent English essay on the subject, trying to point to English *unanimistes,* is pure rubbish, and shows no comprehension on the part of its author. Romains' *unanimisme* is a definite theory, almost a religion. He alone of the better French poets seems to have written at its dictates. The rest of the men of his decade have not written to a theory. Romains has, I think, more intellect than the rest of them, and he is an equally notable poet. He has tried to make, and in places succeeded in making, poetry out of crowd-psychology. Vildrac has been personal and humanitarian. Arcos and Spire have delineated. Romains' portrayal of the collective emotions of a school of little girls out for the day is the most original poem in our generation's French. His series of 'prayers'—to the God-one, the god-couple, the god-house, the god-street, and so on—is extremely interesting. Vildrac's short narrative poems are a progress on the pseudo-Maupassant story, and have parallels in English. Romains has no English parallel. Allowing for personal difference, I should say that Spire and Arcos write 'more or less as I do myself.' I do not mean to make any comparison of merits, but this comparison is the easiest or simplest way of telling the general reader 'what sort of poems' they have written.

I do not think I have copied their work, and they certainly have not copied mine. We are contemporary and as sonnets of a certain sort were once written on both sides of the channel, so these short poems depicting certain phases of contemporary life are now written on both sides of the channel; with, of course, personal differences.

Vildrac has written *Auberge* and *Visite*, and no doubt these poems will be included in any anthology of the period. The thing that puzzles me in attempting to appreciate both Romains and Vildrac is just this question of 'hardness', and a wonder how poetry can get on without it—not by any means demanding that it be ubiquitous. For I do not in the least mean that I want their poems rewritten 'hard'; any more than I should want Jammes' early poems rewritten 'hard'. A critic must spend some of his time asking questions—which perhaps no one can answer. It is much more his business to stir up curiosity than to insist on acceptances.

SWINBURNE VERSUS HIS
BIOGRAPHERS[1]

The Life of Algernon Charles Swinburne, by Edmund Gosse, C.B.
The Macmillan Co.

Gosse's *Life of Swinburne* is merely the attempt of a silly and pompous old man to present a man of genius, an attempt necessarily foredoomed to failure and not worth the attention of even the most cursive reviewer. Gosse has written one excellent book: *Father and Son,* prompted according to gossip by his wife's fear that Mr. George Moore, having been rashly allowed access to Mr. Gosse's diaries, proposed to steal the material. Mr. Gosse has also held divers positions of trust under the British government, in one of which, at least, he has fulfilled his functions with great credit and fairness. Apart from that he resembles many literary figures of about his age and generation, who, coming after the more or less drunken and more or less obstreperous real Victorians, acquired only the cant and the fustiness.

Tennyson, 'so muzzy that he tried to go out through the fire-place'; Morris (William, not Lewis) lying on the floor biting the table-leg in a rage because Gabriel had gone off before he, Morris, had finished what he was saying; Swinburne at the Madox Browns' door in a cab, while the house-keeper lectures the cabman: 'Wot! No, sir, my marster is at the 'ead of 'is table carving the j'int. *That's* Mr. Swinburne—tike 'im up to the barth': were all vital and human people. The real pre-raphaelites lived with Ford Madox Brown's hospitable address sewn inside their coats, in case of these little events. Tennyson, personally the North-country ox, might very well take refuge from his deplorable manners in verbal *patisserie;* Thackeray might snivvel over not being allowed to write with desirable open-ness: most of these people surround themselves with extenuations, but for the next generation there is not much to be said save that they go like better men toward extinction. We do not however wish a

[1] Reprinted from *Poetry,* XI, 6 (March 1918).

Swinburne coated with veneer of British officialdom and decked out for a psalm-singing audience.

Gosse in the safety of his annual pension of £666, 16 shillings, 8 pence, has little to fear from the slings of fortune or from the criticisms of younger men. If he preferred to present Swinburne as an epileptic rather than as an intemperate drinker, we can only attribute this to his taste, a taste for kowtowing.

The 'events at the art club', which he so prudishly glozes over, were the outcome of alcohol, and the story is worth while if only for the magnificent tanning that Whistler administered to the Arts Club committee: 'You ought to be proud that there is in London a club where the greatest poet of your time *can* get drunk if he wants to, otherwise he might lie in the gutter.'

There is more Swinburne, and perhaps more is to be told of his tragedy, in a few vignettes than is to be found in all Gosse's fusty volume. Swinburne's tragedy was that he ended as a deaf, querulous old man in Putney, mediocre in his faculties. W. H. Davies tells the story of the little old man looking into a perambulator in front of a pub, and a cockney woman hastily interposing herself and pulling the clothes over the infant's head with, '*Narsty* old man, 'e sharn't look at *my* baby.'

Thus departed his mundane glory, the glory of a red mane, the glory of the strong swimmer, of the swimmer who when he was pulled out of the channel apparently drowned, came to and held his French fishermen rescuers spellbound all the way to shore declaiming page after page of Hugo.

As George Moore, in his writings, nearly always attributes to himself the witty remarks wherewith other men have extinguished him in conversation, we may be pardoned for another tale, which may as likely as not contain verity. It is said that Moore desired greatly to look upon Swinburne, and having obtained his address, repaired to the Temple, and heavily climbing the stairs heard noises

come fa mar per tempesta.

They proceeded from Swinburne's rooms. Moore knocked—the door was already open. No answer was given. The booming increased and diminished and increased. Moore entered—the room was empty; he proceeded to the next open door, and to still another. He stood aghast; Swinburne, hair on end and stark naked, strode

backwards and forwards howling Aeschylus. Moore stood paralysed.
Swinburne after some moments caught sight of him; thundered
'What the hell do *you* want?' Moore summoned his waning powers
of expression, and with mountainous effort brought forth the verbal
mouse: 'Please, sir, are these Mr. Jones' chambers?'

'*No*, sir!'

Whereat Mr. George Moore departed.

It is impossible that a self-respecting biographer should not have
found many such tales of Swinburne. The anaemic Gosse prefers the
epileptic version. Any poet might be justified in taking to drink on
finding himself born into a world full of Gosses, Comstocks, and
Sumners.

.   .   .   .

Swinburne's art is out of fashion. The best imitations of him are
by the Germans. The nineties refined upon him, and Kipling has set
his 'cello-tunes to the pilly-wink of one banjo.

Swinburne recognized poetry as an art, and as an art of verbal
music. Keats had got so far as to see that it need not be the pack-
mule of philosophy. Swinburne's actual writing is very often rather
distressing, but a deal of his verse is no worse written than Shelley's
Ode to the West Wind. He habitually makes a fine stanzaic form,
writes one or two fine strophes in it, and then continues to pour into
the mould strophes of diminishing quality.

His biography is perfectly well written in his work. He is never
better than in the *Ballad of Life*, the *Ballad of Death*, and the
Triumph of Time. To the careful reader this last shows quite clearly
that Swinburne was actually broken by a real and not by a feigned
emotional catastrophe early in life; of this his later slow decline is a
witness. There is a lack of intellect in his work. After the poems in
the *Laus Veneris* volume (not particularly the title poem) and the
poems of the time when he made his magnificent adaptations from
Villon, he had few rallies of force, one of them in *Siena*.

He neglected the value of words as words, and was intent on their
value as sound. His habit of choice grew mechanical, and he himself
perceived it and parodied his own systemization.

Moderns more awake to the value of language will read him with
increasing annoyance, but I think few men who read him before their
faculty for literary criticism is awakened—the faculty for purely

literary discrimination as contrasted with melopoeic discrimination
—will escape the enthusiasm of his emotions, some of which were
indubitably real. At any rate we can, whatever our verbal fastidious-
ness, be thankful for any man who kept alive some spirit of paganism
and of revolt in a papier-mâché era, in a time swarming with Long-
fellows, Mabies, Gosses, Harrisons.

After all, the whole of his defects can be summed up in one—that
is, inaccurate writing; and this by no means ubiquitous. To quote
his magnificent passages is but to point out familiar things in our
landscape. *Hertha* is fit for professors and young ladies in boarding-
school. The two ballads and the *Triumph of Time* are full of sheer
imagism, of passages faultless.

No one else has made such music in English, I mean has made his
kind of music; and it is a music which will compare with Chaucer's
Hide Absalon thi gilte tresses clere or with any other maker you like.

The Villon translations stand with Rossetti's and the *Rubaiyat*
among the Victorian translations. The ballad, *Where ye droon ane
man I droon twa*, is as fine as any reconstruction, and the cross-
rhythms are magnificent. The *Itylus*, the *Ballad of Burdens*—what is
the use of naming over poems so familiar to all of us!

'As yet you get no whole or perfect poet.' He and Browning are
the best of the Victorian era; and Browning wrote to a theory of the
universe, thereby cutting off a fair half of the moods for expression.

No man who cares for his art can be deaf to the rhythms of
Swinburne, deaf to their splendour, deaf also to their bathos. The
sound of *Dolores* is in places like that of horses' hooves being pulled
out of mud. The sound in a poem of sleep is so heavy that
one can hardly read it aloud, the voice is drawn into a slumber.
(I am not sure that this effect is not excessive, and that it does not
show the author over-shooting his mark; but for all that it shows
ability in his craft, and has, whatever one's final opinion, an indisputable value as experiment.) Swinburne's surging and leaping
dactyllics had no comparable forerunners in English.

His virtues might be largely dug from the Greeks, and his faults
mostly traceable to Victor Hugo. But a perception of the beauties
of Greek melopoeia does not constitute a mastery in the creation of
similar melopoeia. The rhythm-building faculty was in Swinburne,
and was perhaps the chief part of his genius. The word-selecting,
word-castigating faculty was nearly absent. Unusual and gorgeous

words attracted him. His dispraisers say that his vocabulary is one of the smallest at any poet's command, and that he uses the same adjectives to depict either a woman or a sunset. There are times when this last is not, or need not be, *ipso facto* a fault. There is an emotional fusion of the perceptions, and a certain kind of verbal confusion has an emotive value in writing; but this is of all sorts of writing the most dangerous to an author, and the unconscious collapse into this sort of writing has wrecked more poets in our time than perhaps all other faults put together.

> Forth, ballad, and take roses in thine arms,
> Even till the top rose prick thee in the throat
> Where the least thorn-prick harms;
> And gird thee in the golden singing coat. . . .
> Borgia, thy gold hair's colour burns in me. . . .

The splendid lines mount up in one's memory and overwhelm any minute restrictions of one's praise. It is the literary fashion to write exclusively of Swinburne's defects; and the fashion is perhaps not a bad one, for the public is still, and will presumably remain, indiscriminate. Defects are in Swinburne by the bushelful: the discriminating reader will not be able to overlook them, and need not condone them; neither will he be swept off his feet by detractors. There are in Swinburne fine passages, like fragments of fine marble statues; there are fine transcripts from the Greek:

A little soul for a little bears up this corpse which is man.

And there is, underneath all the writing, a magnificent passion for liberty—a passion dead as mutton in most of his contemporaries, and immeasurably deader than mutton in a people who allow their literature to be blanketed by a Comstock and his successors; for liberty is not merely a catchword of politics, nor a right to shove little slips of paper through a hole. The passion not merely for political, but also for personal, liberty is the bedrock of Swinburne's writing. The sense of tragedy, and of the unreasoning cruelty of the gods, hangs over it. He fell into facile writing, and he accepted a facile compromise for life; but no facile solution for his universe. His belief did not desert him; no, not even in Putney.

HENRY JAMES[1]

This essay on James is a dull grind of an affair, a Baedecker to a continent.

I set out to explain, not why Henry James is less read than formerly—I do not know that he is. I tried to set down a few reasons why he ought to be, or at least might be, more read.

Some say that his work was over, well over, finely completed; there is mass of that work, heavy for one man's shoulders to have borne up, labour enough for two lifetimes; still we would have had a few more years of his writing. Perhaps the grasp was relaxing, perhaps we should have had no strongly-planned book; but we should have had paragraphs here and there, and we should have had, at least, conversation, wonderful conversation; even if we did not hear it ourselves, we should have known that it was going on somewhere. The massive head, the slow uplift of the hand, *gli occhi onesti e tardi*, the long sentences piling themselves up in elaborate phrase after phrase, the lightning incision, the pauses, the slightly shaking admonitory gesture with its 'wu-a-wait a little, wait a little, something will come'; blague and benignity and the weight of so many years' careful, incessant labour of minute observation always there to enrich the talk. I had heard it but seldom, yet it is all unforgettable.

The man had this curious power of founding affection in those who had scarcely seen him and even in many who had not, who but knew him at second hand.

No man who has not lived on both sides of the Atlantic can well appraise Henry James; his death marks the end of a period. *The Times* says: 'The Americans will understand his changing his nationality', or something of that sort. The 'Americans' will understand nothing whatsoever about it. They have understood nothing about it. They do not even know what they lost. They have not stopped for eight minutes to consider the meaning of his last public act. After a year of ceaseless labour, of letter writing, of argument, of striving in every way to bring in America on the side of civilization, he

[1] *Little Review*, Aug. 1918.

died of apoplexy. On the side of civilization—civilization[1] against barbarism, civilization, not Utopia, not a country or countries where the right always prevails in six weeks! After a lifetime spent in trying to make two continents understand each other, in trying, and only his thoughtful readers can have any conception of how he had tried, to make three nations intelligible one to another. I am tired of hearing pettiness talked about Henry James's style. The subject has been discussed enough in all conscience, along with the minor James. Yet I have heard no word of the major James, of the hater of tyranny; book after early book against oppression, against all the sordid petty personal crushing oppression, the domination of modern life; not worked out in the diagrams of Greek tragedy, not labelled 'epos' or 'Aeschylus'. The outbursts in *The Tragic Muse*, the whole of *The Turn of the Screw*, human liberty, personal liberty, the rights of the individual against all sorts of intangible bondage![2] The passion of it, the continual passion of it in this man who, fools said, didn't 'feel'. I have never yet found a man of emotion against whom idiots didn't raise this cry.

And the great labour, this labour of translation, of making America intelligible, of making it possible for individuals to meet across national borders. I think half the American idiom is recorded in Henry James' writing, and whole decades of American life that otherwise would have been utterly lost, wasted, rotting in the unhermetic jars of bad writing, of inaccurate writing. No English reader will ever know how good are his New York and his New England; no one who does not see his grandmother's friends in the pages of the American books. The whole great assaying and weighing, the research for the significance of nationality, French, English, American.

[1] 1929. I should probably be incapable of writing this paragraph now. But that is how things looked in 1918 and I see no reason to pretend that I saw them otherwise. I still believe that a Hohenzollern victory would have meant an intolerable post-war world. I think I write this without animus, and that I am quite aware of the German component indispensable to a complete civilization.

[2] This holds, despite anything that may be said of his fuss about social order, social tone. I naturally do not drag in political connotations, from which H. J. was, we believe, wholly exempt. What he fights is 'influence', the impinging of family pressure, the impinging of one personality on another; all of them in highest degree damn'd, loathsome and detestable. Respect for the peripheries of the individual may be, however, a discovery of our generation; I doubt it, but it seems to have been at low ebb in some districts (not rural) for some time.

'An extraordinary old woman, one of the few people who are really doing anything good.' There were the cobwebs about connoisseurship, etc. but what do they matter? Some yokel writes in the village paper, as Henley had written before, 'James's stuff was not worth doing.' Henley has gone pretty completely. America has not yet realized that never in history had one of her great men abandoned his citizenship out of shame. It was the last act—the last thing left. He had worked all his life for the nation and for a year he had laboured for the national honour. No other American was of sufficient importance for his change of allegiance to have constituted an international act; no other American would have been welcome in the same public manner. America passes over these things, but the thoughtful cannot pass over them.

Armageddon, the conflict? I turn to James' *A Bundle of Letters;* a letter from 'Dr Rudolph Staub' in Paris, ending:

'You will, I think, hold me warranted in believing that between precipitate decay and internecine enmities, the English-speaking family is destined to consume itself and that with its decline the prospect of general pervasiveness to which I allude above, will brighten for the deep-lunged children of the fatherland!'

We have heard a great deal of this sort of thing since; it sounds very natural. My edition of the volume containing these letters was printed in 1883, and the imaginary letters were written somewhat before that. I do not know that this calls for comment. Henry James' perception came thirty years before Armageddon. That is all I wish to point out. Flaubert said of the War of 1870: 'If they had read my *Education Sentimentale,* this sort of thing wouldn't have happened.' Artists are the antennae of the race, but the bullet-headed many will never learn to trust their great artists. If it is the business of the artist to make humanity aware of itself; here the thing was done, the pages of diagnosis. The multitude of wearisome fools will not learn their right hand from their left or seek out a meaning.

It is always easy for people to object to what they have not tried to understand.

I am not here to write a full volume of detailed criticism, but two things I do claim which I have not seen in reviewers' essays. First, that there was emotional greatness in Henry James' hatred of tyranny; secondly, that there was titanic volume, weight, in the masses he sets in opposition within his work. He uses forces no whit less

specifically powerful than the proverbial 'doom of the house'—
Destiny, *Deus ex machina*,—of great traditional art. His art was
great art as opposed to over-elaborate or over-refined art by virtue
of the major conflicts which he portrays. In his books he showed race
against race, immutable; the essential Americanness, or Englishness
or Frenchness—in *The American*, the difference between one nation
and another; not flag-waving and treaties, not the machinery of
government, but 'why' there is always misunderstanding, why men
of different race are not the same.

We have ceased to believe that we conquer anything by having
Alexander the Great make a gigantic 'joy-ride' through India. We
know that conquests are made in the laboratory, that Curie with his
minute fragments of things seen clearly in test tubes, in curious
apparatus, makes conquests. So, too, in these novels, the essential
qualities which make up the national qualities, are found and set
working, the fundamental oppositions made clear. This is no
contemptible labour. No other writer had so assayed three great
nations or even thought of attempting it.

Peace comes of communication. No man of our time has so laboured to create means of communication as did the late Henry James.
The whole of great art is a struggle for communication. All things
that oppose this are evil, whether they be silly scoffing or obstructive
tariffs.

And this communication is not a levelling, it is not an elimination
of differences. It is a recognition of differences, of the right of differences to exist, of interest in finding things different. Kultur is an
abomination; philology is an abomination, all repressive uniforming
education is an evil.

A SHAKE DOWN

I have forgotten the moment of lunar imbecility in which I conceived the idea of a 'Henry James' number.[1] The pile of typescript
on my floor can but annoyingly and too palpably testify that the
madness has raged for some weeks.

Henry James was aware of the spherical form of the planet, and
susceptible to a given situation, and to the tone and tonality of
persons as perhaps no other author in all literature. The victim and

[1] *Little Review*, Aug. 1918.

the votary of the 'scene', he had no very great narrative sense, or at
the least, he attained the narrative faculty but *per aspera*, through
very great striving.

It is impossible to speak accurately of 'his style', for he passed
through several styles which differ greatly one from another; but in
his last, his most complicated and elaborate, he is capable of great
concision; and if, in it, the single sentence is apt to turn and perform
evolutions for almost pages at a time, he nevertheless manages to say
on one page more than many a more 'direct' author would convey
only in the course of a chapter.

His plots and incidents are often but adumbrations or symbols of
the quality of his 'people', illustrations invented, contrived, often
factitiously and almost transparently, to show what acts, what
situations, what contingencies would befit or display certain
characters. We are hardly asked to accept them as happening.[1]

He did not begin his career with any theory of art for art's sake,
and a lack of this theory may have damaged his earlier work.

If we take *French Poets and Novelists* as indication of his then
(1878) opinions, and novels of the nineties showing a later bias, we
might contend that our subject began his career with a desire to
square all things to the ethical standards of a Salem mid-week
Unitarian prayer meeting, and that to almost the end of his course he
greatly desired to fit the world into the social exigencies of Mrs
Humphry Ward's characters.

Out of these unfortunate cobwebs, he emerged into his greatness,
I think, by two causes: first by reason of his hatred of personal
intimate tyrannies working at close range; and secondly, in later life,
because the actual mechanism of his scriptorial processes became so
bulky, became so huge a contrivance for record and depiction, that
the old man simply couldn't remember or keep his mind on or
animadvert on anything but the authenticity of his impression.

I take it as the supreme reward for an artist; the supreme return
that his artistic conscience can make him after years spent in its
service, that the momentum of his art, the sheer bulk of his processes,
the (*si licet*) size of his fly-wheel, should heave him out of himself,
out of his personal limitations, out of the tangles of heredity and of
environment, out of the bias of early training, of early predilections,

[1] Cf. Stendhal's rather unconvincing apology for the ultimate female in *Le
Rouge et le Noir*.

whether of Florence, A.D. 1300, or of Back Bay of 1872, and leave him simply the great true recorder.

This reward came to Henry James in the ripeness of his talents; even further perhaps it entered his life and his conversation. The stages of his emergence are marked quite clearly in his work. He displays himself in *French Poets and Novelists*, constantly balancing over the question of whether or no the characters presented in their works are, or are not, fit persons to be received in the James family back-parlour.

In *The Tragic Muse* he is still didactic quite openly. The things he believes still leap out nakedly among the people and things he is portraying; the parable is not yet wholly incarnate in the narrative.

To lay all his faults on the table, we may begin with his self-confessed limitations, that 'he never went down town'. He displayed in fact a passion for high life comparable only to that supposed to inhere in the readers of a magazine called *Forget-me-not*.

Hardy, with his eye on the Greek tragedians, has produced an epic tonality, and *The Mayor of Casterbridge* is perhaps more easily comparable to the Grettir Saga than to the novels of Mr Hardy's contemporaries. Hardy is, on his other side, a contemporary of Sir Walter Scott.

Balzac gains what force his crude writing permits him by representing his people under the ἀνάγκη of modernity, cash necessity; James, by leaving cash necessity nearly always out of the story, sacrifices, or rather fails to attain, certain intensities.

He never manages the classic, I mean as Flaubert gives us in each main character: *Everyman*. One may conceivably be bored by certain pages in Flaubert, but one takes from him a solid and concrete memory, a property. Emma Bovary and Frederic and M. Arnoux are respectively every woman and every man of their period. Maupassant's *Bel Ami* is not. Neither are Henry James' people. They are always, or nearly always, the bibelots.

But he does, nevertheless, treat of major forces, even of epic forces, and in a way all his own. If Balzac tried to give a whole civilization, a whole humanity, James was not content with a rough sketch of one country.

As Armageddon has only too clearly shown, national qualities are the great gods of the present and Henry James spent himself from the beginning in an analysis of these potent chemicals; trying to determine from the given microscopic slide the nature of the Frenchness, Englishness, Germanness, Americanness, which chemicals too little regarded, have in our time exploded for want of watching. They are the permanent and fundamental hostilities and incompatibles. We may rest our claim for his greatness in the magnitude of his protagonists, in the magnitude of the forces he analysed and portrayed. This is not the bare matter of a number of titled people, a few duchesses and a few butlers.

Whatever Flaubert may have said about his *Education Sentimentale* as a potential preventive of the débâcle of 1870, *if people had* read it, and whatever Gautier's friend may have said about *Emaux et Camées* as the last resistance to the Prussians, from Dr Rudolph Staub's paragraph in *The Bundle of Letters* to the last and almost only public act of his life, James displayed a steady perception and a steady consideration of the qualities of different Western races, whose consequences none of us can escape.

And these forces, in precisely that they are not political and executive and therefore transient, factitious, but in precisely that they are the forces of race temperaments, are major forces and are indeed as great protagonists as any author could have chosen. They are firmer ground than Flaubert's when he chooses public events as in the opening of the third part of *Education Sentimentale*.

The portrayal of these forces, to seize a term from philology, may be said to constitute 'original research'—to be Henry James' own addendum; not that this greatly matters. He saw, analysed, and presented them. He had most assuredly a greater awareness than was granted to Balzac or to Mr Charles Dickens or to M. Victor Hugo who composed the *Légende des Siècles*.

His statement that he never went down town has been urged greatly against him. A butler is a servant, tempered with upper-class contacts. Mr Newman, the American, has emerged from the making of wash-tubs; the family in *The Pupil* can scarcely be termed upperclass, however, and the factor of money, Balzac's ἀνάγκη, scarcely enters his stories.

We may leave Hardy writing Sagas. We may admit that there is a greater *robustezza* in Balzac's messiness, simply because he is perpetually concerned, inaccurately, with the factor of money, of earning one's exiguous living.

We may admit the shadowy nature of some of James' writing,

and agree whimsically with 'R.H.C.'[1] (in the *New Age*) that James will be quite comfortable after death, as he had been dealing with ghosts all his life.

James' third donation is perhaps a less sweeping affair and of more concern to his compatriots than to any one who might conceivably translate him into an alien tongue, or even to those who publish his writings in England.

He has written history of a personal sort, social history well documented and incomplete, and he has put America on the map both in memoir and fiction, giving to her a reality such as is attained only by scenes recorded in the arts and in the writing of masters. Mr Eliot has written, and I daresay most other American admirers have written or will write, that, whatever any one else thinks of Henry James, no one but an American can ever know, really know, how good he is at the bottom, how good his 'America' is.

No Englishman can, and in less degree can any continental, or in fact any one whose family was not living on, say, West 23rd Street in the old set-back, two-story-porched red brick vine-covered houses, etc. when Henry James was being a small boy on East 23rd Street; no one whose ancestors had not been presidents or professors or founders of Ha'vawd College or something of that sort, or had not heard of a time when people lived on 14th Street, or had known of some one living in Lexington or Newton 'Old Place' or somewhere of that sort in New England, or had heard of the New York that produced 'Fanny', New York the jocular and uncritical, or of people who danced with General Grant or something of that sort, would quite know *Washington Square* or *The Europeans* to be so autochthonous, so authentic to the conditions. They might believe the things to be 'real', but they would not know how closely they corresponded to an external reality.

Perhaps only an exile from these things will get the range of the other half of James' presentations! Europe to the Transpontine New York of brown stone that he detested, the old and new New York in *Crapey Cornelia* and in *The American Scene*, which more than any other volumes give us our peculiar heritage, an America with an interest, with a tone of time not overstrained, not jejunely oversentimentalized, which is not a re-doing of school histories or the laying out of a fabulous period; and which is in relief, if you like,

[1] Pseudonym used by A. R. Orage.

from Dickens or from Mark Twain's *Mississippi*. He was not without sympathy for his compatriots as is amply attested by Mr and Mrs B. D. Hayes of New York (*vide The Birthplace*) with whom he succeeds, I think, rather better than with most of his princely continentals. They are, at any rate, his bow to the Happy Genius of his country—as distinct from the gentleman who displayed the 'back of a banker and a patriot', or the person whose aggregate features could be designated only as a 'mug'.

In his presentation of America he is greatly attentive, and, save for the people in *Coeur Simple*, I doubt if any writer has done more of 'this sort of thing' for his country, this portrayal of the typical thing in timbre and quality—balanced, of course, by the array of spittoons in the Capitol (*The Point of View*).

Still if one is seeking a Spiritual Fatherland, if one feels the exposure of what he would not have scrupled to call, two clauses later, such a wind-shield, *The American Scene* greatly provides it. It has a mermaid note, almost to outvie the warning, the sort of nickel-plate warning which is hurled at one in the saloon of any great transatlantic boat; the awfulness that engulfs one when one comes, for the first time unexpectedly on a pile of all the *Murkhn* magazines laid, shingle-wise, on a brass-studded, screwed-into-place, baize-covered steamer table. The first glitter of the national weapons for driving off quiet and all closer signs of intelligence.[1]

Attempting to view the jungle of the work as a whole, one notes that, despite whatever cosmopolitan upbringing Henry James may have had, as witness *A Small Boy's Memoirs* and *Notes of a Son and Brother*, he nevertheless began in *French Poets and Novelists* with a provincial attitude from which it took him a long time to work free. Secondly, we see various phases of the 'style' of his presentation or circumambience.

There is a small amount of prentice work. Let us say *Roderick Hudson, Casamassima*. There are lucky first steps in *The American* and *The Europeans*, as precocity of result, for certainly some of his early work is as permanent as some of the ripest, and more so than a

---

[1] I differ, beyond that point, with our author. I enjoy ascent as much as I loathe descent in an elevator. I do not mind the click of brass doors. I had indeed for my earliest toy, if I was not brought up in it, the rather slow and well-behaved elevator in a quiet and quietly bright huge sanatorium. The height of high buildings, the chasms of New York are delectable; but this is beside the point; one is not asked to share the views and tastes of a writer.

deal of the intervening. We find (for in the case before us criticism must be in large part a weeding-out) that his first subject matter provides him with a number of good books and stories: *The American, The Europeans, Eugene Pickering, Daisy Miller, The Pupil, Brooksmith, A Bundle of Letters, Washington Square, The Portrait of a Lady,* before 1882 and, rather later, *Pandora, The Four Meetings,* perhaps *Louisa Pallant.* He ran out of his first material.

We next note a contact with the *Yellow Book,* a dip into 'cleverness', into the epigrammatic genre, the bare epigrammatic style. It was no better than other writers, not so successful as Wilde. We observe him to be not so hard and fine a satirist as is George S. Street.

We come then to the period of allegories (*The Real Thing, Dominick Ferrand, The Liar*). There ensues a growing discontent with the short sentence, epigram, etc. in which he does not at this time attain distinction; the clarity is not satisfactory, was not satisfactory to the author, his *donnée* being radically different from that of his contemporaries. The 'story' not being really what he is after, he starts to build up his medium; a thickening, a chiaroscuro is needed, the long sentence; he wanders, seeks to add a needed opacity, he overdoes it, produces the cobwebby novel, emerges or justifies himself in *Maisie* and manages his long-sought form in *The Awkward Age.* He comes out the triumphant stylist in the *American Scene* and in all the items of *The Finer Grain*[1] collection and in the posthumous *Middle Years.*

This is not to damn incontinent all that intervenes, but I think the chief question addressed to me by people of good-will who do not, but are yet ready and willing to, read James, is: Where the deuce shall I begin? One cannot take even the twenty-four volumes, more or less selected volumes of the Macmillan edition all at once, and it is, alas, but too easy to get so started and entoiled as never to finish this author or even come to the best of him.

The laziness of an uncritical period can be nowhere more blatant than in the inherited habit of talking about authors as a whole. It is perhaps the sediment from an age daft over great figures, or a way of displaying social gush, the desire for a celebrity at all costs, rather than a care of letters.

[1] Volume now labelled *Maud Evelyn* in the Macmillan collected edition. The titles in my essay are those of their 'New York' edition.

To talk in any other way demands an acquaintance with the work of an author, a price few conversationalists care to pay, *ma chè*! It is the man with inherited opinions who talks about 'Shelley', making no distinction between the author of the Fifth Act of *The Cenci* and of the *Sensitive Plant*. Not but what there may be a personal *virtù* in an author—appraised, however, from the best of his work when, that is, it is correctly appraised. People ask me what James to read. He is a very uneven author; not all of his collected edition has marks of permanence.

One can but make one's own suggestion:

The American, French Poets and Novelists, The Europeans, Daisy Miller, Eugene Pickering, Washington Square, A Bundle of Letters, Portrait of a Lady, Pandora, The Pupil, Brooksmith, What Maisie Knew and *The Awkward Age* (if one is 'doing it all'), *Europe, Four Meetings, The Ambassadors, The American Scene, The Finer Grain* (all the volume, i.e. *The Velvet Glove, Mona Montravers, Round of Visits, Crapey Cornelia, Bench of Desolation*), *The Middle Years* (posthumous), *The Ivory Tower* (notes first) and *The Sacred Fount.*

I 'go easy' on the more cobwebby volumes; the most Jamesian are indubitably *The Wings of a Dove* and *The Golden Bowl;* upon them devotees will fasten, but the potential devotee may as well find his aptitude in the stories of *The Finer Grain* volume where certain exquisite titillations will come to him as readily as anywhere else. If he is to bask in Jamesian tickle, nothing will restrain him and no other author will to any such extent afford him equal gratifications.

If, however, the reader does not find delectation in the list given above, I think it fairly useless for him to embark on the rest.

Part of James is a caviare, part I must reject according to my lights as bad writing; another part is a *spécialité*, a pleasure for certain temperaments only; the part I have set together above seems to me maintainable as literature. One can definitely say: 'this is good'; hold the argumentative field, suffer comparison with other writers; with, say, the Goncourt, or Maupassant. I am not impertinently throwing books on the scrap-heap; there are certain valid objections to James; there are certain standards which one may believe in, and having stated them, one is free to state that any author does not comply with them; always granting that there may be other standards with which he complies, or over which he charmingly or brilliantly triumphs.

James does not 'feel' as solid as Flaubert; he does not give us

Everyman, but, on the other hand, he was aware of things whereof Flaubert was not aware and in certain things supersedes the author of *Madame Bovary.*

He appears at times to write around and around a thing and not always to emerge from the 'amorous plan' of what he wanted to present, into definite presentation.

He does not seem to me at all times evenly skilful in catching the intonations of speech. He recalls the New England 'a' in the 'Ladys' small brothers 'Ha-ard' (Hnaah-d) but only if one is familiar with the phonetics described; but (*vide* the beginning of *The Birthplace*) one is not convinced that he really knows (by any sure instinct) how people's voices would sound. Some remarks are in key, some obviously factitious.

He gives us more of his characters by description than he can by any attribution of conversation, save perhaps by the isolated and discreet remarks of Brooksmith.

His emotional centre is in being sensitive to the feel of the place or to the tonality of the person.

It is with his own so beautiful talk, his ability to hear his own voice in the rounded paragraph, that he is aptest to charm one. I find it often, though not universally, difficult to 'hear' his characters speaking. I have observed various places where the character notably stops speaking and the author interpolates words of his own; sentences that no one but Henry James could in any circumstances have used. Beyond which statements I see no great concision or any clarity to be gained by rearranging my perhaps too elliptical comments on individual books.

Honest criticism, as I conceive it, cannot get much further than saying to one's reader exactly what one would say to the friend who approaches one's bookshelf asking: 'What the deuce shall I read?' Beyond this there is the 'parlour game', the polite essay, and there is the official pronouncement, with neither of which we are concerned.

Of all exquisite writers James is the most colloquial, yet in the first edition of his *French Poets and Novelists,* his style, save for a few scattered phrases, is so little unusual that most of the book seems, superficially, as if it might have been written by almost anyone. It contains some surprising lapses ... as bad as any in Mr Hueffer or even in Mr Mencken. It is interesting largely in that it shows us what our subject had to escape from.

Let us grant at once that his novels show him, all through his life, possessed of the worst possible taste in pictures,[1] of almost as great a lack of taste as that which he attributes to the hackwork and newspaper critiques of Théophile Gautier. Let us admit that 'painting' to Henry James probably meant, to the end of his life, the worst possible late Renaissance conglomerations.

Let us admit that in 1876, or whenever it was, his taste in poetry inclined to the swish of De Musset; that it very likely never got any further. By 'poetry' he very possibly meant the 'high-falutin' and he eschewed it in certain forms; himself taking still higher falutes in a to-be-developed mode of his own.

I doubt if he ever wholly outgrew that conception of the (by him so often invoked) Daughters of Memory. He arrived truly at a point from which he could look back upon people who 'besought the deep blue sea to roll'. Poetry to him began, perhaps, fullfledged, springing Minerva-like from the forehead of George Gordon, Lord Byron, and went pretty much to the bad in Charles Baudelaire; it did not require much divination by 1914 (*The Middle Years*) to note that he had found Tennyson rather vacuous and that there 'was something in' Browning.

James was so thoroughly a recorder of people, of their atmospheres, society, personality, setting; so wholly the artist of this particular genre, that it was, perhaps, impossible for him ever to hold a critical opinion of art out of key with the opinion about him—except in so far as he might have ambitions for the novel, for his own particular métier. His critical opinions were simply an extension of his being in key with the nice people who 'impressed' themselves on his gelatine 'plate'. (This is a theoretical generalization and must be taken *cum grano*.)

We may, perhaps, take his adjectives on De Musset as a desperate attempt to do 'justice' to a man with whom he knew it impossible for him to sympathize. There is, however, nothing to hinder our supposing that he saw in De Musset's 'gush' something for him impossible and that he wished to acknowledge it. Side by side with this are the shreds of Back Bay or Buffalo, the mid-week-prayer-meeting point of view.

His most egregious slip is in the essay on Baudelaire, the sentence

[1] 1929. There are, however, signs of personal observation and appreciation of paintings in his sketches of Italy.

quoted by Hueffer.[1] Notwithstanding this, he does effectively put his nippers on Baudelaire's weakness:

'A good way to embrace Baudelaire at a glance is to say that he was, in his treatment of evil, exactly what Hawthorne was not— Hawthorne, who felt the thing at its source, deep in the human consciousness. Baudelaire's infinitely slighter volume of genius apart, he was a sort of Hawthorne reversed. It is the absence of this metaphysical quality in his treatment of his favourite subjects (Poe was his metaphysician, and his devotion sustained him through a translation of 'Eureka!') that exposes him to that class of accusations of which M. Edmond Scherer's accusation of feeding upon *pourriture* is an example; and, in fact, in his pages we never know with what we are dealing. We encounter an inextricable confusion of sad emotions and vile things, and we are at a loss to know whether the subject pretends to appeal to our conscience or—we were going to say—to our olfactories. 'Le Mal?' we exclaim; 'you do yourself too much honour. This is not Evil; it is not the wrong; it is simply the nasty!' Our impatience is of the same order as that which we should feel if a poet, pretending to pluck 'the flowers of good', should come and present us, as specimens, a rhapsody on plum-cake and *eau de Cologne*'.

Here as elsewhere his perception, apart from the readability of the work, is worthy of notice.

Hueffer says that[2] James belauds Balzac. I cannot see it. I can but perceive Henry James wiping the floor with the author of *Eugénie Grandet*, pointing out all his qualities, but almightily wiping the floor with him. He complains that Gautier is lacking in a concern about supernatural hocus-pocus and that Flaubert is lacking. If Balzac takes him to any great extent in, James with his inherited Swedenborgianism is perhaps thereby laid open to Balzac.

It was natural that James should write more about the bulky author of *La Comédie Humaine* than about the others; here was his richest quarry, here was there most to note and to emend and to apply so emended to processes of his own. From Maupassant, the Goncourt or Baudelaire there was nothing for him to acquire.

His dam'd fuss about furniture is foreshadowed in Balzac, and all the paragraphs on Balzac's house-furnishing propensities are of

---

[1] 'For a poet to be realist is of course nonsense', and, as Hueffer says, such a sentence from such a source is enough to make one despair of human nature.

[2] Ford Madox Hueffer's volume on Henry James.

interest in proportion to our interest in, or our boredom with, this part of Henry James' work.

What, indeed, could he have written of the Goncourt save that they were a little dull but tremendously right in their aim? Indeed, but for these almost autobiographical details pointing to his growth out of Balzac, all James would seem but a corollary to one passage in a Goncourt preface:

'Le jour où l'analyse cruelle que mon ami, M. Zola, et peut-être moi-même avons apportée dans la peinture du bas de la société sera reprise par un écrivain de talent, et employée à la reproduction des hommes et des femmes du monde, dans les milieux d'éducation et de distinction—ce jour-là seulement le classicisme et sa queue seront tués. . . .

'Le Réalisme n'a pas en effet l'unique mission de décrire ce qui est bas, ce qui est répugnant. . . .

'Nous avons commencé, nous, par la canaille, parce que la femme et l'homme du peuple, plus rapprochés de la nature et de la sauvagerie, sont des créatures simples et peu compliquées, tandis que le Parisien et la Parisienne de la société, ces civilisés excessifs, dont l'originalité tranchée est faite toute de nuances, toute de demi-teintes, toute de ces riens insaisissables, pareils aux riens coquets et neutres avec lesquels se façonne le caractère d'une toilette distinguée de femme, demandent des années pour qu'on les perce, pour qu'on les sache, pour qu'on les *attrape*—et le romancier du plus grand génie, croyez-le bien, ne les devinera jamais ces gens de salon, avec les *racontars* d'amis qui vont pour lui à la découverte dans le monde. . .

Ce projet de roman qui devait se passer dans le grand monde, dans le monde le plus quintessencié, et dont nous rassemblions lentement et minutieusement les éléments délicats et fugaces, je l'abandonnais après la mort de mon frère, convaincu de l'impossibilité de le réussir tout seul.'

But this particular paragraph could have had little to do with the matter. *French Poets and Novelists* was published in 1878 and Edmond de Goncourt signed the preface to *Les Frères Zemganno* in 1879. The paragraphs quoted are interesting, however, as showing Goncourt's state of mind in that year. He had probably been preaching in this vein long before setting the words on paper, before getting them printed.

If ever one man's career was foreshadowed in a few sentences of another, Henry James' is to be found in this paragraph.

It is very much as if he said: I will not be a megatherium botcher like Balzac; there is nothing to be said about these Goncourt, but one must try to be rather more interesting than they are in, let us say, *Madame Gervaisais*.[1]

Proceeding with the volume of criticism, we find that 'Le Jeune H.' simply didn't 'get' Flaubert; that he was much alive to the solid parts of Turgenev. He shows himself very apt, as we said above, to judge the merits of a novelist on the ground that the people portrayed by the said novelist are or are not suited to reception into the household of Henry James senior; whether, in short, Emma Bovary or Frederic or M. Arnoux would have spoiled the so delicate atmosphere; have juggled the so fine susceptibilities of a refined 23rd Street family at the time of the Philadelphia 'Centennial'.

I find the book not so much a sign that Henry James was 'disappointed', as Hueffer puts it, as that he was simply and horribly shocked by the literature of his continental forebears and contemporaries.

It is only when he gets to the Théâtre Français that he finds something which really suits him. Here there is order, tradition, perhaps a slight fustiness (but a quite pardonable fustiness, an arranged and suitable fustiness having its recompense in a sort of spiritual quiet); here, at any rate, was something decorous, something not to be found in Concord or in Albany. And it is easy to imagine the young James, not illuminated by Goncourt's possible conversation or writing, not even following the hint given in his essay on Balzac and Balzacian furniture, but sitting before Madame Nathalie in *Le Village* and resolving to be the Théâtre Français of the novel.

A resolution which he may be said to have carried out to the great enrichment of letters.

Strictures on the work of this period are no great detraction. *French Poets and Novelists* gives us a point from which to measure Henry James' advance. Genius showed itself partly in the escape from some

[1] It is my personal feeling at the moment that *La Fille Elisa* is worth so much more than all Balzac that the things are as out of scale as a sapphire and a plum pudding, and that *Elisa*, despite the dull section, is worth most of James' writing. This is, however, aside from the question we are discussing. 1929. Not having re-read *Elisa* in the interim, this earlier opinion of mine now appears to me gross exaggeration. E. P.

of his original limitations, partly in acquirements. His art at length became 'second nature', became perhaps half unconscious; or in part wholly unconscious; in other parts perhaps too highly conscious. At any rate in sunnier circumstances he talked exactly as he wrote, the same elaborate paragraph beautifully attaining its climax; the same sudden incision when a brief statement could dispose of a matter.

Be it said for his style; he is seldom or never involved when a direct bald statement will accurately convey his own meaning, *all of it*. He is not usually, for all his wide leisure, verbose. He may be highly and bewilderingly figurative in his language (*vide* Mr Hueffer's remarks on this question).

Style apart, I take it that the hatred of tyrannies was as great a motive as any we can ascribe to Galileo or Leonardo or to any other great figure, to any other mythic Prometheus; for this driving force we may well overlook personal foibles, the early Bostonese bias, the heritage from his father's concern in commenting Swedenborg, the later fusses about social caution and conservation of furniture. Hueffer rather boasts about Henry James' innocence of the classics. It is nothing to brag of, even if a man struggling against natural medievalism have entrenched himself in impressionist theory. If James *had* read his classics, the better Latins especially, he would not have so excessively cobwebbed, fussed, blathered, worried about minor mundanities. We may *conspuer* with all our vigour Henry James' concern with furniture, the Spoils of Poynton, connoisseurship, Mrs Ward's tea-party atmosphere, the young Bostonian of the immature works. We may relegate these things mentally to the same realm as the author's pyjamas and collar buttons, to his intellectual instead of his physical valeting. There remains the capacious intelligence, the searching analysis of things that cannot be so relegated to the scrap-heap and to the wash-basket.

Let us say that English freedom legally and traditionally has its basis in property. Let us say, à la Balzac, that most modern existence is governed by, or at least interfered with by, the necessity to earn money; let us also say that a Frenchman is not an Englishman or a German or an American, and that despite the remark that the aristocracies of all people, the upper classes, are the same everywhere, racial differences are *au fond* differences; they are likewise major subjects.

Writing, as I am, for the reader of good-will, for the bewildered person who wants to know where to begin, I need not apologize for the following elliptical notes. James, in his prefaces, has written explanation to death (with sometimes a very pleasant necrography). Leaving the *French Poets and Novelists*, I take the novels and stories as nearly as possible in their order of publication (as distinct from their order as rearranged and partially weeded out in the collected edition[1]).

1875 (U.S.A.) *A Passionate Pilgrim and other Tales. Eugene Pickering* is the best of this lot and most indicative of the future James. Contains also the title story and *Madame de Mauves*. Other stories inferior.

1876 (U.S.A.) *Roderick Hudson*, prentice work. First novel not up to the level of *Pickering*.

1877. *The American;* essential James, part of the permanent work. *Watch and Ward*, discarded by the author.

1878. *French Poets and Novelists*, already discussed.

1878. *Daisy Miller*. (The big hit and one of his best.) *An International Episode, Four Meetings*, good work.

1880. Short stories first printed in England with additions, but no important ones.

1880. *Confidence*, not important.

1881. *Washington Square*, one of his best, 'putting America on the map', giving us a real past, a real background. *Pension Beaurepas* and *Bundle of Letters*, especially the girls' letters, excellent, already mentioned.

1881. *The Portrait of a Lady*, one of his best. Charming Venetian preface in the collected edition.

1884. *Tales of Three Cities*, stories dropped from the collected edition, save *Lady Barbarina*.

1884. *Lady Barbarina*, a study in English blankness comparable to that exposed in the letters of the English young lady in *A Bundle of Letters*. There is also New York of the period.

'But if there was one thing Lady Barb disliked more than another it was describing Pasterns. She had always lived with people who knew of themselves what such a place would be, without demanding these pictorial effects, proper only, as she vaguely felt, to persons belonging to the classes whose trade was the arts of expression. Lady Barb of course had never gone into it; but she knew that in her own

---

[1] Either the New York or present 'collected'.

class the business was not to express but to enjoy, not to represent but to be represented.'

'Mrs Lemon's recognition of this river, I should say, was all it need have been; she held the Hudson existed for the purpose of supplying New Yorkers with poetical feelings, helping them to face comfortably occasions like the present, and in general, meet foreigners with confidence. . . .'

'He believed, or tried to believe, the *salon* now possible in New York on condition of its being reserved entirely for adults; and in having taken a wife out of a country in which social traditions were rich and ancient he had done something toward qualifying his own house—so splendidly qualified in all strictly material respects—to be the scene of such an effort. A charming woman accustomed only to the best on each side, as Lady Beauchemin said, what mightn't she achieve by being at home—always to adults only—in an easy early inspiring comprehensive way and on the evening of the seven, when worldly engagements were least numerous? He laid this philosophy before Lady Barb in pursuance of a theory that if she disliked New York on a short acquaintance she couldn't fail to like it on a long. Jackson believed in the New York mind—not so much indeed in its literary, artistic, philosophic or political achievements as in its general quickness and nascent adaptability. He clung to this belief for it was an indispensable neat block in the structure he was attempting to rear. The New York mind would throw its glamour over Lady Barb if she would only give it a chance; for it was thoroughly bright, responsive and sympathetic. If she would only set up by the turn of her hand a blest social centre, a temple of interesting talk in which this charming organ might expand and where she might inhale its fragrance in the most convenient and luxurious way, without, as it were, getting up from her chair; if she would only just try this graceful good-natured experiment—which would make every one like her so much too—he was sure all the wrinkles in the gilded scroll of his fate would be smoothed out. But Lady Barb didn't rise at all to his conception and hadn't the least curiosity about the New York mind. She thought it would be extremely disagreeable to have a lot of people tumbling in on Sunday evening without being invited, and altogether her husband's sketch of the Anglo-American salon seemed to her to suggest crude familiarity, high vociferation—she had already made a remark to him about 'screeching women'—and random extravagant laughter. She didn't tell him—for this somehow it wasn't in her power to express and, strangely enough, he never completely guessed it—that she was singularly deficient in any natural, or indeed, acquired understanding of what a salon might be. She had never seen or dreamed of one—and for the most part was incapable of imagining a thing she hadn't seen. She had seen great dinners and balls and meets and runs and races; she had seen garden-parties and bunches of people, mainly women—who, however, didn't screech—at dull stuffy teas, and distinguished companies collected in splendid castles; but all this gave her no clew to a train of conversation, to any idea of a social agreement that the interest of talk, its continuity, its accumulations from season to season shouldn't be lost. Conversation, in Lady Barb's experience, had never been continuous; in such a case it would surely have been a bore. It had been occasional and fragmentary, a trifle jerky, with allusions that were never explained; it had a dread of detail—it seldom pursued anything very far or kept hold of it very long.'

1885. *Stories Revived,* adding to earlier tales, *The Author of Beltraffio,* which opens with excess of the treading-on-eggs manner, too much to be borne for twenty-four volumes. The pretence of extent of 'people' interested in art and letters, *sic*: 'It was the most complete presentation that had yet been made of the gospel of art; it was a kind of aesthetic war cry. 'People' had endeavoured to sail nearer 'to truth', etc.

He implies too much of art smeared on limited multitudes. One wonders if the eighties did in any great aggregate gush up to this extent. Doesn't he try to spread the special case out too wide?

The thinking is magnificently done from this passage up to page sixteen or twenty, stated with great concision. Compare it with *Madame Gervaisais* and we find Henry James much more interesting than the Goncourt when on the upper reaches. Compare his expressiveness, the expressiveness of his indirectness with that of constatation. The two methods are curiously mixed in the opening of *Beltraffio.* Such sentences as (page 30) '*He said the most interesting and inspiring things*' are, however, pure waste, pure 'leaving the thing undone', inconcrete, unimagined; just simply bad writing or bad novelisting. As for his special case he does say a deal about the author or express a deal by him, but one is bothered by the fact that Pater, Burton, Hardy, Meredith were not, in mere history, bundled into one; that Burton had been to the East and the others had not; that no English novelist of that era would have taken the least notice of anything going on in foreign countries, presumably European, as does the supreme author of *Beltraffio*.

Doubtless he is in many ways the author Henry James would have liked to meet and more illustrative of certain English tones and limitations than any historical portrait might have been. Still Henry James does lay it on—more I think, than the story absolutely requires. In *Beltraffio* he certainly presents (not that he does not comment to advantage) the two damn'd women appended to the gentlemanly hero of the tale. The most violent post-Strindbergian school would perhaps have called them bitches *tout bonnement*, but this word did not belong to Henry James' vocabulary and besides it is of too great an indistinctness. Author, same 'bloody' (in the English sense) author with his passion for 'form' appears in *Lesson of Master*, and most of H. J.'s stories of literary *milieux*. Perpetual Grandisonism or Grandisonizing of this author with the passion for form, all of 'em have it. *Ma ché!* There is, however, great intensity in these same 'be-deared' and be-'poor-old'-ed pages. He has really got a main theme, a great theme, he chooses to do it in silver point rather than in the garish colours of, — well, of Cherbuliez, or the terms of a religious maniac with three-foot long carving knife.

Novel of the gilded pill, an aesthetic or artistic message, dogma, no better than a moral or ethic one, novel a cumbrous camouflage, substitute not for 'that parlour game'[1] the polite essay, but for the impolite essay or conveyance of ideas; novel to do this should completely incarnate the abstraction.

Finish of *Beltraffio* not perhaps up to the rest of it. Not that one at all knows how else. . . .

Gush on page 42[2] from both conversationalists. Still an adumbration of the search for the just word emerges on pages 43-44, real cut at barbarism and bigotry on the bottom of page 45 (of course not labelled by these monstrous and rhetorical brands, scorched on to their hides and rump sides). 'Will it be a sin to make the most of that one too, so bad for the dear old novel?' Butler and James on the same side really chucking out the fake; Butler focussed on Church of England; opposed to him the fakers booming the Bible 'as literature'

[1] T. S. Eliot's phrase.
[2] Page numbers in New York edition.

in a sort of last stand, a last ditch; seeing it pretty well had to go as history, cosmogony, etc., or the old tribal Daddy-slap-'em-with-slab of the Jews as anything like an ideal:

'He told me more about his wife before we arrived at the gate of home, and if he be judged to have aired overmuch his grievance I'm afraid I must admit that he had some of the foibles as well as the gifts of the artistic temperament; adding, however, instantly that hitherto, to the best of my belief, he had rarely let this particular cat out of the bag. "She thinks me immoral—that's the long and short of it", he said as we paused outside a moment and his hand rested on one of the bars of his gate; while his conscious, expressive, perceptive eyes— the eyes of a foreigner, I had begun to account them, much more than of the usual Englishman—viewing me now evidently as quite a familiar friend, took part in the declaration. "It's very strange when one thinks it all over, and there's a grand comicality in it that I should like to bring out. She's a very nice woman, extraordinarily well-behaved, upright and clever and with a tremendous lot of good sense about a good many matters. Yet her conception of a novel—she has explained it to me once or twice and she doesn't do it badly as exposition—is a thing so false that it makes me blush. It's a thing so hollow, so dishonest, so lying, in which life is so blinked and blinded, so dodged and disfigured, that it makes my ears burn. It's two different ways of looking at the whole affair", he repeated, push- ing open the gate. "And they're irreconcilable!" he added with a sigh. We went forward to the house, but on the walk, halfway to the door, he stopped and said to me: "If you're going into this kind of thing there's a fact you should know beforehand; it may save you some disappointment. There's a hatred of art, there's a hatred of literature —I mean of the genuine kinds. Oh, the shams—*those* they'll swallow by the bucket!" I looked up at the charming house, with its genial colour and crookedness, and I answered with a smile that those evil passions might exist, but that I should never have expected to find them there. "Ah, it doesn't matter, after all", he a bit nervously laughed; which I was glad to hear, for I was reproaching myself with having worked him up.'

Literature in the nineteenth and the beginning of the twentieth centuries was and is where science was in the days of Galileo and the Inquisition. Henry James not blinking it, neither can we. 'Poor dears' and 'dear olds' always a little too plentiful.

1885 (continued). *Pandora,* of the best. Let it pass as a sop to America's virginal charm; as counterweight to *Daisy Miller,* or to the lady of *The Portrait.* Henry James alert to the Teuton.

'The process of enquiry had already begun for him in spite of his having as yet spoken to none of his fellow passengers; the case being that Vogelstein enquired not only with his tongue, but with his eyes —that is with his spectacles—with his ears, with his nose, with his palate, with all his senses and organs. He was a highly upright young man, whose only fault was that his sense of comedy, or of the humour of things, had never been specifically disengaged from his several other senses. He vaguely felt that something should be done about this, and in a general manner proposed to do it, for he was on his way to explore a society abounding in comic aspects. This consciousness of a missing measure gave him a certain mistrust of what might be said of him; and if circumspection is the essence of diplomacy our young aspirant promised well. His mind contained several millions of facts, packed too closely together for the light breeze of the imagination to draw through the mass. He was impatient to report himself to his superior in Washington, and the loss of time in an English port could only incommode him, inasmuch as the study of English institutions was no part of his mission. On the other hand the day was charming; the blue sea, in Southampton Water pricked all over with light, had no movement but that of its infinite shimmer. Moreover, he was by no means sure that he should be happy in the United States, where doubtless he should find himself soon enough disembarked. He knew that this was not an important question and that happiness was an unscientific term, such as a man of his education should be ashamed to use even in the silence of his thoughts. Lost none the less in the inconsiderate crowd and feeling himself neither in his own country nor in that to which he was in a manner accredited, he was reduced to his mere personality; so that during the hour, to save his importance, he cultivated such ground as lay in sight for a judgement of this delay to which the German steamer was subjected in English waters. Mightn't it be proved, facts, figures and documents—or at least watch—in hand, considerably greater than the occasion demanded?

'Count Vogelstein was still young enough in diplomacy to think it necessary to have opinions. He had a good many, indeed, which had been formed without difficulty; they had been received ready-made from a line of ancestors who knew what they liked. This was of course—and under pressure, being candid, he would have admitted it—an unscientific way of furnishing one's mind. Our young man was a stiff conservative, a Junker of Junkers; he thought modern democracy a temporary phase and expected to find many arguments against it in the great Republic. In regard to these things it was a pleasure to him to feel that, with his complete training, he had been taught thoroughly to appreciate the nature of evidence. The ship was heavily laden with German emigrants, whose mission in the United States differed considerably from Count Otto's. They hung over the bulwarks, densely grouped; they leaned forward on their elbows for hours, their shoulders kept on a level with their ears: the men in furred caps, smoking long-bowled pipes, the women with babies hidden in remarkably ugly shawls. Some were yellow Germans and some were black, and all looked greasy and matted with the sea-damp. They were destined to swell still further the huge current of the Western democracy; and Count Vogelstein doubtless said to himself that they wouldn't improve its quality. Their numbers, however, were striking and I know not what he thought of the nature of this particular evidence.'

For further style in vignette:

'He could see for himself that Mr and Mrs Day had not at all her grand air. They were fat plain serious people who sat side by side on the deck for hours and looked straight before them. Mrs Day had a white face, large cheeks and small eyes; her forehead was surrounded with a multitude of little tight black curls; her lips moved as if she had always a lozenge in her mouth. She wore entwined about her head an article which Mrs Dangerfield spoke of as a 'nuby', a knitted pink scarf concealing her hair, encircling her neck and having among its convolutions a hole for her perfectly expressionless face. Her hands were folded on her stomach, and in her still swathed figure her bead-like eyes, which occasionally changed their direction, alone represented life. Her husband had a stiff gray beard on his chin and a bare spacious upper lip, to which constant shaving had imparted a hard glaze. His eyebrows were thick and his nostrils wide, and when he was uncovered, in the saloon, it was visible that his grizzled hair was dense and perpendicular. He might have looked rather grim and truculent hadn't it been for the mild familiar accommodating gaze with which his large light-coloured pupils—the leisurely eyes of a

silent man—appeared to consider surrounding objects. He was
evidently more friendly than fierce, but he was more diffident than
friendly. He liked to have you in sight, but wouldn't have pretended
to understand you much or to classify you, and would have been
sorry it should put you under an obligation. He and his wife spoke
sometimes, but seldom talked, and there was something vague and
patient about them as if they had become victims of a wrought spell.
The spell, however, was of no sinister cast; it was the fascination of
prosperity, the confidence of security, which sometimes makes
people arrogant, but which had had such a different effect on this
simple satisfied pair, in whom further development of every kind
appeared to have been happily arrested.'

Pandora's approach to her parents:

'These little offices were usually performed deftly, rapidly, with
the minimum of words, and when their daughter drew near them, Mr
and Mrs Day closed their eyes after the fashion of a pair of household
dogs who expect to be scratched.'

The tale is another synthesis of some of the million reasons why
Germany will never conquer the world.

In describing *Pandora's* success as 'purely personal', Henry James
has hit on the secret of the Quattrocento, 1450 to 1550, the vital part
of the Renaissance. Aristocracy decays when it ceases to be selective
when the basis of selection is not personal. It is a critical acute
ness, not a snobbism, which last is selection on some other principle than that of a personal quality. It is servility to rule-of-thumb
criteria, and a dullness of perception, a timidity in acceptance.
The whole force of the Renaissance was in the personality of its
selection.

There is no faking the amount of perceptive energy concentrated
in Henry James' vignettes in such phrases as that on the parents like
domestic dogs waiting to be scratched, or in the ten thousand phrases
of this sort which abound in his writings. If we were back in the time
of Bruyère, we could easily make a whole book of 'Characters' from
Henry James' vignettes.[1] The vein holds from beginning to end of

[1] Since writing the above I find that some compilation has been attempted;
had indeed been planned by the anthologist, and, in plan, approved by H. J.:
Pictures and Passages from Henry James, selected by Ruth Head (Chatto and
Windus, 1916), if not exactly the book to convince the rising generation of
H. J.'s powers of survival, is at any rate a most charming tribute to our subject
from one who had begun to read him in 'the eighties'.

his work; from this writing of the eighties to *The Ivory Tower*. As for example, Gussie Braddon:

'Rosanna waited facing her, noting her extraordinary perfection of neatness, of elegance, of arrangement, of which it couldn't be said whether they most handed over to you, as on some polished salver, the clear truth of her essential commonness or transposed it into an element that could please, that could even fascinate, as a supreme attestation of care. "Take her as an advertisement of all the latest knowledges of how to 'treat' every inch of the human surface and where to 'get' every scrap of the personal envelope, so far as she *is* enveloped, and she does achieve an effect sublime in itself and thereby absolute in a wavering world." '

We note no inconsiderable progress in the actual writing, in *maestria*, when we reach the ultimate volumes.

1886. *Bostonians*. Other stories in this collection mostly rejected from collected edition.

Princess Casamassima, inferior continuation of *Roderick Hudson*. His original subject matter is beginning to go thin.

1888. *The Reverberator*, process of fantasia beginning.

Fantasia of Americans versus the 'old aristocracy', *The American* with the sexes reversed. Possibly the theme shows as well in *Les Transatlantiques*, the two methods give one at least a certain pleasure of contrast.

1888. *Aspern Papers*, inferior. *Louisa Pallant*, a study in the maternal or abysmal relation, good James. *Modern Warning*, rejected from New York edition.

1889. *A London Life. The Patagonia.*

The Patagonia, not a masterpiece. Slow in opening, excellent in parts, but the sense of the finale intrudes all along. It seems true but there is no alternative ending. One doubts whether a story is really constructed with any mastery when the end, for the purpose of making it a story, is so unescapable. The effect of reality is produced, of course, by the reality of the people in the opening scene; there is no doubt about that part being 'to the life'.

The Liar is superb in its way, perhaps the best of the allegories, of the plots invented purely to be an exposition of impression. It is magnificent in its presentation of the people, both the old man and the masterly Liar.

Mrs Temperly is another such excellent delineation and shows

James as an excellent hater, but G. S. Street expresses a concentration of annoyance with a greater polish and suavity in method; and neither explains, theorizes, nor comments.

James never has Maupassant's reality by sequence of events. His (H. J.'s) people almost always convince, i.e. we believe implicitly that they exist. We also think that Henry James has made up some sort of story as an excuse for writing his impression of the people.

One sees the slight vacancy of the stories of this period, the short clear sentence, the dallying with *jeu d'esprit*, with epigram no better than, though not inferior to, the run of epigram in the nineties. It all explains James' need of opacity, his reaching out for a chiaroscuro to distinguish himself from his contemporaries and in which he could put the whole of his much more complex apperception.

Then comes, roughly, the period of cobwebs and of excessive cobwebs and of furniture, finally justified in *The Finer Grain*, a book of tales with no mis-fire, and the style so vindicated in the triumphs of the various books of Memoirs and *The American Scene*.

Fantasias: *Dominic Ferrand, Nona Vincent* (tales obviously aimed at the *Yellow Book*, but seem to have missed it, a detour in James' career). All artists who discover anything make such detours and must, in the course of things (as in the cobwebs), push certain experiments beyond the right curve of their art. This is not so much the doom as the function of all 'revolutionary' or experimental art, and I think masterwork is usually the result of the return from such excess. One does not know, simply does not know, the true curve until one has pushed one's method beyond it. Until then it is merely a frontier, not a chosen route. It is an open question, and there is no dogmatic answer, whether an artist should write and rewrite the same story (à la Flaubert) or whether he should take a new canvas.

The Papers, a fantasia, diverting; *The Birthplace*, fairy-godmother element mentioned above, excellent; *Edmund Orme*, inferior; *Yellow Book* tale, not accepted by that periodical.

1889-93. Period of this entoilment in the *Yellow Book*, short sentences, the epigrammatic. He reacts from this into the allegorical. In general the work of this period is not up to the mark. *The Chaperon, The Real Thing*, fantasias of 'wit'. By fantasias I mean sketches in which the people are 'real' or convince one of their verity, but where the story is utterly unconvincing, is not intended to convince, is merely a sort of exaggeration of the fitting situation or the situation which ought to result in order to display some type at its apogee. Thus the lady and gentleman models in *The Real Thing*, rather better than other stories in this volume. London society is finely ladled in *The Chaperon*, which is almost as a story, romanticism.

Greville Fane is a scandalous photograph from the life about which the great blagueur scandalously lies in his preface (New York edition). I have been too diverted comparing it with *an* original to give a sane view of its art.

1890. *The Tragic Muse*, uneven, full of good things but showing Henry James in the didactic rôle a little too openly. He preaches, he also displays fine perception of the parochialism of the British political career. It is a readable novel with tracts interpolated. (Excellent and commendable tracts arguing for the right thing, enjoyable, etc.) Excellent text-book for young men with ambitions, etc.

1892. *Lesson of the Master* (cobweb). *The Pupil*, a masterpiece, one of his best and keenest studies. *Brooksmith* of the best.

1893. *The Private Life*. Title story, waste verbiage at the start, ridiculous to put all this camouflage over something *au fond* merely an idea. Not life, not people, allegory, dated to *Yellow Book* era. Won't hold against *Candide*. H. J.'s tilting against the vacuity of the public figure is, naturally, pleasing, i.e. it is pleasing that he should tilt, but the amusement partakes of the nature of seeing coconuts hurled at an aunt sally.

There are other stories, good enough to be carried by H. J.'s best work, not detrimental, but not enough to have 'made him': *Europe* (Hawthorny), *Paste*, *The Middle Years*, *Broken Wings*, etc. Part of the great man's work can perhaps only be criticized as 'etc.'

1895. *Terminations, Coxon Fund*, perhaps best of this lot, a disquisition, but entertaining, perhaps the germ of Galsworthy to be found in it (to no glory of either author) as perhaps a residuum of Dickens in Maisie's Mrs Wix. Verbalism, but delightful verbalism in Coxon affair, *sic*:

'Already, at hungry twenty-six, Gravener looked as blank and parliamentary as if he were fifty and popular.'

or

'a deeply wronged, justly resentful, quite irreproachable and insufferable person',

or (for the whole type)
'put such ignorance into her cleverness?'

Miss Anvoy's echo concerning 'a crystal' is excellently introduced, but is possibly in the nature of a sleight of hand trick (contemporary with *Lady Windermere's Fan*). Does H. J.'s 'politics' remind one of Dizzy's scribbling, just a little? 'Confidence, under the new Ministry, was understood to be reviving', etc.

Perhaps one covers the ground by saying that the James of this period is 'light literature', entertaining if one have nothing better to do. Neither *Terminations* nor (1896) *Embarrassments* would have founded a reputation.

1896-7. Improvement through *Other House* and *Spoils of Poynton*. I leave the appreciation of these, to me, detestable works to Mr Hueffer. They seem to me full of a good deal of needless fuss, though I do not mean to deny any art that may be in them.

1897. The emergence in *What Maisie Knew*. Problem of the adolescent female. Carried on in:

1899. *The Awkward Age*, fairy godmother and spotless lamb and all the rest of it. Only real thing the impression of people, not observation or real knowledge. Action only to give reader the tone, symbolizing the tone of the people. Opening *tour de force*, a study in punks, a cheese *soufflé* of the leprous crust of society done to a turn and a niceness save where he puts on the *dolcissimo, vox humana* stop. James was not the dispassionate observer. He started with the moral obsession; before he had worked clear of it he was entoiled in the obsession of social tone. He has pages of clear depiction, even of satire, but the sentimentalist is always lurking just around the corner. This softens his edges. He has not the clear hardness, the cold satiric justness that G. S. Street has displayed in treating situations, certain struggles between certain idiocies and certain vulgarities. This book is a *specialité* of local interest. It is an *étude* in ephemera. If it contained any revelation in 1899, it no longer contains it. His characters are reduced to the status of *voyeurs*, elaborate analysis of the much too special cases, a bundle of swine and asses who cannot mind their own business, who do not know enough to mind their own business. James' lamentable lack of the classics is perhaps responsible for his absorption in bagatelles. . . . He has no real series of backgrounds of *mœurs du passé*, only the 'sweet dim faded lavender' tone in opposition to modernity, plush nickel-plated, to the disparagement, naturally, of the latter.

Kipling's 'Bigod, I-know-all-about-this' manner, is an annoyance, but one wonders if parts of Kipling by the sheer force of content, of tale to tell, will not outlast most of James' cobwebs. There is no substitute for narrative-sense, however many different and entrancing charms may be spread before us.

The Awkward Age might have been done, from one point of view, as satire, in one-fourth the space. On the other hand, James does give us the subtly graded atmospheres of his different houses most excellently. And indeed, this may be regarded as *his* subject.

If one were advocate instead of critic, one would definitely claim that these atmospheres, nuances, impressions of personal tone and quality *are his subject;* that in these he gets certain things that almost no one else had done before him. These timbres and tonalities are his stronghold, he is ignorant of nearly everything else. It is all very well to say that modern life is largely made up of velleities, atmospheres, timbres, nuances, etc., but if people really spent as much time fussing, to the extent of the Jamesian fuss about such normal, trifling, age-old affairs, as slight inclinations to adultery, slight disinclinations to marry, to refrain from marrying, etc., etc., life would scarcely be worth the bother of keeping on with it. It is also contendable that one must depict such mush in order to abolish it.[1]

---

[1] Most good prose arises, perhaps, from an instinct of negation; is the detailed, convincing analysis of something detestable; of something which one wants to eliminate. Poetry is the assertion of a positive, i.e. of desire, and endures for a longer period. Poetic satire is only an assertion of this positive, inversely, i.e. as of an opposite hatred.

This is a highly untechnical, unimpressionist, in fact almost theological manner of statement; but is perhaps the root difference between the two arts of literature.

Most good poetry asserts something to be worth while, or damns a contrary; at any rate asserts emotional values. The best prose is, has been a presentation (complicated and elaborate as you like) of circumstances, of conditions, for the most part abominable or, at the mildest, amendable. This assertion of the more or less objectionable only becomes doctrinaire and rotten art when the narrator mis-states from dogmatic bias, and when he suggests some quack remedy (prohibition, Christianity, social theory of one sort or another), the only cure being that humanity should display more intelligence and goodwill than humanity is capable of displaying.

Poetry = Emotional synthesis, quite as real, quite as realist as any prose (or intellectual) analysis.

Neither prose nor drama can attain poetic intensity save by construction, almost by scenario; by so arranging the circumstance that some perfectly simple speech, perception, dogmatic statement appears in abnormal vigour. Thus when Frederic in *L'Education* observes Mme Arnoux's shoe-laces as she is descending the stair; or in Turgenev the quotation of a Russian proverb about the 'heart of another', or 'Nothing but death is irrevocable' toward the end of *Nichée de Gentilshommes*.

The main feeling in *The Awkward Age* is satiric. The dashes of sentiment do not help the work as literature. The acute observer is often referred to:

Page 131. 'The ingenious observer just now suggested might even have detected. . . .'

Page 133. 'And it might have been apparent still to our sharp spectator. . . .'

Page 310. 'But the acute observer we are constantly taking for granted would perhaps have detected. . . .'

Page 323. 'A supposititious spectator would certainly have imagined. . . .' (This also occurs in *Ivory Tower*, page 196.)

This scrutinous person wastes a great deal of time in pretending to conceal his contempt for Mrs Brook, Vanderbank, the other punks, and lays it on so *thick* when presenting his old sentimentalist Longdon, who at the one critical moment behaves *with a stupidity*, with a lack of delicacy, since we are dealing with these refinements. Of course neither this stupidity of his action nor the tone of the other characters would have anything to do with the question of *maestria*, if they *were* dispassionately or impartially rendered. The book is weak because all through it James is so manifestly carrying on a long *tenzone* so fiercely and loudly, a long argument *for* the old lavender. There is also the constant implication that Vanderbank ought to want Nanda, though why the devil he should be supposed to be even mildly under this obligation, is not made clear. A basis in the classics, castor oil, even Stevenson's *Virginibus Puerisque* might have helped matters. One's complaint is not that people of this sort don't exist, that they aren't like everything else a subject for literature, but that James doesn't anywhere in the book get down to bed-rock. It is too much as if he were depicting stage scenery not *as* stage scenery, but as nature.

All this critique is very possibly an exaggeration. Take it at half its strength; I do not intend to defend it.

Epigrammatic manner in opening, compare Kipling; compare Maupassant, superb ideas, verity, fantasia, fantasia group, reality, charming stories, poppycock. *Yellow Book* touches, in *The Real Thing*, general statements about their souls, near to bad writing, perfectly lucid.

Nona Vincent, he writes like an adolescent, might be a person of eighteen doing first story.

Page 201. 'Public interest in spiritual life of the army.' (*The Real Thing.*)

Page 201. German Invasion.

Loathsome prigs, stiff conventions, editor of cheap magazine ladled in Sir Wots-his-name.

1893. In the interim he had brought out *In the Cage,* excellent opening sentence, matter too much talked around and around, and *The Two Magics.* This last a Freudian affair which seems to me to have attracted undue interest, i.e. interest out of proportion to its importance as literature and *as part of* Henry James' own work, because of its subject matter. The obscenity of *The Turn of the Screw* has given it undue prominence. People now 'drawn' by the obscene as were people of Milton's period by an equally disgusting bigotry; one unconscious on author's part; the other, a surgical treatment of a disease. This much for progress on part of authors if public has not progressed. The point of my remarks is that an extraneous criterion comes in. One must keep to the question of literature, not of irrelevancies. Galdos' *Lo Prohibido* does Freud long before the sex crank got to it. Kipling really does the psychic, ghosts, etc., to say nothing of his having the 'sense of story'.

1900. *The Soft Side,* collection containing: *The Abasement of the Northmores,* good; again the motif of the vacuity of the public man, the 'figure'; he has tried it in *The Private Life,* which, however, falls into the allegorical. A rotten fall it is too, and Henry James at his worst in it, i.e. the allegorical. *Fordham's Castle* appears in the collected edition only—it may belong to this period but is probably earlier, comedietta, excellently, perhaps flawlessly done. Here, as so often, the circumstances are mostly a description of the character, of the personal tone of the 'sitters'; for his people are so much more, or so much more often, 'sitters' than actors. Protagonists it may be. When they act, they are apt to stage-act, which reduces their action again to being a mere attempt at description. (*The Liar,* for example.) Compare Maupassant's *Toine* for treatment of case similar to *Fordham Castle.*

1902-5. *The Sacred Fount, Wings of a Dove, Golden Bowl* period. *Dove* and *Bowl* certainly not models for other writers, a caviare not part of the canon (metaphors be hanged for the moment).

Henry James is certainly not a model for narrative novelists, for young writers of fiction; perhaps not even a subject of study till they

have attained some sublimity of the critical sense or are at least ready
to be constantly alert, constantly on guard.

I cannot see that he will harm a critic or a describer of places, a
recorder of impressions, whether they be of people, places, music.

In *The Sacred Fount* he attains form, perfect form, his form. It is
almost the only novel about which he says not a word in his prefaces.
Whether or no this was intentional, it seems to be one work that he
could afford to sit back, look at, and find completed. I don't in the
least imply that he did so.

1903. *Better Sort*, mildish.

1903. *The Ambassadors*, rather clearer than the other work. Etude
of Paris versus Woollett. Exhortation to the idle, well-to-do, to
leave home.

1907. *The American Scene*, triumph of the author's long practice.
A creation of America. A book no 'serious American' will neglect.
How many Americans make any attempt toward a realization of that
country is of course beyond our power to compute. The desire to
see the national face in a mirror may be in itself an exotic. I know of no
such grave record, of no such attempt at faithful portrayal as *The
American Scene*. Thus America is to the careful observer; this volume
and the American scenes in the fiction and memoirs, in *The Europeans*, *The Patagonia*, *Washington Square*, etc., bulk large in the very
small amount of writing which can be counted as history of *mœurs
contemporaines*, of national habit of our time and of the two or three
generations preceding us. Newport, the standardized face, the Capitol,
Independence Hall, the absence of penetralia, innocence, essential
vagueness, etc., language 'only definable as not *in intention* Yiddish',
the tabernacle of Grant's ashes, the public collapse of the individual,
the St Gaudens statue. There is nothing to be gained by making
excerpts; the volume is large, but one should in time drift through it.
I mean any American with pretences to an intellectual life should
drift through it. It is not enough to have perused 'The Constitution'
and to have 'heerd tell' of the national founders.

1910. *The Finer Grain*, collection of short stories without a slip.
The Velvet Glove, *Mona Montravers*, *A Round of Visits* (the old
New York versus the new), *Crapey Cornelia*, *The Bench of Desol-
ation*.

It is by beginning on this collection, or perhaps taking it after such
stories as *The Pupil* and *Brooksmith*, that the general literate reader

will best come to James, must in brief be convinced of him and can tell whether or not the 'marginal' James is for him. Whether or no the involutions of the *Golden Bowl* will titillate his arcane sensibilities. If the reader does not 'get' *The Finer Grain* there is no sense in his trying the more elaborate *Wings of a Dove, Sacred Fount, Golden Bowl.* If, on the contrary, he does feel the peculiar, unclassic attraction of the author he may or may not enjoy the uncanonical books.

1911. *The Outcry,* a relapse. Connoisseurship fad again, inferior work.

1913. *A Small Boy and Others,* the beginning of the memoirs. Beginning of this volume disgusting. First three pages enough to put one off Henry James once and for all, damn badly written, atrocious vocabulary. Page 33, a few lines of good writing. Reader might start about here, any reader, that is, to whom New York of that period is of interest. New York of the fifties is significant, in so far as it is typical of what a hundred smaller American cities have been since. The tone of the work shows in excerpts:

'The special shade of its identity was thus that it was not conscious —really not conscious of anything in the world; or was conscious of so few possibilities at least, and these so immediate and so a matter of course, that it came almost to the same thing. That was the testimony that the slight subjects in question strike me as having borne to their surrounding medium—the fact that their unconsciousness could be preserved. . . .'

Of later, when dealing with a pre-Y.M.C.A. America.

'Infinitely queer and quaint, almost incongruously droll, the sense somehow begotten in ourselves, as very young persons, of our being surrounded by a slightly remote, yet dimly rich, outer and quite kindred circle of the tipsy. I remember how, once, as a very small boy, after meeting in the hall a most amiable and irreproachable gentleman, all but closely consanguineous, who had come to call on my mother, I anticipated his further entrance by slipping in to report to that parent that I thought *he* must be tipsy. And I was to recall perfectly afterwards the impression I so made on her—in which the general proposition that the gentlemen of a certain group or connection might on occasion be best described by the term I had used, sought to destroy the particular presumption that our visitor wouldn't, by his ordinary measure, show himself for one of these. He didn't to all appearance, for I was afterwards disappointed at the lapse of lurid evidence: that memory remained with me, as well as a considerable subsequent wonder at my having leaped to so baseless a view. . . .'

'The grim little generalization remained, none the less, and I may speak of it—since I speak of everything—as still standing: the striking evidence that scarce aught but disaster *could,* in that so unformed and unseasoned society, overtake young men who were in the least exposed. Not to have been immediately launched in business of a rigorous sort was to *be* exposed—in the absence, I mean, of some fairly abnormal predisposition to virtue; since it was a world so simply constituted that whatever wasn't business, or exactly an office or a 'store', places in which people sat close and made money, was just simply pleasure, sought, and sought only, in places in which people got tipsy. There was clearly no mean, least of all the golden one, for it was just the ready, even when the moderate, possession of gold that determined, that hurried on disaster. There were whole sets and groups, there were 'sympathetic', though too susceptible, races, that seemed scarce to recognize or to find possible any practical application of moneyed, that is, of transmitted ease, however limited, but to go more or less rapidly to the bad with it—which meant even then going as often as possible to Paris. . . .

'The field was strictly covered, to my young eyes, I make out, by three classes, the busy, the tipsy, and Daniel Webster. . . .

'It has carried me far from my rather evident proposition that if we saw the "natural" so happily embodied about us—and in female maturity, or comparative maturity, scarce less than in female adolescence—this was because the artificial, or in other words the complicated, was so little there to threaten it. . . .'

On page 72 he quotes his father on 'flagrant morality'. In Chapter X we have a remarkable portrayal of a character by almost nothing save vacuums.

'timorous philistine in a world of dangers.'

Our author notes the 'finer civility' but does not see that it is a thing of no period. It is the property of a few individuals, personally transmitted. Henry James had a mania for setting these things in an era or a 'faubourg', despite the continued testimony that the worst manners have constantly impinged upon the most brilliant societies; that decent detail of conduct is a personal talent.

The production of *Il Corteggiano* proves nothing more than

the degree in which Castiglione's contemporaries 'needed to be told'.

On page 236 (*Small Boy and Others*) the phrase 'presence without type'.

On page 286, the people 'who cultivated for years the highest instructional, social and moral possibilities of Geneva'.

Page 283, 'discussion of a work of art mainly hung in these days on that issue of the producible *name*.'

Page 304, 'For even in those days some Americans were rich and several sophisticated.'

Page 313, the real give away of W. J. Page 341, Scarification of Ste-Beuve. Page 179, Crystal Palace. Page 214, Social relativity.

One is impatient for Henry James to do people.

A Little Tour in France. The disadvantage of giving impressions of real instead of imaginary places is that they conflict with other people's impressions. I do not see Angoulême viâ Balzac, nor do I feel Henry James' contacts with the places where our tracks have crossed, very remarkable. I dare say it is a good enough guide for people more meagrely furnished with associations or perceptions. Allow me my *piéton's* shrug for the man who has gone only by train.

Henry James is not very deep in ancient associations. The American's enjoyment of England in *The Passionate Pilgrim* is more searching than anything continental. Windy generality in *Tour de France*, and perhaps indication of how little Henry James' tentacles penetrated into any era before 1600, or perhaps before 1780.

Vignette bottom of pages 337-8 (*Passionate Pilgrim*) 'full of glimpses and responses, of deserts and desolations'. 'His perceptions would be fine and his opinions pathetic.' Commiseration of Searle versus detachment, in *Four Meetings*.

Of the posthumous work, *The Middle Years* is perhaps the most charming. *The Ivory Tower*, full of accumulated perceptions, swift illuminating phrases, perhaps part of a masterpiece. *The Sense of the Past*, less important. I leave my comment on *The Middle Years* as I wrote it, but have recast the analysis of notes to *The Ivory Tower*.

Flaubert is in six volumes, four or five of which every literate man must at one time or another assault. James is strewn over above forty—part of which must go into desuetude, has perhaps done so already.

I have not in these notes attempted the Paterine art of appreciation,

e.g. as in taking the perhaps sole readable paragraph of Pico
Mirandola and writing an empurpled descant.

The problem—discussion of which is about as 'artistic' as a street
map—is: can we conceive a five or six volume edition of James so
selected as to hold its own internationally? My contention is for this
possibility.

My notes are no more than a tentative suggestion, to wit: that some
such compact edition might be, to advantage, tried on the less patient
public. I have been, alas, no more fortunate than our subject in
keeping out irrelevant, non-aesthetic, non-literary, non-technical
vistas and strictures.

THE MIDDLE YEARS

The Middle Years is a tale of the great adventure; for, putting aside a
few simple adventures, sentimental, phallic, Nimrodic, the remaining
great adventure is precisely the approach to the Metropolis; for the
provincial of our race the specific approach to London, and no
subject surely could more heighten the pitch of writing than that the
treated approach should be that of the greatest writer of our time and
of our own particular language. We may, I think, set aside Thomas
Hardy as of an age not our own; of perhaps Walter Scott's or of
L'Abbé Prévost's, but remote from us and things familiarly under
our hand; and we skip over the next few crops of writers as lacking
in any comparative interest, interest in a writer being primarily in his
degree of sensitization; and on this count we may throw out the whole
Wells-Bennett period, for what interest can we take in instruments
which must by nature miss two-thirds of the vibrations in any conceivable situation? In James the maximum sensibility compatible
with efficient writing was present. Indeed, in reading these pages one
can but despair over the inadequacy of one's own literary sensitization, one's so utterly inferior state of awareness; even allowing for
what the author himself allows: his not really, perhaps, having felt
at twenty-six, all that at seventy he more or less read into the memory
of his feeling. The point is that with the exception of exceptional
moments in Hueffer,[1] we find no trace of such degree of awareness in
the next lot of writers, or until the first novels of Lewis[2] and Joyce,

[1] F. Madox Ford, name changed by deed poll.
[2] Wyndham Lewis, author of *Tarr*.

whose awareness is, without saying, of a nature greatly different in kind.

The section of reminiscences called *The Middle Years* is not the book for any reader to tackle who has not read a good deal of James, or who has not, in default of that reading, been endowed with a natural Jamesian sensibility (a case almost negligible by any likelihood); neither is it a book of memoirs, I mean one does not turn to it seeking information about Victorian worthies; any more than one did, when the old man himself was talking, want to be told anything; there are encyclopedias in sufficiency, and statistics, and human mines of information, boring sufficiency; one asked and asks only that the slow voice should continue—evaluating, or perhaps only tying up the strands of a sentence: 'And how my old friend ... *Howells* ...', etc.

The effects of H. J.'s first breakfasts in Liverpool, or invited upstairs in Half Moon Street, are of infinitely more value than any anecdotes of the Laureate (even though H. J.'s inability not to see all through the Laureate is compensated by a quip melting one's personal objection to anything Tennyson touched, by making him merely any old gentleman whatsoever with a gleam of fun in his make-up).

All comers to the contrary, and the proportionate sale of his works, and statistics whatsoever to the contrary, only an American who has come abroad will ever draw *all* the succulence from Henry James' writings; the denizen of Manchester or Wellington may know what it feels like to reach London, the Londoner born will not be able quite to reconstruct even this part of the book; and if for intimacy H. J. might have stayed at the same hotel on the same day as one's grandfather; and if the same American names had part in one's own inceptions in London, one's own so wholly different and less padded inceptions; one has perhaps a purely personal, selfish, unliterary sense of intimacy: with, in my own case, the vast unbridgeable difference of settling-in and escape.

The essence of James is that he is always 'settling-in', it is the ground-tone of his genius.

Apart from the state of James' sensibility on arrival nothing else matters, the 'mildness of the critical air', the fatuity of George Eliot's husband, the illustrational and accomplished lady, even the faculty for a portrait in a paragraph, not to be matched by contemporary effects in half-metric, are indeed all subordinate to one's curiosity as to what Henry James knew, and what he did not know on landing. The portrait of the author on the cover showing him bearded, and looking rather like a cross between a bishop and a Cape Cod long-shoreman, is an incident gratuitous, interesting, but in no way connected with the young man of the text.

The England of a still rather whiskered age, never looking inward, in short, the Victorian, is exquisitely embalmed, and 'mounted', as is, I think, the term of microscopy. The book is just the right length as a volume, but one mourns there not being twenty more, for here is the unfinished work ... not in *The Sense of the Past*, for there the pen was weary, as it had been in *The Outcry*, and the talent that was never most worth its own while when gone off on connoisseurship, was, conceivably, finished; but here in his depiction of his earlier self the verve returned in full vigour.

THE NOTES TO 'THE IVORY TOWER'[1]

The great artists among men of letters have occasionally and by tradition burst into an *Ars Poetica* or an *Arte nuevo de hacer Comedias*, and it should come as no surprise that Henry James has left us some sort of treatise on novel-writing—no surprise, that is, to the dis-criminating reader who is *not*, for the most part, a writer of English novels. Various reviewers have hinted obscurely that some such treatise is either adumbrated or concealed in the Notes for *The Ivory Tower* and for *The Sense of the Past;* they have said, indeed, that novelists will 'profit greatly', etc., but no one has set forth the gist of the generalities which are to be found in these notes.

Divested of its fine verbiage, of its clichés, of its provincialisms of American phrase, and of the special details relating to the particular book in his mind, the formula for building a novel (any novel, not merely any ' psychological' novel); the things to have clearly in mind before starting to write it are enumerated in *The Ivory Tower* notes somewhat as follows:

1. Choice of names for characters; names that will 'fit' their owners, and that will not 'joggle' or be cacophonic when in juxta-position on the page.

2. Exposition of one group of characters and of the 'situation'.

[1] Recast from an article in Chas. Granville's magazine, *The Future*.

(In *The Ivory Tower* this was to be done in three subdivisions. 'Book I' was to give the 'Immediate Facts'.)

3. One character at least is hitched to his 'characteristic'. We are to have one character's impression on another.

4. (Book III.) Various reactions and interactions of characters.

5. The character, i.e. the main character, is 'faced with the situation'.

6. For *The Ivory Tower* and probably for any novel, there is now need to show clearly and definitely the 'antecedents', i.e. anything that had happened before the story started. And we find Henry James making up his mind which characters have interacted before this story opens, and which things are to be due to fresh impacts of one character on another.

7. Particular consideration of the special case in hand. The working-free from incongruities inherent in the first vague preconceptions of the plot. Thus:

(*a*) The hinge of the thing is not to be the effect of A. on B. or of B. on A.; nor of A. on C. or of C. on B.; but is to be due to an effect all round, of A. and B. and C. working on each other.

(*b*) James' care not to repeat figures from earlier novels. Not a categoric prohibition, but a caution not to sail too near the wind in this matter.

(*c*) A care not to get too many 'personally remarkable' people, and not enough stupid ones into the story.

(*d*) Care for the relative 'weight' as well as the varied 'tone' of the characters.

(We observe, in all this, the peculiarly American passion for 'art'; for having a system in things, cf. Whistler.)

(*e*) Consideration how far one character 'faces' the problems of another character's 'character'.

(This and section (*d*) continue the preoccupation with 'moral values' shown in James' early criticism in *French Poets and Novelists*.)

8. Definite 'joints'; or relations of one character to another finally fitted and settled.

This brings us again to point 5. The character, i.e. the main character definitely 'faced' with the situation.

9. The consequences.

10. (*a*) Further consideration of the state of character C. before contact with B., etc.

(*b*) The effect of further characters on the mind, and thence on the action of A.

(*c*) Considerations of the effect of a fourth main character; of introducing a subsidiary character, and its effect, i.e. that of having an extra character for a particular function.

11. The great *coup* foreshadowed.

(In this case the mild Othello, more and more drifting consciously into the grip of the mild Iago—I use the terms 'Othello' and 'Iago' merely to avoid, if not 'hero', at least 'villain'; the sensitive temperament allowing the rapacious temperament to become effective.)

(*a*) The main character in perplexity as to how far he shall combat the drift of things.

(*b*) The opposed character's perception of this.

(These sub-sections are, of course, sub-sections for a psychological novel; one would have different but equivalent 'joints' in a novel of action.)

(*c*) Effect of all this on third character. (In this case female, attracted to 'man-of-action' quality.)

(*d*) A.'s general perceptions of these things and his weighing of values, a phase solely for the psychological novel.

(*e*) Weighing of how much A.'s perception of the relations between B. and C. is to be *dénouement*, and how much, more or less, known.

12. Main character's 'solution' or vision of what course he will take.

13. The fourth character's 'break into' things, or into a perception of things.

(*a*) Actions of an auxiliary character, of what would have been low life in old Spanish or Elizabethan drama. This character affects the main actions (as sometimes a *gracioso* (servant, buffoon, Sancho Panza) affects the main action in a play, for example, of Lope de Vega).

(*b*) Caution not to let author's interest in fascinating auxiliary character run away with his whole plan and design.

(This kind of restraint is precisely what leaves a reader 'wanting more'; which gives a novel the 'feel' of being full of life; convinces the reader of an abundant energy, an abundant sense of life in an author.)

14. Effects of course of the action on fourth main character and on

the others. The scale being kept by the relation here not being between main character and *one* antagonist, but with a group of three people, relations 'different' though their 'point' is the same; cf. a 'main character' versus a Rosenkrantz and Guildenstern, or 'attendant lords'. James always has half an eye on play construction; the scene.

(*a*) The second auxiliary character brought out more definitely. (This is accidental. It might happen at any suitable point in a story wherever needed.)

(*b*) Act of this auxiliary person reaches through to main action.

15. We see the author determining just how bad a case he is going to make his villain.

(*a*) Further determination of his hero. (In this case an absolute non-producer, non-accumulator.)

(*b*) Care not to get an unmixed 'bad' in his 'villain' but to keep a right balance, a dependency, in this case, on the main character's weakness or easiness.

(*c*) Decision how the main *coup* or transfer shall slide through.

16. Effect upon C. Effect upon main character's relations to D., E. and F.

At this point, in the consideration of eight of the ten 'books' of his novel, we see the author most intent on his composition or architecture, most anxious to get all the sections fitted in with the greatest economy, a sort of crux of his excitement and anxiety, a fullness of his perception that the thing must be so tightly packed that no sentence can afford to be out of place.

17. Climax. The *Deus* or, in this case, *Dea, ex machina*. Devices for prolonging climax. The fourth main character having been, as it were, held back for a sort of weight or balance here, and as a 'resolution' of the tangles.

Finis.

18. Author's final considerations of time scheme, i.e. fitting the action into time not too great for unity, and great enough to allow for needed complexity. Slighter consideration of place scheme; where final scenes shall be laid, etc.

Here in a few paragraphs are the bare bones of the plan described in eighty of Henry James' pages. The detailed thoroughness of this plan, the complicated consciousness displayed in it, give us the measure of this author's superiority, as conscious artist, over the 'normal' British novelist, i.e. over the sort of person who tells you that when he did his first book he 'just sat down and wrote the first paragraph', and then found he 'couldn't stop'. This he tells you in a manner clearly implying that, from that humble beginning to the shining hour of the present, he has given the matter no further thought, and that his succeeding works were all knocked off with equal simplicity.

I give this outline with such fullness because it is a landmark in the history of the novel as written in English. It is inconceivable that Fielding or Richardson should have left, or that Thomas Hardy should leave, such testimony to a comprehension of the novel as a 'form'. The Notes are, on the other hand, quite distinct from the voluminous prefaces which so many French poets write before they have done anything else. James, we note, wrote no prefaces until there were twenty-four volumes of his novels and stories waiting to be collected and republished. The Notes are simply the accumulation of his craftsman's knowledge, they are, in all their length, the summary of the things he would have, as a matter of habit, in his mind before embarking on composition.

I take it rather as a sign of editorial woodenheadedness that these notes are printed at the *end* of *The Ivory Tower;* if one have sense enough to suspect that the typical mentality of the elderly heavy reviewer has been shown, one will for oneself reverse the order; read the notes with interest and turn to the text already with the excitement of the sport or with the zest to see if, with this chance of creating the masterpiece so outlined, the distinguished author is going to make good. If on the other hand one reads the unfinished text, there is no escaping the boredom of re-reading in skeleton, with tentative and confusing names, the bare statement of what has been, in the text, more fully set before us.

The text is attestation of the rich, banked-up perception of the author. I dare say the snap and rattle of the fun, or much of it, will be only half perceptible to those who do not know both banks of the Atlantic; but enough remains to show the author at his best; despite the fact that occasionally he puts in the mouths of his characters sentences or phrases that no one but he himself could have used. I cannot attribute this to the unfinished state of the manuscript. These oversights are few, but they are the kind of slip which occurs in his earlier work. We note also that his novel is a descriptive novel, not a novel that simply depicts people speaking and moving. There is a constant dissertation going on, and in it is our major enjoyment.

The Notes to *The Sense of the Past* are not so fine a specimen of method, they are the plan not of a whole book, but only of the latter section. The editor is quite right to print them at the end of the volume.

Of the actual writing in the three posthumous books, far the most charming is to be found in *The Middle Years* ... inn-rooms, breakfasts, butlers. ... There is no need for its being 'memoirs' at all; call the protagonist Mr Ponsonby or Mr Hampton, obliterate the known names of celebrities and half celebrities, and the whole thing becomes a James novel, and, so far as it goes, a mate to the best of them.

Retaining the name of the author, any faithful reader of James, or at any rate the attentive student, finds a good deal of amusement in deciphering the young James, his temperament as mellowed by recollection and here recorded forty years later, and then in contrasting it with the young James as revealed or even 'betrayed' in his own early criticisms, *French Poets and Novelists,* a much cruder and more savagely puritanical and plainly New England product with, however, certain permanent traits of his character already in evidence, and with a critical faculty keen enough to hit on certain weaknesses in the authors analysed, often with profundity, and with often a 'rightness' in his mistakes. I mean that apparent errors are at times only an excess of zeal, an overshooting of his mark, which was to make for an improvement, by him, of certain defects.

The prefaces are a special study belonging chronologically to the date of the New York edition with the Coburn photos, and the memory of his having travelled about with the photographer. I intended my notes as a study of H. J.'s art in the novel, not as a critique of his own criticism; though I seem to have neglected to say so. There is a marvellous passage on Ninevites in the Preface to *Lady Barberina,* and in another place he had already written his defence against charges which had been levelled at him, saying that if such people don't exist we ought at least, for the honour of the race, to pretend that they do.

REMY DE GOURMONT[1]

A DISTINCTION

followed by notes

The mind of Remy de Gourmont was less like the mind of Henry James than any contemporary mind I can think of. James' drawing of *mœurs contemporaines* was so circumstantial, so concerned with the setting, with detail, nuance, social aroma, that his transcripts were 'out of date' almost before his books had gone into a second edition; out of date that is, in the sense that his interpretations of society could never serve as a guide to such supposititious utilitarian members of the next generation as might so desire to use them.

He has left his scene and his characters, unalterable as the little paper flowers permanently visible inside the lumpy glass paperweights. He was a great man of letters, a great artist in portrayal; he was concerned with mental temperatures, circumvolvulous social pressures, the clash of contending conventions, as Hogarth with the cut of contemporary coats.

On no occasion would any man of my generation have broached an intimate idea to H. J., or to Thomas Hardy, O.M., or years since, to Swinburne, or even to Mr Yeats with any feeling that the said idea was likely to be received, grasped, comprehended. However much one may have admired Yeats' poetry; however much one may have been admonished by Henry James' prose works, one has never thought of agreeing with either.

You could, on the other hand, have said to Gourmont anything that came into your head; you could have sent him anything you had written with a reasonable assurance that he would have known what you were driving at. If this distinction is purely my own, and subjective, and even if it be wholly untrue, one will be very hard pressed to find any other man born in the 'fifties' of whom it is even suggestible.

Gourmont prepared our era; behind him there stretches a limitless

---

[1] From *Instigations* (1920).

darkness; there *was* the counter-reformation, still extant in the English printer; there *was* the restoration of the Inquisition by the Catholic Roman Church, holy and apostolic, in the year of grace 1824; there was the Mephistopheles period, morals of the opera left over from the Spanish seventeenth-century plays of 'capa y espada'; Don Juan for subject matter, etc.; there was the period of English Christian bigotry, Saml. Smiles, exhibition of 1851 ('Centennial of 1876') machine-made building 'ornament', etc., enduring in the people who did not read Saml. Butler; there was the Emerson-Tennysonian plus optimism period; there was the 'aesthetic' era during which people 'wrought' as the impeccable Beerbohm has noted; there was the period of funny symboliste trappings, 'sin', satanism, rosy cross, heavy lilies, Jersey Lilies, etc.,

> 'Ch' hanno perduto il ben dell' intelletto';

all these periods had mislaid the light of the eighteenth century; though in the symbolistes Gourmont had his beginning.

In contradiction to, in wholly antipodal distinction from, Henry James, Gourmont was an artist of the nude. He was an intelligence almost more than an artist; when he portrays, he is concerned with hardly more than the permanent human elements. His people are only by accident of any particular era. He is poet, more by possessing a certain quality of mind than by virtue of having written fine poems; you could scarcely contend that he was a novelist.

He was intensely aware of the differences of emotional timbre; and as a man's message is precisely his *façon de voir*, his modality of apperception, this particular awareness was his 'message'.

Where James is concerned with the social tone of his subjects, with their entourage, with their *superstes* of dogmatized 'form', ethic, etc., Gourmont is concerned with their modality and resonance in emotion.

Mauve, Fanette, Neobelle, La Vierge aux Plâtres, are all studies in different *permanent* kinds of people; they are not the results of environments or of 'social causes', their circumstance is an accident and is on the whole scarcely alluded to. Gourmont differentiates his characters by the modes of their sensibility, not by sub-degrees of their state of civilization.

He recognizes the right of individuals to *feel* differently. Confucian, Epicurean, a considerer and entertainer of ideas, this complicated sensuous wisdom is almost the one ubiquitous element, the 'self' which keeps his superficially heterogeneous work vaguely 'unified'.

The study of emotion does not follow a set chronological arc: it extends from the *Physique de l'Amour* to *Le Latin Mystique;* from the condensation of Fabre's knowledge of insects to

'Amas ut facias pulchram'

in the Sequaire of Goddeschalk (*Le Latin Mystique*).

He had passed the point where people take abstract statement of dogma for 'enlightenment'. An 'idea' has little value apart from the modality of the mind which receives it. It is a railway from one state to another, and as dull as steel rails in a desert.

The emotions are equal before the aesthetic judgment. He does not grant the duality of body and soul, or at least suggests that this medieval duality is unsatisfactory; there is an interpenetration, an osmosis of body and soul, at least for hypothesis.

'My words are the unspoken words of my body.'

And in all his exquisite treatment of all emotion he will satisfy many whom August Strindberg, for egregious example, will not. From the studies of insects to Christine evoked from the thoughts of Diomède, sex is not a monstrosity or an exclusively German study.[1] And the entire race is not bound to the habits of the *mantis* or of other insects equally melodramatic. Sex, in so far as it is not a purely physiological reproductive mechanism, lies in the domain of aesthetics, the junction of tactile and magnetic senses; as some people have accurate ears both for rhythm and for pitch, and as some are tone deaf, some impervious to rhythmic subtlety and variety, so in this other field of the senses some desire the trivial, some the processional, the stately, the master-work.

As some people are good judges of music, and insensible to painting and sculpture, so the fineness of one sense may entail no corresponding fineness in another, or at least no corresponding critical perception of differences.

Emotions to Henry James were more or less things that other people had and that one didn't go into; at any rate not in drawing rooms. The gods had not visited James, and the Muse, whom he so

[1] 'A German study, Hobson, A German study!' *Tarr.*

frequently mentions, appeared doubtless in corsage, the narrow waist, the sleeves puffed at the shoulders, *à la mode* 1890-2.

Gourmont is interested in hardly anything save emotions and the ideas that will go into them, or take life in emotional application. (Apperceptive rather than active.)

One reads *Les Chevaux de Diomède* (1897) as one would have listened to incense in the old Imperial court. There are many spirits incapable. Gourmont calls it a 'romance of possible adventures'; it might be called equally an aroma, the fragrance of roses and poplars, the savour of wisdoms, not part of the canon of literature, a book like *Daphnis and Chloe* or like Marcel Schwob's *Livre de Monelle;* not a solidity like Flaubert; but a pervasion.

'My true life is in the unspoken words of my body.'

In *Une Nuit au Luxembourg,* the characters talk at more length, and the movement is less convincing. *Diomède* was Gourmont's own favourite and we may take it as the best of his art, the most complete expression of his particular 'façon d'apercevoir'; if, even in it, the characters do little but talk philosophy, or drift into philosophic expression out of a haze of images, they are for all that very real. It is the climax of his method of presenting characters differentiated by emotional timbre, a process which had begun in *Histoires Magiques* (1895); and in *D'un Pays Lointain* (published 1898, in reprint from periodicals of 1892-4).

Songe d'une Femme (1899) is a novel of modern life, Gourmont's sexual intelligence, as contrasted to Strindberg's sexual stupidity well in evidence. The work is untranslatable into English, but should be used before thirty by young men who have been during their undergraduate days too deeply inebriated with the *Vita Nuova.*

'Tout ce qui se passe dans la vie, c'est de la mauvaise littérature.'

'La vraie terre natale est celle où on a eu sa première émotion forte.'

'La virginité n'est pas une vertu, c'est un état; c'est une sous-division des couleurs.'

Livres de chevet for those whom the Strindbergian school will always leave aloof.

'Les imbéciles ont choisi le beau comme les oiseaux choisissent ce qui est gras. La bêtise leur sert de cornes.'

Cœur Virginal (1907) is a light novel, amusing, and accurate in its psychology.

I do not think it possible to overemphasize Gourmont's sense of beauty. The mist clings to the lacquer. His spirit was the spirit of Omakitsu; his *pays natal* was near to the peach-blossom-fountain of the untranslatable poem. If the life of Diomède is overdone and done badly in modern Paris, the wisdom of the book is not thereby invalidated. It may be that Paris has need of some more Spartan corrective, but for the descendants of witch-burners Diomède is a needful communication.

As Voltaire was a needed light in the eighteenth century, so in our time Fabre and Frazer have been essentials in the mental furnishings of any contemporary mind qualified to write of ethics or philosophy or that mixed molasses religion. *The Golden Bough* has supplied the data which Voltaire's incisions had shown to be lacking. It has been a positive succeeding his negative. It is not necessary perhaps to read Fabre and Frazer entire, but one must be aware of them; people unaware of them invalidate all their own writing by simple ignorance, and their work goes ultimately to the scrap heap.

Physique de L'Amour (1903) should be used as a text-book of biology. Between this biological basis in instinct, and the 'Sequaire of Goddeschalk' in *Le Latin Mystique* (1892) stretch Gourmont's studies of amour and aesthetics. In Diomède we find an Epicurean receptivity, a certain aloofness, an observation of contacts and auditions, in contrast to the Propertian attitude:

'Ingenium nobis ipsa puella fecit',

this is perhaps balanced by

'Sans vous, je crois bien que je n'aimerais plus beaucoup et que je n'aurais plus une extrême confiance ni dans la vie ni moi-même.' (In *Lettres à l'Amazone*.)

But there is nothing more unsatisfactory than saying that Gourmont 'had such and such ideas' or held 'such and such views', the thing is that he held ideas, intuitions, perceptions in a certain personal exquisite manner. In a criticism of him, 'criticism' being an over-violent word, in, let us say, an indication of him, one wants merely to show that one has himself made certain dissociations; as here, between the aesthetic receptivity of tactile and magnetic values, of the perception of beauty in these relationships and the conception of love, passion, emotion as an intellectual instigation; such as

Propertius claims it; such as we find it declared in the King of Navarre's

                    'De fine amor vient science et beauté';
and constantly in the troubadours.

(I cannot repeat too often that there was a profound psychological knowledge in medieval Provence, however Gothic its expression; that men, concentrated on certain validities, attaining an exact and diversified terminology, have there displayed considerable penetration; that this was carried into early Italian poetry; and faded from it when metaphors became decorative instead of interpretative; and that the age of Aquinas would not have tolerated sloppy expression of psychology concurrent with the exact expression of 'mysticism'. There is also great wisdom in Ovid. *Passons!*)

Gourmont's wisdom is not wholly unlike the wisdom which those ignorant of Latin may, if the gods favour their understanding, derive from Golding's *Metamorphoses*.

Barbarian ethics proceed by general taboos. Gourmont's essays collected into various volumes, *Promenades, Epilogues,* etc., are perhaps the best introduction to the ideas of our time that any unfortunate, suddenly emerging from Peru, Peoria, Oshkosh, Iceland, Kochin, or other out-of-the-way lost continent could desire. A set of Landor's collected works will go further towards civilizing a man than any university education now on the market. Montaigne condensed Renaissance awareness. Even so small a collection as Lionel Johnson's *Post Liminium* might save a man from utter barbarity.

But if, for example, a raw graduate were contemplating a burst into intellectual company, he would be less likely to utter unutterable *bêtises, gaffes,* etc., after reading Gourmont than before. One cannot of course create intelligence in a numbskull.

Needless to say, Gourmont's essays are of uneven value as the necessary subject matter is of uneven value. Taken together, proportionately placed in his work, they are a portrait of the civilized mind. I incline to think them the best portrait available, the best record that is, of the civilized mind from 1885-1915.

There are plenty of people who do not know what the civilized mind is like, just as there were plenty of mules in England who did not read Landor contemporaneously, or who did not in his day read Montaigne. Civilization is individual.

Gourmont arouses the senses of the imagination, preparing the mind for receptivities. His wisdom, if not of the senses, is at any rate viâ the senses. We base our 'science' on perceptions, but our ethics have not yet attained this palpable basis.

In 1898, *Pays Lointain* (reprinted from magazine publication of 1892-4), Gourmont was beginning his method:

'Douze crimes pour l'honneur de l'infini.'

He treats the special case, cases as special as any of James' but segregated on different demarcative lines. His style had attained the vividness of

'Sa vocation était de paraître malheureuse, de passer dans la vie comme une ombre gémissante, d'inspirer de la pitié, du doute et de l'inquiétude. Elle avait toujours l'air de porter des fleurs vers une tombe abandonnée'. *La Femme en Noir*.

In *Histoires Magiques* (1894): *La Robe Blanche, Yeux d'eau, Marguerite Rouge, Sœur de Sylvie, Danaette,* are all of them special cases, already showing his perception of neurosis, of hyperaesthesia. His mind is still running on tonal variations in *Les Litanies de la Rose*.

'Pourtant il y a des yeux au bout des doigts.'

'Femmes, conservatrices des traditions milésiennes.'

Epilogues (1895-8). Pleasant re-reading, a book to leave lying about, to look back into at odd half hours. A book of accumulations. Full of meat as a good walnut.

Heterogeneous as the following paragraphs:

'Ni la croyance en un seul Dieu, ni la morale ne sont les fondements vrais de la religion. Une religion, même le Christianisme, n'eut jamais sur les mœurs qu'une influence dilatoire, l'influence d'un bras levé; elle doit recommencer son prêche, non pas seulement avec chaque génération humaine, mais avec chaque phase d'une vie individuelle. N'apportant pas des vérités évidentes en soi, son enseignement oublié, elle ne laisse rien dans les âmes que l'effroi du peut-être et la honte d'être asservi à une peur ou à une espérance dont les chaînes fantômales entravent non pas nos actes mais nos désirs.

. . . . . .

'L'essence d'une religion, c'est sa littérature. Or la littérature religieuse est morte.' *Religions*.

'Je veux bien que l'on me protège contre des ennemis inconnus, l'escarpe ou le cambrioleur—mais contre moi-même, vices ou passions, non.' *Madame Boulton.*

'Si le cosmopolitisme littéraire gagnait encore et qu'il réussît à éteindre ce que les différences de race ont allumé de haine de sang parmi les hommes, j'y verrais un gain pour la civilisation et pour l'humanité tout entière.' *Cosmopolitisme.*

'Augier! Tous les lucratifs rêves de la bourgeoise économe; tous les soupirs des vierges confortables: toutes les réticences des consciences soignées; toutes les joies permises aux ventres prudents; toutes les veuleries des bourses craintives; tous les siphons conjugaux; toutes les envies de la robe montante contre les épaules nues; toutes les haines du waterproof contre la grâce et contre la beauté! Augier, crinoline, parapluie, bec-de-corbin, bonnet grec. . . .' *Augier.*

'Dieu aime la mélodie grégorienne, mais avec modération. Il a soin de varier le programme quotidien des concerts célestes, dont le fond reste le plain-chant liturgique, par des auditions de Bach, Mozart, Haendel, Haydn, "et même Gounod". Dieu ignore Wagner, mais il aime la variété.' *Le Dieu des Belges.*

'La propriété n'est pas sacrée; elle n'est qu'un fait acceptable comme nécessaire au développement de la liberté individuelle.

.   .   .   .   .

'L'abominable loi des cinquante ans—contre laquelle Proudhon lutta en vain si courageusement—commence à faire sentir sa tyrannie. La veuve de M. Dumas a fait interdire la reprise d'Antony. Motif: son bon plaisir. Des caprices d'héritiers peuvent d'un jour à l'autre nous priver pendant cinquante ans de toute une oeuvre.

.   .   .   .   .

'Demain les œuvres de Renan, de Taine, de Verlaine, de Villiers peuvent appartenir à un curé fanatique ou à une dévote stupide.' *La Propriété Littéraire.*

'M. Desjardins, plus modeste, inaugure la morale artistique et murale, secondé par l'excellent M. Puvis de Chavannes qui n'y comprend rien, mais s'avoue tout de même bien content de figurer sur les murs.' *U.P.A.M.*

'Les auteurs, 'avertis par le Public. . . .' Il y a dans ces mots toute une esthétique, non seulement dramatique, mais démocratique. Plus d'insuccès. Plus de fours. Admirable invention par laquelle, sans doute, le peuple trouvera enfin l'art qui lui convient et les auteurs qu'il mérite.' *Conscience Littéraire.*

'Le citoyen est une variété de l'homme; variété dégénérée ou primitive il est à l'homme ce que le chat de gouttière est au chat sauvage.

·   ·   ·   ·   ·   ·

'Comme toutes les créations vraiment belles et noblement utiles, la sociologie fut l'œuvre d'un homme de génie, M. Herbert Spencer, et le principe de sa gloire.

·   ·   ·   ·   ·   ·

'La saine Sociologie traite de l'évolution à travers les âges d'un groupe de métaphores, Famille, Patrie, Etat, Société, etc. Ces mots sont de ceux que l'on dit collectifs et qui n'ont en soi aucune signification, l'histoire les a employés de tous temps, mais la Sociologie, par d'astucieuses définitions, précise leur néant tout en propageant leur culte.

'Car tout mot collectif, et d'abord ceux du vocabulaire sociologique, sont l'objet d'un culte. A la Famille, à la Patrie, à l'Etat, à la Société, on sacrifie des citoyens mâles et des citoyens femelles; les mâles en plus grand nombre; ce n'est que par intermède, en temps de grève ou d'émeute, pour essayer un nouveau fusil que l'on perfore des femelles; elles offrent au coup une cible moins défiante et plus plaisante; ce sont là d'inévitables petits incidents de la vie politique. Le mâle est l'hostie ordinaire.

·   ·   ·   ·   ·   ·

'Le caractère fondamental du citoyen est donc le dévouement, la résignation et la stupidité; il exerce principalement ces qualités selon trois fonctions physiologiques, comme animal reproducteur, comme animal électoral, comme animal contribuable.

·   ·   ·   ·   ·   ·

'Devenu animal électoral, le citoyen n'est pas dépourvu de subtilité. Ayant flairé, il distingue hardiment entre un opportuniste et un radical. Son ingéniosité va jusqu'à la méfiance: le mot Liberté le fait aboyer, tel un chien perdu. A l'idée qu'on le laisse seul dans les ténèbres de sa volonté, il pleure, il appelle sa mère, la République, son père, l'Etat.

·   ·   ·   ·   ·   ·

'Du fond de sa grange ou de son atelier, il entretient volontiers ceux qui le protègent contre lui-même.

·   ·   ·   ·   ·   ·

'Et puis songe; si tu te révoltais, il n'y aurait plus de lois, et quand tu voudrais mourir, comment ferais-tu, si le régistre n'était plus là pour accueillir ton nom?' *Paradoxes sur le Citoyen.*

'Si l'on est porté à souhaiter un déraillement, il faut parler, il faut écrire, il faut sourire, il faut s'abstenir—c'est le grand point de toute vie civique. Les actuelles organisations sociales ont cette tare fondamentale que l'abstention légale et silencieuse les rend inermes et ridicules. Il faut empoisonner l'Autorité, lentement, en jouant. C'est si charmant de jouer et si utile au bon fonctionnement humain! Il faut se moquer. Il faut passer, l'ironie dans les yeux, à travers les mailles des lois anti-libérales, et quand on promène à travers nos vignes, gens de France, l'idole gouvernemental, gardez-vous d'aucun acte vilain, des gros mots, des violences—rentrez chez vous, et mettez les volets. Sans avoir rien fait que de très simple et de très innocent vous vous réveillerez plus libres le lendemain.' *Les Faiseurs de Statues.*

'Charmant Tzar, tu la verras chez toi, la Révolution, stupide comme le peuple et féroce comme la bourgeoisie; tu la verras, dépassant en animalité et en rapacité sanglante tout ce qu'on t'a permis de lire dans les tomes expurgés qui firent ton éducation.' *Le Délire Russe.*

'Or un écrivain, un poète, un philosophe, un homme des régions intellectuelles n'a qu'une patrie: sa langue.' *Querelles de Belgique.*

'Il faut encore, pour en revenir aux assassins, noter que le crime, sauf en des rares cas passionnels, est le moyen et non le but.' *Crimes.*

'Le vers traditionnel est patriotique et national; le vers nouveau est anarchiste et sans patrie. Il semble que la rime riche fasse partie vraiment de la richesse nationale: on vole quelque chose à l'Etat en adoucissant la sonorité des ronrons: 'La France, Messieurs, manque de consonnes d'appui!' D'autre part, l'emploi de l'assonance a quelque chose de rétrograde qui froisse les vrais démocrates.

. . . . . .

'Il est amusant de voir des gens qui ne doivent leur état 'd'hommes modernes' qu'à la fauchaison brutale de toutes les traditions Françaises, protester aussi sottement contre des innovations non seulement logiques, mais inévitables. Ce qui donne quelque valeur à leur acrimonie, c'est qu'ils ignorent tout de cette question si complexe; de là leur liberté critique, n'ayant lu ni Gaston Paris, ni Darmesteter, ni aucun des écrivains récents qui étudièrent avec

prudence tant de points obscurs de la phonétique et de la rythmique,
ils tirent autorité évidente de leur incompétence même.' *Le Vers
Libre et les Prochaines Élections.*

Pèlerin du Silence (1896) contains: *Fleurs de Jadis* (1893), *Château
Singulier* (1894), *Livres des Litanies, Litanie de la Rose*[1] (1892)
Théâtre Muet, Le Fantôme (1893).

Livres des Masques (1896) not particularly important, though the
preface contains a good reformulation, as, for example:

'Le crime capital pour écrivain, c'est le conformisme, l'imitativité,
la soumission aux règles et aux enseignements. L'œuvre d'un
écrivain doit être non seulement le reflet, mais le reflet grossi de sa
personnalité. La seule excuse qu'un homme ait d'écrire c'est de
s'écrire lui-même, de dévoiler aux autres la sorte de monde qui se
mire en son miroir individuel; Sa seule excuse est d'être original; il
doit dire des choses non encore dites, et les dire en une forme non
encore formulée. Il doit se créer sa propre esthétique—et nous
devrons admettre autant d'esthétiques qu'il y a d'esprits originaux et
les juger d'après ce qu'elles sont, et non d'après ce qu'elles ne sont pas.

.   .   .   .   .

'L'esthétique est devenue elle aussi, un talent personnel.'[2] *Préface.*

'Comme tous les écrivains qui sont parvenus à comprendre la vie,
c'est-à-dire son inutilité immédiate, M. Francis Poictevin, bien que
né romancier, a promptement renoncé au roman.

.   .   .   .   .

'Il est très difficile de persuader à de certains vieillards—vieux
ou jeunes—qu'il n'y a pas de sujets; il n'y a en littérature qu'un
sujet, celui qui écrit, et toute la littérature, c'est-à-dire toute la
philosophie, peut surgir aussi bien à l'appel d'un chien écrasé qu'aux
acclamations de Faust interpellant la Nature: "Ou te saisir, ô Nature
infinie? Et vous, mamelles?" ' *Francis Poictevin.*

This book is of the nineties, of temporary interest, judgment in
mid-career, less interesting now that the complete works of the
subject are available, or have faded from interest. This sort of criticism is a duty imposed on a man by his intelligence. The doing it a
duty, a price exacted for his possession of intelligence.

In places the careless phrase, phrases careless of sense, in places the
thing *bien dit* as in his 'Verlaine'. Here and there a sharp sentence, as :

[1] Quoted in *Little Review*, Feb. 1918.
[2] Each of the senses has its own particular eunuchs.

'M. Moréas ne comprendra jamais combien il est ridicule d'appeler Racine le Sophocle de la Ferté Milon.'

or:

'Parti de la chanson de Saint Léger, il en est, dit-on, arrivé au XVIIième siècle, et cela en moins de dix années; ce n'est pas si décourageant qu'on l'a cru. Et maintenant que les textes se font plus familiers, la route s'abrège; d'ici peu de haltes, M. Moréas campera sous le vieux chêne Hugo et, s'il persévère, nous le verrons atteindre le but de son voyage, qui est sans doute de se rejoindre lui-même.' *Jean Moréas.*

This first *Livre des Masques* is of historical interest, as a list of men interesting at that time. It is work done in establishing good work, a necessary scaffolding, the debt to Gourmont, because of it, is ethical rather than artistic. It is a worthy thing to have done. One should not reproach flaws, even if it appears that the author wastes time in this criticism, although this particular sort of half energy probably wouldn't have been any use for more creative or even more formulative writing. It is not a carving of statues, but only holding a torch for the public; ancillary writing. Local and temporal, introducing some men now better known and some, thank heaven, unknown and forgotten.

Deuxième Livre des Masques (1898), rather more important, longer essays, subjects apparently chosen more freely, leaves one perhaps more eager to read Alfred Vallette's *Le Vierge* than any other book mentioned.

'Etre nul arrêté dans développement vers une nullité équilibrée.'

We find typical Gourmont in the essay on Rictus:

'Ici c'est l'idée de la résignation qui trouble le Pauvre; comme tant d'autres, il la confond avec l'idée bouddhiste de non-activité. Cela n'a pas d'autre importance en un temps ou l'on confond tout, et ou un cerveau capable d'associer et de dissocier logiquement les idées doit être considéré comme une production miraculeuse de la Nature.

.   .   .   .   .   .

'Or l'art ne joue pas; il est grave, meme quand il rit, même quand il danse. Il faut encore comprendre qu'en art tout ce qui n'est pas nécessaire est i 'utile; et tout ce qui inutile est mauvais'. *Jehan Rictus.*

He almost convinces one of Ephraim Milkhail's poetry, by his skilful leading up to quotation of:

'Mais le ciel gris est plein de tristesse caline
Ineffablement douce aux cœurs chargés d'ennuis.'

The essay on the Goncourt is important, and we find in it typical
dissociation.

'Avec de la patience, on atteint quelquefois l'exactitude, et avec de
la conscience, la véracité; ce sont les qualités fondamentales de
l'histoire.

.   .   .   .   .   .

'Quand on a goûté à ce vin on ne veut plus boire l'ordinaire
vinasse des bas littérateurs. Si les Goncourt étaient devenus popul-
aires, si la notion du style pouvait pénétrer dans les cerveaux
moyens! On dit que le peuple d'Athènes avait cette notion.

.   .   .   .   .   .

'Et surtout quel mémorable désintéressement. En tout autre
temps nul n'aurait songé à louer Edmond de Goncourt pour ce
dédain de l'argent et de la basse popularité, car l'amour est exclusif
et celui qui aime l'art n'aime que l'art: mais après les exemples de
toutes les avidités qui nous ont été donnés depuis vingt ans par les
boursiers des lettres, par la coulisse de la littérature, il est juste et
nécessaire de glorifier, en face de ceux qui vivent pour l'argent, ceux
qui vécurent pour l'idée et pour l'art.

.   .   .   .   .   .

'La place des Goncourt dans l'histoire littéraire de ce siècle sera
peut-être même aussi grande que celle de Flaubert, et ils la devront
à leur souci si nouveau, si scandaleux, en une littérature alors encore
toute rhétoricienne, de la 'non-imitation'; cela a révolutionné le
monde de l'écriture. Flaubert devait beaucoup à Chateaubriand: il
serait difficile de nommer le maître des Goncourt. Ils conquirent
pour eux, ensuite pour tous les talents, le droit à la personnalité
stricte, le droit pour un écrivain de s'avouer tel quel, et rien qu'ainsi,
sans s'inquiéter des modèles, des règles, de tout le pédantisme
universitaire et cénaculaire, le droit de se mettre face-à-face avec la
vie, avec la sensation, avec le rêve, avec l'idée, de créer sa phrase—et
même, dans les limites du génie de la langue, sa syntaxe.' *Les
Goncourt.*

One is rather glad M. Hello is dead. Ghil is mentionable, and the
introductory note on Félix Fénéon is of interest.

Small periodicals are praised in the notes on Dujardins and Alfred
Vallette.

'Il n'y a rien de plus utile que ces revues spéciales dont le public élu parmi les vrais fidèles admet les discussions minutieuses, les admirations franches.' *Edouard Dujardins.*

'Il arrive dans l'ordre littéraire qu'une revue fondée avec quinze louis a plus d'influence sur la marche des idées et, par conséquent, sur la marche du monde (et peut-être sur la rotation des planètes) que les orgueilleux recueils de capitaux académiques et de dissertations commerciales.' *Alfred Vallette.*

Promenades Philosophiques (1905-8). One cannot brief such work as the *Promenades.* The sole result is a series of aphorisms, excellent perhaps, but without cohesion; a dozen or so will show an intelligence, but convey neither style nor personality of the author:

'Sans doute la religion n'est pas vraie, mais l'anti-religion n'est pas vraie non plus: la vérité réside dans un état parfait d'indifférence.

    .   .   .   .   .

'Peu importe qu'on me sollicite par des écrits ou par des paroles; le mal ne commence qu'au moment où on m'y plie par la force.' *Autre Point de Vue.*

'L'argent est le signe de la liberté. Maudire l'argent c'est maudire la liberté, c'est maudire la vie qui est nulle si elle n'est libre.' *L'Argent.*

'Quand on voudra définir la philosophie du XIXième siècle, on s'apercevra qu'il n'a fait que de la théologie.

    .   .   .   .   .

'Apprendre pour apprendre est peut-être aussi grossier que manger pour manger.

    .   .   .   .   .

'C'est singulier en littérature, quand la forme n'est pas nouvelle, le fond ne l'est pas non plus.

    .   .   .   .   .

'Le nu de l'art contemporain est un nu d'hydrothérapie.

    .   .   .   .   .

'L'art doit être à la mode ou créer la mode.

    .   .   .   .   .

'Les pacifistes, de braves gens à genoux, près d'une balance et priant le ciel qu'elle s'incline, non pas selon les lois de la pesanteur, mais selon leurs vœux.

    .   .   .   .   .

'La propriété est nécessaire, mais il ne l'est pas qu'elle reste toujours dans les mêmes mains.

. . . . .

'Il y a une simulation de l'intelligence comme il y a une simulation de la vertu.

. . . . .

'Le roman historique. Il y a aussi la peinture historique, l'architecture historique, et, à la mi-carême, le costume historique.

. . . . . .

'Etre impersonnel c'est être personnel selon un mode particulier: Voyez Flaubert. On dirait en jargon: l'objectif est une des formes du subjectif.

. . . . .

La maternité, c'est beau, tant qu'on n'y fait pas attention. C'est vulgaire dès qu'on admire.

. . . . .

'L'excuse du christianisme, a été son impuissance sur la réalité. Il a corrompu l'esprit bien plus que la vie.

'Je ne garantis pas qu'aucune de ces notes ne se trouve déjà dans un de mes écrits, ou qu'elle ne figurera pas dans un écrit futur. On les retrouvera peut-être même dans des écrits qui ne seront pas les miens.' *Des Pas sur le Sable.*

Those interested in the subject will take *Le Problème du Style* (1902) entire; the general position may perhaps be indicated very vaguely by the following quotations:

'Quant à la peur de se gâter le style, c'est bon pour un Bembo, qui use d'une langue factice. Le style peut se fatiguer comme l'homme même; il vieillira de même que l'intelligence et la sensibilité dont il est le signe; mais pas plus que l'individu, il ne changera de personnalité, à moins d'un cataclysme psychologique. Le régime alimentaire, le séjour à la campagne ou à Paris, les occupations sentimentales et leurs suites, les maladies ont bien plus d'influence sur un style vrai que les mauvaises lectures. Le style est un produit physiologique, et l'un des plus constants; quoique dans la dépendance des diverses fonctions vitales.

. . . . . .

'Les Etats-Unis tomberaient en langueur, sans les voyages en Europe de leur aristocratie, sans la diversité extrême des climats, des sols et par conséquent des races en évolution dans ce vaste empire.

Les échanges entre peuples sont aussi nécessaires à la révigoration de chaque peuple que le commerce social à l'exaltation de l'énergie individuelle. On n'a pas pris garde à cette nécessité quand on parle avec regret de l'influence des littératures étrangères sur notre littérature.

. . .

'Aujourd'hui l'influence d'Euripide pourrait encore déterminer en un esprit original d'intéressantes œuvres; l'imitateur de Racine dépasserait à peine le comique involontaire. L'étude de Racine ne deviendra profitable que dans plusieurs siècles et seulement à condition que, complètement oublié, il semble entièrement nouveau, entièrement étranger, tel que le sont devenus pour le public d'aujourd'hui Adenès li Rois ou Jean de Meung. Euripide était nouveau au XVIIième siècle. Théocrite l'était alors que Chénier le transposait. 'Quand je fais des vers, insinuait Racine, je songe toujours à dire ce qui ne s'est point encore dit dans notre langue.' André Chénier a voulu exprimer cela aussi dans une phrase maladroite; et s'il ne l'a dit il l'a fait. Horace a bafoué les serviles imitateurs; il n'imitait pas les Grecs, il les étudiait.

. . .

' "Le style est l'homme même" est un propos de naturaliste, qui sait que le chant des oiseaux est déterminé par la forme de leur bec, l'attache de leur langue, le diamètre de leur gorge, la capacité de leurs poumons.

. . .

'Le style, c'est de sentir, de voir, de penser, et rien plus.

. . .

'Le style est une spécialisation de la sensibilité.

. . .

'Une idée n'est qu'une sensation défraîchie, une image effacée.

. . .

'La vie est un dépouillement. Le but de l'activité propre d'un homme est de nettoyer sa personnalité, de la laver de toutes les souillures qu'y déposa l'education, de la dégager de toutes les empreintes qu'y laissèrent nos admirations adolescentes.

. . .

'Depuis un siècle et demi, les connaissances scientifiques ont augmenté énormément; l'esprit scientifique a rétrogradé; il n'y a plus de contact immédiat entre ceux qui lisent et ceux qui créent la science, et (je cite pour la seconde fois la réflexion capitale de Buffon): "On n'acquiert aucune connaissance transmissible, qu'en voyant par soi-même": Les ouvrages de seconde main amusent l'intelligence et ne stimulent pas son activité.

.   .   .   .   .

'Rien ne pousse à la concision comme l'abondance des idées.' *Le Problème du Style*, 1902.

Christianity lends itself to fanaticism.Barbarian ethics proceed by general taboos. The relation of two individuals is so complex that no third person can pass judgment upon it. Civilization is individual. The truth is the individual. The light of the Renaissance shines in Varchi when he declines to pass judgment on Lorenzaccio.

One might make an index of, but one cannot write an essay upon, the dozen volumes of Gourmont's collected discussions. There was weariness towards the end of his life. It shows in even the leisurely charm of *Lettres à l'Amazone*. There was a final flash in his drawing of M. Croquant.

The list of his chief works published by the *Mercure de France*, 26 Rue de Condé, Paris, is as follows:

Sixtine.
Le Pèlerin du Silence.
Les Chevaux de Diomède.
D'un Pays Lointain.
Le Songe d'une Femme.
Lilith, suivi de Théodat.
Une Nuit au Luxembourg.
Un Cœur Virginal.
Couleurs, suivi de Choses Anciennes.
Histoires Magiques.
Lettres d'un Satyre.
Le Chat de Misère.
Simone.

CRITIQUE

Le Latin Mystique.
Le Livre des Masques (Iier et IIième).
La Culture des Idées.
Le Chemin de Velours.

Le Problème du Style.

Physique de l'Amour.

Epilogues.

Esthétique de la Langue Française.

Promenades Littéraires.

Promenades Philosophiques.

Dialogue des Amateurs sur les Choses du Temps.

Nouveaux Dialogues des Amateurs sur les Choses du Temps.

Dante, Béatrice et la Poésie Amoureuse.

Pendant l'Orage.

Gourmont's readiness to co-operate in my first plans for establishing some sort of periodical to maintain communications between New York, London and Paris, was graciously shown in the following (post-mark June 13, 1915):

Dimanche

Cher Monsieur:

J'ai lu avec plaisir votre longue lettre, qui m'expose si clairement la nécessité d'une revue unissant les efforts des Américains, des Anglais, et des Français. Pour cela, je vous servirai autant qu'il sera en mon pouvoir. Je ne crois pas que je puisse beaucoup. J'ai une mauvaise santé et je suis extrêmement fatigué; je ne pourrai vous donner que des choses très courtes, des indications d'idées plutôt que des pages accomplies, mais je ferai de mon mieux. J'espère que vous réussirez à mettre debout cette petite affaire littéraire et que vous trouverez parmi nous des concours utiles. Evidemment si nous pourrions amener les Américains à mieux sentir la vraie littérature française et surtout à ne pas la confondre avec tant d'œuvres courantes si médiocres, cela serait un résultat très heureux. Sont-ils capables d'assez de liberté d'esprit pour lire, sans être choqués, mes livres par exemple? Il est bien douteux et il faudrait pour cela un long travail de préparation. Mais pourquoi ne pas l'entreprendre? En tous les pays, il y a un noyau de bons esprits, d'esprits libres, il faut leur donner quelque chose qui les change de la fadeur des magazines, quelque chose qui leur donne confiance en eux-mêmes et leur soit un point d'appui. Comme vous le dites, il faudra pour commencer les amener à respecter l'individualisme français, le sens de la liberté que quelquesuns d'entre nous possèdent à un si haut point. Ils comprennent cela en théologie. Pourquoi ne le comprendraient-ils pas en art, en poésie, en littérature, en philosophie. Il faut leur faire voir—s'ils ne le voient pas déjà—que l'individualisme français peut, quand il le faut, se plier aux plus dures disciplines.

Conquérir l'Américain n'est pas sans doute votre seul but. Le but du *Mercure* a été de permettre à ceux qui en valent la peine d'écrire franchement ce qu'ils pensent—seul plaisir d'un écrivain. Cela doit aussi être le vôtre.

Votre bien dévoué,
REMY DE GOURMONT.

'The aim of the *Mercure* has been to permit any man, who is worth it, to write down his thought frankly—this is a writer's sole pleasure. And this aim should be yours.'

'Are they capable of enough mental liberty to read my books, for example, without being horrified? I think this very doubtful, and it will need long preparation. But why not try it? There are in all countries knots of intelligent people, open-minded; one must give something to relieve them from the staleness of magazines, something which will give them confidence in themselves and serve as a rallying point. As you say, one must begin by getting them to respect French individualism; the sense of liberty which some of us have in so great degree. They understand this in theology, why should they not understand it in art, poetry, literature?'

If only my great correspondent could have seen letters I received about this time from English alleged intellectuals!!!!!! The incredible stupidity, the ingrained refusal of thought!!!!! Of which more anon, if I can bring myself to it. Or let it pass? Let us say simply that Gourmont's words form an interesting contrast with the methods employed by the British literary episcopacy to keep one from writing what one thinks, or to punish one (financially) for having done so.

Perhaps as a warning to young writers who cannot afford the loss, one would be justified in printing the following:

"50*a* Albemarle Street, London, W.
22 October, 1914.

Dear Mr Pound,
Many thanks for your letter of the other day. I am afraid that I must say frankly that I do not think I can open the columns of the

Q.R.—at any rate, at present—to any one associated publicly with such a publication as *Blast*. It stamps a man too disadvantageously.

Yours truly,

G. W. PROTHERO.

Of course, having accepted your paper on the *Noh*, I could not refrain from publishing it. But other things would be in a different category."

I need scarcely say that *The Quarterly Review* is one of the most profitable periodicals in England, and one of one's best 'connections', or sources of income. It has, of course, a tradition.

'It is not that Mr Keats (if that be his real name, for we almost doubt that any man in his senses would put his real name to such a rhapsody)'—

wrote their Gifford of Keats' *Endymion*. My only comment is that the *Quarterly* has done it again. Their Mr A. Waugh is a lineal descendant of Gifford, by the way of mentality. A century has not taught them manners. In the eighteen forties they were still defending the review of Keats. And more recently Waugh has lifted up his senile slobber against Mr Eliot. It is indeed time that the functions of both English and American literature were taken over by younger and better men.

As for their laying the birch on my pocket, I compute that my support of Lewis and Brzeska has cost me at the lowest estimate about £20 per year, from one source alone since that regrettable occurrence, since I dared to discern a great sculptor and a great painter in the midst of England's artistic desolation ('European and Asiatic papers please copy.')

Young men, desirous of finding before all things smooth berths and elderly consolations, are cautioned to behave more circumspectly.

The generation that preceded us does not care much whether we understand French individualism, or the difference between the good and bad in French literature. Nor is it conceivable that any of them would write to a foreigner: 'indications of ideas, rather than work accomplished, but I will send you my best.'

Gourmont's next communication to me was an inquiry about Gaudier-Brzeska's sculpture.

PART III
Contemporaries

LIONEL JOHNSON[1]

ATraditionalist of traditionalists, his poems are criticism for the most part. One might almost say they are literary criticism in verse, for that is the impression which they leave, if one have laid them by for long enough to have an impression of the book as a whole, and not a confusion, not the many little contradictory impressions of individual poems. I am accustomed to meeting his friends, and his friends, with the sole exception of Mr Yeats, seem to regard him as a prose writer who inadvertently strayed into verse. His language is formal. It has an old-fashioned kind of precision that is very different from the sort of precision now sought, yet, in the dozen places where this stately and meticulous speech is moved by unwonted passion, Lionel Johnson has left poems as beautiful as any in English; as in the poem:

> Fair face gone from sight
>
> .   .   .   .
>
> Fair lips hushed in death
> Now their glad breath
> Breathes not upon our air
> Music, that saith
> Love only, and things fair.

Or in the poem to O'Leary:

> From Howth to Achil, the glad noise
> Rings: and the heirs of glory fall.

Or in the poem to Oliver Georges Destrée:

> In Merioneth, over the sad moor
> Drives the rain, the cold wind blows;
> Past the ruinous church door,
> The poor procession without music goes.
>
> The curlew cries
> Over her laid down beside
> Death's lonely people:

[1] Originally published as the Preface to *Poetical Works of Lionel Johnson*: Elkin Mathews, London, 1915.

I think I have been chosen to write this Preface largely because I am known to hold theories which some people think new, and which several people know to be hostile to much that hitherto had been accepted as 'classic' in English poetry; that is to say, I reverence Dante and Villon and Catullus; for Milton and Victorianism and for the softness of the 'nineties' I have different degrees of antipathy or even contempt. Mr Elkin Mathews wanted, I think, some definite proof that Lionel Johnson was still respected by a generation, or, if you will, by a clique, of younger poets who scoff at most things of his time. Now Lionel Johnson cannot be shown to be in accord with our present doctrines and ambitions. His language is a bookish dialect, or rather it is not a dialect, it is a curial speech and our aim is natural speech, the language as spoken. We desire the words of poetry to follow the natural order. We would write nothing that we might not say actually in life—under emotion. Johnson's verse is full of inversions, but no one has written purer Imagisme than he has, in the line

> Clear lie the fields, and fade into blue air.

It has a beauty like the Chinese.

Having held out for a uniform standard of appreciation, having insisted that one should weigh Theocritus and one's neighbour in one balance I cannot, for the sake even of courtesy, cast that standard aside. I do not, however, contradict it when I say that the natural speech of one decade is not the natural speech of another. In 1590 it was the fashion of the court to parley Euphues. Shakespeare's characters use a florid speech to show their good breeding, and 'Multitudinous seas incarnadine' probably got as much applause *quia* magniloquent as a witticism of Wilde's *quia* witty. In 1600 people were interested in painted speech. It was vital. It was part of the time. For a later age it is rank affectation. Some say the 'nineties' spoke as they wrote. I have heard it said that 'A generation of men came down from Oxford resolved to talk as prose had been written'. They had, presumably, the conviction that the speech of life and of poetry should be the same. They were quixotic. They loved the speech of books and proposed to make daily speech copy it.

Men of the Renaissance had done something like this. They wrote excellent Latin, but daily speech did not follow it. Lorenzo Valla wrote invectively as Johnson might have written elegiacally, 'linguam

latinam magnum sacramentum est.' And, indeed, Johnson wrote
Latin, as beautifully as Flaminius, so far did his reverence lead him.

> Defecit inter tenebris cor triste.

He would have been content always writing Latin, I think, but failing that, he set himself the task of bringing into English all that he
could of the fineness of Latinity. He wrote an English that had grown
out of Latin. He, at his worst, approached the Miltonian quagmire;
the old error of supposing that an uninflected language can be written
according to rules of order fit for an inflected speech and for that only.

Yet, because he is never florid, one remembers his work, or one
thinks of his work in one's memory as if it were speech in unruffled
order. One does this in spite of his inversion, in spite of the few
treasured archaisms, in spite of his 'spelling it *chaunted*'.

One thinks that he had read and admired Gautier, or that at least,
he had derived similar ambitions from some traditional source. One
thinks that his poems are in short hard sentences. The reality is that
they are full of definite statement. For better or worse they are
doctrinal and nearly always dogmatic. He had the blessed habit of
knowing his own mind, and this was rare among writers of his
decade.

The 'nineties' have chiefly gone out because of their muzziness,
because of a softness derived, I think, not from books but from
impressionist painting. They riot with half decayed fruit.

The impression of Lionel Johnson's verse is that of small slabs of
ivory, firmly combined and contrived. There is a constant feeling of
neatness, a sense of inherited order. Above all he respected his art.

From the Elizabethans to Swinburne, through all that vast hiatus,
English poetry had been the bear-garden of doctrinaires. It had been
the 'vehicle' of opinion. For Swinburne it was at least the art of
musical wording. For Johnson it was the art of good writing. The
last is a rare thing in England.

I think we respect Johnson to-day, in part for his hardness, in
part for his hatred of amateurishness. His sense of criticism is to be
gathered from his own prose, though I think it is never more clear
than in the notes sent to Katharine Tynan and printed by her after
his death (*Dublin Review*, October 1907). He had a tradition that the
printed page should be courteous, but here we find only his judgment stark naked. The list is as follows:

WATSON

An almost unfailing dignity of *external* manner; and always an *attempt* at an internal gravity and greatness, which sometimes succeeds, but most often when he is reflecting and commenting, not imagining. An understudy, as actors say, of the great men, Arnold, Wordsworth, etc., capable of deceiving you for a time by his airs of being the true master instead of a very serious and accomplished substitute. At his best he impresses by his frequent stateliness and purity of phrase, his freedom from positively bad work, and his sincere *desire* to be lofty and impassioned and fine. He will tell you, in felicitous phrases and with a grand air, that Duty is difficult and divine: and the poem will be just an honest and thoughtful moral essay aptly versified. Read Wordsworth's *Ode to Duty*, and Watson vanishes. He has *worked at poetry*, and has made himself a sonorous *orator*, a fine declaimer, a dexterous manager of words. He respects himself and the English language.

DAVIDSON

Powerful is the word: fervour, ardour, energy, rapid imagination and passion, sometimes heated and turbulent—a dash of Watson's sobriety would improve him. Intensely interested in *life* and its questions: a Scotch metaphysician turned into a romantic and realistic poet, without losing his *curiosity* about things. Versatile, experimentalist, prolific: writes ballads, which are psychological problems dramatically conceived and put, with wonderful beauty of language at moments, but with a certain lack of delicacy—the poems rush and dash at you, overpower and invigorate you, rather than charm and enchant you. A restless poet—a true countryman of Burns and Carlyle, who has read the Elizabethans, and Keats and Browning. Earthly in a good sense; loves facts and Darwin: dreams and wonders and imagines, but always with kind of robust consciousness. His beauty and his strength not in perfect accord. Take a poem of Watson; no amount of alteration would improve its decent and decorous mediocrity: Davidson's work often requires a last refining touch to transfigure it into a very wonderful thing. Hardest to estimate of all the younger poets: has tried so many ways and done so much. Has put genuine passion into his poetry, not an 'artistic' pose: full-blooded, generous, active: very human. Has not quite 'found himself' in literature or in life.

Le Gallienne

Prettiness; not beauty, which implies more imaginative thought and faith, than he possesses. Sensitive by temperament, and feels the *sentiment* of beautiful things in art and life, not their *truth*. A persistent note of—not vulgarity, nor bad taste—but of unconscious familiarity in a bad sense. He belittles things by his touch. When his subject is in itself trivial he can be charming: when it is high he does not rise to it. He prattles, chatters, which he thinks natural and simple: in dread of the 'academic' he becomes impertinent. A real love of poetry, utterly undisciplined and unintelligent: he is never to be trusted. Has enough culture not to be a 'self-taught' genius: and not enough to desire the discipline, the labour, the pains of art. Now and then is happily inspired, and is never quite contemptible: but usually very irritating. Conceivable, that he might write an Endymion: impossible, that he should ever write Hyperion or the Odes. Is too much the 'professional' poet, thinking of Chatterton and Keats and Shelley. Should take a long course of Arnold and Dr Johnson. Contrives to get a certain curious *personality* into his work, which either fascinates or exasperates.

Symons

A singular power of technique, and a certain imaginativeness of conception, mostly wasted upon insincere obscenities. Baudelaire and Verlaine generally ring true, and their horrors and squalors and miseries and audacities have the value and virtue of touching the reader to something of compassion or meditation. Symons no more does that than a teapot. 'This girl met me in the Haymarket, with a straw hat and a brown paper parcel, and the rest was a delirious delight: that girl I met outside a music hall, we had champagne, and the rest was an ecstasy of shame.' That is Symons. And this sort of thing in cadences of remarkable cleverness and delicacy! He can be pleasant and cleanly when he chooses: has written things of power and things of charm. But is a slave to impressionism, whether the impression be precious or no. A London fog, the blurred, tawny lamplights, the red omnibus, the dreary rain, the depressing mud, the glaring gin-shop, the slatternly shivering women: three dexterous stanzas, telling you that and nothing more. And in nearly every poem, one line or phrase of absolutely pure and fine imagination. If he would wash and be clean, he might be of the elect.

THOMPSON

Magnificently faulty at times, magnificently perfect at others. The ardours of poetry, taking you triumphantly by storm: a surging sea of verse, rising and falling and irresistibly advancing. Drunk with his inspiration, sometimes helplessly so: more often, he is merely fired and quickened, and remains master of himself. Has done more to harm the English language than the worst American newspapers: *corruptio optimi pessima*. Has the opulent, prodigal manner of the seventeenth century; a profusion of great imagery, sometimes excessive and false: and another opulence and profusion, that of Shelley in his lyric choruses. Beneath the outward manner, a passionate reality of thought: profound, pathetic, full of faith without fear. 'Words that, if you pricked them, would bleed,' as was said of Meredith. Incapable of prettiness and pettiness: for good and bad, always vehement and burning and—to use a despised word—sublime. *Sublime*, rather than *noble!* too fevered to be austere: a note of ardent suffering, not of endurance.

MICHAEL FIELD

Alone of the younger poets aims at tragedy above all other forms of poetry: the lyrics and sonnets are well enough, but the play is the thing. An imaginative grasp of historic tragedy, the clash of high passions and forces, the sense of destiny at work. Vigorous language, sometime over-Elizabethan, but never flat and tame. The earlier work the best: is becoming too subtle and eccentric, less broad and strong. Not afraid of attempting great work: no mincing delicacy, in the prevailing fashion. The plays are *dramatic*, moving, urgent: some scenes of extraordinary force, others of extraordinary grace. In a way, like Mrs Browning: ambitious, vehement, sometimes turbid and turgid and strained, but at least enamoured of strength and largeness.

VARIOUS

Horne and Image, both artists in many arts, both have published one book of verse: infinitely refined work; inspired scholarship; awaiting upon perfection, an admirable restraint; a somewhat old-world daintiness, clothing rather than concealing a very true and fine passion. Binyon: a beautiful seriousness, a gracious pensiveness, a sort of Puritanism and mild austerity: an artist in rhythms and music. Rhys: best in Celtic things of the gentler sort and in a kind of shy and reverent love-poetry. Benson: a quaint charm of moral meditation and loving intimacy with nature's 'little' things.

So sorry to have delayed: I have not been up to anything. These notes are very poor and hasty stuff, barely intelligible: but they try to be true. I say nothing of Beeching: you know him better than I. John Gray, perhaps, a sometimes beautiful oddity: not more. I send my *Chronicle* review of Yeats: will you return it at your leisure? Among the women poets, Madame Darmesteter comes high; far above Mrs Bland and Miss Blind and Mrs Marriott Watson. You might mention Dowson and Victor Plarr as men sure to be successful when their first books appear: Dowson you appreciate, I know: but Plarr is delightful, a kind of half-French, half-Celtic Dobson with nature and the past and dying traditions and wild races for his Theme. Radford: a very limited, but very true, lyrical gift of singular simplicity and 'forthrightness'.

If this rigmarole be of any service to you, 'twill be a wonder. L. J.

Allowing for a certain friendliness and for temporary enthusiasm, these judgments remain as he made them; that is, the estimates remain for us, in each case, true in kind, if a little less in degree.

He never pardoned in himself a fault which he would have detected, and perhaps even have condoned, in another. These criticisms were written about '95. Johnson is not the first poet of the 'nineties' to reach one. Perhaps that is only a confusion of my personal memory. In America ten or twelve years ago one read Fiona MacLeod, and Dowson, and Symons. One was guided by Mr Mosher of Bangor. I think I first heard of Johnson in an odd sort of post-graduate course conducted by Dr Weygandt. One was drunk with 'Celticism', and with Dowson's 'Cynara', and with one or two poems of Symons' 'Wanderers' and 'I am the torch she saith':

> I am the flame of beauty
> And I burn that all may see
> Beauty.

Johnson's poems were almost the last to catch one's attention. Their appeal is not so much to the fluffy, unsorted imagination of adolescence as to more hardened passion and intellect of early middle-age. I cannot speak of more than that. They hold their own now, not perhaps as a whole, but because of certain passages, because of that effect of neatness and hardness.

In the midst of enthusiasms one thinks perhaps that, if Gautier had not written, Johnson's work might even take its place in Welt-literatur, that it might stand for this clearness and neatness. In English literature it has some such place, with the writings of Arnold and of Christina Rossetti.[1] His attitude toward the past was prag-matical. He seemed to regard what had been as good, or as, at least, bearable. His taste was catholic. There is no use regretting this fault. He had its virtues. The 'Post Liminium' is a complete world of culture; his own, wrought out of worthy things. His mind was open-ly receptive. This gentleness sets him apart from our decade. But if he was traditionalist, he was so in the finest sense of that term. He really knew the tradition, the narrow tradition, that is, of English, Latin, and Greek. This intelligent acquaintance with the past differen-tiates him from the traditionalists of his time, and of ours.

He would, for instance, have welcomed good *vers libre;* he would have known how the Greeks had used it. You could have discussed with him any and every serious problem of technique, and this is certainly a distinction among 'the poets of England'. He might have differed from your views of good writing but he would have believed in good writing. His hatred of slovenliness would have equalled your own.

Accepting his belief that poetry was not 'a rendering of one's own time in the terms of one's own time' but a using of the lineal term in the purest sense of that lineage, one might well say of his few best poems, as Parrhasius said of his own:

φημὶ γὰρ ἤδη
τέχνης εὑρῆσθαι τέρματα τῆσδε σαφῆ
χειρὸς ὑφ' ἡμετέρης· ἀνυπέρβλητος δε πέπηγεν
οὖρος· ἀμώμητον δ' οὐδὲν ἔγεντο βροτοῖς.

And even without my restriction his language is, in a sense, *of* his time, though it would never have deigned to be the common speech. It was part of his fear of life, a fear that he was not afraid of, but which he openly acknowledged (Nihilism):

I shall be calm soon, with the calm death brings.
The skies are grey there, without any star.

[1] The *Wykehamist* contains a premature appreciation of Christina by L. J., but as it was written at a time when he was appreciating nearly everything indiscriminately, one cannot lay great store by it. He was also mad over Hugo.

His sense of traditional book-speech and his sense of traditional form combine to make him somewhat unreadable. He falls into stanza poems, that is to say into vain repetitions and weakenings of the original statement. For instance, the complete poem

> Man is a shadow's dream!
> Opulent Pindar saith:
> Yet man may win a gleam
> Of glory, before death.

is carried on into a series of strophes and is probably weakened by quoting 'golden Shakespear' in the second of them. The inversions do not lend it vitality. The beautiful poem beginning 'In Merioneth' is to my sense complete without the last stanza, though I dare say our fashion is no more permanent than his fashion, but we are done with imaginative reason—at least for our time. Poetry is concerned with statement, not with arguments and conversions. This is no more than saying of Johnson what one must say of all save the greatest poets; that a part of his work is transient. *Pars labitinam vitabit.*[1]

II

As the editor of this complete book of his verse it is perhaps rash for me to discriminate between the few scattered poems which were not included in the two volumes published during his lifetime. His last volume appeared five years before his death. He died suddenly. He had no time to put his house in order. A hospitality to late work should not however apply to early work rejected by him, I mean, to the boy's poems published, often under pseudonyms in a school paper, the *Wykehamist*.

It was quite natural that Johnson at seventeen should have been writing Swinburniania:

> Before the winds awaken
>   The sleeping years;
> Before the stars are shaken
>   Within high spheres;
> Enough of old caresses, etc.

[1] Naturally one does not condemn 'the stanza poem' categorically. It has its use and its place. The villanelle, even, can at its best achieve the closest intensity, I mean when, as with Dowson, the refrains are an emotional fact, which the intellect, in the various gyrations of the poem, tries in vain and in vain to escape.

The above appears over the signature 'ICH' which Mr Scott Moncrieff, who has kindly lent us the *Wykehamist,* supposes to mean L. J., the editor himself. It is neither better nor worse than some of the other school verse, as for example an earlier version of the sapphics to Hugo, ending, 'Sappho salutes thee.' Though he never quite freed himself from slightly obvious alliterations, he was, by the time he came to publish, quite capable of discarding such lines as

> Tumult of monochordal mastery.

and

> Diaphanous lawns of dawn-light.

and one would do little credit to his memory by reprinting these verses. The first song printed over the 'ICH' signature opens gracefully:

> My lady lieth low along
>   A rippling rill;
> Smiling her little laugh-light song
> Lulling the air still
>
> Sweeter lady liveth none
>   Than my lady lives;
> To whom the burning red round sun
>   Clear beauty gives.

This was promptly parodied by someone signing himself 'V'. An early and more lengthy draft of *Julian at Eleusis* appeared in the *Wykehamist* in '86, but I think it better to print only his final version as it appeared in *Ireland and Other Poems* (1897). This is the earliest of his poems to which he later gave sanction. I omit also a long verse-letter to the editor of the *Wykehamist,* containing numerous names of poets, and the one pleasing passage:

> How many woo the beautiful
> To end in adoration of the dull!
> The dull is too much with you . . . .

I trust I have not transgressed in reprinting some few of the earlier poems.

THE PROSE TRADITION IN VERSE[1]

In a country in love with amateurs, in a country where the incompetent have such beautiful manners, and personalities so fragile and charming, that one cannot bear to injure their feelings by the introduction of competent criticism, it is well that one man should have a vision of perfection and that he should be sick to the death and disconsolate because he cannot attain it.

Mr Yeats wrote years ago that the highest poetry is so precious that one should be willing to search many a dull tome to find and gather the fragments. As touching poetry this was, perhaps, no new feeling. Yet where nearly everyone else is still dominated by an eighteenth-century verbalism, Mr Hueffer[2] has had this instinct for prose. It is he who has insisted, in the face of a still Victorian press, upon the importance of good writing as opposed to the opalescent word, the rhetorical tradition. Stendhal had said, and Flaubert, de Maupassant and Turgenev had proved, that 'prose was the higher art'—at least their prose.

Of course it is impossible to talk about perfection without getting yourself very much disliked. It is even more difficult in a capital where everybody's Aunt Lucy or Uncle George has written something or other, and where the victory of any standard save that of mediocrity would at once banish so many nice people from the temple of immortality. So it comes about that Mr Hueffer is the best critic in England, one might say the only critic of any importance. What he says to-day the press, the reviewers, who hate him and who disparage his books, will say in about nine years' time, or possibly sooner. Shelley, Yeats, Swinburne, with their 'unacknowledged legislators', with 'Nothing affects these people except our conversation', with 'The rest live under us'; Rémy de Gourmont, when he says that most men think only husks and shells of the thoughts that have been already lived over by others, have shown their very just appreciation of the system of echoes, of the general vacuity of public

---

[1] *Poetry* (Chicago), 1914.

[2] Ford Madox Ford, the novelist. He changed his name from Hueffer to Ford at some time after the outbreak of the war of 1914-18.—Ed.

opinion. America is like England, America is very much what England would be with the two hundred most interesting people removed. One's life is the score of this two hundred with whom one happens to have made friends. I do not see that we need to say the rest live under them, but it is certain that what these people say comes to pass. They live in their mutual credence, and thus they live things over and fashion them before the rest of the world is aware. I dare say it is a Cassandra-like and useless faculty, at least from the world's point of view. Mr Hueffer has possessed the peculiar faculty of 'foresight', or of constructive criticism, in a pre-eminent degree. Real power will run any machine. Mr Hueffer said fifteen years ago that a certain unknown Bonar Law would lead the conservative party. Five years ago he said with equal impartiality that D. H. Lawrence would write notable prose, that Mr de la Mare could write verses, and that *Chance* would make Conrad popular.

Of course if you think things ten or fifteen or twenty years before anyone else thinks them you will be considered absurd and ridiculous. Mr Allen Upward, thinking with great lucidity along very different lines, is still considered absurd. Some professor feels that if certain ideas gain ground he will have to re-write his lectures, some parson feels that if certain other ideas are accepted he will have to throw up his position. They search for the forecaster's weak points.

Mr Hueffer is still underestimated for another reason also: namely, that we have not yet learned that prose is as precious and as much to be sought after as verse, even its shreds and patches. So that, if one of the finest chapters in English is hidden in a claptrap novel, we cannot weigh the vision which made it against the weariness or the confusion which dragged down the rest of the work. Yet we would do this readily with a poem. If a novel have a form as distinct as that of a sonnet, and if its workmanship be as fine as that of some Pleiade rondel, we complain of the slightness of the motive. Yet we would not deny praise to the rondel. So it remains for a prose craftsman like Arnold Bennett to speak well of Mr Hueffer's prose, and for a verse-craftsman like myself to speak well of his verses. And the general public will have little or none of him because he does not put on pontifical robes, because he does not take up the megaphone of some known and accepted pose, and because he makes enemies among the stupid by his rather engaging frankness.

We may as well begin reviewing the *Collected Poems* with the knowledge that Mr Hueffer is a keen critic and a skilled writer of prose, and we may add that he is not wholly unsuccessful as a composer, and that he has given us, in 'On Heaven', the best poem yet written in the 'twentieth-century fashion'.

I drag in these apparently extraneous matters in order to focus attention on certain phases of significance, which might otherwise escape the hurried reader in a volume where the actual achievement is uneven. Coleridge has spoken of 'the miracle that might be wrought simply by one man's feeling a thing more clearly or more poignantly than anyone had felt it before'. The last century showed us a fair example when Swinburne awoke to the fact that poetry was an art, not merely a vehicle for the propagation of doctrine. England and Germany are still showing the effects of his perception. I cannot belittle my belief that Mr Hueffer's realization that poetry should be written at least as well as prose will have as wide a result. He himself will tell you that it is 'all Christina Rossetti', and that 'it was not Wordsworth', for Wordsworth was so busied about the ordinary word that he never found time to think about *le mot juste*.

As for Christina, Mr Hueffer is a better critic than I am, and I would be the last to deny that a certain limpidity and precision are the ultimate qualities of style; yet I cannot accept his opinion. Christina had these qualities, it is true—in places, but they are to be found also in Browning and even in Swinburne at rare moments. Christina very often sets my teeth on edge—and so for that matter does Mr Hueffer. But it is the function of criticism to find what a given work is, rather than what it is not. It is also the faculty of a capital or of high civilization to value a man for some rare ability, to make use of him and not hinder him or itself by asking of him faculties which he does not possess.

Mr Hueffer may have found certain properties of style first, for himself, in Christina, but others have found them elsewhere, notably in Arnaut Daniel and in Guido, and in Dante, where Christina herself would have found them. Still there is no denying that there is less of the *ore rotundo* in Christina's work than in that of her contemporaries, and that there is also in Hueffer's writing a clear descent from such passages as:

> 'I listened to their honest chat:
> Said one: 'To-morrow we shall be

Plod plod along the featureless sands
    And coasting miles and miles of sea.'
Said one: 'Before the turn of tide
    We will achieve the eyrie-seat.'
Said one: 'To-morrow shall be like
    To-day, but much more sweet."

We find the qualities of what some people are calling 'the modern cadence' in this strophe, also in 'A Dirge', in 'Up Hill', in—

'Somewhere or other there must surely be
The face not seen, the voice not heard.'

and in—

'Sometimes I said: 'It is an empty name
I long for; to a name why should I give
The peace of all the days I have to live?'—
Yet gave it all the same.'

Mr Hueffer brings to his work a prose training such as Christina never had, and it is absolutely the devil to try to quote snippets from a man whose poems are gracious impressions, leisurely, low-toned. One would quote 'The Starling', but one would have to give the whole three pages of it. And one would like to quote patches out of the curious medley, 'To All the Dead'—save that the picturesque patches aren't the whole or the feel of it; or Sussmund's capricious 'Address', a sort of 'Inferno' to the 'Heaven' which we are printing for the first time in another part of this issue. But that also is too long, so I content myself with the opening of an earlier poem, 'Finchley Road'.

'As we come up at Baker Street
Where tubes and trains and 'buses meet
There's a touch of fog and a touch of sleet;
And we go on up Hampstead way
Toward the closing in of day. . . .

You should be a queen or a duchess rather,
Reigning, instead of a warlike father,
In peaceful times o'er a tiny town,
Where all the roads wind up and down
From your little palace—a small, old place
Where every soul should know your face
And bless your coming.'

I quote again, from a still earlier poem where the quiet of his manner is less marked:

'Being in Rome I wonder will you go
    Up to the hill. But I forget the name . . .
Aventine? Pincio? No: I do not know
    I was there yesterday and watched. You came.'

(I give the opening only to 'place' the second portion of the poem.)

'Though you're in Rome you will not go, my You,
    Up to that Hill. . . but I forget the name.
Aventine? Pincio? No, I never knew. . .
    I was there yesterday. You never came.

I have that Rome; and you, you have a Me,
You have a Rome, and I, I have my You;
My Rome is not your Rome: my You, not you.
     . . . . . For, if man knew woman
I should have plumbed your heart; if woman, man,
Your Me should be true I . . . If in your day—
You who have mingled with my soul in dreams,
You who have given my life an aim and purpose,
A heart, an imaged form—if in your dreams
You have imagined unfamiliar cities
And me among them, I shall never stand
Beneath your pillars or your poplar groves, . . .
Images, simulacra, towns of dreams
That never march upon each other's borders,
And bring no comfort to each other's hearts!'

I present this passage, not because it is an example of Mr Hueffer's no longer reminiscent style, but because, like much that appeared four years ago in 'Songs from London', or earlier still in 'From Inland', it hangs in my memory. And so little modern work does hang in one's memory, and these books created so little excitement when they appeared. One took them as a matter of course, and they're not a matter of course, and still less is the later work a matter of course. Oh well, you all remember the preface to the collected poems with its passage about the Shepherd's Bush exhibition, for it appeared first as a pair of essays in *Poetry*, so there is no need for me to speak further of Mr Hueffer's aims or of his prose, or of his power to render an impression.

There is in his work another phase that depends somewhat upon his knowledge of instrumental music. Dante has defined a poem[1] as a composition of words set to music, and the intelligent critic will demand that either the composition of words or the music shall possess a certain interest, or that there be some aptitude in their jointure together. It is true that since Dante's day—and indeed his day and Casella's saw a re-beginning of it—'music and 'poetry' have drifted apart, and we have had a third thing which is called 'word music'. I mean we have poems which are read or even, in a fashion, intoned, and are 'musical' in some sort of complete or inclusive sense that makes it impossible or inadvisable to 'set them to music'. I mean obviously such poems as the First Chorus of 'Atalanta' or many of Mr Yeats' lyrics. The words have a music of their own, and a second 'musician's' music is an impertinence or an intrusion.

There still remains the song to sing: to be 'set to music', and of this sort of poem Mr Hueffer has given us notable examples in his rendering of Von der Vogelweide's 'Tandaradei' and, in lighter measure, in his own 'The Three-Ten':

'When in the prime and May-day time dead lovers went a-walking,
How bright the grass in lads' eyes was, how easy poet's talking!
Here were green hills and daffodils, and copses to contain them:
Daisies for floors did front their doors agog for maids to chain them.
So when the ray of rising day did pierce the eastern heaven
Maids did arise to make the skies seem brighter far by seven.
Now here's a street where 'bus routes meet, and 'twixt the wheels and paving
Standeth a lout who doth hold out flowers not worth the having.
But see, but see! The clock strikes three above the Kilburn Station,
Those maids, thank God, are 'neath the sod and all their generation.

What she shall wear who'll soon appear, it is not hood nor wimple,
But by the powers there are no flowers so stately or so simple.
And paper shops and full 'bus tops confront the sun so brightly,
That, come three-ten, no lovers then had hearts that beat so lightly

[1] or at any rate a canzone.

As ours or loved more truly,
Or found green shades or flowered glades to fit their loves more
    duly.
And see, and see! 'Tis ten past three above the Kilburn Station,
Those maids, thank God! are 'neath the sod and all their generation.'

Oh well, there are very few song writers in England, and it's a
simple old-fashioned song with a note of futurism in its very lyric
refrain; and I dare say you will pay as little attention to it as I did
five years ago. And if you sing it aloud, once over, to yourself, I dare
say you'll be just as incapable of getting it out of your head, which
is perhaps one test of a lyric.

It is not, however, for Mr Hueffer's gift of song-writing that I
have reviewed him at such length; this gift is rare but not novel. I
find him significant and revolutionary because of his insistence upon
clarity and precision, upon the prose tradition; in brief, upon
efficient writing—even in verse.

THE LATER YEATS[1]

Responsibilities, by W. B. Yeats. The Cuala Press, Churchtown, Dundrum.

I live, so far as possible, among that more intelligently active segment of the race which is concerned with today and tomorrow; and, in consequence of this, whenever I mention Mr Yeats I am apt to be assailed with questions: 'Will Mr Yeats do anything more?', 'Is Yeats in the movement?', 'How *can* the chap go on writing this sort of thing?'

And to these inquiries I can only say that Mr Yeats' vitality is quite unimpaired, and that I dare say he'll do a good deal; and that up to date no one has shown any disposition to supersede him as the best poet in England, or any likelihood of doing so for some time; and that after all Mr Yeats has brought a new music upon the harp, and that one man seldom leads two movements to triumph, and that it is quite enough that he should have brought in the sound of keening and the skirl of the Irish ballads, and driven out the sentimental cadence with memories of *The County of Mayo* and *The Coolun;* and that the production of good poetry is a very slow matter, and that, as touching the greatest of dead poets, many of them could easily have left that *magnam partem,* which keeps them with us, upon a single quire of foolscap or at most upon two; and that there is no need for a poet to repair each morning of his life to the *Piazza dei Signori* to turn a new sort of somersault; and that Mr Yeats is so assuredly an immortal that there is no need for him to recast his style to suit our winds of doctrine; and that, all these things being so, there is nevertheless a manifestly new note in his later work that they might do worse than attend to.

'Is Mr Yeats an Imagiste?' No, Mr Yeats is a symbolist, but he has written *des Images* as have many good poets before him; so that is nothing against him, and he has nothing against them (*les Imagistes*), at least so far as I know—except what he calls 'their devil's metres'.

He has written *des Images* in such poems as *Breasal and the Fisherman;* beginning, 'Though you hide in the ebb and flow of the

[1] Reprinted from *Poetry,* IV, 11 (May 1914).

pale tide when the moon has set'; and he has driven out the inversion and written with prose directness in such lyrics as, 'I heard the old men say everything alters'; and these things are not subject to a changing of the fashions. What I mean by the new note—you could hardly call it a change of style—was apparent four years ago in his *No Second Troy*, beginning, 'Why should I blame her,' and ending—

> Beauty like a tightened bow, a kind
> That is not natural in any age like this,
> Being high and solitary and most stern?
> Why, what could she have done being what she is?
> Was there another Troy for her to burn?

I am not sure that it becomes apparent in partial quotation, but with the appearance of *The Green Helmet and Other Poems* one felt that the minor note—I use the word strictly in the musical sense—had gone or was going out of his poetry; that he was at such a cross roads as we find in

> *Voi che intendendo il terzo ciel movete.*

And since that time one has felt his work becoming gaunter, seeking greater hardness of outline. I do not say that this is demonstrable by any particular passage. *Romantic Ireland's Dead and Gone* is no better than Red Hanrahan's song about Ireland, but it is harder. Mr Yeats appears to have seen with the outer eye in *To a Child Dancing on the Shore* (the first poem, not the one printed in this issue). The hardness can perhaps be more easily noted in *The Magi*.

Such poems as *When Helen Lived* and *The Realists* serve at least to show that the tongue has not lost its cunning. On the other hand, it is impossible to take any interest in a poem like *The Two Kings*— one might as well read the *Idylls* of another. *The Grey Rock* is, I admit, obscure, but it outweighs this by a curious nobility, a nobility which is, to me at least, the very core of Mr Yeats' production, the constant element of his writing.

In support of my prediction, or of my theories, regarding his change of manner, real or intended, we have at least two pronouncements of the poet himself, the first in *A Coat*,[1] and the second, less formal, in the speech made at the Blunt presentation.[2] The verses, *A*

[1] *Vide* this issue, page 60.
[2] *Vide* POETRY for March, 1914, p. 223.

Coat, should satisfy those who have complained of Mr Yeats' four and forty followers, that they would 'rather read their Yeats in the original'. Mr Yeats had indicated the feeling once before with

> Tell me, do the wolf-dogs praise their fleas?

which is direct enough in all conscience, and free of the 'glamour'. I've not a word against the glamour as it appears in Yeats' early poems, but we have had so many other pseudo-glamours and glamourlets and mists and fogs since the nineties that one is about ready for hard light.

And this quality of hard light is precisely what one finds in the beginning of his *The Magi*:

> Now as at all times I can see in the mind's eye,
> In their stiff, painted clothes, the pale unsatisfied ones
> Appear and disappear in the blue depth of the sky
> With all their ancient faces like rain-beaten stones,
> And all their helms of silver hovering side by side.

Of course a passage like that, a passage of *imagisme,* may occur in a poem not otherwise *imagiste,* in the same way that a lyrical passage may occur in a narrative, or in some poem not otherwise lyrical. There have always been two sorts of poetry which are, for me at least, the most 'poetic'; they are firstly, the sort of poetry which seems to be music just forcing itself into articulate speech, and secondly, that sort of poetry which seems as if sculpture or painting were just forced or forcing itself into words. The gulf between evocation and description, in this latter case, is the unbridgeable difference between genius and talent. It is perhaps the highest function of art that it should fill the mind with a noble profusion of sounds and images, that it should furnish the life of the mind with such accompaniment and surrounding. At any rate Mr Yeats' work has done this in the past and still continues to do so. The present volume contains the new metrical version of *The Hour Glass, The Grey Rock, The Two Kings,* and over thirty new lyrics, some of which have appeared in these pages, or appear in this issue. In the poems on the Irish gallery we find this author certainly at *prise* with things as they are and no longer romantically Celtic, so that a lot of his admirers will be rather displeased with the book. That is always a gain for a poet, for his admirers nearly always want him to 'stay put', and they resent any signs of stirring, of new curiosity or of intellectual uneasiness. I have said that *The Grey Rock* was obscure; perhaps I should not have said so, but I think it demands unusually close attention. It is as obscure, at least, as *Sordello*, but I can not close without registering my admiration for it all the same.

ROBERT FROST[1] (TWO REVIEWS)

A Boy's Will, by Robert Frost, David Nutt, London

> I had withdrawn in forest, and my song
> was swallowed up in leaves.

There is another personality in the realm of verse, another American, found, as usual, on this side of the water, by an English publisher long known as a lover of good letters. David Nutt publishes at his own expense *A Boy's Will*, by Robert Frost, the latter having been long scorned by the 'great American editors'. It is the old story.

Mr Frost's book is a little raw, and has in it a number of infelicities; underneath them it has the tang of the New Hampshire woods, and it has just this utter sincerity. It is not post-Miltonic or post-Swinburnian or post-Kiplonian. This man has the good sense to speak naturally and to paint the thing, the thing as he sees it. And to do this is a very different matter from gunning about for the circumplectious polysyllable.

It is almost on this account that it is a difficult book to quote from.

> She's glad her simple worsted gray
> Is silver now with clinging mist—

does not catch your attention. The lady is praising the autumn rain, and he ends the poem, letting her talk.

> Not yesterday I learned to know
>   The love of bare November days,
> Before the coming of the snow;
>   But it were vain to tell her so,
> And they are better for her praise.

Or again:

[1] The review of *A Boy's Will* appeared in *The New Freewoman*, London, in September 1913. The review of *North of Boston* appeared in *Poetry*, V, 3 (December 1914).

> There was never a sound beside the wood but one,
> And that was my long scythe whispering to the ground.
> . . . .
> My long scythe whispered and left the hay to make.

I remember that I was once canoeing and thirsty and I put in to a shanty for water and found a man there who had no water and gave me cold coffee instead. And he didn't understand it, he was from a minor city and he 'just set there watchin' the river' and didn't 'seem to want to go back', and he didn't much care for anything else. And so I presume he entered into Ananda. And I remember Joseph Campbell telling me of meeting a man on a desolate waste of bogs, and he said to him. 'It's rather dull here;' and the man said, 'Faith, ye can sit on a middan and dream stars.'

And that is the essence of folk poetry with distinction between America and Ireland. And Frost's book reminded me of these things.

There is perhaps as much of Frost's personal tone in the following little catch, which is short enough to quote, as in anything else. It is to his wife, written when his grandfather and his uncle had disinherited him of a comfortable fortune and left him in poverty because he was a useless poet instead of a money-getter.

IN NEGLECT

> They leave us so to the way we took,
>   As two in whom they were proved mistaken,
> That we sit sometimes in a wayside nook,
> With mischievous, vagrant, seraphic look,
>   And *try* if we cannot feel forsaken.

There are graver things, but they suffer too much by making excerpts. One reads the book for the 'tone', which is homely, by intent, and pleasing, never doubting that it comes direct from his own life, and that no two lives are the same.

He has now and then such a swift and bold expression as

> The whimper of hawks beside the sun.

He has now and then a beautiful simile, well used, but he is for the most part as simple as the lines I have quoted in opening or as in the poem of mowing. He is without sham and without affectation.

North of Boston, by Robert Frost. David Nutt, London.

It is a sinister thing that so American, I might even say so parochial, a talent as that of Robert Frost should have to be exported before it can find due encouragement and recognition.

Even Emerson had sufficient elasticity of mind to find something in the 'yawp'. One doesn't need to like a book or a poem or a picture in order to recognize artistic vigor. But the typical American editor of the last twenty years has resolutely shut his mind against serious American writing. I do not exaggerate, I quote exactly, when I say that these gentlemen deliberately write to authors that such and such a matter is 'too unfamiliar to our readers'.

There was once an American editor who would even print me, so I showed him Frost's *Death of the Hired Man*. He wouldn't have it; he had printed a weak pseudo-Masefieldian poem about a hired man two months before, one written in a stilted pseudo-literary language, with all sorts of floridities and worn-out ornaments.

Mr Frost is an honest writer, writing from himself, from his own knowledge and emotion; not simply picking up the manner which magazines are accepting at the moment, and applying it to topics in vogue. He is quite consciously and definitely putting New England rural life into verse. He is not using themes that anybody could have cribbed out of Ovid.

There are only two passions in art; there are only love and hate— with endless modifications. Frost has been honestly fond of the New England people, I dare say with spells of irritation. He has given their life honestly and seriously. He has never turned aside to make fun of it. He has taken their tragedy as tragedy, their stubbornness as stubbornness. I know more of farm life than I did before I had read his poems. That means I know more of 'Life'.

Mr Frost has dared to write, and for the most part with success, in the natural speech of New England; in natural spoken speech, which is very different from the 'natural' speech of the newspapers, and of many professors. His poetry is a bit slow, but you aren't held up every five minutes by the feeling that you are listening to a fool; so perhaps you read it just as easily and quickly as you might read the verse of some of the sillier and more 'vivacious' writers.

A sane man knows that a prose story can't be much better than the short stories of De Maupassant or of 'Steve' Crane. Frost's work is interesting, incidentally, because there has been during the last few years an effort to proceed from the prose short story to the short story in verse. Francis Jammes has done a successful novel in verse, in a third of the space a prose novel would have taken—*Existences* in *La Triomphe de la Vie*. Vildrac and D. H. Lawrence have employed verse successfully for short stories. Masefield is not part of this movement. He has avoided all the difficulties of the immeasurably difficult art of good prose by using a slap-dash, flabby verse which has been accepted in New Zealand. Jammes, Vildrac and Lawrence have lived up to the exigencies of prose and have gained by brevity. This counts with serious artists.

Very well, then, Mr Frost holds up a mirror to nature, not an oleograph. It is natural and proper that I should have to come abroad to get printed, or that 'H. D.'—with her clear-cut derivations and her revivifications of Greece—should have to come abroad ; or that Fletcher—with his *tic* and his discords and his contrariety and extended knowledge of everything—should have to come abroad. One need not censure the country; it is easier for us to emigrate than for America to change her civilization fast enough to please us. But why, IF there are serious people in America, desiring literature of America, literature accepting present conditions, rendering American life with sober fidelity— why, in heaven's name, is this book of New England eclogues given us under a foreign imprint?

Professors to the contrary notwithstanding, no one expects Jane Austen to be as interesting as Stendhal. A book about a dull, stupid, hemmed-in sort of life, by a person who has lived it, will never be as interesting as the work of some author who has comprehended many men's manners and seen many grades and conditions of existence. But Mr Frost's people are distinctly real. Their speech is real; he has known them. I don't want much to meet them, but I know that they exist, and what is more, that they exist as he has portrayed them.

Mr Frost has humour, but he is not its victim. *The Code* has a pervasive humor, the humor of things as they are, not that of an author trying to be funny, or trying to 'bring out' the ludicrous phase of some incident or character because he dares not rely on sheer presentation. There is nothing more nauseating to the developed mind than that sort of local buffoonery which the advertisements call 'racy'—the village wit presenting some village joke which is worn out everywhere else. It is a great comfort to find someone who tries to give life, the life of the rural district, as a whole, evenly, and not merely as a hook to hang jokes on. The easiest thing to see about a man is an eccentric or worn-out garment, and one is god-forsakenly tired of the post-Bret-Hartian, post-Mark-Twainian humorist.

Mr Frost's work is not 'accomplished', but it is the work of a man who will make neither concessions nor pretences. He will perform no monkey-tricks. His stuff sticks in your head—not his words, nor his phrases, nor his cadences, but his subject matter. You do not confuse one of his poems with another in your memory. His book is a contribution to American literature, the sort of sound work that will develop into very interesting literature if persevered in.

I don't know that one is called upon to judge between the poems in *North of Boston*. *The Death of the Hired Man* is perhaps the best, or *The Housekeeper*, though here the construction is a bit straggly. There are moments in *Mending Wall*. *The Black Cottage* is very clearly stated.

D. H. LAWRENCE[1]

Love Poems and Others, by D. H. Lawrence. Duckworth.

The *Love Poems,* if by that Mr Lawrence means the middling-sensual erotic verses in this collection, are a sort of pre-raphaelitish slush, disgusting or very nearly so. The attempts to produce the typical Laurentine line have brought forth:

> I touched her and she shivered like a dead snake.

which was improved by an even readier parodist, to

> I touched her and she came off in scales.

Jesting aside, when Mr Lawrence ceases to discuss his own disagreeable sensations, when he writes low-life narrative, as he does in *Whether or Not* and in *Violets,* there is no English poet under forty who can get within shot of him. That Masefield should be having a boom seems, as one takes count of these poems, frankly ridiculous.

It is no more possible to quote from them as illustration than it would be to illustrate a Rembrandt by cutting off two inches of canvas. The first is in mood-ridden *chiaroscuro,* the characters being a policeman, his sweetheart, his mother, and a widow who has taken advantage of his excitement and by whom he has had a child. It is sullen and heavy, and as ugly as such a tale must be.

> Yi, tha'rt a man, tha'rt a fine big man, but never a baby had eyes
> As sulky an' ormin as thine.

> I damn well shanna marry 'er,
> So chew at it no more,
> Or I'll chuck the flamin' lot of you—
> You needn't have swore.

So much for the tonality. Kipling has never done it as well in verse, though he gets something like the same range in his prose of *Bedelia Harrodsfoot.* The comparison with Masefield is, as I have said, ridiculous. It is what Masefield would like to do and can not.

[1] This review of *Love Poems and Others* appeared in *Poetry,* II, 4 (July 1913).

Violets presents two girls and another at the funeral of a young fellow who has died among

> Pals worse n'r any name as you could call.

> Ah know tha liked 'im better nor me. But let
> Me tell thee about this lass. When you had gone
> Ah stopped behind on t' pad i' th' drippin' wet
> An' watched what 'er 'ad on.

If this book does not receive the Polignac prize[1] a year from this November, there will be due cause for scandal.

Mr Lawrence was 'discovered' by Ford Madox Hueffer during the latter's editorship of the *English Review,* about four years ago. Some of his verses appeared then, and he has since made a notable reputation by his prose works, *The White Peacock* and *The Trespasser.*

His prose training stands him in good stead in these poems. The characters are real. They are not stock figures of 'the poor,' done from the outside and provided with *cliché* emotions.

> I expect you know who I am, Mrs Naylor!
> —Who yer are? yis, you're Lizzie Stainwright.
> An 'appen you might guess what I've come for?
> —'Appen I mightn't, 'appen I might.

Mr Lawrence has attempted realism and attained it. He has brought contemporary verse up to the level of contemporary prose, and that is no mean achievement.

[1] This prize, awarded by the British academic committee to Walter de la Mare in 1911, to Masefield in 1912, is given for a work of imagination which must have appeared before the November previous.

DR WILLIAMS' POSITION[1]

I

There is an anecdote told me by his mother, who wished me to understand his character, as follows: The young William Carlos, aged let us say about seven, arose in the morning, dressed and put on his shoes. Both shoes buttoned on the left side. He regarded this untoward phenomenon for a few moments and then carefully removed the shoes, placed shoe *a* that had been on his left foot, on his right foot, and shoe *b*, that had been on the right foot, on his left foot; both sets of buttons again appeared on the left side of the shoes.

This stumped him. With the shoes so buttoned he went to school, but ... and here is the significant part of the story, he spent the day in careful consideration of the matter.

It happens that this type of sensibility, persisting through forty years, is of extreme, and almost unique, value in a land teeming with clever people, all capable of competent and almost instantaneous extroversion; during the last twenty of these years it has distinguished Dr Williams from the floral and unconscious minds of the populace and from the snappy go-getters who'der seen wot wuz rong in er moment.

It has prevented our author from grabbing ready-made conclusions, and from taking too much for granted.

There are perhaps, or perhaps have been milieux where the reflective and examining habits would not have conferred, unsupported, a distinction. But chez nous, for as long as I can remember if an article appeared in Munsey's or McClure's, expressing a noble passion (civic or other) one could bank (supposing one were exercising editorial or quasi-editorial functions) on seeing the same article served up again in some fifty lyric expressions within, let us say, three or four months.

Our national mind hath about it something 'marvellous porous'; an idea or notion dropped into New York harbour emerges in Santa Fé or Galveston, watered, diluted, but still the same idea or notion, pale but not wholly denatured; and the time of transit is very

[1] *Dial*, Nov. 1928.

considerably lower, than any 'record' hitherto known. We have the defects of our qualities, and that very alertness which makes the single American diverting or enlivening in an European assembly often undermines his literary capacity.

For fifteen or eighteen years I have cited Williams as sole known American-dwelling author who could be counted on to oppose some sort of barrier to such penetration; the sole catalectic in whose presence some sort of modification would take place.

Williams has written: 'All I do is to try to understand something in its natural colours and shapes.' There could be no better effort underlying any literary process, or used as preparative for literary process; but it appears, it would seem, almost incomprehensible to men dwelling west of the Atlantic: I don't mean that it appears so in theory, America will swallow anything in theory, all abstract statements are perfectly welcome, given a sufficiently plausible turn. But the concrete example of this literary process, whether by Williams or by that still more unreceived and uncomprehended native hickory Mr Joseph Gould, seems an unrelated and inexplicable incident to our populace and to our 'monde—or whatever it is—littéraire'. We have, of course, distinctly American authors, Mr Frost for example, but there is an infinite gulf between Mr Frost on New England customs, and Mr Gould on race prejudice; Mr Frost having simply taken on, without any apparent self-questioning, a definite type and set of ideas and sensibilities, known and established in his ancestral demesne. That is to say he is 'typical New England'. Gould is no less New England, but parts of his writing could have proceeded equally well from a Russian, a German, or an exceptional Frenchman —the difference between regionalism, or regionalist art and art that has its root in a given locality.

Carlos Williams has been determined to stand or sit as an American. Freud would probably say 'because his father was English' (in fact half English, half Danish). His mother, as ethnologists have before noted, was a mixture of French and Spanish; of late years (the last four or five) Dr Williams has laid claim to a somewhat remote Hebrew connexion, possibly a rabbi in Saragossa, at the time of the siege. He claims American birth, but I strongly suspect that he emerged on shipboard just off Bedloe's Island and that his dark and serious eyes gazed up in their first sober contemplation at the Statue and its brazen and monstrous nightshirt.

At any rate he has not in his ancestral endocrines the arid curse of our nation. None of his immediate forebears burnt witches in Salem,[1] or attended assemblies for producing prohibitions. His father was in the rum trade; the rich ichors of the Indes, Hollands, Jamaicas, Goldwasser, Curaoças provided the infant William with material sustenance. Spanish was not a strange tongue, and the trade profited by discrimination, by dissociations performed with the palate. All of which belongs to an American yesterday, and is as gone as les caves de Mouquin.

From this secure ingle William Carlos was able to look out of his circumjacence and see it as something interesting *but exterior;* and he could not by any possibility resemble any member of the Concord School. He was able to observe national phenomena without necessity for constant vigilance over himself, there was no instinctive fear that if he forgot himself he might be like some really unpleasant Ralph Waldo; neither is he, apparently, filled with any vivid desire to murder the indescribable dastards who betray the work of the national founders, who spread the fish-hooks of bureaucracy in our once, perhaps, pleasant bypaths.

One might accuse him of being, blessedly, the observant foreigner, perceiving American vegetation and landscape quite directly, as something put there for him to look at; and his contemplative habit extends, also blessedly, to the fauna.

When Mr Wanamaker's picture gallery burned in the dead of winter I was able to observe the destruction of faked Van Dykes, etc., *comme spectacle*, the muffler'd lads of the village tearing down gold frames in the light of the conflagration, the onyx-topped tables against the blackness were still more 'tableau' and one could think detachedly of the French Revolution. Mr Wanamaker was nothing to me, he paid his employees badly, and I knew the actual spectacle was all I should ever get out of him. I cannot, on the other hand, observe the nation befouled by Volsteads and Bryans, without anger; I cannot see liberties that have lasted for a century thrown away for nothing, for worse than nothing, for slop; frontiers tied up by an imbecile bureaucracy exceeding 'anything known in Russia under the Czars' without indignation.[2]

---

[1] Note: We didn't burn them, we hanged them. T. S. E.

[2] This comparison to Russia is not mine, but comes from a Czarist official who had been stationed in Washington.

And by just this susceptibility on my part Williams, as author, has the no small advantage. If he wants to 'do' anything about what he sees, this desire for action does not rise until he has meditated in full and at leisure. Where I see scoundrels and vandals, he sees a spectacle or an ineluctable process of nature. Where I want to kill at once, he ruminates, and if this rumination leads to anger it is an almost inarticulate anger, that may but lend colour to style, but which stays almost wholly in the realm of his art. I mean it is a qualificative, contemplative, does not drive him to some ultra-artistic or non-artistic activity.

Even recently where one of his characters clearly expresses a dissatisfaction with the American milieu, it is an odium against a condition of mind, not against overt acts or institutions.

II

The lack of celerity in his process, the unfamiliarity with facile or with established solutions would account for the irritation his earlier prose, as I remember it, caused to sophisticated Britons. 'How any man could go on talking about such things!' and so on. But the results of this sobriety of unhurried contemplation, when apparent in such a book as *The American Grain*, equally account for the immediate appreciation of Williams by the small number of French critics whose culture is sufficiently wide to permit them to read any modern tongue save their own.

Here, at last, was an America treated with a seriousness and by a process comprehensible to an European.

One might say that Williams has but one fixed idea, as an author; i.e., he starts where an European would start if an European were about to write of America: sic: America is a subject of interest, one must inspect it, analyse it, and treat it as subject. There are plenty of people who think they 'ought' to write 'about' America. This is a wholly different kettle of fish. There are also numerous people who think that the given subject has an inherent interest simply because it is American and that this gives it ipso facto a dignity or value above all other possible subjects; Williams may even think he has, or may once have thought he had this angle of attack, but he hasn't.

After a number of years, and apropos of a given incident he has (first quarterly number of *Transition*) given a perfectly clear verbal manifestation of his critical attitude. It is that of his most worthy

European contemporaries, and of all good critics. It is also symptomatic of New York that his analysis of the so-called criticisms of Antheil's New York concert should appear in Paris, a year after the event, in an amateur periodical.

The main point of his article being that no single one of the critics had made the least attempt at analysis, or had in any way tried to tell the reader what the music consisted of, what were its modes or procedures. And that this was, of course, what the critics were, or would in any civilised country have been, there for. This article is perhaps Williams' most important, or at any rate most apposite, piece of critical writing; failing a wide distribution of the magazine in which it appeared, it should be reprinted in some more widely distributable journal.

It would seem that the illusion of 'progress' is limited, chez nous, to the greater prevalence of erotic adventure, whether developed in quality or merely increased in quantity I have no present means of deciding; the illusion as to any corresponding 'progress' or catchingup in affairs of the intellect, would seem to rise from the fact that in our literary milieux certain things are now known that were not known in 1912; but this does not constitute a change of relation, i.e. does not prove that America is not still fifteen years or twenty years or more 'behind the times'. We must breed a non-Mabie, non-Howells type of author. And of the possible types Williams and Gould serve as our best examples—as distinct from the porous types.

I mean, not by this sentence, but by the whole trend of this article: when a creative act occurs in America 'no one' seems aware of what is occurring. In music we have chefs d'orchestre, not composers, and we have something very like it in letters, though the distinction is less obvious.

Following this metaphor, it is undeniable that part of my time, for example, has been put into orchestral directing. Very little of Dr Williams' energy has been so deflected. If he did some Rimbaud forty years late it was nevertheless composition, and I don't think he knew it was Rimbaud until after he finished his operation.

Orchestral directing is 'all right' mais c'est pas la même chose. We are still so generally obsessed by monism and monotheistical backwash, and ideas of orthodoxy that we (and the benighted Britons) can hardly observe a dissociation of ideas without thinking a censure is somehow therein implied.

We are not, of course we are not, free from the errors of post-reformation Europe. The triviality of philosophical writers through the last few centuries is extraordinary, in the extent that is, that they have not profited by modes of thought quite common to biological students; in the extent that they rely on wholly unfounded assumptions, for no more apparent reason than that these assumptions are currently and commonly made. Reputed philosophers will proceed (four volumes at a time) as if the only alternative for monism were dualism; among distinguished literati, si licet, taking personal examples: Mr Joyce will argue for hours as if one's attack on Christianity were an attack on the Roman church *in favour of* Luther or Calvin or some other half-baked ignoramus and the 'protestant' conventicle. Mr Eliot will reply, even in print, to Mr Babbitt as if some form of Christianity or monotheism were the sole alternative to irreligion; and as if monism or monotheism were anything more than an hypothesis agreeable to certain types of very lazy mind too weak to bear an uncertainty or to remain in 'uncertainty'.

And, again, for such reasons William Williams, and may we say, his Mediterranean equipment, have an importance in relation to his temporal intellectual circumjacence.

Very well, he does not 'conclude'; his work has been 'often formless', 'incoherent', opaque, obscure, obfuscated, confused, truncated, etc.

I am not going to say: 'form' is a non-literary component shoved on to literature by Aristotle or by some non-litteratus who told Aristotle about it. Major form is not a non-literary component. But it can do us no harm to stop an hour or so and consider the number of very important chunks of world-literature in which form, major form, is remarkable mainly for absence.

There is a corking plot to the *Iliad*, but it is not told us in the poem or at least not in the parts of the poem known to history as The Iliad. It would be hard to find a worse justification of the theories of dramatic construction than the *Prometheus* of Aeschylus. It will take a brighter lad than the author of these presents to demonstrate the element of form in Montaigne or in Rabelais; Lope has it, but it is not the 'Aristotelian' beginning, middle and end, it is the quite reprehensible: BEGINNING WHOOP and then any sort of a trail off. *Bouvard and Pécuchet* wasn't even finished by its author. And of all these Lope is the only one we could sacrifice without inestimable loss and impoverishment.

The component of these great works and *the* indispensable component is texture; which Dr Williams indubitably has in the best, and in increasingly frequent, passages of his writing.

III

In current American fiction that has, often, quite a good deal of merit, and which has apparently been concocted with effort and goodish intentions, the failure to attain first-rateness seems to be mainly of two sorts: The post-Zolas or post-realists deal with subject matter, human types, etc., so simple that one is more entertained by Fabre's insects or Hudson's birds and wild animals. The habits or the reactions of 'an ant' or 'a chaffinch' emerge in a more satisfactory purity or at least in some modus that at least seems to present a more firm and sustaining pabulum to reflection.

Secondly: there are the perfumed writers. They aim, one believes, at olde lavender; but the ultimate aroma lacks freshness. 'Stale meringue', 'last week's custard' and other metaphorical expressions leap to mind when one attempts to give an impression of their quality. One 'ought' perhaps to make a closer analysis and give the receipt for the fadeur; though like all mediocre dilutations it is harder to analyse than the clearer and fresher substance. When I was fourteen, people used to read novels of the same sort, let us say *The House of a Thousand Candles*, etc., of which one may remember a title, but never remembers anything else, and of which the author's name has, at the end of five or ten years, escaped one.

It is perfectly natural that people wholly surrounded by roughnecks, whether in mid-nineteenth century or in The Hesperian present, should want to indicate the desirability of sweetness and refinement, but . . . these things belong to a different order of existence, different that is from pity, terror, τὸ καλόν, and those things with which art, plastic or that of the writer, is concerned.

Now in reading Williams, let us say this last book *A Voyage to Pagany* or almost anything else he has written, one may often feel: he is wrong. I didn't mean wrong in idea, but: that is the wrong way to write it. He oughtn't to have said that. But there is a residue of effect. The work is always distinct from writing that one finds merely hopeless and in strict sense irremediable.

There is a difference in kind between it and the mass of current writing, about which there is just nothing to be done, and which no series of re-touches, or cuttings away, would clarify, or leave hard.

Art very possibly *ought* to be the supreme achievement, the 'accomplished'; but there is the other satisfactory effect, that of a man hurling himself at an indomitable chaos, and yanking and hauling as much of it as possible into some sort of order (or beauty), aware of it both as chaos and as potential.

Form is, indeed, very tiresome when in reading current novels, we observe the thinning residue of pages, 50, 30, and realize that there is now only time (space) for the hero to die a violent death, no other solution being feasible in that number of pages.

To come at it another way: There are books that are clever enough, good enough, well enough done to fool the people who don't know, or to divert one in hours of fatigue. There are other books—and they may be often less clever, and may often show less accomplishment— which, despite their ineptitudes, and lack of accomplishment, or 'form', and finish, contain something for the best minds of the time, a time, any time. If *Pagany* is not Williams' best book, if even on some counts, being his first long work, it is his worst, it indubitably contains pages and passages that are worth any one's while, and that provide mental cud for any ruminant tooth.

IV

And finally, to comply with those requirements for critics which Dr Williams has outlined in his censure of Mr Antheil's critics: The particular book that is occasion for this general discussion of Williams, *A Voyage to Pagany*,[1] has not very much to do with the 'art of novel writing', which Dr Williams has fairly clearly abjured. Its plot-device is the primitive one of 'a journey', frankly avowed. Entire pages could have found place in a simple autobiography of travel.

In the genealogy of writing it stems from *Ulysses*, or rather we would say better: Williams' *The Great American Novel*, 80 pages, Three Mountains Press, 1923, was Williams' first and strongest derivation from *Ulysses*, an 'inner monologue', stronger and more gnarled, or stronger *because* more gnarled at least as I see it, than the *Pagany*.

---

[1] *A Voyage to Pagany*, by William Carlos Williams (The Macaulay Company 10mo., 338 pages, $2.50).

The other offspring from *Ulysses*, the only other I have seen possessing any value, is John Rodker's *Adolphe*, 1920. The two books are greatly different. *The Great American Novel* is simply the application of Joycean method to the American circumjacence. The *Adolphe*, professedly taking its schema from Benjamin Constant, brings the Joycean methodic inventions into a form; slighter than *Ulysses*, as a rondeau is slighter than a canzone, but indubitably a 'development', a definite step in general progress of writing; having, as have at least two other novels by Rodker, its definite shaped construction. And yet, if one read it often enough, the element of form emerges in *The Great American Novel*, not probably governing the whole, but in the shaping of at least some of the chapters, notably Chapter VII, the one beginning 'Nuevo Mundo'.

As to subject or problem, the *Pagany* relates to the Jamesian problem of U.S.A. *v.* Europe, the international relation, etc.; the particular equation of the Vienna milieu has had recent treatment 'from the other end on' in Joseph Bard's *Shipwreck in Europe*, more sprightly and probably less deeply concerned with the salvation of the protagonist; I think the continental author mentions as a general and known post-war quantity; the American or Americans who comes or come to Vienna to find out why they can't enjoy life, even after getting a great deal of money.

The American Grain remains, I imagine, Dr Williams' book having the greater interest for the European reader. In the looseish structure of the *Pagany* I don't quite make out what, unless it be simple vagary of the printer, has caused the omission of 'The Venus' (July *Dial*), pages obviously written to occur somewhere in the longer work, though they do form a whole in themselves, and pose quite clearly the general question, or at least one phase of the question in the *Pagany*.

In all the books cited,[1] the best pages of Williams—at least for the present reviewer—are those where he has made the least effort to fit anything into either story, book, or (in *The American Grain*) into an essay. I would almost move from that isolated instance to the generalization that plot, major form, or outline should be left to

---

[1] *The Tempers* (Elkin Mathews, 1913); *Al Que Quiere* (The Four Seas Company, 1917); *Kora in Hell* (The Four Seas Company, 1920) *Sour Grapes* (The Four Seas Company, 1921); *The Great American Novel* (Three Mountains Press, 1923); *The American Grain* (Albert and Charles Boni, 1925); *A Voyage to Pagany* (The Macaulay Company, 1928).

authors who feel some inner need for the same; even let us say a very strong, unusual, unescapable need for these things; and to books where the said form, plot, etc., springs naturally from the matter treated. When put on ab exteriore, they probably lead only to dullness, confusion or remplissage or the 'falling between two stools'. I don't mean that Williams 'falls'; he certainly has never loaded on enough shapings to bother one. As to his two dialectical ladies? Of course he may know ladies who argue like that. There may be ladies who so argue, aided by Bacchus. In any case the effect of one human on another is such that Williams may elicit such dialectic from ladies who in presence of a more dialectic or voluble male would be themselves notably less so. No one else now writing would have given us the sharp clarity of the medical chapters.

As to the general value of Carlos Williams' poetry I have nothing to retract from the affirmation of its value that I made ten years ago, nor do I see any particular need of repeating that estimate; I should have to say the same things, and it would be with but a pretence or camouflage of novelty.

When an author preserves, by any means whatsoever, his integrity, I take it we ought to be thankful. We retain a liberty to speculate as to how he might have done better, what paths would conduce to, say, progress in his next opus, etc., to ask whether for example Williams would have done better to have read W. H. Hudson than to have been interested in Joyce. At least there is place for reflection as to whether the method of Hudson's *A Traveller in Little Things* would serve for an author so concerned with his own insides as is Williams; or whether Williams himself isn't at his best—retaining interest in the uncommunicable or the hidden roots of the consciousness of people he meets, but confining his statement to presentation of their objective manifests.

No one but a fantastic impressionist or a fanatic subjectivist or introversionist will try to answer such a question save in relation to a given specific work.

DUBLINERS AND MR JAMES JOYCE[1]

Freedom from sloppiness is so rare in contemporary English prose that one might well say simply, 'Mr Joyce's book of short stories is prose free from sloppiness,' and leave the intelligent reader ready to run from his study, immediately to spend three and sixpence on the volume.[2]

Unfortunately one's credit as a critic is insufficient to produce this result.

The readers of *The Egoist*, having had Mr Joyce under their eyes for some months, will scarcely need to have his qualities pointed out to them. Both they and the paper have been very fortunate in his collaboration.

Mr Joyce writes a clear hard prose. He deals with subjective things, but he presents them with such clarity of outline that he might be dealing with locomotives or with builders' specifications. For that reason one can read Mr Joyce without feeling that one is conferring a favour. I must put this thing my own way. I know about 168 authors. About once a year I read something contemporary without feeling that I am softening the path for poor Jones or poor Fulano de Tal.

I can lay down a good piece of French writing and pick up a piece of writing by Mr Joyce without feeling as if my head were being stuffed through a cushion. There are still impressionists about and I dare say they claim Mr Joyce. I admire impressionist writers. English prose writers who haven't got as far as impressionism (that is to say, 95 per cent of English writers of prose and verse) are a bore.

Impressionism has, however, two meanings, or perhaps I had better say, the word 'impressionism' gives two different 'impressions'.

There is a school of prose writers, and of verse writers for that matter, whose forerunner was Stendhal and whose founder was Flaubert. The followers of Flaubert deal in exact presentation. They are often so intent on exact presentation that they neglect intensity, selection, and concentration. They are perhaps the most clarifying

[1] Reprinted from *Pavannes and Divisions* (1918), but first printed in *The Egoist*, I, 14 (15th July, 1914).

[2] *Dubliners*, by James Joyce. Grant Richards.

and they have been perhaps the most beneficial force in modern writing.

There is another set, mostly of verse writers, who founded themselves not upon anybody's writing but upon the pictures of Monet. Every movement in painting picks up a few writers who try to imitate in words what someone has done in paint. Thus one writer saw a picture by Monet and talked of 'pink pigs blossoming on a hillside', and a later writer talked of 'slate-blue' hair and 'raspberry-coloured flanks'.

These 'impressionists' who write in imitation of Monet's softness instead of writing in imitation of Flaubert's definiteness, are a bore, a grimy, or perhaps I should say, a rosy, floribund bore.

The spirit of a decade strikes properly upon all of the arts. There are 'parallel movements'. Their causes and their effects may not seem, superficially, similar.

This mimicking of painting ten or twenty years late, is not in the least the same as the 'literary movement' parallel to the painting movement imitated.

The force that leads a poet to leave out a moral reflection may lead a painter to leave out representation. The resultant poem may not suggest the resultant painting.

Mr Joyce's merit, I will not say his chief merit but his most engaging merit, is that he carefully avoids telling you a lot that you don't want to know. He presents his people swiftly and vividly, he does not sentimentalize over them, he does not weave convolutions. He is a realist. He does not believe 'life' would be all right if we stopped vivisection or if we instituted a new sort of 'economics'. He gives the thing as it is. He is not bound by the tiresome convention that any part of life, to be interesting, must be shaped into the conventional form of a 'story'. Since De Maupassant we have had so many people trying to write 'stories' and so few people presenting life. Life for the most part does not happen in neat little diagrams and nothing is more tiresome than the continual pretence that it does.

Mr Joyce's *Araby*, for instance, is much better than a 'story', it is a vivid waiting.

It is surprising that Mr Joyce is Irish. One is so tired of the Irish or 'Celtic' imagination (or 'phantasy' as I think they now call it) flopping about. Mr Joyce does not flop about. He defines. He is not an institution for the promotion of Irish peasant industries. He accepts an international standard of prose writing and lives up to it.

He gives us Dublin as it presumably is. He does not descend to farce. He does not rely upon Dickensian caricature. He gives us things as they are, not only for Dublin, but for every city. Erase the local names and a few specifically local allusions, and a few historic events of the past, and substitute a few different local names, allusions and events, and these stories could be retold of any town.

That is to say, the author is quite capable of dealing with things about him, and dealing directly, yet these details do not engross him, he is capable of getting at the universal element beneath them.

The main situations of *Madame Bovary* or of *Doña Perfecta* do not depend on local colour or upon local detail, that is their strength. Good writing, good presentation can be specifically local, but it must not depend on locality. Mr Joyce does not present 'types' but individuals. I mean he deals with common emotions which run through all races. He does not bank on 'Irish character'. Roughly speaking, Irish literature has gone through three phases in our time, the shamrock period, the dove-grey period, and the Kiltartan period. I think there is a new phase in the works of Mr Joyce. He writes as a contemporary of continental writers. I do not mean that he writes as a faddist, mad for the last note, he does not imitate Strindberg, for instance, or Bang. He is not ploughing the underworld for horror. He is not presenting a macabre subjectivity. He is classic in that he deals with normal things and with normal people. A committee room, Little Chandler, a nonentity, a boarding house full of clerks—these are his subjects and he treats them all in such a manner that they are worthy subjects of art.

Francis Jammes, Charles Vildrac and D. H. Lawrence have written short narratives in verse, trying, it would seem, to present situations as clearly as prose writers have done, yet more briefly. Mr Joyce is engaged in a similar condensation. He has kept to prose, not needing the privilege supposedly accorded to verse to justify his method.

I think that he excels most of the impressionist writers because of his more rigorous selection, because of his exclusion of all unnecessary detail.

There is a very clear demarcation between unnecessary detail and irrelevant detail. An impressionist friend of mine talks to me a good deal about 'preparing effects', and on that score he justifies much unnecessary detail, which is not 'irrelevant', but which ends by being wearisome and by putting one out of conceit with his narrative.

Mr Joyce's more rigorous selection of the presented detail marks him, I think, as belonging to my own generation, that is, to the 'nineteen-tens', not to the decade between 'the nineties' and to-day.

At any rate these stories and the novel now appearing in serial form are such as to win for Mr Joyce a very definite place among English contemporary prose writers, not merely a place in the 'Novels of the Week' column, and our writers of good clear prose are so few that we cannot afford to confuse or to overlook them.

ULYSSES[1]

Πολλῶν δ' ἀνθρώπων ἴδεν ἄστεα καὶ νόον ἔγνω

All men should 'Unite to give praise to Ulysses'; those who will not, may content themselves with a place in the lower intellectual orders; I do not mean that they should all praise it from the same viewpoint; but all serious men of letters, whether they write out a critique or not, will certainly have to make one for their own use. To begin with matters lying outside dispute I should say that Joyce has taken up the art of writing where Flaubert left it. In Dubliners and The Portrait he had not exceeded the Trois Contes or L'Education; in Ulysses he has carried on a process begun in *Bouvard et Pécuchet*; he has brought it to a degree of greater efficiency, of greater compactness; he has swallowed the Tentation de St Antoine whole, it serves as comparison for a single episode in Ulysses. Ulysses has more form than any novel of Flaubert's. Cervantes had parodied his predecessors and might be taken as basis of comparison for another of Joyce's modes of concision, but where Cervantes satirized one manner of folly and one sort of highfalutin' expression, Joyce satirizes at least seventy, and includes a whole history of English prose, by implication.

Messrs Bouvard and Pécuchet are the basis of democracy; Bloom also is the basis of democracy; he is the man in the street, the next man, the public, not our public, but Mr Wells' public; for Mr Wells he is Hocking's public, he is *l'homme moyen sensuel;* he is also Shakespeare, Ulysses, The Wandering Jew, the Daily Mail reader, the man who believes what he sees in the papers, Everyman, and 'the goat'... πολλὰ... πάθειν... κατὰ θυμόν.

Flaubert having recorded provincial customs in Bovary and city habits in L'Education, set out to complete his record of nineteenth-century life by presenting all sorts of things that the average man of the period would have had in his head; Joyce has found a more expeditious method of summary and analysis. After Bouvard and his friend have retired to the country Flaubert's incompleted

[1] This formed the author's 'Paris Letter' to The Dial, New York, LXXII, 6 (June 1922). Dated 'May 1922'.

narrative drags; in Ulysses anything may occur at any moment; Bloom suffers *kata thumon;* 'every fellow mousing round for his liver and his lights': he is *polumetis* and a receiver of all things.

Joyce's characters not only speak their own language, but they think their own language. Thus Master Dignam stood looking at the poster: 'two puckers stripped to their pelts and putting up their props. . . .

'Gob that'd be a good pucking match to see, Myler Keogh, that's the chap sparring out to him with the green sash. Two bob entrance, soldiers half price. I could easy do a bunk on ma. When is it? May the twenty second. Sure, the blooming thing is all over.'

But Father Conmee was wonderfully well indeed: 'And her boys, were they getting on well at Belvedere? Was that so? Father Conmee was very glad to hear that. And Mr Sheehy himself? Still in London. The House was still sitting, to be sure it was. Beautiful weather it was, delightful indeed. Yes, it was very probable that Father Bernard Vaughn would come again to preach. O, yes, a very great success. A wonderful man really.'

Father Conmee later 'reflected on the providence of the Creator who had made turf to be in bogs where men might dig it out and bring it to town and hamlet to make fires in the houses of poor people.'

The dialects are not all local, on page 406 we hear that:

'Elijah is coming. Washed in the Blood of the Lamb. Come on, you winefizzling, ginsizzling, booseguzzling existences! Come on, you dog-gone, bullnecked, beetlebrowed, hogjowled, peanutbrained, weaseleyed fourflushers, false alarms and excess baggage! Come on, you triple extract of infamy! Alexander J. Christ Dowie, that's yanked to glory most half this planet from 'Frisco Beach to Vladivostok. The Deity ain't no nickel dime bumshow. I put it to you that he's on the square and a corking fine business proposition. He's the grandest thing yet, and don't you forget it. Shout salvation in King Jesus. You'll need to rise precious early, you sinner there, if you want to diddle Almighty God. . . . Not half. He's got a coughmixture with a punch in it for you, my friend, in his backpocket. Just you try it on.'

This variegation of dialects allows Joyce to present his matter, his tones of mind, very rapidly; it is no more succinct than Flaubert's exhaustion of the relation of Emma and her mother-in-law; or of

Père Rouault's character, as epitomized in his last letter to Emma; but it is more rapid than the record of 'received ideas' in Bouvard et Pécuchet.

Ulysses is, presumably, as unrepeatable as Tristram Shandy; I mean you cannot duplicate it; you can't take it as a 'model', as you could Bovary; but it does complete something begun in Bouvard; and it does add definitely to the international store of literary technique.

Stock novels, even excellent stock novels, seem infinitely long, and infinitely encumbered, after one has watched Joyce squeeze the last drop out of a situation, a science, a state of mind, in half a page, in a catechismic question and answer, in a tirade à la Rabelais.

Rabelais himself rests, he remains, he is too solid to be diminished by any pursuer; he was a rock against the follies of his age; against ecclesiastic theology, and more remarkably, against the blind idolatry of the classics just coming into fashion. He refused the lot, lock, stock, and barrel, with a greater heave than Joyce has yet exhibited; but I can think of no other prose author whose proportional status in pan-literature is not modified by the advent of Ulysses.

James (H.) speaks with his own so beautiful voice, even sometimes when his creations should be using *their* own; Joyce speaks if not with the tongue of men and angels, at least with a many-tongued and multiple language, of small boys, street preachers, of genteel and ungenteel, of bowsers and undertakers, of Gertie McDowell and Mr Deasey.

One reads Proust and thinks him very accomplished; one reads H. J. and knows that he is very accomplished; one begins Ulysses and thinks, perhaps rightly, that Joyce is less so; that he is at any rate less gracile; and one considers how excellently both James and Proust 'convey their atmospheres'; yet the atmosphere of the Gerty-Nausikaa episode with its echoes of vesper service is certainly 'conveyed', and conveyed with a certitude and efficiency that neither James nor Proust have excelled.

And on the home stretch, when our present author is feeling more or less relieved that the weight of the book is off his shoulders, we find if not gracile accomplishments, at any rate such acrobatics, such sheer whoops and hoop-las and trapeze turns of technique that it would seem rash to dogmatize concerning his limitations. The whole of him, on the other hand, lock, stock, and gunny-sacks is wholly outside H. J.'s compass and orbit, outside Proust's circuit and orbit.

If it be charged that he knows 'that provincialism which must be forever dragging in allusions to some book or local custom', it must also be admitted that no author is more lucid or more explicit in presenting things in such a way that the imaginary Chinaman or denizen of the forty-first century could without works of reference gain a very good idea of the scene and habits portrayed.

Poynton with its spoils forms a less vivid image than Bloom's desired two story dwelling house and appurtenances. The recollections of In Old Madrid are not at any rate highbrow; the 'low back car' is I think local. But in the main, I doubt if the local allusions interfere with a *general* comprehension. Local details exist everywhere; one understands them *mutatis mutandis*, and any picture would be perhaps faulty without them. One must balance obscurity against brevity. Concision itself is an obscurity for the dullard.

In this super-novel our author has also poached on the epic, and has, for the first time since 1321, resurrected the infernal figures; his furies are not stage figures; he has, by simple reversal, caught back the furies, his flagellant Castle ladies. Telemachus, Circe, the rest of the Odyssean company, the noisy cave of Aeolus gradually place themselves in the mind of the reader, rapidly or less rapidly according as he is familiar or unfamiliar with Homer. These correspondences are part of Joyce's mediaevalism and are chiefly his own affair, a scaffold, a means of construction, justified by the result, and justifiable by it only. The result is a triumph in form, in balance, a main schema, with continuous inweaving and arabesque.

The best criticism of any work, to my mind the only criticism of any work of art that is of any permanent or even moderately durable value, comes from the creative writer or artist who does the next job; and *not*, not ever from the young gentlemen who make generalities about the creator. Laforgue's Salomé is the real criticism of Salammbô; Joyce and perhaps Henry James are critics of Flaubert. To me, as poet, the Tentations is *jettatura*, it is the effect of Flaubert's time on Flaubert; I mean he was interested in certain questions now dead as mutton, because he lived in a certain period; fortunately he managed to bundle these matters into one or two books and keep

them out of his work on contemporary subjects; I set it aside as one
sets aside Dante's treatise De Aqua et Terra, as something which
matters now only as archaeology. Joyce, working in the same
medium as Flaubert, makes the intelligent criticism: 'We might
believe in it if Flaubert had first shown us St Antoine in Alexandria
looking at women and jewellers' windows.'

Ulysses contains 732 double sized pages, that is to say it is about
the size of four ordinary novels, and even a list of its various points
of interest would probably exceed my allotted space; in the Cyclops
episode we have a measuring of the difference between reality, and
reality as represented in various lofty forms of expression; the satire
on the various dead manners of language culminates in the execution
scene, blood and sugar stewed into clichés and rhetoric; just what the
public deserves, and just what the public gets every morning with its
porridge, in the Daily Mail and in sentimento-rhetorical journalism;
it is perhaps the most savage bit of satire we have had since Swift
suggested a cure for famine in Ireland. Henry James complained of
Baudelaire, 'Le Mal, you do yourself too much honour ... our
impatience is of the same order as ... if for the "Flowers of Good"
one should present us with a rhapsody on plum-cake and eau de
cologne.' Joyce has set out to do an inferno, and he has done an
inferno.

He has presented Ireland under British domination, a picture so
veridic that a ninth rate coward like Shaw (Geo. B.) dare not even
look it in the face. By extension he has presented the whole occident
under the domination of capital. The details of the street map are
local but Leopold Bloom (né Virag) is ubiquitous. His spouse Gea-
Tellus the earth symbol is the soil from which the intelligence strives
to leap, and to which it subsides in saeculum saeculorum. As Molly she
is a coarse-grained bitch, not a whore, an adulteress, il y en a. Her
ultimate meditations are uncensored (bow to psychoanalysis required
at this point). The 'censor' in the Freudian sense is removed, Molly's
night-thoughts differing from those versified in Mr Young's once
ubiquitous poem are unfolded, she says ultimately that her body is a
flower; her last word is affirmative. The manners of the genteel
society she inhabits have failed to get under her crust, she exists
presumably in Patagonia as she exists in Jersey City or Camden.

And the book is banned in America, where every child of seven
has ample opportunity to drink in the details of the Arbuckle case,

or two hundred other equodorous affairs from the 270,000,000 copies of the 300,000 daily papers which enlighten us. One returns to the Goncourt's question, 'Ought the people to remain under a literary edict? Are there classes unworthy, misfortunes too low, dramas too ill set, catastrophes, horrors too devoid of nobility? Now that the novel is augmented, now that it is the great literary form . . . the social inquest, for psychological research and analysis, demanding the studies and imposing on its creator the duties of science . . . seeking facts . . . whether or no the novelist is to write with the accuracy, and thence with the freedom of the savant, the historian, the physician?'

Whether the only class in America that tries to think is to be hindered by a few cranks, who cannot, and dare not interfere with the leg shows on Broadway? Is any one, for the sake of two or three words which every small boy has seen written on the walls of a privy, going to wade through two hundred pages on consubstantiation or the biographic bearing of Hamlet? And ought an epoch-making report on the state of the human mind in the twentieth century (first of the new era) to be falsified by the omission of these half a dozen words, or by a pretended ignorance of extremely simple acts. Bloom's day is uncensored, very well. The faecal analysis, in the hospital around the corner, is uncensored. No one but a Presbyterian would contest the utility of the latter exactitude. A *great literary masterwork is made for minds quite as serious as those engaged in the science of medicine.* The anthropologist and sociologist have a right to equally accurate documents, to equally succinct reports and generalizations, which they seldom get, considering the complexity of the matter in hand, and the idiocy of current superstitions.

A Fabian milk report is of less use to a legislator than the knowledge contained in L'Education Sentimentale, or in Bovary. The legislator is supposed to manage human affairs, to arrange for comity of human agglomerations. *Le beau monde gouverne*—or did once—because it had access to condensed knowledge, the middle ages were ruled by those who could read, an aristocracy received Macchiavelli's treatise before the serfs. A very limited plutocracy now gets the news, of which a fraction (not likely to throw too much light upon proximate markets) is later printed in newspapers. Jefferson was perhaps the last American official to have any general sense of civilization. Molly Bloom judges Griffith derisively by 'the sincerity of his trousers', and the Paris edition of the Tribune tells us that the tailors' congress has declared Pres. Harding to be our best dressed Chief Magistrate.

Be it far from me to depreciate the advantages of having a president who can meet on equal trouserial terms such sartorial paragons as Mr Balfour and Lord (late Mr) Lee of Fareham (and Checquers) but be it equidistant also from me to disparage the public utility of accurate language which can be attained only from literature, and which the succinct J. Caesar, or the lucid Macchiavelli, or the author of the Code Napoléon, or Thos. Jefferson, to cite a local example, would have in no ways despised. Of course it is too soon to know whether our present ruler takes an interest in these matters; we know only that the late pseudo-intellectual Wilson did not, and that the late bombastic Teddy did not, and Taft, McKinley, Cleveland, did not, and that, as far back as memory serves us no American president has ever uttered one solitary word implying the slightest interest in, or consciousness of, the need for an intellectual or literary vitality in America. A sense of style could have saved America and Europe from Wilson; it would have been useful to our diplomats. The *mot juste* is of public utility. I can't help it. I am not offering this fact as a sop to aesthetes who want all authors to be fundamentally useless. We are governed by words, the laws are graven in words, and literature is the sole means of keeping these words living and accurate. The specimen of fungus given in my February letter shows what happens to language when it gets into the hands of illiterate specialists.

Ulysses furnishes matter for a symposium rather than for a single letter, essay, or review.

JOYCE[1]

Despite the War, despite the paper shortage, and despite those old-established publishers whose god is their belly and whose god-father was the late F. T. Palgrave, there is a new edition of James Joyce's *A Portrait of the Artist as a Young Man*.[2] It is extremely gratifying that this book should have 'reached its fourth thousand', and the fact is significant in just so far as it marks the beginning of a new phase of English publishing, a phase comparable to that started in France some years ago by the *Mercure*.

The old houses, even those, or even *more* those, which once had a literary tradition, or at least literary pretensions, having ceased to care a damn about literature, the lovers of good writing have 'struck'; have sufficiently banded themselves together to get a few good books into print, and even into circulation. The actual output is small in bulk, a few brochures of translations, Eliot's *Prufrock*, Joyce's *A Portrait*, and Wyndham Lewis' *Tarr*, but I have it on good authority that at least one other periodical will start publishing its authors after the War, so there are new rods in pickle for the old fat-stomached contingent and for the cardboard generation.

Joyce's *A Portrait* is literature; it has become almost the prose bible of a few people, and I think I have encountered at least three hundred admirers of the book, certainly that number of people who whether they 'like' it or not, are wholly convinced of its merits.

Mr Wells I have encountered in print, where he says that Joyce has a cloacal obsession, *but* he also says that Mr Joyce writes literature and that his book is to be ranked with the works of Sterne and of Swift.

Wells is no man to babble of obsessions, but let it stand to his honour that he came out with a fine burst of admiration for a younger and half-known writer.

From England and America there has come a finer volume of praise for this novel than for any that I can remember. There has also come impotent spitting and objurgation from the back-woods and

[1] *The Future*, May, 1918.
[2] *A Portrait of the Artist as a Young Man*. Egoist, Ltd. London. Huebsch, New York.

from Mr Dent's office boy, and, as offset, interesting comment in modern Greek, French and Italian.

Joyce's poems have been reprinted by Elkin Mathews, his short stories re-issued, and a second novel started in *The Little Review*.

For all the book's being so familiar, it is pleasant to take up *A Portrait* in its new exiguous form, and one enters many speculations, perhaps more than when one read it initially. It is not that one can open to a forgotten page so much as that wherever one opens there is always a place to start; some sentence like—

'Stephen looked down coldly on the oblong skull beneath him overgrown with tangled twine-coloured hair'; *or*

'Frowsy girls sat along the curbstones before their baskets'; *or*

'He drained his third cup of watery tea to the dregs and set to chewing the crusts of fried bread that were scattered near him, staring into the dark pool of the jar. The yellow dripping had been scooped out like a boghole, and the pool under it brought back to his memory the dark turf-coloured water of the bath in Clongowes. The box of pawntickets at his elbow had just been rifled, and he took up idly one after another in his greasy fingers the blue and white dockets, scrawled and sanded and creased and bearing the name of the pledger as Daly or MacEvoy.

1 Pair Buskins, etc.'

I do not mean to imply that a novel is necessarily a bad novel because one man can pick it up without being in this manner caught and dragged into reading: but I do indicate the curiously seductive interest of the clear-cut and definite sentences.

Neither, emphatically, is it to be supposed that Joyce's writing is merely a depiction of the sordid. The sordid is there in all conscience as you would find it in De Goncourt, but Joyce's power is in his scope. The reach of his writing is from the fried breadcrusts and from the fig-seeds in Cranley's teeth to the casual discussion of Aquinas:

'He wrote a hymn for Maundy Thursday. It begins with the words *Pange lingua gloriosi*. They say it is the highest glory of the hymnal. It is an intricate and soothing hymn. I like it; but there is no hymn that can be put beside that mournful and majestic processional song, the Vexilla Regis of Venantius Fortunatus.

'Lynch began to sing softly and solemnly in a deep bass voice:

"Impleta sunt quae concinit
David fideli carmine . . . . ."

'They turned into Lower Mount Street. A few steps from the corner a fat young man, wearing a silk neck-cloth, &c.'

On almost every page of Joyce you will find just such swift alternation of subjective beauty and external shabbiness, squalor, and sordidness. It is the bass and treble of his method. And he has his scope beyond that of the novelists his contemporaries, in just so far as whole stretches of his keyboard are utterly out of their compass.

The conclusion or moral termination from all of which is that the great writers of any period must be the remarkable minds of that period; they must know the extremes of their time; they must not represent a *social status;* they cannot be the 'Grocer' or the 'Dilettante' with the egregious and capital letter, nor yet the professor or the professing wearer of Jaeger or professional eater of herbs.

In the three hundred pages of *A Portrait of the Artist as a Young Man* there is no omission; there is nothing in life so beautiful that Joyce cannot touch it without profanation—without, above all, the profanations of sentiment and sentimentality—and there is nothing so sordid that he cannot treat it with his metallic exactitude.

I think there are few people who can read Shaw, Wells, Bennett, or even Conrad (who is in a category apart) without feeling that there are values and tonalities to which these authors are wholly insensitive. I do not imply that there cannot be excellent art within quite distinct limitations, but the artist cannot afford to be or to appear ignorant of such limitations; he cannot afford a pretence of such ignorance. He must almost choose his limitations. If he paints a snuff-box or a stage scene he must not be ignorant of the fact, he must not think he is painting a landscape, three feet by two feet, in oils.

I think that what tires me more than anything else in the writers now past middle age is that they always seem to imply that they are giving us all modern life, the whole social panorama, all the instruments of the orchestra. Joyce is of another donation.

His earlier book, *Dubliners,* contained several well-constructed stories, several sketches rather lacking in form. It was a definite promise of what was to come. There is very little to be said in praise of it which would not apply with greater force to *A Portrait.* I find that whoever reads one book inevitably sets out in search of the other.

The quality and distinction of the poems in the first half of Mr Joyce's *Chamber Music* (new edition, published by Elkin Mathews, 4A, Cork Street, W 1. at 1s. 3d.) is due in part to their author's strict musical training. We have here the lyric in some of its best traditions, and one pardons certain trifling inversions much against the taste of the moment, for the sake of the clean-cut ivory finish, and for the interest of the rhythms, the cross run of the beat and the word, as of a stiff wind cutting the ripple-tops of bright water.

The wording is Elizabethan, the metres at times suggesting Herrick, but in no case have I been able to find a poem which is not in some way Joyce's own, even though he would seem, and that most markedly, to shun apparent originality, as in:

> Who goes amid the green wood
> With springtide all adorning her?
> Who goes amid the merry green wood
> To make it merrier?
>
> Who passes in the sunlight
> By ways that know the light footfall?
> Who passes in the sweet sunlight
> With mien so virginal?
>
> The ways of all the woodland
> Gleam with a soft and golden fire—
> For whom does all the sunny woodland
> Carry so brave attire?
>
> O, it is for my true love
> The woods their rich apparel wear—
> O, it is for my true love,
> That is so young and fair.

Here, as in nearly every poem, the motif is so slight that the poem scarcely exists until one thinks of it as set to music; and the workmanship is so delicate that out of twenty readers scarce one will notice its fineness. If Henry Lawes were alive again he might make the suitable music, for the cadence is here worthy of his cunning:

O, it is for my true love,
        That is so young and fair.

The musician's work is very nearly done for him, and yet how few
song-setters could be trusted to finish it and to fill in an accompaniment.

The tone of the book deepens with the poem beginning:

O sweetheart, hear you
        Your lover's tale;
A man shall have sorrow
        When friends him fail.

For he shall know then
        Friends be untrue;
And a little ashes
        Their words come to.

The collection comes to its end and climax in two profoundly
emotional poems; quite different in tonality and in rhythm-quality
from the lyrics in the first part of the book:

All day I hear the noise of waters
        Making moan,
Sad as the sea-bird is, when going
        Forth alone,
He hears the wind cry to the waters'
        Monotone.

The gray winds, the cold winds are blowing
        Where I go.
I hear the noise of many waters
        Far below.
All day, all night, I hear them flowing
        To and fro.

The third and fifth lines should not be read with an end stop. I
think the rush of the words will escape the notice of scarcely any one.
The phantom hearing in this poem is coupled, in the next poem, to
phantom vision, and to a *robustezza* of expression:

I hear an army charging upon the land,
 And the thunder of horses plunging, foam above their knees;
Arrogant, in black armour, behind them stand,
 Disdaining the reins, with fluttering whips, the charioteers.

They cry unto the night their battle-name;
 I moan in sleep when I hear afar their whirling laughter;
They cleave the gloom of dreams, a blinding flame,
 Clanging, clanging upon the heart as upon an anvil.

They come shaking in triumph their long green hair;
 They come out of the sea and run shouting by the shore:
My heart, have you no wisdom thus to despair?
 My love, my love, my love, why have you left me alone?

In both these poems we have a strength and a fibrousness of sound which almost prohibits the thought of their being 'set to music' or to any music but that which is in them when spoken; but we notice a similarity of the technique to that of the earlier poems, in so far as the beauty of movement is produced by a very skilful, or perhaps we should say a deeply intuitive, interruption of metric mechanical regularity. It is the irregularity which has shown always in the best periods.

The book is an excellent antidote for whose who find Mr Joyce's prose 'disagreeable' and who at once fly to conclusions about Mr Joyce's 'cloacal obsessions'. I have yet to find in Joyce's published works a violent or malodorous phrase which does not justify itself not only by its verity, but by its heightening of some opposite effect, by the poignancy which it imparts to some emotion or to some thwarted desire for beauty. Disgust with the sordid is but another expression of a sensitiveness to the finer thing. There is no perception of beauty without a corresponding disgust. If the price for such artists as James Joyce is exceedingly heavy, it is the artist himself who pays, and if Armageddon has taught us anything it should have taught us to abominate the half-truth, and the tellers of the half-truth in literature.

ULYSSES

Incomplete as I write this. His profoundest work, most significant —'Exiles' was a side-step, necessary katharsis, clearance of mind from continental contemporary thought—*Ulysses,* obscure, even obscene, as life itself is obscene in places, but an impassioned meditation on life.

He has done what Flaubert set out to do in *Bouvard and Pécuchet,* done it better, more succinct. An epitome.

Bloom answers the query that people made after *The Portrait.* Joyce has created his second character; he has moved from autobiography to the creation of the complementary figure. Bloom on life, death, resurrection, immortality. Bloom and the Venus de Milo.

Bloom brings life into the book. All Bloom is vital. Talk of the other characters, cryptic, perhaps too particular, incomprehensible save to people who know Dublin, at least by hearsay, and who have university education plus medievalism. But unavoidable or almost unavoidable, given the subject and the place of the subject.

NOTE: I am tired of rewriting the arguments for the realist novel; besides there is nothing to add. The Brothers de Goncourt said the thing once and for all, but despite the lapse of time their work is still insufficiently known to the American reader. The program in the preface to *Germinie Lacerteux* states the case and the whole case for realism; one can not improve the statement. I therefore give it entire, ad majoram Dei gloriam.

PRÉFACE

De la première édition

Il nous faut demander pardon au public de lui donner ce livre, et l'avertir de ce qu'il y trouvera.

Le public aime les romans faux: ce roman est un roman vrai.

Il aime les livres qui font semblant d'aller dans le monde: ce livre vient de la rue.

Il aime les petites oeuvres polissonnes, les mémoires de filles, les confessions d'alcôves, les saletés érotiques, le scandale qui se retrousse dans une image aux devantures des libraires, ce qu'il va lire est sévère et pur. Qu'il ne s'attende point à la photographie décolletée du plaisir: l'étude qui suit est la clinique de l'Amour.

Le public aime encore les lectures anodines et consolantes, les aventures qui finissent bien, les imaginations qui ne dérangent ni sa digestion ni sa sérénité: ce livre, avec sa triste et violente distraction, est fait pour contrarier ses habitudes et nuire à son hygiène.

Pourquoi donc l'avons-nous écrit? Est-ce simplement pour choquer le public et scandaliser ses goûts?

Non.

Vivant au dix-neuvième siècle, dans un temps de suffrage universel, de démocratie, de libéralisme, nous nous sommes demandé si ce qu'on appelle 'les basses classes' n'avait pas droit au roman; si ce monde sous un monde, le peuple, devait rester sous le coup de l'interdit littéraire et des dédains d'auteurs qui ont fait jusqu'ici le silence sur l'âme et le coeur qu'il peut avoir. Nous nous sommes demandé s'il y avait encore, pour l'ecrivain et pour le lecteur, en ces années d'égalité où nous sommes, des classes indignes, des malheurs trop bas, des drames trop mal embouchés, des catastrophes d'une terreur trop peu noble. Il nous est venu la curiosité de savoir si cette forme conventionnelle d'une littérature oubliée et d'une société disparue, la Tragédie, était définitivement morte; si, dans un pays sans caste et sans aristocratie légale, les misères des petits et des pauvres parleraient à l'intérêt, à l'émotion, à la pitié aussi haut que les misères des grands et des riches; si, en un mot, les larmes qu'on pleure en bas pourraient faire pleurer comme celles qu'on pleure en haut.

Ces pensées nous avaient fait oser l'humble roman de 'Soeur Philomène', en 1861; elles nous font publier aujourd'hui 'Germinie Lacerteux'.

Maintenant, que ce livre soit calomnié: peu lui importe. Aujourd'hui que le Roman s'élargit et grandit, qu'il commence à être la grande forme sérieuse, passionnée, vivante, de l'étude littéraire et de l'enquête sociale, qu'il devient, par l'analyse et par la recherche psychologique, l'Histoire morale contemporaine, aujourd'hui que le Roman s'est imposé les études et les devoirs de la science, il peut en revendiquer les libertés et les franchises. Et qu'il cherche l'Art et la Vérité; qu'il montre des misères bonnes à ne pas laisser oublier aux heureux de Paris; qu'il fasse voir aux gens du monde ce que les dames de charité ont le courage de voir, ce que les reines d'autrefois faisaient toucher de l'oeil à leurs enfants dans les hospices: la souffrance humaine, présente et toute vive, qui apprend la charité; que le Roman ait cette religion que le siècle passé appelait de ce large et vaste nom: *Humanité;* il lui suffit de cette conscience: son droit est là.

E. et J. de G.'

T. S. ELIOT[1]

Il n'y a de livres que ceux où un écrivain s'est raconté lui-même en racontant les moeurs de ses contemporains—leurs rêves, leurs vanités, leurs amours, et leurs folies—Rémy de Gourmont.

De Gourmont uses this sentence in writing of the incontestable superiority of *Madame Bovary*, *L'Education Sentimentale* and *Bouvard et Pécuchet* to *Salammbô* and *La Tentation de St Antoine*. A casual thought convinces one that it is true for all prose. Is it true also for poetry? One may give latitude to the interpretation of *rêves;* the gross public would have the poet write little else, but De Gourmont keeps a proportion. The vision should have its place in due setting if we are to believe its reality.

The few poems which Mr Eliot has given us maintain this proportion, as they maintain other proportions of art. After much contemporary work that is merely factitious, much that is good in intention but impotently unfinished and incomplete; much whose flaws are due to sheer ignorance which a year's study or thought might have remedied, it is a comfort to come upon complete art, naïve despite its intellectual subtlety, lacking all pretence.

It is quite safe to compare Mr Eliot's work with anything written in French, English or American since the death of Jules Laforgue. The reader will find nothing better, and he will be extremely fortunate if he finds much half as good.

The necessity, or at least the advisability of comparing English or American work with French work is not readily granted by the usual English or American writer. If you suggest it, the Englishman answers that he has not thought about it—he does not see why he should bother himself about what goes on south of the channel; the American replies by stating that you are 'no longer American'. This is the bitterest jibe in his vocabulary. The net result is that it is extremely difficult to read one's contemporaries. After a time one tires of 'promise'.

[1] *Prufrock and Other Observations*, by T. S. Eliot. *The Egoist*, London. Essay first published in *Poetry*, 1917.

I should like the reader to note how complete is Mr Eliot's
depiction of our contemporary condition. He has not confined himself to genre or to society portraiture. His

> lonely men in shirt-sleeves leaning out of windows

are as real as his ladies who

> come and go
> Talking of Michelangelo.

His 'one night cheap hotels' are as much 'there' as are his

> four wax candles in the darkened room,
> Four rings of light upon the ceiling overhead,
> An atmosphere of Juliet's tomb.

And, above all, there is no rhetoric, although there is Elizabethan
reading in the background. Were I a French critic, skilled in their
elaborate art of writing books about books, I should probably go to
some length discussing Mr Eliot's two sorts of metaphor: his wholly
unrealizable, always apt, half ironic suggestion, and his precise
realizable picture. It would be possible to point out his method
of conveying a whole situation and half a character by three
words of a quoted phrase; his constant aliveness, his mingling of a
very subtle observation with the unexpectedness of a backhanded
cliché. It is, however, extremely dangerous to point out such devices.
The method is Mr Eliot's own, but as soon as one has reduced even
a fragment of it to formula, some one else, not Mr Eliot, some one
else wholly lacking in his aptitudes, will at once try to make poetry
by mimicking his external procedure. And this indefinite 'some one'
will, needless to say, make a botch of it.

For what the statement is worth, Mr Eliot's work interests me
more than that of any other poet now writing in English.[1] The most
interesting poems in Victorian English are Browning's *Men and
Women*, or, if that statement is too absolute, let me contend that the
form of these poems is the most vital form of that period of English,
and that the poems written in that form are the least like each other
in content. Antiquity gave us Ovid's *Heroides* and Theocritus'
woman using magic. The form of Browning's *Men and Women* is
more alive than the epistolary form of the *Heroides*. Browning

[1] A.D. 1917.

included a certain amount of ratiocination and of purely intellectual comment, and in just that proportion he lost intensity. Since Browning there have been very few good poems of this sort. Mr Eliot has made two notable additions to the list. And he has placed his people in contemporary settings, which is much more difficult than to render them with medieval romantic trappings. If it is permitted to make comparison with a different art, let me say that he has used contemporary detail very much as Velasquez used contemporary detail in *Las Meninas;* the cold gray-green tones of the Spanish painter have, it seems to me, an emotional value not unlike the emotional value of Mr Eliot's rhythms, and of his vocabulary.

James Joyce has written the best novel of my decade, and perhaps the best criticism of it has come from a Belgian who said, 'All this is as true of my country as of Ireland.' Eliot has a like ubiquity of application. Art does not avoid universals, it strikes at them all the harder in that it strikes through particulars. Eliot's work rests apart from that of the many new writers who have used the present freedoms to no advantage, who have gained no new precisions of language, and no variety in their cadence. His men in shirt-sleeves, and his society ladies, are not a local manifestation; they are the stuff of our modern world, and true of more countries than one. I would praise the work for its fine tone, its humanity, and its realism; for all good art is realism of one sort or another.

It is complained that Eliot is lacking in emotion. 'La Figlia che Piange' is an adequate confutation.

If the reader wishes mastery of 'regular form' the *Conversation Galante* is sufficient to show that symmetrical form is within Mr Eliot's grasp. You will hardly find such neatness save in France; such modern neatness, save in Laforgue.

De Gourmont's phrase to the contrary notwithstanding, the supreme test of a book is that we should feel some unusual intelligence working behind the words. By this test various other new books, that I have, or might have, beside me, go to pieces. The barrels of sham poetry that every decade and school and fashion produce, go to pieces. It is sometimes extremely difficult to find any other particular reason for their being so unsatisfactory. I have expressly written here not 'intellect' but 'intelligence'. There is no intelligence without emotion. The emotion may be anterior or concurrent. There may be emotion without much intelligence, but that does not concern us.

Versification:

A conviction as to the rightness or wrongness of *vers libre* is no guarantee of a poet. I doubt if there is much use trying to classify the various kinds of *vers libre*, but there is an anarchy which may be vastly overdone; and there is a monotony of bad usage as tiresome as any typical eighteenth or nineteenth century flatness.

In a recent article Mr Eliot contended, or seemed to contend, that good *vers libre* was little more than a skilful evasion of the better known English metres. His article was defective in that he omitted all consideration of metres depending on quantity, alliteration, etc.; in fact, he wrote as if all metres were measured by accent. This may have been tactful on his part, it may have brought his article nearer to the comprehension of his readers (that is, those of the *New Statesman* people chiefly concerned with the sociology of the 'button' and 'unit' variety). But he came nearer the fact when he wrote elsewhere: 'No *vers* is *libre* for the man who wants to do a good job.'

Alexandrine and other grammarians have made cubby-holes for various groupings of syllables; they have put names upon them, and have given various labels to 'metres' consisting of combinations of these different groups.[1] Thus it would be hard to escape contact with some group or other; only an encyclopedist could ever be half sure he had done so. The known categories would allow a fair liberty to the most conscientious traditionalist. The most fanatical vers-librist will escape them with difficulty. However, I do not think there is any crying need for verse with absolutely no rhythmical basis.

On the other hand, I do not believe that Chopin wrote to a metronome. There is undoubtedly a sense of music that takes count of the 'shape' of the rhythm in a melody rather than of bar divisions, which came rather late in the history of written music and were certainly not the first or most important thing that musicians attempted to record. The creation of such shapes is part of thematic invention. Some musicians have the faculty of invention, rhythmic, melodic. Likewise some poets.

Treatises full of musical notes and of long and short marks have never been convincingly useful. Find a man with thematic invention

---

[1] A.D. 1940: Prosody is the articulation of the total sound of a poem. E.P.

and all he can say is that he gets what the Celts call a 'chune' in his head, and that the words 'go into it', or when they don't 'go into it' they 'stick out and worry him'.

You can not force a person to play a musical masterpiece correctly, even by having the notes 'correctly' printed on the paper before him; neither can you force a person to feel the movement of poetry, be the metre 'regular' or 'irregular'. I have heard Mr Yeats trying to read Burns, struggling in vain to fit the *Birks o' Aberfeldy* and *Bonnie Alexander* into the mournful keen of the *Wind among the Reeds*. Even in regular metres there are incompatible systems of music.

I have heard the best orchestral conductor in England read poems in free verse, poems in which the rhythm was so faint as to be almost imperceptible. He[1] read them with the author's cadence, with flawless correctness. A distinguished statesman[2] read from the same book, with the intonations of a legal document, paying no attention to the movement inherent in the words before him. I have heard a celebrated Dante scholar and medieval enthusiast read the sonnets of the *Vita Nuova* as if they were not only prose, but the ignominious prose of a man devoid of emotions: an utter castration.

The leader of orchestra said to me, 'There is more for a musician in a few lines with something rough or uneven, such as Byron's

> There be none of Beauty's daughters
> With a magic like thee;

than in whole pages of regular poetry.'

Unless a man can put some thematic invention into *vers libre*, he would perhaps do well to stick to 'regular' metres, which have certain chances of being musical from their form, and certain other chances of being musical through his failure in fitting the form. In *vers libre* his musical chances are but in sensitivity and invention.

Mr Eliot is one of the very few who have given a personal rhythm, an identifiable quality of sound as well as of style. And at any rate, his book is the best thing in poetry since . . . (for the sake of peace I will leave that date to the imagination). I have read most of the poems many times; I last read the whole book at breakfast time and from flimsy proof-sheets: I believe these are 'test conditions'. And, 'confound it, the fellow can write.'

---

[1] Beecham (E.P.).   [2] Birrell (E.P.).

WYNDHAM LEWIS[1]

The signal omission from my critical papers is an adequate book on Wyndham Lewis; my excuses, apart from the limitations of time, must be that Mr Lewis is alive and quite able to speak for himself, secondly that one may print half-tone reproductions of sculpture, for however unsatisfactory they be, they pretend to be only half-tones, and could not show more than they do; but the reproduction of drawings and painting invites all sorts of expensive process impracticable during the years of war. When the public or the 'publishers' are ready for a volume of Lewis, suitably illustrated, I am ready to write in the letterpress, though Mr Lewis would do it better than I could.

He will rank among the great instigators and great inventors of design; there is mastery in his use of various media (my own interest in his work centres largely in the 'drawing' completed with inks, water-colour, chalk, etc.). His name is constantly bracketed with that of Gaudier, Picasso, Joyce, but these are fortuitous couplings. Lewis' painting is further from the public than were the carvings of Gaudier; Lewis is an older artist, maturer, fuller of greater variety and invention. His work is almost unknown to the public. His name is wholly familiar, BLAST is familiar, the 'Timon' portfolio has been seen.

I had known him for seven years, known him as an artist, but I had no idea of his scope until he began making his preparations to go into the army; so careless had he been of any public or private approval. The 'work' lay in piles on the floor of an attic; and from it we gathered most of the hundred or hundred and twenty drawings which now form the bases of the Quinn collection and of the Baker collection (now in the South Kensington museum).

As very few people have seen all of these pictures very few people are in any position to contradict me. There are three of his works in this room and I can attest their wearing capactiy; as I can attest the duration of my regret for the Red drawing now in the Quinn collection which hung here for some months waiting shipment; as I can

[1] Reprinted from *Instigations* (1920).

attest the energy and vitality that filled this place while forty drawings of the Quinn assortment stood here waiting also; a demonstration of the difference between 'cubism', *nature-morte-ism* and the vortex of Lewis: sun, energy, sombre emotion, clean-drawing, disgust, penetrating analysis, from the qualities finding literary expression in *Tarr* to the stasis of the Red Duet, from the metallic gleam of the 'Timon' portfolio to the velvet-suavity of the later 'Timon' of the Baker collection.

The animality and the animal satire, the dynamic and metallic properties, the social satire, on the one hand, the sunlight, the utter cleanness of the Red Duet, are all points in an astounding circumference, which will, until the work is adequately reproduced, have more or less to be taken on trust by the 'wider' public.

The novel *Tarr* is in print and no one need bother to read my critiques of it. It contains much that Joyce's work does not contain, but differentiations between the two authors are to the detriment of neither, one tries solely to discriminate qualities: hardness, fullness, abundance, weight, finish, all terms used sometimes with derogatory and sometimes with laudative intonation, or at any rate valued by one auditor and depreciated by another. The English prose fiction of my decade is the work of this pair of authors.

TARR, BY WYNDHAM LEWIS[1]

Tarr is the most vigorous and volcanic English novel of our time. Lewis is the rarest of phenomena, an Englishman who has achieved the triumph of being also a European. He is the only English writer who can be compared with Dostoievsky, and he is more rapid than Dostoievsky, his mind travels with greater celerity, with more unexpectedness, but he loses none of Dostoievsky's effect of mass and of weight.

Tarr is a man of genius surrounded by the heavy stupidities of the half-cultured latin quarter; the book delineates his explosions in this oleaginous milieu; as well as the débâcle of the unintelligent emotion-dominated Kreisler. They are the two titanic characters in contemporary English fiction. Wells's clerks, Bennett's 'cards' and even Conrad's Russian villains do not 'bulk up' against them.

Only in James Joyce's *Stephen Dedalus* does one find an equal

[1] *Little Review.*

intensity, and Joyce is, by comparison, cold and meticulous, where Lewis is, if uncouth, at any rate brimming with energy, the man with a leaping mind.

Despite its demonstrable faults I do not propose to attack this novel.[1] It is a serious work, it is definitely an attempt to express, and very largely a success in expressing something. The 'average novel', the average successful commercial proposition at 6s. per 300 to 600 pages is nothing of the sort; it is merely a third-rate mind's imitation of a perfectly well-known type-novel; of let us say Dickens, or Balzac, or Sir A. Conan-Doyle, or Hardy, or Mr Wells, or Mrs Ward, or some other and less laudable proto- or necro-type.

A certain commercial interest attaches to the sale of these mimicries and a certain purely technical or trade or clique interest may attach to the closeness of 'skill' in the aping, or to the 'application' of a formula. The 'work', the opus, has a purely narcotic value, it serves to soothe the tired mind of the reader, to take said 'mind' off its 'business' (whether that business be lofty, 'intellectual', humanitarian, sordid, acquisitive, or other). There is only one contemporary English work with which *Tarr* can be compared, namely James Joyce's utterly different *Portrait of the Artist*. The appearance of either of these novels would be a recognized literary event had it occurred in any other country in Europe.

Joyce's novel is a triumph of actual writing. The actual arrangement of the words is worth any author's study. Lewis on the contrary, is, in the actual writing, faulty. His expression is as bad as that of Meredith's floppy sickliness. In place of Meredith's mincing we have something active and 'disagreeable'. But we have at any rate the percussions of a highly energized mind.

In both Joyce and Lewis we have the insistent utterance of men who are once for all through with the particular inanities of Shavian-Bennett, and with the particular oleosities of the Wellsian genre.

The faults of Mr Lewis' writing can be examined in the first twenty-five pages. Kreisler is the creation of the book. He is roundly and objectively set before us. Tarr is less clearly detached from his creator. The author has evidently suspected this, for he has felt the need of disclaiming Tarr in a preface.

[1] Egoist, Ltd., 23 Adelphi Terrace House, Robert Street, W.C. 2. 6s. net Knopf, New York. $1.50. Reviewed in *The Future*.

Tarr, like his author, is a man with an energized mind. When Tarr talks at length; when Tarr gets things off his chest, we suspect that the author also is getting them off his own chest. Herein the technique is defective. It is also defective in that it proceeds by general descriptive statements in many cases where the objective present-ment of single and definite acts would be more effective, more convincing.

It differs from the general descriptiveness of cheap fiction in that these general statements are often a very profound reach for the expression of verity. In brief, the author is trying to get the truth and not merely playing baby-battledore among phrases. When Tarr talks little essays and makes aphorisms they are often of intrinsic interest, are even unforgettable. Likewise, when the author comments upon Tarr, he has the gift of phrase, vivid, biting, pregnant, full of suggestion.

The engaging if unpleasant character, Tarr, is placed in an unpleasant milieu, a milieu very vividly 'done'. The reader retains no doubts concerning the verity and existence of this milieu (Paris or London is no matter, though the scene is, nominally, in Paris). It is the existence where:

'Art is the smell of oil paint, Henri Murger's *Vie de Bohème*, corduroy trousers, the operatic Italian model ... quarter given up to Art.—Letters and other things are round the corner.

' ... permanent tableaux of the place, disheartening as a Tussaud's of The Flood.'

Tarr's first impact is with 'Hobson', whose 'dastardly face attempted to portray delicacies of common sense, and gossamer-like back-slidings into the Inane, that would have puzzled a bile-specialist. He would occasionally exploit his blackguardly appearance and blacksmith's muscles for a short time ... his strong piercing laugh threw A.B.C. waitresses into confusion'.

This person wonders if Tarr is a 'sound bird'. Tarr is not a sound bird. His conversational attack on Hobson proceeds by a brandishing of false dilemma, but neither Hobson nor his clan, nor indeed any of the critics of the novel (to date) have observed that this is Tarr's faulty weapon. Tarr's contempt for Hobson is as adequate as it is justifiable.

'Hobson, he considered, was a crowd.—You could not say he was an individual.—He was a set. He sat there a cultivated audience.—

He had the aplomb and absence of self-consciousness of numbers, of the herd—of those who know they are not alone. . . .

'For distinguishing feature Hobson possessed a distinguished absence of personality . . . . Hobson was an humble investor.'

Tarr addresses him with some frankness on the subject:

'As an off-set for your prying, scurvy way of peeping into my affairs you must offer your own guts, such as they are. . . .

'You have joined yourself to those who hush their voices to hear what other people are saying. . . .

'Your plumes are not meant to fly with, but merely to slouch and skip along the surface of the earth.—You wear the livery of a ridiculous set, you are a cunning and sleek domestic. No thought can come out of your head before it has slipped on its uniform. All your instincts are drugged with a malicious languor, an arm, a respectability, invented by a set of old women and mean, cadaverous little boys.'

Hobson opened his mouth, had a movement of the body to speak. But he relapsed.

'You reply, "What is all this fuss about? I have done the best for myself."—I am not suited for any heroic station, like yours. I live sensibly, cultivating my vegetable ideas, and also my roses and Victorian lilies.—I do no harm to anybody.'

'That is not quite the case. That is a little inexact. Your proceedings possess a herdesque astuteness; in the scale against the individual weighing less than the Yellow Press, yet being a closer and meaner attack. Also you are essentially *spies,* in a scurvy, safe and well-paid service, as I told you before. You are disguised to look like the thing it is your function to betray—What is your position?—You have bought for eight hundred pounds at an aristocratic educational establishment a complete mental outfit, a programme of manners. For four years you trained with other recruits. You are now a perfectly disciplined social unit, with a profound *esprit de corps.* The Cambridge set that you represent is an average specimen, a cross between a Quaker, a Pederast, and a Chelsea artist.—Your Oxford brothers, dating from the Wilde decade, are a stronger body. The Chelsea artists are much less flimsy. The Quakers are powerful rascals. You represent, my Hobson, the *dregs* of Anglo-Saxon civilization! There is nothing softer on earth.—Your flabby potion is a mixture of the lees of Liberalism, the poor froth blown off the decadent nineties, the wardrobe-leavings of a vulgar Bohemianism with its headquarters in Chelsea!

'You are concentrated, systematic slop.—There is nothing in the universe to be said for you. . . .

'A breed of mild pervasive cabbages, has set up a wide and creeping rot in the West of Europe.—They make it indirectly a peril and a tribulation for live things to remain in the neighbourhood. You are a systematizing and vulgarizing of the individual.—You are not an individual. . . .'

and later:

'You are libelling the Artist, by your idleness.' Also, 'Your pseudo-neediness is a sentimental indulgence.'

All this swish and clatter of insult reminds one a little of Papa Karamazoff. Its outrageousness is more Russian than Anglo-Victorian, but Lewis is not a mere echo of Dostoievsky. He hustles his reader, jolts him, snarls at him, in contra-distinction to Dostoievsky, who merely surrounds him with an enveloping dreariness, and imparts his characters by long-drawn osmosis.

Hobson is a minor character in the book, he and Lowndes are little more than a prologue, a dusty avenue of approach to the real business of the book; Bertha, 'high standard Aryan female, in good condition, superbly made; of the succulent, obedient, clear peasant type. . .'.

Kreisler, the main character in the book, a 'powerful' study in sheer obsessed emotionality, the chief foil to Tarr who has, over and above his sombre emotional spawn-bed, a smouldering sort of intelligence, combustible into brilliant talk, and brilliant invective.

Anastasya, a sort of super-Bertha, designated by the author as 'swagger sex'.

These four figures move, lit by the flare of restaurants and cafés, against the frowsy background of 'Bourgeois Bohemia', more or less Bloomsbury. There are probably such Bloomsburys in Paris and in every large city.

This sort of catalogue is not well designed to interest the general reader. What matters is the handling, the vigour, even the violence, of the handling.

The book's interest is not due to the 'style' in so far as 'style' is generally taken to mean 'smoothness of finish', orderly arrangement of sentences, coherence to the Flaubertian method.

It *is* due to the fact that we have a highly-energized mind performing a huge act of scavenging; cleaning up a great lot of rubbish, cultural, Bohemian, romantico-Tennysonish, arty, societish, gutterish.

It is not an attack on the *épicier*. It is an attack on a sort of super-*épicier* desiccation. It is by no means a tract. If Hobson is so drawn as to disgust one with the 'stuffed-shirt', Kreisler is equally a sign-post pointing to the advisability of some sort of intellectual or at least commonsense management of the emotions.

Tarr is, even Kreisler is, very nearly justified by the depiction of the Bourgeois Bohemian fustiness: Fräulein Lippmann, Fräulein Fogs, etc.

What we are blessedly free from is the red-plush Wellsian illusionism, and the click of Mr Bennett's cash-register finish.[1] The book does not skim over the surface. If it does not satisfy the mannequin demand for 'beauty' it at least refuses to accept margarine substitutes. It will not be praised by Katherine Tynan, nor by Mr Chesterton and Mrs Meynell. It will not receive the sanction of Dr Sir Robertson Nicoll, nor of his despicable paper *The Bookman*.

(There will be perhaps some hope for the British reading public, when said paper is no longer to be found in the Public Libraries of the Island, and when Clement Shorter shall cease from animadverting.) *Tarr* does not appeal to these people nor to the audience which they have swaddled. Neither, of course, did Samuel Butler to their equivalents in past decades.

'Bertha and Tarr took a flat in the Boulevard Port Royal, not far from the Jardin des Plantes. They gave a party to which Fräulein Lippmann and a good many other people came. He maintained the rule of four to seven, roughly, for Bertha, with the uttermost punctiliousness. Anastasya and Bertha did not meet.

Bertha's child came, and absorbed her energies for upwards of a year. It bore some resemblance to Tarr. Tarr's afternoon visits became less frequent. He lived now publicly with his illicit and splendid bride.

Two years after the birth of the child, Bertha divorced Tarr. She then married an eye-doctor, and lived with a brooding severity in his company, and that of her only child.

[1] E.P. rather modified his view of part of Bennett's writing when he finally got round to reading *An Old Wives' Tale* many years later. E.P.

Tarr and Anastasya did not marry. They had no children. Tarr, however, had three children by a Lady of the name of Rose Fawcett, who consoled him eventually for the splendours of his 'perfect woman'. But yet beyond the dim though sordid figure of Rose Fawcett, another arises. This one represents the swing-back of the pendulum once more to the swagger side. The cheerless and stodgy absurdity of Rose Fawcett required the painted, fine and inquiring face of Prism Dirkes.'

Neither this well-written conclusion, nor the opening tirade I have quoted, gives the full impression of the book's vital quality, but they may perhaps draw the explorative reader.

'Tarr' finds sex a monstrosity, he finds it 'a German study'; 'Sex Hobson, is a German study. A German study.'

At that we may leave it. 'Tarr' 'Had no social machinery, but the cumbrous one of the intellect. . . . When he tried to be amiable he usually only succeeded in being ominous.'

'Tarr' really gets at something in his last long discussion with Anastasya, when he says that art 'has no inside'. This is a condition of art, '*to have no* inside, nothing you cannot see. It is not something impelled like a machine by a little egoistic inside.'

'Deadness, in the limited sense in which we use that word, is the first condition of art. The second is absence of *soul*, in the sentimental human sense. The lines and masses of a statue are its soul.'

Joyce says something of the sort very differently, he is full of technical scholastic terms: '*stasis, kinesis*', etc. Any careful statement of this sort is bound to be *baffoué*, and fumbled over, but this ability to come to a hard definition of anything is one of Lewis' qualities lying at the base of his ability to irritate the mediocre intelligence. The book was written before 1914, and the depiction of the German was not a piece of war propaganda.

ARNOLD DOLMETSCH[1]

I have seen the God Pan and it was in this manner: I heard a bewildering and pervasive music moving from precision to precision within itself. Then I heard a different music, hollow and laughing. Then I looked up and saw two eyes like the eyes of a wood-creature peering at me over a brown tube of wood. Then someone said: Yes, once I was playing a fiddle in the forest and I walked into a wasps' nest.

Comparing these things with what I can read of the Earliest and best authenticated appearances of Pan, I can but conclude that they relate to similar occurrences. It is true that I found myself later in a room covered with pictures of what we now call ancient instruments, and that when I picked up the brown tube of wood I found that it had ivory rings upon it. And no proper reed has ivory rings on it, by nature. Also, they told me it was a 'recorder', whatever that is.

Our only measure of truth is, however, our own perception of truth. The undeniable tradition of metamorphoses teaches us that things do not remain always the same. They become other things by swift and unanalysable process. It was only when men began to mistrust the myths and to tell nasty lies about the Gods for a moral purpose that these matters became hopelessly confused. Then some unpleasing Semite or Parsee or Syrian began to use myths for social propaganda, when the myth was degraded into an allegory or a fable, and that was the beginning of the end. And the Gods no longer walked in men's gardens. The first myths arose when a man walked sheer into 'nonsense', that is to say, when some very vivid and undeniable adventure befell him, and he told someone else who called him a liar. Thereupon, after bitter experience, perceiving that no one could understand what he meant when he said that he 'turned into a tree' he made a myth—a work of art that is—an impersonal or objective story woven out of his own emotion, as the nearest equation that he was capable of putting into words. That story, perhaps, then gave rise to a weaker copy of his emotion in others, until there arose a cult, a company of people who could understand each other's nonsense about the gods.

[1] Reprinted from *Pavannes and Divisions* 1918.

431

These things were afterwards incorporated for the condemnable 'good of the State', and what was once a species of truth became only lies and propaganda. And they told horrid tales to little boys in order to make them be good; or to the ignorant populace in order to preserve the empire; and religion came to an end and civic science began to be studied. Plato said that artists ought to be kept out of the ideal republic, and the artists swore by their gods that nothing would drag them into it. That is the history of 'civilization', or philology, or Kultur.

When any man is able, by a pattern of notes or by an arrangement of planes or colours, to throw us back into the age of truth, everyone who has been cast back into that age of truth for one instant gives honour to the spell which has worked, to the witch-work or the art-work, or to whatever you like to call it. I say, therefore, that I saw and heard the God Pan; shortly afterwards I saw and heard Mr Dolmetsch. Mr Dolmetsch was talking volubly, and he said some-thing very derogatory to music, which needs 240 (or some such number of) players, and can only be performed in one or two capitals. Pepys writes, that in the Fire of London, when the people were escaping by boat on the Thames, there was scarcely a boat in which you would not see them taking a pair of virginals as among their dearest possessions.

Older journalists tell me it is 'cold mutton', that Mr Dolmetsch was heard of fifteen years ago. This shows a tendency that I have before remarked in a civilization which rests upon journalism, and which has only a sporadic care for the arts. Everyone in London over forty 'has heard of' Mr Dolmetsch, his instruments, etc. The gener-ation under thirty may have heard of him, but you cannot be sure of it. His topical interest is over. I have heard of Mr Dolmetsch for fifteen years, because I am a crank and am interested in such matters. Mr Dolmetsch has always been in France or America, or somewhere I wasn't when he was. Also, I have seen broken-down spinets in portentous and pretentious drawing-rooms. I have heard harpsichords played in Parisian concerts, and they sounded like the scratching of multitudinous hens, and I did not wonder that pianos had superseded them. Also, I have known good musicians and have favoured divers sorts of good music. And I have supposed that clavichords were things you might own if you were a millionaire; and that virginals went with citherns and citoles in the poems of the late D. G. Rossetti.

So I had two sets of adventures. First, I perceived a sound which is undoubtedly derived from the Gods, and then I found myself in a reconstructed century—in a century of music, back before Mozart or Purcell, listening to clear music, to tones clear as brown amber. And this music came indifferently out of the harpsichord or the clavichord or out of virginals or out of odd-shaped viols, or whatever they may be. There were two small girls playing upon them with an exquisite precision; with a precision quite unlike anything I have ever heard from an orchestra. Then someone said in a tone of authority: 'It is nonsense to teach people scales. It is rubbish to make them play *this* (tum, tum, tum, tum tum). They must begin to play music. Three years playing scales, that is what they tell you. How can they ever be musicians?'

It reduces itself to about this. Once people played music. It was gracious, exquisite music, and it was played on instruments which gave out the players' exact mood and personality. 'It is beautiful even if you play it wrong.' The clavichord has the beauty of three or four lutes played together. It has more than that, but no matter. You have your fingers always en rapport with the strings; it is not one dab and then either another dab or else nothing, as with the piano; the music is always lying on your own finger-tips.

This old music was not theatrical. You played it yourself as you read a book of precision. A few people played it together. It was not an interruption but a concentration.

Now, on the other hand, I remember a healthy concert pianist complaining that you couldn't 'really give' a big piano concert unless you had the endurance of an ox; and that 'women couldn't, of course'; and that gradually the person with long hands was being eliminated from the pianistic world, and that only people with little, short fat fingers could come up to the technical requirements. Whether this is so or not, we have come to the pianola. And one or two people are going in for sheer pianola. They cut their rolls for the pianola itself, and make it play as if with two dozen fingers when necessary. That is, perhaps, better art than making a pianola imitate the music of two hands of five fingers each. But still something is lacking.

Oriental music is under debate. We say we 'can't hear it'. Impressionism has reduced us to such a dough-like state of receptivity that we have ceased to like concentration. Or if it has not done this it has at least set a fashion of passivity that has held since the romantic movement. The old music was fit for the old instruments. That was natural. It is proper to play piano music on pianos. But in the end we find that nothing less than a full orchestra will satisfy our modernity.

That is the whole flaw of impressionist or 'emotional' music as opposed to pattern music. It is like a drug; you must have more drug, and more noise each time, or this effect, this impression which works from the outside, in from the nerves and sensorium upon the self— is no use, its effect is constantly weaker and weaker. I do not mean that Bach is not emotional, but the early music starts with the mystery of pattern; if you like, with the vortex of pattern; with something which is, first of all, music, and which is capable of being, after that, many things. What I call emotional, or impressionist music, starts with being emotion or impression and then becomes only approximately music. It is, that is to say, something in the terms of something else. If it produces an effect, if, from sounding as music, it moves at all, it can only recede into the original emotion or impression. Programme music is merely a weaker, more flabby and descriptive sort of impressionist music, needing, perhaps, a guide and explanation.

Mr Dolmetsch was, let us say, enamoured of ancient music. He found it misunderstood. He saw a beauty so great and so various that he stopped composing. He found that the beauty was untranslatable with modern instruments; he has repaired and has entirely remade 'ancient instruments'. The comfort is that he has done this not for a few rich faddists, as one had been led to suppose. He makes his virginals and clavichords for the price of a bad, of a very bad piano. You can have a virginal for £25 if you order it when he is making a dozen; and you can have a clavichord for a few pounds more, even if he is not making more than one.

My interest in these things is not topical. Mr Dolmetsch was a topic some years ago, but you are not *au courant*, and you do not much care for music unless you know that a certain sort of very beautiful music is no longer impossible. It is not necessary to wait for a great legacy, or to inhabit a capital city in order to hear magical voices, in order to hear perfect music which does not depend upon your ability to approximate the pianola, or upon great physical strength. Of the clavichord, one can only say, very inexactly, that it is to the piano what the violin is to the bass viol.

As I believe that Lewis and Picasso are capable of revitalizing the instinct of design so I believe that a return, an awakening to the possibilities, not necessarily of 'Old' music, but of pattern music played upon ancient instruments, is, perhaps, able to make music again a part of life, not merely a part of theatricals. The musician, the performing musician as distinct from the composer, might again be an interesting person, an artist, not merely a sort of manual saltimbanque or a stage hypnotist. It is, perhaps, a question of whether you want music, or whether you want to see an obsessed personality trying to 'dominate' an audience.

I have said little that can be called technical criticism. I have perhaps implied it. There is precision in the making of ancient instruments. Men still make passable violins; I do not see why the art of beautiful-keyed instruments need be regarded as utterly lost. There has been precision in Mr Dolmetsch's study of ancient texts and notation; he has routed out many errors.[1] He has even, with certain help, unravelled the precision of ancient dancing. He has found a complete notation which might not interest us were it not that this very dancing forces one to a greater precision with the old music. One finds, for instance, that certain tunes called dance tunes must be played double the time at which they are modernly taken.

One art interprets the other. It would almost touch upon theatricals, which I am trying to avoid, if I should say that one steps into a past era when one sees all the other Dolmetsches dancing quaint, ancient steps of Sixteenth-Century dancing. One feels that the dance would go on even if there were no audience. That is where real drama begins, and where we leave what I have called, with odium, 'theatricals'. It is a dance, danced for the dance's sake, not a display. It is music that exists for the sake of being music, not for the sake of, as they say, producing an impression.

Of course there are other musicians working with this same ideal. I take Mr Dolmetsch as perhaps a unique figure, as perhaps the one man who knows most definitely whither he is going, and why, and who has given most time to old music.

They tell me 'everyone knows Dolmetsch who knows of old music, but not many people know of it'. Is that sheer nonsense, or what is the fragment of truth or rumour upon which it is based? Why

---

[1] *Vide* his *The Interpretation of the Music of the XVIIth and XVIIIth Centuries.*

is it that the fine things always seem to go on in a corner? Is it a judgment on democracy? Is it that what has once been the pleasure of the many, of the pre-Cromwellian many,[1] has been permanently swept out of life? Musical England? A wild man comes into my room and talks of piles of turquoises in a boat, a sort of shop-house-boat east of Cashmere. His talk is full of the colour of the Orient. Then I find he is living over an old-clothes shop in Bow. 'And there they seem to play all sorts of instruments.'

Is there a popular instinct for anything different from what my ex-landlord calls 'the four-hour-touch'? Is it that the aristocracy, which ought to set the fashion, is too weakened and too unreal to perform the due functions of 'aristocracy'? Is it that nature can, in fact, only produce a certain number of vortices? That the quattro-cento shines out because the vortices of social power coincided with the vortices of creative intelligence? And that when these vortices do not coincide we have an age of 'art in strange corners' and of great dullness among the quite rich? Is it that real democracy can only exist under feudal conditions, when no man fears to recognise creative skill in his neighbour?

[1] Mme. de Genlis notes the efforts of Charles II to restore the language of England after the Cromwellian squalor.

VERS LIBRE AND
ARNOLD DOLMETSCH[1]

P oetry is a composition of words set to music. Most other definitions of it are indefensible, or metaphysical. The proportion or
quality of the music may, and does, vary; but poetry withers and
'dries out' when it leaves music, or at least an imagined music, too far
behind it. The horrors of modern 'readings of poetry' are due to
oratorical recitation. Poetry must be read as music and not as oratory.
I do not mean that the words should be jumbled together and made
indistinct and unrecognizable in a sort of onomatopœic paste. I
have found few save musicians who pay the least attention to the
poet's own music. They are often, I admit, uncritical of his verbal
excellence or deficit, ignorant of his 'literary' value or bathos. But the
literary qualities are not the whole of our art.

Poets who are not interested in music are, or become, bad poets. I
would almost say that poets should never be too long out of touch
with musicians. Poets who will not study music are defective. I do
not mean that they need become virtuosi, or that they need necessarily undergo the musical curriculum of their time. It is perhaps their
value that they can be a little refractory and heretical, for all arts tend
to decline into the stereotype; and at all times the mediocre tend or
try, semi-consciously or unconsciously, to obscure the fact that the
day's fashion is not the immutable.

Music and poetry, melody and versification, alike fall under the
marasmus.

It is too late to prevent vers libre. But, conceivably, one might
improve it, and one might stop at least a little of the idiotic and
narrow discussion based on an ignorance of music. Bigoted attack,
born of this ignorance of the tradition of music, was what we had to
live through.

· · · · · ·

Arnold Dolmetsch's book, *The Interpretation of the Music of the
XVIIth and XVIIIth Centuries*,[2] is full of what we may call either

---

[1] Reprinted from *Pavannes and Divisions* (1918).
[2] (Novello, London, 10*s*. 6*d*; W. H. Gray and Co., New York.)

437

'ripe wisdom' or 'common sense', or 'those things which all good artists at all times have tried (perhaps vainly) to hammer into insensitive heads'. Some of his dicta are, by their nature, applicable only to instrumental music or melody, others are susceptible of a sort of transposition into terms of the sister arts, still others have a direct bearing on poetry, or at least on versification. It is with these last that I shall concern myself. Dolmetsch's style is so clear and his citations of old authors so apt that I had perhaps better quote with small comment.

Mace, *Musick's Monument* (1613):

(1)

... you must Know, That, although in our First Undertakings, we ought to *strive*, for the most Exact Habit of *Time-keeping* that possibly we can attain unto, (and for several good Reasons) yet, when we come to be *Masters*, so that we can *command all manner* of Time, at our own Pleasures; we Then *take Liberty*, (and very often, for Humour, and good Adornment-sake, in certain Places) to *Break Time;* sometimes Faster and sometimes Slower, as we perceive the *Nature of the Thing* Requires, which often adds, much *Grace*, and *Luster*, to the Performance.

(2)

... the thing to be done, is but only to make a kind of *Cessation*, or *standing still* ... in due place an excellent grace.

Again, from Mace, p. 130: '*If you find it uniform, and retortive*, either in its bars or strains' you are told to get variety by the quality of loud and soft, etc. and 'if it expresseth short sentences' this applies. And you are to make pauses on long notes at the end of sentences.

Rousseau, 1687, in 'Maître de Musique et de Viole';

(1)

... At this word 'movement' there are people who imagine that to give the movement is to follow and keep time; but there is much difference between the one and the other, for one may keep time without entering into the movement.

(2)

... You must avoid a profusion of divisions, which only disturb the tune, and obscure its beauty.

(3)

... Mark not the beat too much.

The accompanist is told to imitate the irregularities of the beautiful voice.

François Couperin, 1717, 'L'Art de toucher le Clavecin':

(1)

... We write differently from what we play.

(2)

... I find that we confuse Time, or Measure, with what is called Cadence or Movement. Measure defines the quantity and equality of beats; Cadence is properly the spirit, the soul that must be added.

(3)

... Although these Preludes are written in measured time, there is however a customary style which should be followed.
... Those who will use these set Preludes must play them in an easy manner, WITHOUT BINDING THEMSELVES TO STRICT TIME, unless I should have expressly marked it by the word *mesuré*.

One need seek no further for proof of the recognition of vers libre in music—and this during the 'classical period'.

I have pointed out elsewhere that the even bar measure is certainly NOT the one and important thing, or even the first important thing; and that European musicians, at least, did not begin to record it until comparatively late in the history of notation. Couperin later notes the barring as a convenience:

... One of the reasons why I have measured these Preludes is the facility one will find to teach them or learn them.

That is to say, musical bars are a sort of scaffold to be kicked away when no longer needed.

Disregard of bars is not to be confused with *tempo rubato,* affecting the notes inside a single bar.

．　．　．　．　．　．

Dolmetsch's wisdom is not confined to the demonstration of a single point of topical interest to the poet. I have not space to quote two whole chapters, or even to elaborate brief quotations like: 'You must bind perfectly all that you play.' The serious writer of verse will not rest content until he has gone to the source. I do not wish to give the erroneous impression that old music was all vers libre. I state simply that vers libre exists in old music. Quantzens, 1752, in so far as he is quoted by Dolmetsch, only cautions the player to give the shorter notes 'inequality'. Christopher Simpson, 1655, is much concerned with physical means of getting a regular beat. His date is interesting. The movement toward regularity in verse during the seventeenth century seems condemnable if one compare only Dryden and Shakespeare, but read a little bad Elizabethan poetry and the reason for it appears. On the other hand, Couperin's feeling for irregularity underlying 'classical' forms may give us the clue to a wider unexpressed feeling for a fundamental irregularity which would have made eighteenth-century classicism, classicism of surface, tolerable to those who felt the underlying variety *as strongly as the first regularizers* may have felt it.

These are historical speculations. If I were writing merely a controversial article I should have stopped with the first quotations from Couperin, concerning vers libre. (I have never claimed that vers libre was the only path of salvation. I felt that it was right and that it had its place with the other modes. It seems that my instinct was not wholly heretical and that the opposition was rather badly informed.) Old gentlemen who talk about 'red riot and anarchy', 'treachery to the imperium of poesy', etc., etc., would do well to 'get up their history' and peruse the codices of their laws.[1]

[1] Cf. *The Quarterly*, that hospital for the infirm and aged.

BRANCUSI[1]

'I carve a thesis in logic of the eternal beauty,' writes Rémy de Gourmont in his *Sonnets à l'Amazone*. A man hurls himself toward the infinite and the works of art are his vestiges, his trace in the manifest.

It is perhaps no more impossible to give a vague idea of Brancusi's sculpture in words than to give it in photographs, but it is equally impossible to give an exact sculptural idea in either words or photography. T. J. Everets has made the best summary of our contemporary aesthetics that I know, in his sentence 'A work of art has in it no idea which is separable from the form.' I believe this conviction can be found in either vorticist explanations, and in a world where so few people have yet dissociated form from representation, one may, or at least I may as well approach Brancusi via the formulations by Gaudier-Brzeska, or by myself in my study of Gaudier:

'Sculptural feeling is the appreciation of masses in relation.'
'Sculptural ability is the defining of these masses by planes.'
'Every concept, every emotion presents itself to the vivid consciousness in some primary form. It belongs to the art of that form.'

I don't mean to imply that vorticist formulæ will 'satisfy' Brancusi, or that any formula need ever satisfy any artist, simply the formulæ give me certain axes (plural of *axis*, not of *ax*) for discrimination.

I have found, to date, nothing in vorticist formulæ which contradicts the work of Brancusi, the formulæ left every man fairly free. Gaudier had long since revolted from the Rodin-Maillol mixture; no one who understood Gaudier was fooled by the cheap Viennese Michaelangelism and rhetoric of Mestrovic. One understood that 'Works of art attract by a resembling unlikeness'; that 'The beauty of form in the still stone can not be the same beauty of form as that in the living animal'. One even understood that, as in Gaudier's brown stone dancer, the pure or unadulterated motifs of the circle and triangle have a right to build up their own fugue or sonata in form; as a theme in music has its right to express itself.

[1] Reprinted from *The Little Review*, VIII, 1 (Autumn 1921).

No critic has a right to pretend that he fully understands any artist; least of all do I pretend, in this note, to understand Brancusi (after a few weeks' acquaintance) even as well as I understood Gaudier (after several years' friendship); anything I say here effaces anything I may have said before on the subject, and anything I say the week after next effaces what I say here—a pale reflection of Brancusi's general wish that people would wait until he has finished (i.e., in the cemetery) before they talk aesthetics with or about him.

At best one could but clear away a few grosser misconceptions. Gaudier had discriminated against beefy statues, he had given us a very definite appreciation of stone as stone; he had taught us to feel that the beauty of sculpture is inseparable from its material and that it inheres in the material. Brancusi was giving up the facile success of representative sculpture about the time Gaudier was giving up his baby-bottle; in many ways his difference from Gaudier is a difference merely of degree, he has had time to make statues where Gaudier had time only to make sketches; Gaudier had purged himself of every kind of rhetoric he had noticed; Brancusi has detected more kinds of rhetoric and continued the process of purgation.

When verbally intelligible he is quite definite in the statement that whatever else art is, it is not 'crise des nerfs'; that beauty is not grimaces and fortuitous gestures; that starting with an ideal of form one arrives at a mathematical exactitude of proportion, but *not by* mathematics.

Above all he is a man in love with perfection. Dante believed in the 'melody which most in-centres the soul'; in the preface to my Guido I have tried to express the idea of an absolute rhythm, or the possibility of it. Perhaps every artist at one time or another believes in a sort of elixir or philosopher's stone produced by the sheer perfection of his art; by the alchemical sublimation of the medium; the elimination of accidentals and imperfections.

Where Gaudier had developed a sort of form-fugue or form-sonata by a combination of forms, Brancusi has set out on the maddeningly more difficult exploration toward getting all the forms into one form; this is as long as any Buddhist's contemplation of the universe or as any mediæval saint's contemplation of the divine love, —as long and even as paradoxical as the final remarks in the Divina Commedia. It is a search easily begun, and wholly unending, and the vestiges are let us say Brancusi's 'Bird', and there is perhaps six months' work and twenty years' knowledge between one model of the erect bird and another, though they appear identical in photography. Therein consisting the difference between sculpture and sketches. Plate No. 5 shows what looks like an egg; I give more photos of the bust than of this egg because in the photos the egg comes to nothing; in Plate No. 12 there is at the base of the chimaera an egg with a plane and a groove cut into it, an egg having infantile rotundities and repose.

I don't know by what metaphorical periphrase I am to convey the relation of these ovoids to Brancusi's other sculpture. As an interim label, one might consider them as master-keys to the world of form —not 'his' world of form, but as much as he has found of 'the' world of form. They contain or imply, or should, the triangle and the circle.

Or putting it another way, every one of the thousand angles or approach to a statue ought to be interesting, it ought to have a life (Brancusi might perhaps permit me to say a 'divine' life) of its own. 'Any prentice' can supposedly make a statue that will catch the eye and be interesting from *some* angle. This last statement is not strictly true, the present condition of sculptural sense leaving us with a vastly lower level both of prentises and 'great sculptors'; but even the strictest worshipper of bad art will admit that it is infinitely easier to make a statue which can please from *one* side than to make one which gives satisfaction from no matter what angle of vision.

It is also conceivably more difficult to give this formal-satisfaction by a single mass, or let us say to sustain the formal-interest by a single mass, than to excite transient visual interests by more monumental and melodramatic combinations.

Brancusi's revolt against the rhetorical and the kolossal has carried him into revolt against the monumental, or at least what appears to be, for the instant, a revolt against one sort of solidity. The research for the aerial has produced his bird which stands unsupported upon its diminished base (the best of jade carvers and netsuke makers produce tiny objects which also maintain themselves on extremely minute foundations). If I say that Brancusi's ideal form should be equally interesting from all angles, this does not quite imply that one should stand the ideal temple on its head, but it probably implies a discontent with any combination of proportions which can't be conceived as beautiful even if, in the case of a temple, some earth-quake should stand it up intact and end-ways or turned-turtle. Here I think the concept differs from Gaudier's, as indubitably the metaphysic of Brancusi is outside and unrelated to vorticist manners of thinking.

The great black-stone egyptian patera in the British museum is perhaps more formally interesting than the statues of Memnon.

In the case of the ovoid, I take it Brancusi is meditating upon pure form free from all terrestrial gravitation; form as free in its own life as the form of the analytic geometers; and the measure of his success in this experiment (unfinished and probably unfinishable) is that from some angles at least the ovoid does come to life and appear ready to levitate. (Or this is perhaps merely a fortuitous anecdote, like any other expression.)

Crystal-gazing?? No. Admitting the possibility of self-hypnosis by means of highly polished brass surfaces, the polish, from the sculptural point of view, results merely from a desire for greater precision of the form, it is also a transient glory. But the contemplation of form or of formal-beauty leading into the infinite must be dissociated from the dazzle of crystal; there is a sort of relation, but there is the more important divergence; with the crystal it is a hypnosis, or a contemplative fixation of thought, or an excitement of the 'sub-conscious' or unconscious (whatever the devil they may be), and with the ideal form in marble it is an approach to the infinite *by form*, by precisely the highest possible degree of consciousness of formal perfection; as free of accident as any of the philosophical demands of a 'Paradiso' can make it.

This is not a suggestion that all sculpture should end in the making of abstract ovoids; indeed no one but a genius wholly centred in his art, and more or less 'oriental' could endure the strain of such effort.

But if we are ever to have a bearable sculpture or architecture it might be well for young sculptors to start with some such effort at perfection, rather than with the idea of a new Laocoon, or a 'Triumph of Labour over Commerce'. (This suggestion is mine, and I hope it will never fall under the eye of Brancusi.—But then Brancusi can spend most of his time in his own studio, surrounded by the calm of his own creations, whereas the author of this imperfect exposure is compelled to move about in a world full of junk-shops, a world full of more than idiotic ornamentations, a world where pictures are made for museums, where no man has a front-door that he can bear to look at, let alone one he can contemplate with reasonable pleasure, where the average house is each year made more hideous, and where the sense of form which ought to be as general as the sense of refreshment after a bath, or the pleasure of liquid in time of drouth or any other clear animal pleasure, is the rare possession of an 'intellectual' (heaven help us) 'aristocracy'.

INDEX

New Directions Paperbooks – A Partial Listing

For complete listing request free catalog from
New Directions, 80 Eighth Avenue, New York 10011   † Bilingual